American
Foreign Policy
Since World War II

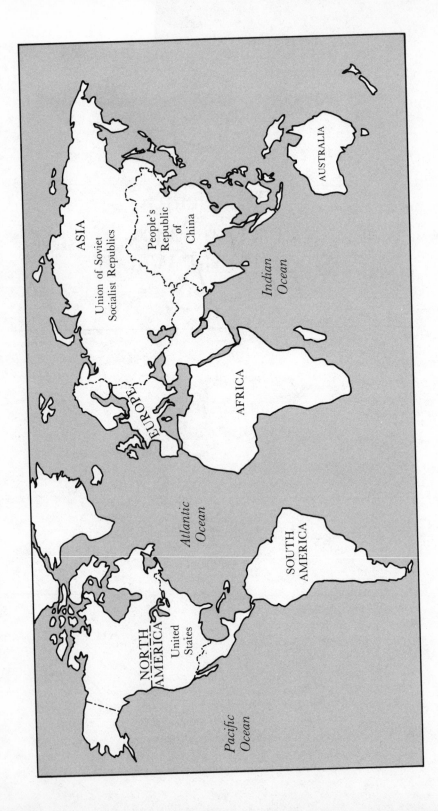

American Foreign Policy Since World War II

Eleventh Edition

John Spanier

University of Florida

A Division of Congressional Quarterly Inc.
1414 22nd Street N.W., Washington, D.C. 20037

Library of Congress Cataloging-in-Publication Data

Spanier, John W.
    American foreign policy since World War II.

    Bibliography: p.
    Includes index.
    1. United States—Foreign relations—1945- I. Title.
E744.S8   1988   327.73   87-24441
ISBN 0-87187-448-2

For David and Lisa

Love, all alike, no season knows, or clime,
Nor hours, days, months, which are the rags of time.

From *The Sun Rising* by John Donne

Contents

c h a p t e r   e i g h t

c h a p t e r   n i n e

c h a p t e r   t e n

chapter eleven

chapter twelve

chapter thirteen

Maps

Preface

The eleventh edition of *American Foreign Policy Since World War II* is the first edition of this book to be published by CQ Press. I am very happy to have this extensively revised edition in the capable hands of such a prestigious political science publisher.

The book presents an account of American foreign policy from the closing days of World War II through most of Ronald Reagan's second term. The focus of the study is the superpower rivalry, which has dominated postwar international politics; but this focus neither excludes the actions of other states nor ignores problems such as the contemporary role of terrorism or the plight of the less-developed countries and their relationships to the Western industrial world.

This book is *not* a diplomatic history—a detailed presentation of American actions in the world since 1945. Rather, it is an interpretation of the roles the United States has played on the world stage for the last four decades. The assumption is that the present cannot be understood without historical context. The Vietnam War, for example, still exerts a powerful influence on the conduct of American foreign policy. Insight into that war and contemporary policy can be gained only by a deeper understanding of the causes and evolution of the conflict between the United States and the Soviet Union, former allies in the struggle against Hitler's Germany.

The framework of the book is what I call the "American style" in foreign policy. The American approach is unlike that of any other major nation in its distaste for "power politics"—it would prefer not to be forced to enhance its security by means of military or economic pressure. If it cannot avoid power politics, however, the United States will moralize it into a crusade against the enemy. The constancy of this style, from Harry Truman and Dwight Eisenhower to Jimmy Carter and Ronald Reagan, is quite amazing and testifies to its tenacity. Richard Nixon was perhaps the only recent president who did not adopt it. Whether the American national style has served the country well or ill is a matter of individual judgment. (My conclusions will be found in the last chapter, which reappraises the policy of containment.) But it cannot be doubted that national style is a useful concept for explaining and understanding American foreign policy.

I have balanced the emphasis on U.S. national style with a section on the Soviet Union's style, which is a composite of czarist Russian and Soviet historical experiences and perceptions. The discussion is included partly to provide a contrast to the United States and to show how antithetical the two styles are and partly to provide a better explanation and understanding of Soviet behavior during World War II and immediately after—when the alliance came apart and the cold war began.

There is a third reason for discussing the Soviet Union: the publication of a number of thought-provoking books that deal with the U.S.-Soviet rivalry in postrevisionist terms. They have added an important balance to other American historical writing on the superpower competition. During the late 1960s and early 1970s—the period of America's deepest involvement in Vietnam—many writers stressed the responsibility of the United States for the cold war, noting America's "arrogance of power," and its never-ending search for profits in foreign markets. These revisionist writers speculated that if the war in Southeast Asia was the result of U.S. leaders' misperceptions of the nature of the Communist threat, perhaps the leaders also misperceived the Soviet Union. Or did the leaders see a threat where none existed? Did Washington therefore overreact to Moscow's purportedly defensive moves in Eastern Europe? Revisionist views of how the cold war began went along with opposition to the war in Vietnam and, more broadly, disapproval of U.S. foreign policy in general.

Postrevisionist writings reject the assumption that U.S. policy made the cold war inevitable because it was insensitive to Soviet security needs. The postrevisionist accounts of Soviet policy focus, as in the days before the Vietnam War, on Soviet expansionist goals. The failure of the United States, according to this view, was not in trying to accommodate Stalin but in not opposing him earlier and consistently. Postwar rivalry could have been avoided, but weakness provoked Stalin. Amid the euphoria of wartime cooperation, Franklin Roosevelt failed to prepare the American people for the possibility that conflict would continue.

This book has always placed a strong emphasis on the international or "state system" in explaining the origins and conduct of the cold war. The environment in which states exist is the primary influence on their behavior. In this edition, I have strengthened this emphasis with a focus on the geopolitics of twentieth-century conflict. This allows me to stress the similarity between the two wars fought between Germany, a land power, and Britain, a maritime power, and the cold war conflict between the Soviet

Union and the United States.

This edition also gives greater emphasis to international economics than did previous editions. There is ample discussion of the Organization of Petroleum Exporting Countries (OPEC) and its manipulation of oil prices and of the plight of the less-developed countries and their debt problems. But greater weight is given to the U.S. economy and its growing uncompetitiveness in an increasingly interdependent world economy. In my judgment, the implications of this development are at least as profound as the arms race.

The swiftness with which the world changes is truly astounding and provides the impetus to incorporate unfolding events into the patterns of foreign policy analysis. Revising this text has been a major task given the number of important developments since the last edition. My burden has been lightened by a number of people. I wish to thank the reviewers, with whom I did not always agree but whose observations put matters in a new perspective. Joanne Daniels, director of CQ Press, has made my relationship with my new publisher effortless and rewarding. I also thank my editor, Carolyn Goldinger, whose work contributed greatly to the readability of this volume, and Jane Gilligan for her tireless assistance.

U.S. Administrations Since World War II

Dates	President	Secretary of State	Secretary of Defense	National Security Assistant
1945–1952	Harry Truman	Edward Stettinius James Byrnes George Marshall Dean Acheson	James Forrestal Louis Johnson Robert Lovett George Marshall	
1953–1960	Dwight Eisenhower	John Dulles Christian Herter	Charles Wilson Neil McElroy Thomas Gates	
1961–1963	John Kennedy	Dean Rusk	Robert McNamara	McGeorge Bundy
1963–1968	Lyndon Johnson	Dean Rusk	Robert McNamara Clark Clifford	McGeorge Bundy W. W. Rostow
1969–1974	Richard Nixon	William Rogers Henry Kissing	Melvin Laird Elliot Richardson James Schlesinger	Henry Kissinger
1974–1976	Gerald Ford	Henry Kissinger	James Schlesinger Donald Rumsfeld	Henry Kissinger Brent Scowcroft
1977–1980	Jimmy Carter	Cyrus Vance Edward Muskie	Harold Brown	Zbigniew Brzezinski
1981–1988	Ronald Reagan	Alexander Haig George Shultz	Caspar Weinberger Frank Carlucci	Richard Allen William Clark Robert McFarlane John Poindexter Frank Carlucci Colin Powell

The American Approach to Foreign Policy

NATIONS, like individuals, face the world differently. How nations see the world, their place in it, and how they act in the international arena depend in large measure on their geography, historical backgrounds, and experiences. These national styles, as we shall call them, vary considerably. The perceptions and behavior of most states are heavily influenced, if not primarily influenced, according to some observers, by the environment or state system in which they coexist. States quickly learn "the rules of the game" or what they must do to ensure their survival and to achieve a measure of security. They ignore or disregard these rules at their peril.

Because for most of its existence the United States had isolated itself from the European state system, its national style was molded to a far greater extent than that of other states by its domestic experiences and democratic values and outlook. Not schooled by continuous involvement in international politics, as were the Europeans, the Americans approached foreign policy in a way that was not only peculiarly theirs, but also significantly different from that of other Great Powers. The contrast was particularly strong between the American experience and that of the Soviet Union, which emerged after World War II as the United States' chief adversary. The United States felt absolutely secure in the Western Hemisphere, but czarist Russia (later Soviet Russia) could never feel secure because of its proximity to other great powers who, over the centuries, had their own problems and ambitions. During the postwar decades of conflict with the Soviet Union, the United States learned to play the international game with increasing skill, but its distinctive national style exerted a strong influence for most of that period.[1]

---

1. John Spanier, *Games Nations Play*, 6th ed. (Washington, D.C.: CQ Press, 1987), especially 110-139.

The State System

American foreign policy since World War II is the story of the interaction and tension between the state system and the American style of dealing with other countries. In the state system, each member—especially the great powers, its principal actors—tends to feel a high degree of insecurity. In the absence of a world government that could safeguard it, each state knows that it can depend only on itself for its preservation and safety. Self-protection is the only protection in an essentially anarchical system; understandably, states tend to regard one another as potential adversaries, menaces to one another's territorial integrity and political independence. In short, the very nature of the state system breeds feelings of insecurity, distrust, suspicion, and fear.

This atmosphere produces a constant scramble for power. To reduce its insecurity, each state seeks to enhance its power relative to that of a possible foe. If a state perceives its neighbor as a potential enemy, it tries to deter an attack or political coercion by becoming a little stronger than its neighbor. The neighbor, in turn, also fears attack or political intimidation. It understands that its best interests lie in increasing its strength to forestall either contingency or if necessary, to win a war, should matters go that far.

It is not the alleged aggressive instinct of humans as "naked apes" or their presumed desire for acquiring ever greater power that accounts for what is popularly called "power politics." Rather, power politics stems from each state's continuous concern with its security, which is the prerequisite for each for the enjoyment of its particular way of life. Because the external environment is seen as menacing to their security, states react fearfully against what they believe to be threats. In such a context it does not take much for one state to arouse another's apprehensions and to stimulate reciprocal images of hostility that each finds easy to substantiate by its opponent's behavior. Indeed, in most instances this enmity is maintained despite contradictory evidence and even avowedly friendly acts. Conciliatory behavior is likely to be seen as an indicator of weakness and may invite exploitation. Or it may be regarded as a trick to persuade a state to relax its guard.

It is easy to understand why in these circumstances a balance of power is what keeps the state system from breaking down. A balance or equilibrium makes victory in a war less probable and more costly. Therefore, a balance is presumed to be that distribution of power most likely to deter an attack. By contrast, possession of disproportionate power might tempt a state to undertake aggression by making it far less costly to gain a predominant position and impose its will upon other states. In other words, the fundamental assumption underlying the state system is that its members cannot be trusted with power because they will be tempted to abuse it. Unrestrained power in the system constitutes a threat to all states; power is, therefore, the best antidote to power. As one close observer of international politics, Arnold Wolfers, has noted:

> Under these conditions of anarchy the expectations of violence and even of annihilation is ever-present. To forget this and thus fail in the concern for enhanced power spells the doom of a state. This does not mean open constant warfare; expansion of power at the expense of others will not take place if there is enough counterpower to deter or to stop states from undertaking it. Although no state is interested in a mere balance of power, the efforts of all states to maximize power may lead to equilibrium. If and when that happens, there is "peace" or, more exactly, a condition of stalemate or truce. Under the conditions described here, this balancing of power process is the only available "peace" strategy.[2]

Power thus elicits countervailing power. The basic rule of the "international game" is to resist attempts by any state to expand and seek a predominant position in the international system. Therefore, when the balance is disturbed, equilibrium tends to be restored by the emergence of counterpower. States ignore at their peril the rule to maintain the balance of power.

The Balance of Power
and the End of U.S. Isolationism

What all this means is that any state's behavior can be explained to a very significant degree in terms of the ever-changing distribution of power. As that distribution changes, so does a state's behavior or foreign policy. For example, the impact of a shift in the distribution of power is evident in U.S. participation in the two world wars of this century. During most of the nineteenth century and early twentieth century, the United States was able to preserve its historical isolation from power politics and enjoy an unprecedented degree of security because the balance of power on the European continent was maintained by Britain.

Germany's unification in 1870 and its subsequent rapid industrialization eventually forced the United States to end its isolation. The immediate impact of Germany's growing strength was the relative decline of British power. The early years of World War I showed clearly that even when British power was thrown in on the side of France and Russia, the three allies could barely contain Germany. With the collapse of czarist Russia in 1915 and the transfer of almost 2 million German soldiers from the Russian front to the western front, a German victory became a distinct possibility. The United States would then have faced a Germany astride an entire continent, dominating European Russia and, in alliance with Austria-Hungary, the Ottoman Empire, extending German influence into the Balkans and the Middle East as far

---

2. Arnold Wolfers, *Discord and Collaboration* (Baltimore: Johns Hopkins University Press, 1965), 83.

as the Persian Gulf. It was at that point that Germany's unrestricted submarine warfare, which included attacks on American shipping, led to a U.S. declaration of war. America's entry into the war was what made it possible to contain the German spring offensive of 1918, leading to Germany's defeat.

After its victory, the United States retreated into its customary isolationism. American bankers, with the tacit approval of the government, maintained ties to Europe, playing an important role in its economic recovery and stabilization during the 1920s. Their primary motive, however, was to recover money loaned to the European allies during World War I. Although the U.S. economy rivaled that of all of Europe and the United States exercised some economic influence, it refused to define for itself a political and military role consistent with its economic power. U.S. military power had been decisive in Germany's defeat, but the United States wanted nothing to do with international politics. It began to play a political role again only when the balance of European power was upset once more by the eruption of World War II in 1939 and the unexpected defeat of France in 1940. The United States faced the possibility of Britain's defeat and the control of Eurasia by Germany, Italy, and Japan, all antidemocratic states. To prevent this, President Franklin Roosevelt undertook a number of measures to help Britain withstand any Nazi assault. He sent fifty old destroyers to defend the English Channel, and he set up the lend-lease program, which provided munitions, food, and other material support. This commitment to Britain was necessary, even though such actions increased the risk of war with Germany. In fact, by the time of the bombing of Pearl Harbor in December 1941, the United States was already engaged in an undeclared naval war with Germany in the Atlantic, and full-scale war was merely a matter of time.

The U.S. Definition of Security

Two points deserve emphasis. First, the defense of U.S. security has always involved more than physical security. The German threat during World War I was not the likelihood of an immediate invasion; nor was invasion the main threat even after the defeat of France early in World War II. Then why should the United States twice have forsaken its isolationism? Surely, the width of the Atlantic and Pacific oceans would protect the United States.

American security was threatened because any state, especially a state that was antidemocratic as well as undemocratic, that controlled all the resources—human, natural, and industrial—of Eurasia, the Middle East, and Africa, and that organized these resources and transformed them into military power, might some day be able to attack North America. This would be particularly true had Britain been defeated and the British navy no longer guarded the sea highway to the Western Hemisphere. Even if Britain sank its navy rather than see it joined with the fleets of Germany and its allies (Italy in World War II) and defeated nations (like France in World War II), the German navy might come to dominate the Atlantic approaches to the Western Hemisphere. This would certainly be true if Germany absorbed the British fleet. Such circumstances would require the United States to mobilize its resources fully and be on constant alert for a possible attack by an opponent with more people and superior resources. Most probably, the only way the United States could match this dominant Eurasian power would be by transforming itself into a "garrison state," a disciplined, militarized state, which, in the name of security, would have to sacrifice democracy and individual liberty as ideological excess baggage.

The more immediate reason for U.S. intervention was that the security of a democratic America was inextricably interwoven with the survival of other democracies, especially France and Britain. After France collapsed in 1940, Roosevelt explained to the American public why the United States had to assist Britain: the United States could not survive as a lone democratic island surrounded by totalitarian seas. Democracy in America could not flourish unless democratic values prospered in other societies. There might be no physical threat to the nation, but the aim of American foreign policy has never been just the security of the United States as a piece of real estate; the purpose has been to defend the security of a democratic America. A democratic America required democratic values to flourish internationally.

The other point to be emphasized is that, despite the U.S. concern with security in Europe, the timing of the interventions in 1917 and 1941 were not rational decisions made by Washington. It was Berlin's decision in 1917 to launch unrestricted submarine warfare against all shipping to England that brought the United States into the war; and it was Tokyo's decision to sink the U.S. fleet at anchor in Hawaii that led to the American declaration of war against Japan. But for Hitler's reckless declaration of war against the United States—a country he held in great contempt—U.S. power would have been directed only against Japan, and Germany, the far stronger power, would have faced only Britain and Russia, both already reeling from German blows. But for German and Japanese mistakes, the United States would *not* have entered the two world wars. At the very least, the timing would have been different. The decisions to go to war were not made by the United States even though the balance of power in Europe and Asia were imperiled and American security was at stake. The United States was saved from itself by its enemies.

Great powers usually do not leave decisions about their security to their adversaries. The strategy of the major states in the state system is—or should be—to oppose any state that seeks predominance because this constitutes a grave threat to its own security. Power is the best antidote to power, and a balance of power provides the best protection for all members of the state system. The failure of the United States twice to act according to the logic dictated by the balance of power is due largely to its particular national style.

Each nation is the product of its geography, historical experiences, economic resources, and political values and organization; each tends to see the world and its role in it differently. Each nation has a unique history from which, correctly or incorrectly, it draws certain lessons. Each therefore develops a specific personality and behavior patterns that is its national style.

The American National Style

The particular style reflected in the American response to war in Europe and later to the cold war was the product of domestic experience. The priority of internal political and economic tasks, a characteristic of the United States since its beginning, demonstrated that the United States had successfully isolated itself from European power politics. As a nation with nonthreatening neighbors to the north and south, and fish to the east and west, the United States could take security for granted. Free from external threat, it could focus on its development as a democratic society.

The American Sense of Destiny

The ability of the United States to live in isolation during the nineteenth century and the first decade of the twentieth century cannot be attributed *only* to the nation's distance from Europe, or to Europe's preoccupation with industrialization and class conflict at home and colonialism abroad, or to the strength of the Royal Navy. The nature of democracy also must be considered. The United States saw itself as more than just the world's first "new nation"; it was also the world's first democracy and, as such, the first country in history with the desire to improve the lot of ordinary people, to grant them the opportunity to enrich and ennoble their lives. ("Give me your tired, your poor, your huddled masses yearning to breathe free," reads the inscription on the Statue of Liberty.) The more perfect union was to be an egalitarian society. European concepts of social hierarchy, nobility and titles, and bitter class struggles were not to be planted in its democratic soil.

From the very beginning of their national life, Americans professed a strong belief in what they considered their destiny—to spread, *by example,* freedom and social justice to all and to lead humankind away from its wicked ways to the New Jerusalem on earth. The massive immigration of the nineteenth century—particularly after 1865—was to reinforce this sense of destiny. "Repudiation of Europe," John Dos Passos once said, "is, after all, America's main excuse for being." Europe stood for war, poverty, and exploitation; America, for peace, opportunity, and democracy. But the United States was not merely to be a beacon of a superior democratic domestic way of life. It was also to be an example of a morally superior democratic pattern of international behavior. The United States would voluntarily reject power politics as unfit for the conduct of its foreign policy. Democratic theory posits that people are rational and moral and that differences among them can be settled by rational persuasion and moral exhortation. Indeed, granted this assumption, the only differences that could arise would simply be misunderstandings, and, since people are endowed with reason and a moral sense, what quarrels could not be settled, given the necessary good will? Peace—the result of harmony among people—was considered the natural or normal state.

Conversely, conflict was considered a deviation caused primarily by wicked leaders whose morality and reason had been corrupted by their exercise of uncontrolled authority. Power politics was an instrument of selfish and autocratic rulers—that is, leaders unrestrained by democratic public opinion—who love to wield it for personal advantage. To them, war was a grand game. They could remain in their palatial homes, continuing to eat well and to enjoy the luxuries of life. They suffered none of the hardships of war. These fell upon the ordinary people, who had to leave their families to fight, to endure the higher taxes to pay for the war, and possibly to see their homes and families destroyed. The conclusion was clear: undemocratic states were inherently warlike and evil; democratic nations, in which the people controlled and regularly changed their leaders, were peaceful and moral.

The American experience seemed to support this conclusion: the United States was a democracy, and it was at peace. Furthermore, peace seemed to be the normal state of affairs. It was logical that democracy and peaceful behavior and intentions should be thought of as synonymous. Americans never asked themselves whether democracy was responsible for the peace they enjoyed, or whether peace was the product of other forces. The constant wars of Europe appeared to provide the answer: European politics was power politics, and this was because of the undemocratic nature of European regimes. Americans had cut themselves off from Europe and its class conflicts and power politics after the Revolutionary War. America had to guard its democratic purity and abstain from any involvement in the affairs of Europe lest it be soiled and corrupted. Nonalignment or isolationism, therefore, was the morally correct policy, for it allowed the United States to quarantine itself from Europe's hierarchical social structures and immoral international habits.

By confusing the results of geography and Europe's focus on Asia, the Middle East, and Africa with the virtues of American democracy, Americans could smugly enjoy their self-conferred moral superiority as the world's first democracy. It was the Monroe Doctrine, proclaimed in 1823, that first stressed, officially and explicitly, this ideological difference between the New World and the Old World. It declared specifically that the American political system was "essentially different" from that of Europe, whose nations were constantly engaged in warfare. The implication was very clear: democratic government equals peace, and aristocratic government—which was identified with despotism—means war.

The Depreciation of Power in International Politics

But this association of peace with democracy was not the only reason for the American depreciation of power politics. Another was that the United States was overwhelmingly a one-class society, in which most shared belief in a common set of middle-class, capitalistic, and democratic values. America was unique among nations in this respect. The European countries were, by contrast, three-class societies. In addition to the middle class, they contained in their bodies politic an aristocratic class, whose energies were devoted either to maintaining itself in power or to recapturing power and returning to the glorious days of a feudal past. Moreover, European urbanization and industrialization during the nineteenth century had given birth to a proletariat, which, because it felt it did not receive a fair share of the national income, became a revolutionary class. The nations of the Old World were a composite of these three elements: a reactionary aristocracy, a democratic middle class, and a revolutionary proletariat. These nations had, in an intellectual as well as a political sense, a right, a center, and a left.

The United States had only a center, both intellectually and politically. It had never experienced a feudal past and therefore possessed no large, powerful aristocratic class on the right. Because it was, by and large, an egalitarian society, it also lacked a genuine left-wing movement of protest, such as socialism and communism. America was, as Alexis de Tocqueville had said, "born free" as a middle-class, individualist, capitalistic, and democratic society. It was not divided by the kind of deep ideological conflicts that in France, for instance, set one class of people against another. No one class was ever so afraid of another that it preferred national defeat to domestic revolution—as in France in the late 1930s, when the *haute bourgeoisie* was so apprehensive of a proletarian upheaval that its slogan became "Better Hitler than Blum" (Léon Blum, the French Socialist leader).

This overwhelming agreement on the fundamental values of American society and Europe's intense class struggles reinforced the American misunderstanding of the nature and functions of power on the international scene. Dissatisfied groups never developed a revolutionary ideology because the growing prosperity spread to them before they could translate their grievances against the capitalist system into political action. (Black Americans were the exception because they never shared this wealth or political power.) With the exception of the Civil War, America—politically secure, socially cohesive, and economically prosperous—was able to resolve most of its differences peacefully. Living in isolation, this country could believe in an evolutionary, democratic, economically prosperous historical process; revolution and radicalism were considered bad. In sharp contrast, because of their internal class struggles and external conflicts among themselves, the nations of Europe fully appreciated that social conflict is natural and that power plays a role in resolving conflict.

Americans in the past have been so in accord on basic values that whenever the nation has been threatened externally it has also become fearful of internal disloyalty. It is one of the great ironies of American society that, while Americans possess this unity of shared beliefs to a greater degree than any other people, their apprehension of external danger repeatedly has led them, first, to insist upon a general and somewhat dogmatic reaffirmation of loyalty to the "American way of life," and then to hunt for internal groups that might betray this way of life. Disagreement tended to become suspect as disloyalty; people were accused of "un-American" thinking and behavior and labeled "loyalty or security risks." Perhaps only a society so overwhelmingly committed to one set of values could have been so sensitive to internal subversion and so fearful of internal betrayal. Perhaps only a society in which two or more ideologies have long since learned to live together can genuinely tolerate diverse opinions: Who has ever heard of "un-British" or "un-French" activities? The United States has often been called a "melting pot" because of the many different nationality groups it comprises, but, before each generation of immigrants has been fully accepted into American society, it has had to be "Americanized." Few Americans have ever accepted diversity as a value. American society has, in fact, taken great pride in destroying diversity through assimilation.

Politics did not, in any event, seem very important to Americans. The United States matured during the nineteenth century, the era of *laissez-faire* capitalism, the basic assumption of which was that people were economically motivated. Self-interest governed behavior. It might be referred to as "enlightened self-interest," but it was self-interest nevertheless. Individuals, seeking to maximize their wealth, responded to the demand of the free market. In an effort to increase profits, they produced what the consumers wanted. The laws of supply and demand therefore transformed each person's economic selfishness into socially beneficial results. In this way, the entire society would prosper. The free market was considered the central institution that provided "the greatest good for the greatest number." Politics mattered little in this self-adjusting economic system based upon individuals whose combined efforts resulted in the general welfare. The best government was the government that governed least. Arbitrary political interference with the economic laws of the market only upset the results these laws were intended to produce. Private property, profit, and the free market were the keys to ensuring the happiness of people by providing them with abundance. Capitalism, in short, reflected the materialism of the age of industrialization.

To state the issue even more bluntly: economics was good and politics was bad. This simple dichotomy came naturally to the capitalist middle class. Were the benefits of economic freedom not as "self-evident" as the truths stated in the Declaration of Independence? And had this economic freedom not been gained only by a long and bitter struggle of the European middle class to cut down the authority of the powerful monarchical state, and finally to overthrow it by revolution in France? The middle class, as it had grown more prosperous and numerous, had become increasingly resentful of paying taxes from which the aristocracy was usually exempt, of the restrictions placed upon trade and industry, of the absence of institutions in which middle-class economic and political interests were represented, of the class barriers to the social status that came with careers in the army and in the bureaucracy, and of the general lack of freedom of thought and expression. Because the middle class identified the power of the state with its own lack of freedom, its aim was to restrict this power. Only by placing restraints upon the authority of the state could it gain the individual liberty and, above all, the right to private enterprise it sought. Democratic philosophy stated these claims in terms of the individual's "natural rights." The exercise of political authority was equated with the abuse of that authority and the suppression of personal freedoms. The power of the state had to be restricted to the minimum to ensure the individual's maximum political and economic liberties. It was with this purpose in mind that the American Constitution divided authority between the states and the federal government, and, within the latter, among the executive, legislative, and judicial branches. Federalism and the separation of powers were deliberately designed to keep all governments—and especially the national government—weak. Secular problems would be resolved not by the state's political actions, but by the individual's own economic actions in society in peacetime.

The American experience reflected this philosophy; millions came to the United States from other lands to seek a better way of life. America was the earthly paradise where everyone could earn a respectable living. A virgin land, America presented magnificent opportunities for individual enterprise. First, there was the Western frontier with its rich soil; later, during the Industrial Revolution, the country's bountiful natural resources. The environment, technology, individual enterprise, and helpful governmental policies enabled the American people to become the "people of plenty." But to earn money was not only economically necessary to attain a comfortable standard of living; it was also psychologically necessary to gain social status and to earn the respect of one's fellow citizens.

It follows logically that, if material gain confers social respect and position, everyone will pursue the "almighty dollar." If people in an egalitarian society are judged primarily by their economic achievements, they will concentrate on getting ahead. It is not surprising, therefore, that money comes closer to being the common standard of value in the United States than in any other country. Money is the symbol of power and prestige; it is the sign of success, just as failure to earn enough money is a token of personal failure. It has been said, not without some justice, that the American male prefers two cars to two mistresses.

It was hardly surprising that in these circumstances the solution to international problems should be considered matters of economics rather than politics. Economics was identified with social harmony and the welfare of all peoples; politics was equated with conflict, war, and death. Just as the "good society" was to be the product of free competition, so the peaceful international society would be created by free trade. An international *laissez-faire* policy would benefit all states just as a national *laissez-faire* policy benefited each individual within these states. Consequently, people all over the world had a vested interest in peace in order to carry on their economic relations. Trade and war were incompatible. Trade depended upon mutual prosperity (the poor do not buy much from one another). War impoverishes and destroys and creates ill will among nations. Commerce benefits all the participating states; the more trade, the greater the number of individual interests involved. Commerce created a vested interest in peace; war was economically unprofitable and therefore obsolete. Free trade and peace, in short, were one and the same cause.

The Penchant for Crusading

One result of this American depreciation of power politics was that the United States historically has drawn a clear-cut distinction between war and peace in its approach to foreign policy. Peace was characterized by a state of harmony among nations; power politics, on the other hand, was considered abnormal and war a crime. In peacetime, one needed to pay little or no attention to foreign problems; indeed, to do so would have diverted people from their individual, materialistic concerns and upset the whole scale of social values. The effect of this attitude was clear: Americans turned their attention toward the outside world with reluctance and usually only when provoked—that is, when the foreign menace had become so clear that it could no longer be ignored. Or, to state it somewhat differently, the United States rarely initiated policy; the stimuli responsible for the formulation of American foreign policy came from beyond America's frontiers.

Once Americans were provoked and the United States had to resort to force, the employment of this force was justified in terms of the moral principles with which the United States, as a democratic country, identified itself. War could be justified only by presuming noble purposes and completely destroying the immoral enemy who threatened the integrity, if not the existence, of these principles. American power had to be "righteous" power; only its full exercise could ensure salvation or the absolution of sin. A second result of the depreciation of power politics was, therefore, that the national aversion to violence became transformed on occasion into a national glorification of violence, and wars became ideological crusades to destroy the enemy state and then send its people to democratic reform school. Making the world safe for democracy—the stated objective during World War I—was to be achieved by democratizing the populace of the offending nation, making its new rulers responsible to the people they governed and thereby converting the formerly authoritarian or totalitarian state into a peaceful democratic state and banishing power politics for all time. Once that aim had been achieved, the United States could again withdraw into itself, secure in the knowledge that American works had again proved to be "good works." In this context, foreign affairs were an annoying diversion from more important domestic matters. But such a diversion was only temporary because maximum force was applied to the aggressor as punishment and as instruction that aggression was immoral and would not be rewarded. As a result, American wars were total wars to end war itself, but once the wars were over, the United States would once more withdraw from international politics. Normalcy having been restored, the pendulum would swing back.

This is the pattern of American foreign policy: from isolationism to interventionism, from withdrawal to crusading and back again. As a self-proclaimed morally and politically superior country, the United States could remain uncontaminated only by abstaining from involvement in a corrupt world or, if the world would not leave it alone, destroying the source of evil. In short, both the isolationist and the crusading impulses sprang from the same moralism. These swings tended, moreover, to be accompanied by radical shifts of mood: from one of optimism, which sprang from the belief that America was going to reform the world, to one of disillusionment as the grandiose objectives the United States had set for itself proved beyond its capacity to reach. Feeling too good for this world, which clearly did not want to be reformed but preferred its old corrupt habits, the nation retreated into isolationism to perfect and protect its way of life. Having expected too much from the use of its power, the United States then also tended to feel guilty and ashamed about having used its power at all.

The third result of the depreciation of power politics was that Americans divorced force from diplomacy. In peacetime, diplomacy unsupported by force was supposed to preserve the harmony among states. But, in time of war, political considerations were subordinated to force. Once the diplomats had failed to keep the peace with appeals to morality and reason, military considerations became primary, and the soldier was placed in charge.

The United States, then, had traditionally rejected the concept of war as a political instrument and Carl von Clausewitz's definition of war as the continuation of politics by other means.[3] Instead, it had regarded war as a politically neutral operation that should be guided by its own professional rules and imperatives. The military officer was a nonpolitical man who conducted his campaign in a strictly military, technically efficient manner. And war was a purely military instrument whose sole aim was the destruction of the enemy's forces and despotic regime. Policy and strategy were unrelated;

---

3. This phrase sums up the essence of Carl von Clausewitz's famous book, *On War*. First published in 1832, it remains the most outstanding effort in Western history to understand war's internal dynamics and its relationship to political policy and goals. The best modern translation and editing is by Michael Howard and Peter Paret, *On War* (Princeton, N.J.: Princeton University Press, 1976).

strategy began where policy ended. After the Japanese attack on Pearl Harbor, the secretary of state turned to the secretary of war (as he was then called) and said the situation was now out of his hands; it was all up to the War Department. As the war in Europe was coming to a close, the British asked General George C. Marshall, architect of the Western allies' victory, to send U.S. forces to liberate Prague and as much of Czechoslovakia as possible before the Soviet army arrived. Marshall responded that he would not risk American lives for "purely political purposes"—a commendable sentiment, but what is war about if not the achievement of political purposes?

War was a means employed to abolish power politics; war was conducted to end all wars. This same moralistic attitude, which was responsible for the Americans' all-or-nothing approach to war, also militated against the use of diplomacy in its classical sense: to compromise interests, to conciliate differences, and to moderate and isolate conflicts. Although Americans regarded diplomacy as a rational process for straightening out misunderstandings between nations, they were also extremely suspicious of it. If the United States was by definition moral, it obviously could not compromise; for a nation endowed with a moral mission could hardly violate its own principles. That constituted appeasement and national humiliation. The nation's principles would be transgressed, the nation's interests improperly defended, the national honor stained. To compromise with the immoral enemy was to be contaminated with evil. Moreover, to reach a settlement with enemies, rather than wiping them out in order to safeguard those principles, would be to acknowledge American weakness. This attitude toward diplomacy, which, in effect, made its use as an instrument of compromise difficult, reinforced the predilection for violence as a means of settling international problems. War allowed the nation to destroy its evil opponent, but permitted it to keep its moral mission intact and unsullied by any compromises.

The Contrast Between the United States and Traditional Great Powers

On the eve of the cold war, then, the American approach to foreign policy contrasted sharply in a number of important respects with the conduct of states long immersed in international politics. As a highly secure state, it needed neither a large army nor navy to protect it. The military and its values were basically despised because they were believed to be contrary to those of a democracy, and it was the building of democracy that the nation considered its first task. The result has been the pattern just described: a swing from an isolationist position in which the country served as an example of social justice on earth to a posture of massive and violent intervention. Consistent continuous participation in the international system has not been the norm.

Furthermore, the American perception of an international harmony of interests stood in stark contrast to the state system's emphasis on the inevitability of conflict and differences of interests among states. The former view regarded conflict as an abnormal condition; the latter perceived harmony as an illusion. The United States, long isolated from Europe and therefore not socialized by the state system, did not accept the reality and permanence of conflicts among its members. Differences between states were considered unnatural; certainly such differences should not be deep or long-lasting. Rather, they were attributed to wicked leaders (who could be eliminated), authoritarian political systems (which could be reformed), or misunderstandings (which could be straightened out if the adversaries approached each other with sincerity and empathy). Once these obstacles had been removed, peace, harmony, and good will would reign supreme.

Because the United States considered itself a morally and politically superior society, its attitude toward the use of power internationally was dominated by the belief that the struggle for power did not exist or could be avoided by isolating the country from it or could be eliminated by crusading against those countries indulging in power politics. Moralism in foreign policy proscribed the use of power in peacetime; power could be employed only in confrontations with unambiguous aggression, transformed then into an obligation to fight on behalf of righteous causes. In short, power could be legitimated only by democratic purposes; otherwise, its exercise would be evil and would necessarily arouse guilt feelings.

The great American compulsion to feel moral about the nation's behavior reinforced the cyclical swings from isolationism to crusading and back again. The perception of power as simply the raw material of international politics—its use as an instrument of compromise, conciliation, and moderation of interstate politics, its discriminating application toward achievement of specific and less-than-total objectives—was clearly antithetical to the American understanding of power. The term *power politics* was itself kind of "dirty," an anathema, a reminder of a way of doing things that the New World hoped it had left behind, and a potential threat to its virtue if the nation were to indulge in that kind of immoral Old World behavior.

One of the most telling symptoms of America's national style in conducting foreign policy is that after every major war the reasons for the country's participation in struggle and bloodshed have been reinterpreted.[4] These revisionist histories have certain common themes: the conflicts in which the nation had become entangled did not in fact threaten its security interests; it became involved because the politicians saw a menace where none existed, and this illusion had been promoted by propagandists who aroused and manipulated public opinion, by soldiers with bureaucratic motives, and, above all else, by bankers and industrialists—the "merchants of death" of the 1930s,

---

4. See bibliography, p. 389.

the "military-industrial complex" of the 1960s—whose economic interests benefited from the struggle. America's engagements in the two world wars of this century (as in the cold war later) were mistakes; they were really unnecessary or immoral, if not both. The enemy identified yesterday as the aggressor and *provocateur* apparently did not represent a threat to American security at all; to the contrary, the threat turns out to have come from within. But for certain *domestic forces* the United States could have continued to isolate itself from international politics. Note also that these internal groups propelling the nation into war were said, in characteristic American fashion, to be motivated by profit.

The fundamental revisionist assumption, then, has been that the nation had a choice whether it wanted to employ power politics. Conversely, revisionism rejected the idea that the distribution of power in the state system left the United States—or any other country, for that matter—with a choice only of whether it would help maintain the balance of power. Power was equated with its abuse. Abstention from its use and the creation of a truly just society at home were considered wiser and more moral policies. Crusading, allegedly for the reform of the world, risked corrupting America's very soul because it diverted attention and resources from reform at home to military preparation and war. Revisionism, then, was essentially an argument for continued isolation from power politics. International involvements, especially wars, were aberrations from the normalcy of harmony.

But if one could no longer avoid power politics or abolish it, there was yet another solution: to escape from it, to flee the troublesome and divisive world of power into the more peaceful and united world of economics. The belief that political conflict among states could be transformed into cooperation among nations when they focused on what was truly important—the improvement of humanity's material and social life—was another major characteristic of American style. If power politics and concern for security led to conflict and war, economics with its concern for raising everyone's standard of living bound all people together, regardless of nationality or race. They had to cooperate for their common good. The revulsion against the concept of maintaining the balance of power and a renewed emphasis on "interdependence" that followed the Vietnam War was hardly novel. Even while the republic was still young there were already those who felt that

> The [national political] barriers that existed seemed artificial and ephemeral in comparison with the fine net by which the merchants tied the individuals of the different nations together like "threads of silk.". . . [T]he merchants—whether they are English, Dutch, Russian, or Chinese—do not serve a single nation; they serve everyone and are citizens of the whole world. Commerce was believed to bind the nations together and to create not only a community of interests but also a distribution of labor among them—a new comprehensive principle placing the isolated sovereign nations in a higher political unit. In the eighteenth century, writers were likely to say that the various nations belonged to "one society"; it was stated that all

states together formed "a family of nations," and the whole globe a "general and unbreakable confederation." [5]

The United States after World War II, therefore, faced the world with attitudes and behavior patterns formed by its long period of isolationism from Europe. More specifically, the nation confronted the Soviet Union, a state with long experience in power politics.

The Soviet Style

The Russian Background

Russia was not blessed by geography. Unprotected by natural barriers such as oceans or mountains, Russia suffered frequent invasions. During the thirteenth and fourteenth centuries, Russia was ruled by the Mongols from the East. By the middle of the fifteenth century Mongol domination had been repelled, and Moscow emerged as the capital of a Russian state that was the equivalent of the European and Great Russian-speaking part of the contemporary Soviet Union. In more modern times, Napoleon's armies invaded and captured Moscow in 1812; British and French armies landed in the Crimea in 1854-1856; Japan attacked and defeated Russia in 1904-1905. Germany twice invaded Russia during the twentieth century, defeating it in 1917—which led to the collapse of the monarchy and brought the Bolsheviks into power—and almost defeating it again within a few months after the attack in June 1941. In between, the Western allies intervened on the anti-Bolshevik side, and the Poles in 1920 almost defeated a Russia exhausted by civil war. Historically, therefore, Russia could not take its security for granted or give priority to domestic affairs. Not surprisingly in these circumstances, political power became centralized in the state, and the possession of large standing military forces was thought to be a necessity. Indeed, Russia's experiences led its leaders to believe that there was no such thing as too much military power, and their forces have been considerably larger than those of the other European Great Powers, although this numerical superiority has not prevented their defeat.

Historian Richard Pipes has remarked, however, that Russia no more became the world's largest territorial state by repelling repeated invasions than a man becomes rich by being robbed. As the map (page 38) shows, Russia spans the European continent. Its people, 280 million in 1986 (compared to 241 million for the United States), composed of just over 100 nationalities, occupy almost 9 million square miles, spread over eleven time zones, and speak 130 languages. Occupying Eurasia's heartland, Russia

---

5. Felix Gilbert, *To the Farewell Address: Ideas of Early American Foreign Policy* (Princeton, N.J.: Princeton University Press, 1961), 57.

borders on Europe, the Middle East, and Asia, the regions which together possess most of the world's population and resources. The same lack of natural frontiers that fail to protect Russia from invasion also allow Russian power to extend outward all around its frontier, which is precisely the course Russia has followed since the fourteenth century. Sustained territorial expansion has been called the "Russian way." President Jimmy Carter's former national security assistant, Zbigniew Brzezinski, said that any list of aggressions against Russia in the last two centuries would be dwarfed by Russian expansionist moves against its neighbors.[6]

Historically, whether Russian motives were defensive or offensive, the result has been a pattern of expansionism. To the degree that Russian rulers have feared attacks, they have pushed outward to keep the enemy as far away as possible. Territorial extension became a partial substitute for the lack of wide rivers or mountains that might have afforded a degree of natural protection. Individual rulers' ambitions, such as Peter the Great's determination to have access to the sea, also resulted in territorial conquest and defeat of the power blocking that aim (in this instance, Sweden). This pattern of insecurity and appetite set up a vicious cycle. Expansion might momentarily satisfy Russian ambitions and relieve Russian fears, but it intensified its neighbors' insecurities, leading to new conflicts; this, in turn, stimulated Russian insecurity once more, leading to another round of expansion. Even before the Bolsheviks seized power in 1917, the idea of good neighbors was an alien concept. The basic "rules" of the state system—the emphasis on national interests, distrust of other states, expectation of conflict, self-reliance, and the possession of enough power, especially, military power—were deeply ingrained in Russia's leaders.

The Soviet Ingredient

These attitudes were strengthened by the outlook of the new regime after 1917. Russia was a state; Soviet Russia was also a church. The new leaders' ideological outlook did not tell them what to do in a specific foreign policy situation, but it gave them a broad framework for perceiving and understanding the world. Theirs was essentially a revolutionary perspective. Why were most human beings poor, illiterate, and unhealthy? Why did states fight wars? Their answer was that a small minority of capitalists, who controlled both the wealth and power in capitalist states, exploited those who worked in their factories to maximize profits. To keep wages down, they kept food prices low so that agricultural labor also lived in destitution. Wars were the result of these states' constant search for profits internationally and the resulting conflicts over dividing up the non-European colonial world. If human beings

---

6. Zbigniew Brzezinski, "The Soviet Union: The Aims, Problems, and Challenges to the West" in *The Conduct of East-West Relations in the 1980s,* Adelphi Paper No. 189, Part I (London: International Institute for Strategic Studies, 1984), 4.

were ever to live in freedom and enjoy a decent standard of living in peace and fraternity with other countries, capitalism would have to be replaced by communism. This line of thinking made the domestic order of other states a key issue for the Soviet leaders.

Ideology was more than a way of viewing the world; it also gave the Soviet leaders a mission. Their perspective that capitalism was the chief obstacle to humanity's liberation meant that from the moment the Soviets seized power they defined capitalist states as enemies. Soviet leaders considered the American and West European governments as enemies because of what they were—capitalist. Believing the West to be hostile, the Soviets interpreted all Western actions that way. Sooner or later, a state that considers other states as enemies and acts accordingly will be proven correct as other states reciprocate. Whereas in the traditional state system, states had no permanent friends and enemies, changing allies as the distribution of power changed, Soviet ideology clearly discriminated friend from foe on a permanent basis. Because the Soviet Union defined the capitalist states as foes, the relationship between it and them would be marked by conflict until the victory of what the Soviets call *socialism* and the defeat of capitalism. Soviet leaders, moreover, took it for granted that the capitalist states were equally hostile to them and equally determined to eliminate the Soviet Union, if only to avoid their own demise. Although the fervor of their mission faded over the decades following 1917 and the impact of ideology declined, the Soviet leaders' continued to see the capitalist states as enemies and the Soviet relationship with them as one of constant struggle.

The overall effect was to accentuate historic Russian suspicions of foreigners and feelings of insecurity so strong they might be described as paranoia. The Soviet leaders believed that the state system, composed of capitalist states, was a very hostile environment. They were unwilling to accept the latter's professions of good will and peaceful intentions, regarding them as duplicitous, and they committed the Soviet Union to the "inevitable and irreconcilable struggle" against these states. They fostered a strong emphasis on self-reliance and an equally intense concern with the Soviet Union's relative power. They were convinced that when an enemy makes concessions in negotiations or becomes more accommodating, it is not because the enemy wants a friendlier relationship but because it is *forced* to do so by the Soviet Union's growing strength—a viewpoint that obviously leads to a self-sustaining rationale for more military power.

These attitudes reinforce the traditional Russian tendency toward expansionism: fear of capitalist states demands that they be kept away from Soviet frontiers. But, as the physical embodiment of a cause, the Soviet Union's task was also to wage an unrelenting struggle to liberate humanity from the chains of capitalist exploitation and oppression. Russian history stands as a warning to Soviet leaders that peace is but a preparation for the next war; their ideological perceptions also strengthen the view that peace is but the continuation of the last war by other means. The Soviet mentality, in short, reinforces the historically repetitious cycles that have always resulted in a further expansion of power. Even if it were to be granted that insecurity drives this expansion, rather than any historical mission, the result for neighboring states remains the same—they are endangered. A drive to achieve absolute security in a system in which no state can achieve that aim, short of total domination, leaves other states very insecure.

The contrast between American culture and national style, which emphasizes peace as normal and conflict as abnormal, and that of the Soviet Union, which stresses precisely the opposite view, could not be more striking. The key question is not which style is morally more appealing or intellectually more satisfying, but which one is operationally more relevant—that is, which one allows the policy makers to make their state more secure and create a more hospitable environment for that state to enjoy its particular way of life.

The Beginning of
the Cold War

BEFORE the 1945 Quebec conference between Prime Minister Winston Churchill and President Franklin Roosevelt, a U.S. War Department memorandum forecasting the Soviet Union's postwar position concluded that the Soviet Union would be the dominant power on the continent of Europe: "With Germany crushed, there is no power in Europe to oppose her tremendous military forces. . . . The conclusions from the foregoing are obvious. Since Russia is the decisive factor in the war, she must be given every assistance, and every effort must be made to obtain her friendship. Likewise, since without question she will dominate Europe on the defeat of the Axis, it is even more essential to develop and maintain the most friendly relations with Russia." [1]

The importance of this assessment lies less in its prediction of the Soviet Union's postwar position—which was, after all, fairly obvious—than in its reflection of American expectations about future Soviet-American relations. American policy makers apparently accepted without any major misgivings the prospect of the Soviets as the new dominant power in Europe; they did not conceive of it replacing Nazi Germany as a grave threat to the European and global balance of power. The United States twice in the twentieth century had been propelled into Europe's wars at exactly those moments when Germany became so powerful that it almost destroyed this balance. The lessons of history—specifically, the impact upon American security of any nation's domination of Europe—had not yet been absorbed. Roosevelt and the American government did not aim at reestablishing a balance of power in Europe to safeguard the United States; they expected this security to stem from mutual Soviet-American good will, unsupported by considerations of

---

1. Robert E. Sherwood, *Roosevelt and Hopkins*, vol. 2 (New York: Bantam Books), 363-364.

power. This reliance upon mere good will and mutual esteem was to prove foolish at best and, at worst, might have been fatal.

American Wartime Illusions

The expectation of a postwar "era of good feeling" between the Soviet Union and the United States was characteristic of the unsuspecting and utopian nature of American wartime thinking, which held that war was an interruption of the normal state of harmony among nations, that military force was an instrument for punishing the aggressor or war criminals, that those who cooperated with their country in its ideological crusade were equally moral and peace-loving, and that, once the war was finished, the natural harmony would be restored and the struggle for power ended. The implication was clear: the United States need take no precautionary steps against its noble wartime allies in anticipation of a possible disintegration of the alliance and potential hostility among its partners. Instead, it was hoped that the friendly relations and mutual respect that American leaders believed had matured during war would preserve the common outlook and goals and guarantee an enduring peace.

These optimistic expectations of future Soviet-American relations made it necessary, however, to explain away continuing signs of Soviet suspicion of American and British intentions and hostility toward its two Western allies. This was particularly true with regard to the Western delay in opening up a second front. When the front was postponed from 1942 to 1943 to 1944, Joseph Stalin, dictator of the Soviet Union, became very bitter. He brusquely rejected Allied explanations that they were not yet properly equipped for such an enormous undertaking, and he especially denounced Churchill for declaring that there would be no invasion until the Germans were so weakened that Allied forces would not have to suffer forbiddingly high losses. To Stalin, this was no explanation, for the Soviets accepted huge losses of men as a matter of course. "When we come to a minefield," Marshal G. K. Zhukov explained to General Dwight Eisenhower after the war, "our infantry attacks exactly as if it were not there. The losses we get from personnel mines we consider only equal to those we would have gotten from machine guns and artillery if the Germans had chosen to defend that particular area with strong bodies of troops instead of with minefields." [2]

It was no wonder, then, that the Soviets should dismiss Allied explanations and fasten instead upon what was for them a more reasonable interpretation of American and British behavior. From the Marxist viewpoint, the Allies were doing exactly what they should be doing—namely, postponing the second front until the Soviet Union and Germany had

---

2. Quoted by Dwight Eisenhower, *Crusade in Europe* (New York: Doubleday, 1948), 514.

exhausted each other. Then the two Western powers could land in France, march into Germany without heavy losses, and dictate the peace to Germany and the Soviet Union. The Western delay was seen as a deliberate attempt by the world's two leading capitalist powers to destroy their two major ideological opponents at one and the same time. Throughout the war, the Russians displayed again and again this almost paranoid fear of hostile Western intentions.

American leaders, however, found a ready explanation for these repeated indications of Soviet suspicion. They thought of Soviet foreign policy not in terms of the internal dynamics of the regime and its enmity toward all non-Communist nations, but solely in terms of Soviet reactions to Western policies; new to international politics, they had little knowledge of Russian history and, therefore, of Russia's historical goals under czarist and Soviet rule. The few experts the State Department had were ignored; in fact, Roosevelt never took the secretary of state along to any of the wartime conferences with Churchill and Stalin. The Soviet attitude was viewed by the president against the pattern of prewar anti-Soviet Western acts: the Allied intervention in Russia at the end of World War I aimed at overthrowing the Soviet regime and, after the failure of that attempt, the establishment of the *cordon sanitaire* in Eastern Europe to keep the Soviet virus from spreading; the West's rejection of Soviet offers in the mid- and late 1930s to build an alliance against Hitler; and especially, the Munich agreement in 1938, which, by destroying Czechoslovakia, opened Hitler's gateway to the East. Western efforts to ostracize and ultimately destroy the Soviet Union, as well as attempts to turn Adolf Hitler's threat away from the West and toward Russia, were considered the primary reasons for the existence of Soviet hostility.

To overcome this attitude, American leaders thought they had only to demonstrate good intentions and prove their friendliness. The question was not whether Soviet cooperation could be won for the postwar world, but how it could be gained. And if these efforts bore fruit and created good will, what conflicts of interest could not be settled peacefully in the future? Various Soviet policies and acts during the war—the disbanding of the Comintern (the instrument of international communism), the toning down of Communist ideology and placing new emphasis placed on Soviet nationalism, the relaxation of restrictions upon the church and, above all, the statement of Soviet war aims in the same language of peace, democracy, and freedom used by the West—all seemed to prove that if the Western powers demonstrated their friendship they could convert the Soviets into friends.

Roosevelt's efforts to gain this cooperation focused on Stalin. In that respect Roosevelt's instincts were correct: if he could gain Stalin's trust, postwar Soviet-American relations would be peaceful. "To win a friend is to be a friend" is, after all, a deeply felt American belief. But in another respect his instincts were poor. Roosevelt's political experience was in the domestic arena. He had dealt successfully with all sorts of politicians and managed to resolve differences by finding compromise solutions. As a result he had great confidence in his ability to win Stalin's friendship. He would talk to Stalin as "one politician to another." In short, Roosevelt saw Stalin as a Russian version of himself, who, as a fellow politician, could be won over by a mixture of concessions and good will. It did not occur to Roosevelt that all of his considerable skills and charm might not suffice. At home, these qualities were enough because he and his opponents agreed on goals; differences were over the means. But between the United States and the Soviet Union, the differences were over the ends, the kind of world each expected to see when the war was over.

Roosevelt and his advisers believed that they had firmly established amicable and lasting relations with the Soviet Union at the Yalta Conference of the Big Three—Roosevelt, Stalin, and Churchill—in February 1945. Stalin had made concessions on a number of vital issues and promised good will for the future. He had accepted the United Nations on the basis of the American formula that the veto in the Security Council should be applied only to enforcement action, and not to peaceful attempts at the settlement of disputes. Moreover, in the "Declaration of Liberated Europe," he had promised to support self-government and allow free elections in Eastern Europe. He also had responded to the wishes of the American military and promised to enter the war against Japan. Finally, he had repeatedly expressed his hope for fifty years of peace and "big power" cooperation.

At the end of the conference the American delegation felt a mood of "supreme exaltation." The new era of good will was to be embodied in the United Nations. Here the peoples of the world could exercise vigilance over their national leaders. The United Nations was regarded as democracy working on an international scale: just as citizens within democratic states could constantly watch their representatives and prevent them from effecting compromises injurious to their interests, so the people of all countries would now be able to keep an eye on their leaders, making it impossible for them to arrange any secret deals that would betray the people's interests and shatter the peace of the world. Peace-loving world public opinion, expressing itself across national boundaries, would maintain a constant guard over the diplomats and hold them accountable. Covenants were to be open, and "openly arrived at," as President Woodrow Wilson had once expressed it.

Power politics would be banned once and for all. In the words of Secretary of State Cordell Hull: "There will no longer be need for spheres of influence, for alliances, balance of power, or any other of the special arrangements through which, in the unhappy past, the nations strove to safeguard their security or promote their interests." [3] Reliance would instead

3. Quoted by Herbert Feis, *Churchill, Roosevelt, Stalin: The War They Waged and the Peace They Sought* (Princeton, N.J.: Princeton University Press, 1957), 238.

be placed upon sound principles and good fellowship. In almost identical words, but more pointedly, the president upon his return from Yalta told Congress and the American people that his recent conference with Stalin and Churchill "ought to spell the end of the system of unilateral action, the exclusive alliances, the spheres of influence, the balances of power, and all the other expedients that have been tried for centuries—and have always failed." Instead, "We propose to substitute for all these, a universal organization in which all peace-loving nations will fully have a chance to join." [4] The Advisory Commission on Postwar Foreign Policy to the State Department had been even more emphatic on the subordination of power politics to principles. Its Subcommittee on Territorial Problems specifically stated that "the vital interests of the United States lay in following a 'diplomacy of principle'—of moral disinterestedness instead of power politics." [5] No comment could have summed up more aptly the American habit of viewing international politics in terms of abstract moral principles instead of clashes of interest and power. And no institution could have embodied more fully the immediate postwar hope for a return to "normalcy," the desire for minimum international involvement, and the expectation that the wartime cooperation with the Soviet Union would continue, than the United Nations, which was essentially seen as a *substitute* for the vigorous, self-reliant, national conduct of foreign policy.

Soviet Postwar Expansion

The American dream of postwar peace and Big Three cooperation was shattered as the Red Army, having finally halted the Nazi armies and decisively defeated the Germans at Stalingrad in late 1942, began slowly to drive the enemy out of the Soviet Union and then relentlessly pursued the retreating Germans to Berlin. The Soviet Union, which on the eve of World War II had absorbed the three Baltic States (Latvia, Lithuania, and Estonia), thus expanded into Eastern and Central Europe and began to impose its control upon Poland, Hungary, Bulgaria, Romania, and Albania, even before the end of the war. (Yugoslavia was by then under the Communist control of Marshal Tito, the Yugoslav partisan leader who had fought bravely against the German occupation, and Czechoslovakia was under the threat of the Red Army.)

In each of the nations of Eastern Europe where the Soviets had their troops, they unilaterally established pro-Soviet coalition governments. The key posts in these regimes—the ministries of the interior, which usually controlled the police, and defense, which controlled the army—were in the

---

4. Quoted by James MacGregor Burns, *Roosevelt, The Soldier of Freedom* (New York: Harcourt, Brace, Jovanovich, 1970), 582.
5. Quoted by Feis, *Churchill, Roosevelt, Stalin,* 207.

hands of the Communists. With this decisive lever of power in their grasp, it was an easy matter to extend their domination and subvert the independence of these countries. As the war drew to a close, it became clear that the words of the Yalta Declaration, in which the Soviets had committed themselves to free elections and democratic governments in Eastern Europe, meant quite different things to the Soviets and to the Americans. For the Soviet Union, control of Eastern Europe, and especially Poland, was essential. This area constituted a vital link in its security belt. After suffering two German invasions in less than thirty years, it was perhaps inevitable that the Soviet Union would try to establish "friendly" governments throughout the area. To the Soviets, democratic governments meant Communist governments, and free elections meant elections from which parties not favorable to the Communists were barred. The peace treaties with the former German satellite states (Hungary, Bulgaria, Romania), which were painfully negotiated by the victors in a series of foreign ministers' conferences during 1945 and 1946, could not therefore loosen the tight Soviet grip on what were by now Soviet satellite states.

In terms of the state system, this Soviet behavior is understandable. Each state must act as its own guardian against potential adversaries in a system characterized by conflict among states and a sense of insecurity and fear on the part of its members. As the alliance against the common enemy came to an end, the Soviet Union predictably would strengthen itself against the power most likely to be its new opponent. As czarist Russia, with a long history of invasions from the East and West, it had learned the basic rules of the international game through bitter experience; as *Soviet* Russia, its sense of peril and mistrust had been intensified by an ideology that posited capitalist states as implacable enemies. In the war, it had suffered 20 million casualties, soldiers and civilians, and saw the establishment of non-Communist regimes in Eastern Europe as unacceptable. The American insistence upon free elections was seen as an attempt to push the Soviet Union out of Europe. The assumption was that a non-Communist government would be an anti-Communist one.

U.S.-USSR Differences

No issue could have reflected more accurately the differences between the Soviet Union and the United States. Roosevelt acted precisely upon the assumption that non-Communist did not have to mean anti-Soviet. During the war, he had been all too aware of the consequences of a possible Soviet-American clash in the wake of Germany's defeat. As the leader of a nation that had *not* been socialized by the state system, he accurately represented American attitudes and expectations when he single-mindedly pursued his policy of friendship toward the Soviet Union. Roosevelt, who explained Soviet behavior almost exclusively as a reaction to past hostile actions of the West, did not view free elections in that area in terms of the creation of a new anti-Soviet belt. For him, free elections, non-Communist coalition governments in which Communists might participate if they gained a sizable vote, and a friendly attitude toward West *and* East were quite compatible.

The model he had in mind was Czechoslovakia. As the only democracy in that area, Czechoslovakia had maintained close ties with the West since its birth after World War I. But because France and Britain had failed to defend Czechoslovakia at Munich in 1938, and betrayed it by appeasing Hitler, it had also become friendly with the Soviet Union. After 1945 Czechoslovakia, like the other East European states, knew that it lay in the Soviet sphere of influence and that its security depended upon getting along with, not irritating, its powerful neighbor. Czech leaders expressed only amicable feelings for the Soviet Union and signed a security treaty with it; and, in one of the rare free elections the Soviets allowed in Eastern Europe, the Communist party received the largest vote of any party and therefore the key posts in the government. To share power in a coalition government, however, was to share power with class enemies. A "friendly" state, to the Soviets, was one totally controlled by the Communist party. A "friendly" state, in Roosevelt's eyes, was sensitive to Soviet security interests but retained its domestic autonomy. A Communist party monopoly of power was not a necessary prerequisite for the states of Eastern Europe to adopt a pro-Soviet foreign policy. Great powers historically have dominated their neighbors, who have usually accommodated themselves to this fact because they have recognized the wisdom of doing so.

During the war, the heroic Soviet war effort and sacrifices had created an enormous "reservoir of good will" in the West. Had the Soviets acted with greater restraint after the war and accepted states that, regardless of their governments' composition, would have adjusted to their great power neighbor, Stalin could have had the security he was seeking. But Stalin did not trust Roosevelt. No matter how personable the president was, no matter how sincere his statements of good will and postwar friendship, Stalin saw him as the leader of a capitalist nation: as a "tool of Wall Street," Roosevelt could not be sincere in his peaceful professions. To Stalin, Roosevelt was an American version of himself, a man who was fully aware of the impending postwar Soviet-American struggle and equally determined to weaken his adversary and gain the advantage for his nation. In Eastern Europe Soviet bayonets enforced Stalin's will. The Soviet style ensured that the wartime alliance would break up and that eventually the Western allies would return Stalin's hostility, thus proving to him that he had been right all along about Western enmity!

Ignoring a Lesson of History

The power vacuum created by Germany's defeat was virtually a replay of the situation that existed after the end of the war against Napoleon. The czar's troops entered Paris, and his alliance with Prussia and control over what then constituted Poland presented his allies—Austria-Hungary and

England—with the possibility of Russian continental hegemony. These two states plus their former enemy, France, signed a secret agreement pledging to go to war with Russia if the czar refused a peace treaty that distributed power in such a manner that all the principal states could feel reasonably secure. When the news of this secret arrangement was leaked, the czar became more compliant.

The United States did not follow this strategy. Churchill, concerned about Stalin's behavior in Eastern Europe, urged the United States to send forces to capture the symbolically important German capital of Berlin instead of rounding up the remnants of Germany's defeated army; to advance the U.S. armies as far east as possible, including farther into Czechoslovakia; not to pull back U.S. forces to their agreed-upon occupation zones in Germany until Stalin observed his agreements in Eastern Europe; and until then not to shift the bulk of American military power from Europe to the Far East for the final offensive against Japan. Washington declined all these suggestions. Roosevelt had assured Stalin that all American troops would be withdrawn within two years after the war. Why then should Stalin worry about American opposition to his efforts to control Eastern Europe? Stalin exercised caution when he encountered opposition, but he ignored diplomatic notes of protest. Carefully waiting to see what the United States would do, Stalin allowed free elections in Czechoslovakia and Hungary, the two states nearest to American power. But continued U.S.—and British—verbal protests, unsupported by action, did not impress Stalin. Consequently, Hungary's freedom was soon destroyed by the Soviets; finally in 1948, even the Czech government, in which the Communist party had the largest plurality, was overthrown by the Soviets in a *coup d'état*. Contrary to Roosevelt's earlier expectations, not even a Communist-controlled coalition government was acceptable to Stalin. Indeed, as the Soviet satellization of Eastern Europe was to show, the failure of the United States was not the failure of efforts to accommodate Soviet interests in Eastern Europe, but the failure to resist Stalin earlier. Because Stalin apparently saw no limits to Soviet expansion and his conception of Soviet security left little, if any, security for his neighbors, that limit had to be defined by the two Western powers, of whom the United States was, at the end of the war, by far the stronger. Setting that limit first occurred on the Soviet Union's southern perimeter.

The Soviet Push to the South

As in the two world wars, in which Britain had led the effort to contain Germany, it was London—not Washington—that took the first steps in opposing the Soviet Union after 1945. Indeed, the United States at first tried to play the role of mediator between the Soviet Union and Britain. Only when British power proved to be insufficient did the United States take over the task of balancing Soviet power. American initiative evolved gradually in the 1946-1947 period and was precipitated by Stalin's attempt to extend Soviet influence beyond Eastern Europe. The United States had accommodated itself to Soviet control over Eastern Europe, especially Poland, the corridor through which Germany had attacked Russia twice in a quarter-century. Moscow's security interests were understandable, and Washington, despite its disappointment over the Soviet failure to fulfill its Yalta obligations in Poland, quickly recognized the new Polish government as well as the other Soviet-installed regimes in Eastern Europe. The United States tried to convince Stalin that it was not hostile, understood Soviet security concerns, and wished to get along with the Soviet Union in peace.

But then the Soviets began moving toward the Persian Gulf and into the Mediterranean. Greece, Turkey, and Iran were the first to feel Soviet pressure. If Soviet behavior in Eastern Europe could be explained in defensive terms, this was less true for the area south of the Soviet Union, the line that runs from Turkey to India. Long before Stalin, the czars had sought access to the Mediterranean via the Dardanelles; simultaneously, they had tried to expand to the south to bring Russian power closer to the Middle East and the Persian Gulf.

The pressure on Iran began in 1946, when the Soviets refused to withdraw their troops from that country. These troops had been there since late 1941, when the Soviet Union and Britain had invaded Iran to forestall increased Nazi influence and to use Iran as a corridor through which the West could ship military aid to the Soviet Union. The Soviets had occupied northern Iran, the British the central and southern sections. When the British withdrew, the Soviets sought to convert Iran into a Soviet satellite. The Iranian prime minister's willingness to offer oil concessions to get the Soviets to withdraw was rebuffed. Moscow's goal was nothing less than detaching the northern area of Azerbaijan and then by various means pressuring Iran into a servile status.

During this period, the Soviet Union also exerted pressure on Turkey. Indeed, the Soviets had begun to do this as early as June 1945, when they made several demands: the cession of several Turkish districts lying on the Turkish-Soviet frontier, the revision of the Montreux Convention governing the Dardanelles Straits in favor of a joint Soviet-Turkish administration, the severance of Turkey's ties with Britain and the conclusion of a treaty with the Soviet Union similar to those that the Soviet Union had concluded with its Balkan satellites, and finally, the leasing to the Soviet Union of bases for naval and land forces in the Dardanelles for its "joint defense." Moscow rejected a compromise proposal that would have given the Soviet Union a veto over any non-Black Sea powers' warships seeking passage through the straits. This suggested that the Soviet motive was not primarily defensive. (In fact, after Stalin's death in 1953, Moscow renounced its claims on Turkey.) In August 1946 the Soviet Union, in a note to the United States and Britain, renewed its demand for a new administration of the straits. By now, the United States was convinced that the Soviet goal was nothing less than domination of

Turkey and fulfillment of the historic Soviet ambition to control Constantinople and gain access to the Mediterranean. Control of Turkey, of course, would have left Moscow in a better position to intimidate Iran and Greece.

In Greece, Communist pressure was exerted on the government through wide-scale guerrilla warfare, which began in the fall of 1946. Civil war in Greece was nothing new; the Communist and anti-Communist guerrillas had spent much of their energy battling each other instead of the Germans. When the British landed in Greece and the Germans withdrew, the Communists had attempted to take over Athens. Only after several weeks of bitter street fighting and the landing of British reinforcements was the Communist control of Athens dislodged; a truce was signed in January 1945. Just over a year later—in March 1946—the Greeks held a general election in which right-wing forces captured the majority of votes.

The Greek situation did not improve, however. The country was exhausted from the Italian and German invasions, the four years of occupation, and the Germans' scorched-earth policy as they retreated. Moreover, Greece had always depended on imports that were paid for by exports; now its traditional market in Central Europe was closed. While the masses lived at a bare subsistence level, the black market flourished. The inability of any government to deal with this situation aroused a good deal of social discontent. And the 100,000-man army that Greece needed to protect itself from its Communist neighbors (Albania, Yugoslavia, and Bulgaria) had brought the country to near-bankruptcy. If Britain had not helped finance, train, and equip the army and kept troops in the country, Greece probably would have collapsed. In August 1946 the Communist forces renewed the war in the north, where the Soviet satellites could keep the guerrillas well supplied. A victory for these forces would have been another way for the Soviets to reach the Mediterranean and Turkey.

In all these situations, the American government was once more confronted with the need to support Britain, the traditional guardian of this area. In the case of Iran, the United States and Britain delivered firm statements that strongly implied that they would use force to defend Iran. The Soviet response, in late March 1946, was the announcement that the Red Army would be withdrawn during the next five to six weeks. In the case of Turkey, the United States sent a naval task force into the Mediterranean immediately after the Soviets made their demand over the Dardanelles. Twelve days later, the United States formally replied to the Soviets by rejecting their demand to share responsibility for the defense of the straits with Turkey. Britain sent a similar reply. The Greek situation had not yet come to a head, and the need for American action could have been postponed for a while longer.

But it should be pointed out that President Harry Truman's actions in support of Iranian and Turkish political independence and territorial integrity were merely swift reactions to immediate crises. They were not the product of an overall American strategy. Such a coherent strategy came only after a new assessment of Soviet foreign policy had been made.

Toward the Strategy of Containment

Eighteen months passed before the United States undertook that reassessment—from the surrender of Japan on September 2, 1945, until the announcement of the Truman Doctrine on March 12, 1947. Perhaps such a reevaluation could not have been made any more quickly. Public opinion in a democratic country does not normally shift drastically overnight. It would have been too much to expect the American public to change suddenly from an attitude of friendliness toward the Soviet Union—inspired largely by the picture of Soviet wartime bravery and endurance and by hopes for peaceful postwar cooperation—to hostility. The United States wished only to be left alone to occupy itself once more with domestic affairs. The end of the war signaled the end of power politics and the restoration of normal peacetime harmony among nations.

In response to this expectation, the public demanded a speedy demobilization. In May 1945, at the end of the war with Germany, the United States had an army of 3.5 million organized into 68 divisions in Europe, supported by 149 air groups. By March 1946, only ten months later, the United States had only 400,000 troops left, mainly new recruits; the homeland reserve was six battalions. The army made further reductions, as did the air force and navy. This deliberate reduction of military strength, as a symptom of America's psychological demobilization, no doubt encouraged Soviet intransigence in Europe and attempts to extend their influence. American diplomacy and force retained their traditional separation. America's large and powerful armed forces and its enormous industrial strength, which could have provided the basis for serious negotiations about Eastern Europe, were respectively dismantled and converted back to the production of consumer goods. American policy, unsupported by sufficient conventional military power, was impotent. And "atomic diplomacy," despite what later revisionists have written, was not used either in the immediate post war period. Or, if it was used, as was claimed, it certainly did not frighten Stalin or deter him from strengthening his grip on Eastern Europe or trying to expand Soviet power into new areas.

A Change in Direction

These Soviet efforts finally provoked the United States and led to a reevaluation of American policy. Three positions became clear during this period. At one extreme stood that old realist Winston Churchill. At the end of the European war, he had counseled against the withdrawal of American troops. He had insisted that they stay, together with British troops, to force the Soviet Union to live up to its Yalta obligations regarding free elections in Eastern Europe and the withdrawal of the Red Army from eastern Germany. The United States had rejected Churchill's plea. In March 1946, at Fulton, Missouri, Churchill took his case directly to the American public. The Soviet Union, he asserted, was an expansionist state. "From Stettin in the Baltic to Trieste in the Adriatic, an iron curtain has descended across the continent. Behind that line lie all the capitals of the ancient states of Central and Eastern Europe. Warsaw, Berlin, Prague, Vienna, Budapest, Belgrade, Bucharest, and Sofia, all the famous cities and populations around them lie in the Soviet sphere and all are subject in one form or another, not only to Soviet influence but to a very high and increasing measure of control from Moscow." Churchill did not believe that the Soviets wanted war: "What they desire is the fruits of war and the indefinite expansion of their power and doctrines." This could be prevented only by the opposing power of the British Commonwealth and the United States. Churchill, in short, said bluntly that the cold war had begun, that Americans must recognize this fact and give up their dreams of Big Three unity in the United Nations. International organization was no substitute for the balance of power. "Our difficulties and dangers will not be removed by closing our eyes to them. They will not be removed by mere waiting to see what happens; nor will they be relieved by a policy of appeasement." [6] An alliance of the English-speaking peoples was the prerequisite for American and British security and world peace.

At the other extreme stood Secretary of Commerce Henry Wallace, who felt it was precisely the kind of aggressive attitude expressed by Churchill that was to blame for Soviet hostility. The United States and Britain, he said, had no more business in Eastern Europe than had the Soviet Union in Latin America; to each, the respective area was vital for national security. Western interference in nations bordering on the Soviet Union was bound to arouse Soviet suspicion, just as Soviet intervention in countries neighboring on the United States would. "We may not like what Russia does in Eastern Europe," said Wallace. "Her type of land reform, industrial expropriation, and suspension of basic liberties offend the great majority of the people of the United States. But whether we like it or not, the Russians will try to socialize their sphere of influence just as we try to democratize our sphere of influence (including Japan and Western Germany)." The tough attitude that Churchill and other "reactionaries" at home and abroad demanded was precisely the wrong policy; it would only increase international tension. "We must not let British balance-of-power manipulations determine whether and when the United States gets into a war ... 'getting tough' never bought anything real and lasting—whether for schoolyard bullies or world powers. The tougher we get, the tougher the Russians will get." [7] Only mutual trust

6. *Vital Speeches*, March 25, 1946, 329-332.
7. *Vital Speeches*, October 1, 1946, 738-741.

would allow the United States and the Soviet Union to live together peacefully, and such trust could not be created by an unfriendly American attitude and policy.

The American government and public wavered between these two positions. The administration recognized that Big Three cooperation had ended, and it realized that the time had passed when the United States needed to demonstrate good will toward the Soviet Union to overcome its suspicions. The United States would make no further concessions to preserve the appearance of friendship with the Soviet Union. America had tried to gain Soviet amity by being a friend; it was now up to Soviet leaders to demonstrate a friendly attitude toward America as well. Paper agreements, written in such general terms that they actually hid divergent purposes, were regarded as having little value. Something more than paper agreements was needed: Soviet words would have to be matched by Soviet deeds.

The American secretary of state, James Byrnes, called this new line the "policy of firmness and patience." This phrase meant that the United States would take a firm position whenever the Soviet Union became intransigent and that it would not compromise simply to reach a quick agreement. This change in the official American attitude toward the Soviet Union was not, however, a fundamental one. A firm line was to be followed only on specific issues. The assumption was that if the United States took a tougher bargaining position and no longer seemed in a hurry to resolve particular points of tension, the Soviet rulers would see the pointlessness of their obduracy and agree to fair compromise solutions of their differences with the United States and the West. In short, American firmness would make the Soviets "reasonable." But there was no suggestion in this call for a tactical shift in how to negotiate with Moscow that the United States needed to organize international opposition to the Soviet Union. The new American position, as one political analysis has aptly summed it up, "meant to most of its exponents that the Soviet Union had to be induced by firmness to play the game in the American way. There was no consistent official suggestion that the United States should begin to play a different game." [8] The prerequisite for such a suggestion was that American policy makers recognize that the Soviet Union was no longer just a difficult ally but an enemy.

Kennan and the New American Policy

George Kennan, the Foreign Service's foremost expert on the Soviet Union, in 1946 first presented the basis of what was to be a new American policy that recognized the hostile character of the Soviet regime. Kennan's analysis focused on the Communist outlook on world affairs. In the Soviet

---

8. William Reitzel, Morton A. Kaplan, and Constance G. Coblenz, *United States· Foreign Policy 1945-1955* (Washington, D.C.: The Brookings Institution, 1956), 89.

leaders' pattern of thought, he said, the Soviet Union had no community of interest with the capitalist states; indeed, they saw their relationship with the Western powers in terms of an innate antagonism. Communist ideology had taught them "that the outside world was hostile and that it was their duty eventually to overthrow the political forces beyond their borders. The powerful hands of Russian history and tradition reached up to sustain them in this feeling. Finally, their own aggressive intransigence with respect to the outside world began to find its own reaction. . . . It is an undeniable privilege for every man to prove himself right in the thesis that the world is his enemy; for if he reiterates it frequently enough and makes it the background for his conduct, he is bound to be right." [9] According to Kennan, this Soviet hostility was a constant factor; it would continue until the capitalist world had been destroyed: "Basically, the antagonism remains. It is postulated. And from it flow many of the phenomena which we find disturbing in the Kremlin's conduct of foreign policy: the secretiveness, the lack of frankness, the duplicity, the war suspiciousness, and the basic unfriendliness of purpose. . . . These characteristics of the Soviet policy, like the postulates from which they flow, are basic to the *internal* nature of Soviet power, and will be with us . . . until the nature of Soviet power is changed [italics added]." [10] Until that moment, he said, Soviet strategy and objectives would remain the same.

The American-Soviet struggle would thus be a long one, but Kennan stressed that Soviet hostility did not mean that the Soviets would embark upon a do-or-die program to overthrow capitalism by a fixed date. They had no timetable for conquest. In a brilliant passage, Kennan outlined the Soviet concept of the struggle:

> The Kremlin is under no ideological compulsion to accomplish its purposes in a hurry. Like the Church, it is dealing in ideological concepts which are of a long-term validity, and it can afford to be patient. It has no right to risk the existing achievements of the revolution for the sake of vain baubles of the future. The very teachings of Lenin himself require great caution and flexibility in the pursuit of Communist purposes. Again, these precepts are fortified by the lessons of Russian history: of centuries of obscure battles between nomadic forces over the stretches of a vast unfortified plain. Here caution, circumspection, flexibility, and deception are the valuable qualities; and their value finds natural appreciation in the Russian, or the Oriental mind. Thus the Kremlin has no compunction about retreating in the face of superior force. And being under the compulsion of no timetable, it does not get panicky under the necessity of such a retreat. Its political action is a fluid stream which moves constantly, wherever it is permitted to move, toward a given goal. Its main concern is to make sure that it has filled every nook and cranny available to it in the basin of world power. But if it finds

9. George F. Kennan, *American Diplomacy 1900-1950* (Chicago: University of Chicago Press, 1951), 111-112.
10. Kennan, *American Diplomacy 1900-1950*, 115.

unassailable barriers in its path, it accepts these philosophically and accommodates itself to them. The main thing is that there should always be pressure, increasing constant pressure, toward the desired goal. There is no trace of any feeling in Soviet psychology that the goal must be reached at any given time.[11]

How could the United States counter such a policy—a policy that was always pushing, seeking weak spots, attempting to fill power vacuums? Kennan's answer was that American policy would have to be one of "long-term, patient, but firm and vigilant containment." The United States would find Soviet diplomacy both easier and more difficult to deal with than that of dictatorships. "On the one hand, it [Soviet policy] is more sensitive to contrary force, more ready to yield on individual sectors of the diplomatic front when that force is felt to be too strong, and thus more rational in the logic and rhetoric of power. On the other hand, it cannot be easily defeated or discouraged by a single victory on the part of its opponents. And the patient persistence by which it is animated means that it can be effectively countered not by sporadic acts which represent the momentary whims of democratic opinion, but only intelligent long-range policies on the part of Russia's adversaries—policies no less steady in their purpose, and no less variegated and resourceful in their application, than those of the Soviet Union itself."

Kennan viewed containment as a test of American democracy to conduct an effective, responsible foreign policy *and* contribute to changes within the Soviet Union that might bring about a moderation of its revolutionary aims. The United States, he emphasized, "has it in its power to increase enormously the strains under which Soviet policy must operate, to force upon the Kremlin a far greater degree of moderation and circumspection than it has had to observe in recent years, and in this way to promote tendencies which must eventually find their outlet in either the breakup or the gradual mellowing of Soviet power. For no mystical, messianic movement—and particularly not that of the Kremlin—can face frustration indefinitely without eventually adjusting itself in one way or another to the logic of that state of affairs."

Why was the United States so favorably positioned for a long-term struggle with the Soviet Union? The reason was, Kennan argued, that industry was the key ingredient of power and the United States controlled most of the centers of industry. There were five such centers in the world: the United States, Britain, West Germany, Japan, and the Soviet Union. The United States and its future allies possessed four of these centers, the Soviet Union just one. Containment meant confining the Soviet Union to that one. The question, Kennan said, was not whether the United States had sufficient power to contain the Soviet Union but whether it had the patience and wisdom to do so.

---

11. Kennan, *American Diplomacy 1900-1950*, 118.

Alternatives to Containment

The policy of containment implicitly discarded two other courses of action. The first rejected was a retreat into historic isolationism. That became clear when, on the afternoon of February 21, 1947, the first secretary of the British Embassy in Washington visited the State Department and handed American officials two notes from His Majesty's government. One concerned Greece, the other Turkey, but, in effect, they said the same thing: Britain could no longer meet its traditional responsibilities in those two countries. Because both were on the verge of collapse, the meaning of the British notes was clear: a Soviet breakthrough could be prevented only by an all-out American commitment.

February 21 was a turning point for the West. Great Britain, the only remaining power in Europe, acknowledged its exhaustion. It had fought Philip II of Spain, Louis XIV and Napoleon of France, Kaiser Wilhelm II and Adolf Hitler of Germany. It had preserved the balance of power that had protected the United States for so long that it seemed almost natural for it to continue to do so. But its ability to protect that balance had steadily declined in the twentieth century. Twice it had needed American help. Each time, however, Britain had fought the longer battle; the United States had entered the wars when it was clear that Germany and its allies were too strong for Great Britain and that America would have to help safeguard its own security. Now there was no power to protect the United States but the United States itself; no one stood between that country and the present threat to its security. All the other major powers of the world had collapsed—except the Soviet Union. A bipolar or two-power world suddenly faced the United States. That was also the difference between Britain in the two world wars and the United States: Britain could fall back on American power, but the United States had no one to back it up.

The immediate crisis was in the eastern Mediterranean. Iran and Turkey had so far successfully resisted direct Soviet pressure, but Greece's northern Communist neighbors, Yugoslavia and Bulgaria, were helping the Communists in the Greek civil war, while Stalin watched to see what would happen. If Greece should fall, as Washington feared, it would be only a matter of time until Turkey and Iran also fell. But the collapse of Greece would not only affect its neighbors to the east and inject Soviet power into the Mediterranean and Persian Gulf; it would also lead to an increase of Communist pressure on Italy because Italy would then have two Communist states to its east—Yugoslavia and Greece—as well as the largest Communist party in Western Europe within its borders. To the northwest of Italy lay France, with the second largest Communist party in the West. If the security of all of Western Europe were endangered, a policy of isolationism would not protect the United States.

The other course rejected in the adoption of the strategy of containment was a preventive war. The United States had an atomic monopoly until late 1949. (By 1950 the United States had fifty bombs plus the means to deliver them, and the Soviet Union had none.) For a short time, then, the United States had possessed the opportunity of establishing a *Pax Americana* or world domination. Certainly, if that had been the U.S. intention, it could have built up its atomic stockpile and means of delivery. But exploiting this atomic monopoly was never seriously considered. Quite apart from the relatively small size of the stockpile, launching an atomic "Pearl Harbor" on the Soviet Union was contrary to American tradition and morality. Indeed, after Hiroshima, the conviction grew that atomic weapons were too horrible to use and that in a future war there would be no winners. The bomb signaled a significant change: historically, the principal task of the military had been to win wars; from now on its main purpose was to deter wars. Atomic weapons could have no other rationale. In future years, after both superpowers had tested nuclear devices and the range of destruction had taken a quantum leap from kilotons (thousands of tons of TNT) to megatons (millions of tons of TNT), this conviction grew to absolute certainty. Such weapons could not defend a nation; rather, their use would destroy it.

The consequences of the potentially suicidal nature of atomic or nuclear warfare were profound: the United States was committed to a long struggle, and this struggle was to be carried on in a new way. Conflicts between great powers—between Athens and Sparta for the control of ancient Greece, between Rome and Carthage for control of the Mediterranean, or, in more modern times, between Germany and England for control of Europe, if not Eurasia—had been settled on the battlefield. Such a solution was no longer feasible. This required the United States, a country that, when provoked by an enemy, had usually set out to destroy and punish its enemy by force of arms, to conduct a *protracted conflict* alien to its style. The term frequently given to this conflict—cold war—was apt indeed. *War* signified that the U.S.-Soviet rivalry was serious; *cold* referred to the fact that nuclear weapons were so utterly destructive that war could not be waged with "hot" (nuclear) weapons, but only with "cold" weapons (which included the use of limited conventional force but not nuclear force). But for existence of nuclear weapons, the superpower conflict at some point might well have escalated into a shooting war, as had already happened twice in the twentieth century.

The nonuse of force meant the continuation of that conflict. The resulting cold war may therefore be defined as a relationship characterized by perpetual hostility and by a mutual determination not to use force to decide who is the winner. As it took over Britain's role as the keeper of the balance of power, the United States had to learn power politics; but, in protecting itself, it also had to learn how to conduct a protracted conflict in peacetime, a completely new experience and one at odds with its historic ways of dealing with an enemy state.

The Changing of the Guard:
Sea Power Versus Land Power

The U.S. role, then, was historically similar to Britain's: primarily a naval power, it was to contain the outward thrust of a land power from the Eurasian "heartland." After World War I, a British geographer, Halford MacKinder, interested in the relationship of geographic position to international politics (referred to as *geopolitics*) stated the following axiom: "Who rules East Europe commands the Heartland [Eurasia]; Who rules the Heartland commands the World-Island [Eurasia and Africa, which, on the map, look like a centrally located island]; Who rules the World-Island commands the World." Some years later, an American geopolitician, Nicholas Spykman, coined a reply to MacKinder: "Who controls the Rimland [the peripheral areas around Eurasia] controls Eurasia; who rules Eurasia controls the destinies of the world." Although these axioms may be considered too simplistic, and there is some danger in accepting geography as too deterministic a factor in explaining the behavior of states, they explain rather well the essence of the British-German and the U.S.-Soviet conflicts. As the heartland power sought domination over Eurasia, if not the World-Island, which would have made it the dominant global power, the "off-shore" naval power sought control of the Eurasian rimlands in order to deny that domination to the heartland power and thereby contain it.

Indeed, before World War I, before the German threat received Britain's primary attention, it had been *czarist* Russia—then incorporating Finland, the three Baltic States, and Poland—that had been London's concern. Russian power was spreading eastward to the Pacific, southward from Siberia into Manchuria and into northern China, southward from the Caucasus to Turkey and into Iran toward the Persian Gulf, and southeasterly toward the frontier of British India, the area of today's Afghanistan and Pakistan. British power along the rim running from Turkey to India guarded the perimeter around Russia. When Russia pushed into Korea toward Japan, Japan attacked and defeated Russia, thereby also limiting the spread of Russian influence in northern China. After that, Russia focused on the Balkans where it came into conflict with Austria-Hungary, the ally of Germany, which had become the Continent's most powerful country. Germany became the great threat to British interests, and Britain twice went to war with Germany which, in each conflict, invaded Russia. A victorious Germany would have controlled the heartland—indeed, in World War II, victory would have given Germany control from the Atlantic to the Pacific—plus the Middle East, the area linking Europe, Asia, and Africa.

After Germany's second defeat in 1945, the Russian threat reemerged. Already the heartland power, Russia extended its power into the center of Europe, reclaimed its dominant position in northern China, and sought to

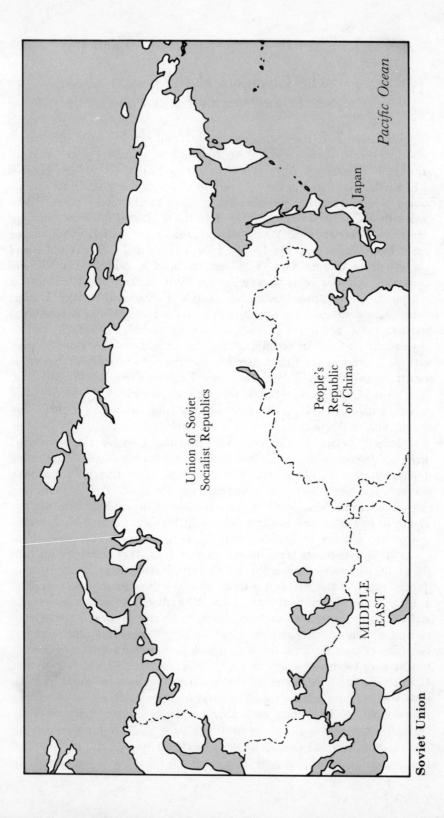

Soviet Union

exploit weaknesses along its southern border from Turkey to Pakistan. Thus, one reason for the postwar conflict was geopolitical: Russian land power expanded but was countered by the countervailing power exerted by a maritime nation. These clashes occurred along the perimeter from Turkey to Iran and then in Western Europe.

It is important to understand the location of the initial conflicts because revisionists argue that whatever the Soviet Union's intentions were, its lack of a large fleet and intercontinental air power meant that it represented no threat to the United States. They point out, moreover, that the United States held an atomic monopoly. Thus, the demobilization from a military force of 12.1 million to 1.6 million and the reduction from a budget of more than $80 billion to approximately $13 billion counted for little. Only one part of this argument is correct: the Soviet Union did not represent a threat to the security of the United States in the Western Hemisphere. But the Red Army, despite demobilization, retained a sufficient superiority to drive to the English Channel. American military observers feared this possibility, as did the West Europeans, who sought U.S. assistance for their defense. The small number of U.S. bombs might have inflicted great damage on Russia, but could not have stopped the Red Army from overrunning Western Europe. This threat, plus that to the Soviet Union's south, were the United States' concern, as earlier they had been Britain's.

What was new about this bipolar clash was that this Russia was *Soviet* Russia. By Soviet definition (as noted in chapter 1), the United States was its primary enemy, the object of permanent hostility. Indeed, the Soviet leadership's legitimacy was tied to its claim that it was waging this conflict for the liberation of humanity; to relax from the struggle against world capitalism would be a betrayal of its Marxist-Leninist legacy. Whether the leadership believed in Communist ideology was beside the point; it needed it to justify its rule and monopoly of power. Unable to rule by divine right, as the czars had, and unwilling to submit to democratic elections despite its claim to govern on behalf of the people, it legitimated its hold on political power by its self-acclaimed historical duty to create a better life not only for the people of Russia but also for the people of the world. The struggle to bring about a postcapitalist socialist international order became a rationale for both dictatorial and eternal power. Asserting that the Soviet Union was besieged by enemies, the regime asserted that it must retain its grip on power and maintain its vigilance against external threats and internal subversion and dissension. The Soviet leadership, in brief, not only required a foreign enemy, but the ideology that legitimated its power also conveniently defined that enemy. The character of the Soviet state, therefore, was an additional cause of the U.S.-Soviet tension. Indeed, former Soviet foreign minister Maxim Litvinov, said after the war that the "root cause" of the cold war was Moscow's ideological preconception that conflict between capitalism and communism was "inevitable." When asked if Western compliance with

Stalin's demands would have created good will and an end to U.S.-Soviet tensions, he replied that after a short time it would have led to the United States' being faced with the next set of Stalin's demands.[12]

The U.S. Declaration of (Cold) War

On March 12, 1947, President Harry Truman went before a joint session of Congress to deliver one of the most important speeches in American history. After outlining the situation in Greece, he spelled out what was to become known as the Truman Doctrine. The United States, he said, could survive only in a world in which freedom flourished. And it would not realize this objective

> unless we are willing to help free peoples to maintain their institutions and their national integrity against aggressive movements that seek to impose upon them totalitarian regimes. *This is no more than a frank recognition that totalitarian regimes imposed on free peoples, by direct or indirect aggression, undermine the foundations of international peace and hence the security of the United States. . . .*
>
> At the present moment in world history nearly every nation must choose between alternative ways of life. The choice is often not a free one.
>
> One way of life is based upon the will of the majority, and is distinguished by free institutions, representative government, free elections, guarantees of individual liberty, freedom of speech and religion, and freedom from political oppression.
>
> The second way of life is based upon the will of a minority forcibly imposed upon the majority. It relies upon terror and oppression, a controlled press and radio, fixed elections, and the suppression of personal freedoms.
>
> I believe it must be the policy of the United States to support free peoples who are resisting attempted subjugations by armed minorities or by outside pressure.
>
> I believe that we must assist free peoples to work out their own destinies in their own way.
>
> I believe that our help should be primarily through economic and financial aid which is essential to economic stability and orderly political processes.[13]

The president asked Congress to appropriate $400 million for economic aid and military supplies for Greece and Turkey and to authorize the dispatch of American personnel to assist with reconstruction and to provide their armies with appropriate instruction and training. The United States thus began the policy of containment.

A number of points about what was to be called the Truman Doctrine need special emphasis because of its universal nature and call for a new anti-

---

12. Quoted by William Taubman in *Stalin's American Policy* (New York: W. W. Norton, 1982), 133.
13. Italics added. The drama of this period and Truman's speech to Congress are still best captured by Joseph M. Jones, *The Fifteen Weeks* (New York: Viking Press, 1955), 17-23.

Communist crusade. First, Soviet expansionist efforts left the United States little choice but to adopt a countervailing policy. With the war over, the United States would have much preferred to concentrate on domestic affairs, as the massive postwar demobilization clearly demonstrated. Americans were about to unleash their pent-up and postponed demands for consumer goods as U.S. industry converted from wartime to peacetime production. Not dependent upon exports for economic growth, the United States did not need extensive foreign markets; the domestic market sufficed and the United States within a decade became the "affluent society." The change from isolationism to internationalism was the product of the postwar bipolar distribution of power in which a gain of power and security by one tends to be seen as a loss of power and security for the other. As one side pushes, the opponent pushes back.

Second, anticommunism was not the major ingredient of American policy during and immediately after World War II. During the war, the United States had sought to overcome the Kremlin's suspicions of the West to lay the foundation for postwar harmony and peace. At the end of the war, the principal concern of American policy makers was not to eliminate the self-proclaimed bastion of world revolution and enemy of Western capitalism, nor to push the Soviet Union out of Eastern Europe, but to forestall a complete return to the historic position of isolationism. The public mood was all too evident in the hasty military demobilization, the riots of some overseas units that felt that their demobilization was not rapid enough, and the cries of America's children heard by both Congress and the White House: "We want our daddies." For the United States to have pursued the assertive foreign policy complete with atomic threats that the revisionists have claimed it did would have required a dictatorial disregard for the widespread demands of public opinion.

It was not until a year and a half after World War II ended that the Truman Doctrine was enunciated. Containment was launched after further attempts to reconcile differences with Moscow failed and after continued Soviet pressure, denunciations, and vilifications. Hostile Soviet behavior and words were the reasons for the gradual shift of American policy and public opinion from amity to enmity. American policy was not the product of a virulent and preexisting anti-Communist ideology; rather, it was activated by the same concern for preventing a major nation from achieving dominance in Europe that had twice in the twentieth century led the United States into war. American policy after 1945 was consistent with U.S. behavior in 1917 and 1940-1941; in both cases, the nation had gone to war to prevent such an outcome. This was not fundamentally an ideological issue. In the two world wars, the enemy was Germany; in the initial engagement, Germany was led by a conservative monarchy, in the second, by an extreme right-wing fascist regime. In the cold war, the adversary was Soviet Russia, a radical left-wing regime. American action, however, remained the same, regardless of the ideological nature of the opponent.

Third, the role of anticommunism in American policy was essentially to mobilize congressional and public support for the policy once it had been decided upon. A nation that had historically condemned power politics as immoral and as a corruption of the democratic ideal needed a moral basis for its new use of power. For a people weary after four years of war, who identified the termination of war with the end of power politics, who were used to isolation from Europe's wicked affairs, and who were preoccupied with the pursuit of happiness, success, and the dollar at home, anticommunism was like the cavalry's bugle call to charge; it fitted neatly into the traditional American dichotomy of the world into extremes of good and evil, thereby arousing the nation for yet another foreign policy mission. Truman was conscious (as were Eisenhower and Kennedy later) of the U.S. desire to retreat into isolationism after a war, and he was unsure the American public was ready to commit itself to a potential conflict. He recognized the need to "sell" the public on the United States' new role in foreign policy by exaggerating the threat the nation faced.

The Truman Doctrine with its dichotomy between the free world and communism and the United States' universal mission served this purpose well. In 1950, following the first Soviet atomic test in 1949, years before it had been expected, the National Security Council issued a report depicting the all-encompassing character of the Soviet threat and the possibility of a possible Soviet atomic strike against the United States by 1954.[14] The report was intended to arouse the foreign policy bureaucracy and alert it to the need for military rearmament to block Soviet designs. Until the Vietnam War undermined this anti-Communist consensus, it served the policy makers' purposes; the policy of containment received widespread public and congressional support from both Democrats and Republicans. (Asian policy was to be the major exception to this rule, as we shall see.)

Fourth is that, despite the universalism of the Truman Doctrine, its application was intended to be specific and limited, not global. American policy makers were well aware that the United States, although a great power, was not omnipotent; therefore, national priorities—which interests were vital and which were not—had to be decided carefully and power applied discriminately. American responses would depend, then, both on where the external challenges occurred and on how Washington defined the relationship of such challenges to the nation's security. Containment was to be implemented only where the Soviet state appeared to be expanding its power. The priority given to balance-of-power considerations was evident from the very beginning. Despite the democratic purposes stated by the Truman Doctrine, its first application was to Greece and Turkey, neither of which

---

14. Samuel F. Wells, Jr., "Sounding the Tocsin: NSC 68 and the Soviet Threat," *International Security*, (Fall 1979): 116-158.

was democratic. Their strategic location was considered more important than their domestic nature.

In Western Europe, of course, America's strategic and power considerations were compatible with its democratic values. The containment of the Soviet Union could be equated with the defense of democracy. But outside of Western Europe, strategy and values were often incompatible with one another. The United States confronted a classic dilemma: protecting strategically located, but undemocratic nations, such as Iran, Turkey, and Greece, might make the containment of Soviet power possible, but also risked America's reputation and weakened the credibility of the policy—the defense of the free world. However, to align itself only with democratic states, of which there were all too few, might make it impossible for the United States to carry out the containment policy. The purity of the cause might be preserved, but the security of democracy would be weakened. This dilemma continues to plague U.S. policy.

The fifth point, and perhaps the most important, is the contrasting nature of American and Soviet expansion. The Soviet Union, which had already annexed the Baltic states, imposed Communist regimes on its neighbors and stationed Soviet forces there to ensure the loyalty of these states. By contrast, Iran, Turkey, and Greece invited American assistance because they feared Soviet pressure and intimidation. Soviet expansion meant their loss of independence; America's expansion guaranteed it. If ever there was a defensively motivated expansion, it was the U.S. commitment in the eastern Mediterranean, which was followed by an even larger commitment to first revive and then defend the nations of Western Europe. All shared the U.S. perception of the Soviet Union as a threat to their political independence and territorial integrity and urged Washington to redress the post-1945 imbalance. Their concern was not U.S. expansion, but U.S. isolationism.

What then, was America's responsibility in precipitating the cold war? If the Soviet contribution was one of commission, that of the United States was basically one of omission. Perhaps the United States could have done no more than protest Soviet satellization of Eastern Europe. It was also true that the American people, like the British, enormously admired the heroic efforts of the Red Army in stopping and driving back the Nazi forces. Moreover, the staggering Soviet losses, compared to the relatively light losses of the Allies, who until 1944 fought the Germans only in North Africa and Italy, made Western leaders and the public feel guilty. In these circumstances, the hope for good postwar relations with the Soviet Union was understandable, and that this would feed the desire to believe the best of the Russians, to find explanations and excuses for their continued suspicions of and hostility toward their Western allies, and minimize the problems among the Big Three was very natural.

But could Roosevelt, whose optimistic assessments of the future were largely responsible for the nation's expectations, not have prepared the public better for what was to happen after the war? National self-determination was the fundamental Western principle underlying the war effort. On that basis, the president was quite willing to push a reluctant Churchill to give national independence to British colonies: self-determination was not to be limited to the conquered nations of Europe. Yet, could Roosevelt not have rallied the nation around this principle as Stalin's conquest of Eastern Europe proceeded and deflated its exaggerated hopes for future U.S.-Soviet harmony? World War II had started over the independence of Poland; it ended with Poland under Soviet domination. By contrast, the United States proceeded with its hasty demobilization, encouraging Stalin to expand Soviet power. Not content with surrounding his country with subservient states, Stalin appeared to have no limit to his ambitions. Where did Soviet security interests end? Did they include control of all of Germany so that the states of Western Europe would then accommodate themselves to Soviet supremacy? Could Soviet security interests be met without creating insecurity problems for all states beyond the Soviet Union's new sphere of influence? The answer clearly was no, and the threatened states took the initiative in asking the United States to exert countervailing power. The United States finally took the necessary measures to oppose Stalin and draw the lines beyond which Soviet expansion would not be tolerated. Stalin, incapable of defining the limits of his ambitions, now found that the United States would do it for him.

Containment in Europe

IT PROBABLY would not be amiss to label American foreign policy just after 1945 as revolutionary. Today, we can look back at the long years of containment, criticize it for its lack of adaptability to a changing world, or even condemn it for its lack of sensitivity to Soviet postwar concerns. But the title of former secretary of state Dean Acheson's book *Present at the Creation* says it best. After more than a century of isolationism, the United States made a quick shift to assuming the leadership of the West, and this period was perhaps the most imaginative of U.S. postwar policy. During these years, President Harry Truman together with first, Secretary of State George Marshall—who during the war had been General Marshall, America's top soldier and the architect of victory in Europe and the Pacific—and then Acheson, reconstructed a prosperous and democratic Western Europe, edged its nations away from their past rivalries toward cooperation and unity, created West Germany and admitted it into the Western community, and provided Europe with security. This alliance of Western Europe and the United States has survived more than four decades and has been a key reason for the avoidance of nuclear war.

Western Europe's Collapse

The commitment to Greece and Turkey had been only the first act under the new American policy of containing Soviet expansion. The war in Europe had devastated the economies of all the countries, winners and losers alike. The deepest fear was that Moscow would be able to exploit Europe's postwar economic and psychological vulnerability. Britain's state of near collapse was symptomatic of the situation throughout Europe. Basically, Britain's crisis was economic. An island nation, Britain depended upon international trade for its livelihood. The Industrial Revolution of the nineteenth century had almost completely urbanized England, and less than 5 percent of the population was engaged in agriculture. This meant that Britain had to import much of its food and, except for coal, almost all the raw materials needed by its industries.

Before 1939 Britain had paid for food and raw materials three ways: services such as shipping, income from foreign investments, and manufactured exports. But the war had crippled its merchant marine, liquidated most of its investments, and destroyed many of its factories. With the first two means of financing its imports all but gone, Britain had to increase its exports; just to maintain the 1939 standard of living it had to raise its exports by 75 percent. By December 1946, despite an American loan and a severe austerity program that included the rationing of bread, Britain had reached only its prewar level of production. It was in these circumstances that nature delivered what proved to be almost a knockout blow. In the winter of 1946-1947, Europe suffered one of its severest cold periods in history; temperatures went below zero. The British transportation system came to a virtual standstill. Industries could not be supplied with the fuel to keep them running, and factories were closed. By February 1947 more than half of Britain's factories lay idle. Coal was not mined, and gas and electricity were in short supply. When the thaw finally arrived, Britain was beset by floods.

The export drive came to a halt, and Britain was at the end of its rope. The financial editor of Reuters saw the true measure of the winter disaster: "This is not the story of a couple of snowstorms. It is the story of the awful debility in which a couple of snowstorms could have such effects." The future looked bleak and ominous: millions of Britons were unemployed, cold and hungry, worn out by the long years of war and the determined postwar efforts to recover. Despite all the sacrifices they had made, their efforts had come to nothing. Britain's fate could have been worse only if the war had been lost.

Postwar conditions in Germany were also dreadful. The war had been carried into the heart of Germany, and few cities or towns had escaped Allied bombing, street fighting, or willful destruction by the Nazis as they retreated. To make matters worse, 10 million additional Germans came into these ruins from former German territory annexed by Poland. Millions of people were without food, shelter, or work. There was only one word to describe Germany in 1945—chaos.

One indication of Germany's financial devastation was that the cigarette replaced money as the prevailing unit of exchange. Cigarettes could buy almost anything, and the black market flourished. Even as late as 1947, a package of cigarettes was equivalent to a working man's monthly wages. Most people did not receive the Allied target ration of 1550 calories per day, which was hardly sufficient to sustain a healthy human being. Everywhere people were hungry. There was no fuel for heating. Three-quarters of the factories still standing in the American and British zones of occupation were closed. In January 1947 production fell to 31 percent of the 1936 level, Germany's best year; by February it had declined to 29 percent. Even before this industrial shutdown German steel production during 1946 had reached only 2 million tons—approximately one-third of Allied authorization.

Allied policy was not designed to alleviate this situation. The Allies were primarily engaged with Germany's disarmament and demilitarization, and with the elimination of all industries whose output could be used for military production. The United States and Britain were not particularly anxious to rebuild Germany's industrial power; after all, it had taken the combined efforts of three world powers to bring the Nazi war machine to a halt and defeat it. Nor were the Allies especially concerned with the lot of the German people during the immediate postwar days. After six years of brutal warfare, such concern could hardly have been expected. The revelations of Nazi atrocities and crimes, of wanton destruction, and of millions of innocent people slaughtered in concentration camps were too recent to be dismissed. The hatred the Nazis had engendered could not be erased overnight, and the Allies were unlikely to display much forgiveness and compassion toward them.

The French, above all others, were not likely to forget the Nazis. Although the French economy had been badly damaged during the war, by late 1946 they had made a remarkable recovery. But iron and steel production had reached only half the prewar total. Here, too, coal was the key factor because the iron and steel industries were dependent upon imported coal. But European coal production was still well below the pre-1939 annual average. German production was low, and Britain needed for itself all the coal it mined. Scarce dollars had to be spent for high-cost American coal. The result was a vivid demonstration of the division of labor between the industrial and agricultural sectors of a modern economy. France's industry was unable to produce sufficient goods for its sizable farm population to buy. Farmers withdrew fields from crop cultivation and used them for grazing. They kept more food for their families and fed more grain to their livestock. Meanwhile, the urban population was short of food, and the government had to spend its few remaining dollars—which it needed for reconstruction—to buy food from abroad. Matters grew even worse during the winter of 1946-1947 when an estimated 3 to 4 million acres of wheat were destroyed.

This situation was made to order for the large, well-organized French Communist party. One-quarter of France's electorate—practically the entire working class—voted for the Communists. (In Italy, the figure was one-third of the electorate.) The reason for this was simple: French and Italian capitalism had alienated these voters. The workers were, in effect, internal *émigrés* who voted Communist in protest against a system they felt had long mistreated them; unlike workers in Britain and the United States, they had suffered all the hardships of capitalism while enjoying few of its benefits, such as good wages and social opportunities. As a result, the Communist party in France enjoyed a powerful position in politics and trade unions. The party was the largest in France and could prevent any reforms from being adopted, thereby preserving its *raison d'être*. The party also controlled the largest French trade union, which had a membership of 80 percent of the workers during the immediate postwar years. In 1947, as U.S.-Soviet tensions increased, the party used this control to initiate or exploit strikes to paralyze the entire economy and bring France to its knees.

With Europe on the verge of not only economic ruin, but also a complete political and social breakdown, everything seemed to force it into dependence upon America. Most of the items needed for reconstruction—wheat, cotton, sulphur, sugar, machinery, trucks, and coal—could be obtained in sufficient quantities only from the United States. Short of food and fuel and with its cities and factories destroyed, Europe could not earn the dollars to pay for these goods. Moreover, the United States was so well supplied with everything that it did not have to buy much from abroad. The countries of Europe, therefore, were unable to obtain enough dollars for the purchase of the commodities required for their recovery. The result was the ominous *dollar gap*—a term that frightened the Europeans as much as *cold war*.

The Marshall Plan

Europe's collapse posed once again the fundamental question whether Europe was vital to U.S. security. America's two previous interventions suggest that the answer was obvious. But both times the United States had been drawn in by Germany. The wars were crusades for democracy; the public had never been made to understand the relationship between U.S. security and the European balance of power. At the end of each conflict the United States had tried to regain its isolationism. For the first time the United States was forced to clarify its relationship with Europe because this time it alone had the resources to take the initiative. Europe's vital importance became starkly clear in the emerging bipolar world. It ranked second only to the United States in its potential power: in industry, productivity, skilled manpower, scientists, and engineers. If these assets shifted toward the Soviet side, the military balance would swing so sharply that U.S. security would be endangered. Given its enormous potential and its geographic position, Europe's security was indeed inseparable from U.S. security.

Because the United States could not permit the Soviet Union to control the western approaches to the Atlantic, it had to find a way to help Europe recover. The prescribed cure was a massive injection of dollars. Only a tremendous program of economic aid could restore Europe's economy, enable it to surpass its prewar agricultural and industrial production, close the dollar gap, and lead Europe to the recovery of its *élan vital*, political stability, and economic prosperity. If these measures succeeded, France and Italy might reintegrate their working classes into their bodies politic.

Europe

American aid was made conditional, however, upon economic cooperation among the European states. In this respect, the United States clearly held itself up as a model. The Economic Cooperation Act of 1948 called specifically for European economic integration. America, it stated, was "mindful of the advantage which the United States has enjoyed through the existence of a large-scale domestic market with no internal trade barriers and [believed] that similar advantages can accrue to the countries of Europe." In official American opinion, integration became the prerequisite for Europe's recovery and the necessary basis for long-range prosperity.

It is not difficult to see why American policy makers, with their belief in low-cost mass production, should have felt that Europe's economic recovery and health were dependent upon the creation of a mass market. The

European nations, living together on a continent one-fourth the size of the United States, had shut their markets off from one another with tariff walls, quota systems, and import and export licenses. By this means, manufacturers assured themselves of the lion's share of their national markets. Sheltered from external competition, they had little incentive to modernize their equipment or techniques, for they minimized domestic competition by dividing their relatively small domestic markets among themselves. The American aim was to modernize this machinery, to overcome the cartelization of industry and the inefficiency of small family enterprises (as in France), and to erase national divisions. Europe's industries were expected to enlarge and become competitive by the creation of a United States of Europe.

Secretary of State Marshall first stressed the economic cooperation required by the United States; he called upon the European states to devise a plan for their *common* needs and *common* recovery. The United States would furnish the funds, but the Europeans had to assume the initiative and do the planning. The result was the Organization for European Economic Cooperation (OEEC). Its estimate of the cost of Europe's recovery over a four-year period was $33 billion. The president asked for $17 billion, which Congress cut to $13 billion. The amount actually used by the Economic Cooperation Administration (ECA) between 1948 and the end of 1951, when the program ended, was just over $12 billion. Britain, France, and West Germany received more than half of this amount.

Europe's Split into East and West

The original invitation by the United States to the nations of Europe to plan their joint recovery was deliberately extended to *all* European countries, including the Soviet Union and the nations of Eastern Europe. If the United States had invited only the nations of Western Europe, it would have placed itself in a politically disadvantageous position in which it would have been blamed for the division of Europe and the intensification of the cold war. Actually, had the Soviets participated, it seems unlikely that Congress would have supported the Marshall Plan for two reasons: first, the costs would have risen astronomically as a result of the very heavy damage suffered by the Soviet Union during the war; and second, anti-Soviet feeling was growing. The risk had to be accepted, however; it had to be the Soviets, who, by their rejection of Marshall Plan aid, would be responsible for the division of Europe.

The likelihood that the Soviets would do precisely that were very strong. European cooperation would mean that the Soviet Union would have to disclose full information about its economy and allow the United States to have some control in its economic planning, as well as in that of its satellites. This was unthinkable to a totalitarian state; a Communist state could hardly permit capitalists to have a voice in its economic development. Soviet participation also would have required the Soviet Union and its satellites to contribute toward Europe's recovery with food and raw materials, in return for the help they were receiving from the United States. The Soviets would actually be helping to stabilize Europe. But if they did not participate, preferring to exploit Europe's misery, they would be blamed for continuing and aggravating the cold war. In either case, the United States could not lose by invoking Karl Marx's slogan, "From each according to his ability, to each according to his need." When Soviet foreign minister V. M. Molotov came to Paris with a large delegation of experts, he gave American policy makers a scare. But only for a moment. Molotov denounced the plan as an attempt to interfere with Soviet sovereignty and withdrew. Western Europe could now plan the use of America's dollars for its recovery.

Was the Marshall Plan a success? The results tell their own story. By 1950, when the Korean War broke out, Europe was already exceeding its prewar production by 25 percent; two years later, this figure was 200 percent higher. British exports were doing well, French inflation was slowing, and German production had reached its 1936 level. The dollar gap had been reduced from $12 billion to $2 billion. In human terms, Europe's cities were being rebuilt, its factories were busy, the stores restocked, and its farmers productive. The Marshall Plan was a huge success, and at a cost that represented only a tiny fraction of the U.S. national income over the same four-year period. Indeed, it was smaller than America's liquor bill for the same years! These were the State Department's best years as it took the lead in organizing U.S. foreign policy. This policy reflected some of the best characteristics of the country: its self-confidence and generosity, its energy and imagination. These were years of excitement as the United States emerged as a great power and as young men from government, business, finance, and academia flocked to Washington and Western Europe to ensure the success of the Marshall Plan. Winston Churchill called it "the most unsordid act in history."

U.S. Commitment to Europe's Defense

Soon after the Marshall Plan was launched, however, it became clear that the plan by itself would not suffice. In February 1948 the Soviets engineered a *coup d'état* in Prague, and—ten years after Munich and Hitler's subsequent seizure of that hapless nation—Czechoslovaki~ ~~ared behind the iron curtain. A few months later, in June, the Sc blockade on Berlin in an effort to dislodge the Western p surprising that the Europeans felt extremely jittery at the Soviet hostility and aggressive intent. In this atmospher insecurity, in which comparisons of Joseph Stalin's Ru Germany seemed all too valid, it became obvious that recovery was impossible. People do not make the nece work hard to recuperate today if they feel that tomorrow they will be conquered and that their efforts will all have been in vain. In short, it suddenly became crystal clear that a prerequisite for Europe's recovery was military security.

The Europeans had already made some moves in this direction. In March 1947 France and Britain had signed the Treaty of Dunkirk to provide for their mutual defense against a threat to their security. Exactly a year later, Great Britain, France, the Netherlands, Belgium, and Luxembourg signed the Brussels Pact of collective self-defense. The Brussels Pact was established as a military counterpart to the OEEC. Just as the OEEC was dedicated to economic cooperation, the pact was committed to military cooperation. And just as the vitality of the OEEC had depended upon the influx of American capital for its success, the pact members expected their alliance to attract American military support.

The Formation of NATO

They were not disappointed. In April 1949 Belgium, Canada, Denmark, France, Great Britain, Iceland, Italy, Luxembourg, the Netherlands, Norway, Portugal, and the United States created the North Atlantic Treaty Organization (NATO). For the United States, the NATO commitment set a precedent: for the first time in its history, the country had committed itself to an alliance in peacetime. Europe had become "Our first line of defense." It was precisely the knowledge that the United States would fight to preserve Europe's freedom that was supposed to prevent a Soviet attack. American participation in two world wars had proved Europe's vital importance to American security. Instead of again allowing the balance of power to be upset and once more becoming drawn into a war after it had started, the United States now expected to prevent this by committing itself to the preservation of the European balance in peacetime. The presumption was that the fear of meeting American resistance and fighting an all-out war with the United States would deter a potential aggressor.

The policy of deterrence relied almost exclusively upon American strategic air power—that is, upon the ability of the Strategic Air Command (SAC) to destroy completely the Soviet Union with atomic bombs. This strategy was based upon two assumptions: first, that a future war would be a total war, which would be precipitated by a direct Soviet attack upon the United States or Western Europe, and second, that deterrence could be achieved by air power and its ability to inflict such heavy damage that an enemy would, in effect, be committing suicide if it launched an attack.

Two events were to change this reliance upon air power alone to deter or destroy the enemy. The first was the explosion of the first Soviet atomic bomb in late 1949. This foreshadowed a time when the Soviet Union, too, would ess a stockpile and the means to deliver them. The second event was the Korean attack upon South Korea in June 1950. Because it was presumed that such an attack could not have occurred without Soviet permission, the North Korean aggression suggested a change in Soviet intentions. This possibility was strengthened in Washington's view by Communist China's intervention in North Korea in late November. The Western response was large-scale rearmament.

This involved three tasks for NATO: the establishment of a command structure, the formulation of a strategy by which to defend Europe on the ground, and the rebuilding of its ground forces. These efforts began with the appointment of General Dwight Eisenhower to serve as Supreme Allied Commander in Europe.

The 'Forward Strategy'

The strategy NATO adopted was known as the "forward strategy"— that is, Europe's defense was to be established at the line between East Germany and West Germany, the so-called intra-German border. Politically, the Europeans wanted no part of a strategy that called for a withdrawal that would bring the Soviet army to their borders, if not into their countries. They had no desire to be a battlefield again. And liberation in a war in which atomic bombs would be dropped was no liberation at all: one could not liberate a corpse. From a political standpoint, Allied forces could not retreat.

Such a defense required troops and proper logistical support. When Eisenhower arrived in Europe, he found, including the Americans, only twelve divisions—none of which was at full strength, properly trained, or fully equipped with the latest weapons. Nor were there any effective reserves to back them up. Perhaps neither of these facts was surprising: the European powers had greater needs and more important things to do in the immediate postwar days than to maintain or rebuild sizable military forces. In addition, because of America's atomic monopoly, it seemed quite safe to rely solely upon SAC for deterrence and to use the troops in Germany mainly for occupation duties.

But Eisenhower needed more ground forces for two purposes. First, they would act as a "tripwire." In case the Soviets harbored doubts that the United States would defend Western Europe, the tripwire troops were to make the U.S. commitment credible. An attack by the Red Army would cost American lives; this would ensure American retaliation against the Soviet Union. Second, the NATO army was to act as a "shield" by holding the Soviet army at the point of attack while SAC destroyed the Soviet Union. Military planners believed that such shield forces would have to be quite large because of the size of the Soviet army.

But the need for an ample number of divisions faced the European states with a painful dilemma. They were still in the midst of economic recovery and not able to devote too large a share of national budgets to rearmament. The American answer was the rearmament of Germany. If France and Britain could not supply the necessary troops, Germany would have to supply them. Moreover, this decision seemed eminently correct because the forward strategy required that NATO would try to hold West Germany. It was only fitting that the Germans should contribute to their own defense. In turn, of course, German rearmament reinforced the need for a forward strategy. The West Germans could hardly be persuaded to rearm if they could not be assured that West Germany would not be turned into a battlefield and that German troops would not be used merely for the defense of France and Britain. Thus, the question of Germany once more raised its head. It was not a new question, but this time it received new answers.

The Revival of Germany

Germany has held the key to the European balance of power since at least 1870 when Prussia defeated France, Europe's preeminent land power, and established a united Germany. This was true of Germany even in defeat in 1945. Almost from the cessation of hostilities, the Soviet Union and the United States began their contest over Germany. East Germany was in Soviet hands; the Western powers occupied West Germany. Actually, the Allies were lucky, for West Germany contained the great majority of Germany's population and the heart of its industrial power. West Germany, in short, was the chief prize in Europe.

During the war Joseph Stalin, Winston Churchill, and Franklin Roosevelt had decided to govern Germany through a four-power Allied Control Commission (with France as the fourth power), which would administer the entire country as a single economic unit. In practice, this task proved impossible. The Soviet Union, Britain, and France, as well as the smaller European nations, had been promised reparations payments in compensation for the widespread destruction the Germans had caused. The Soviets were to receive all the industrial equipment in the Soviet zone, plus one-quarter of the far greater industrial complex in West Germany (it was somehow assumed during the war that Germany's industrial power would be intact at the end of the war). But—and these were the decisive points—the United States and Great Britain had insisted upon two restrictions on these reparations payments. First, Germany was to be left enough of its nonmilitary industries to maintain its standard of living at the same level as the rest of Europe (but definitely not higher); and second, no reparations were to be paid out of current production until Germany had earned enough money with its exports to pay for the imports it needed. Germany was to support itself. The Allies had no desire to spend their money supporting their former enemy.

The Soviets quickly began demolishing the industry in their zone without informing the Western powers how much they were taking. The Soviets also cut off the regular food supply from East Germany, which traditionally had been Germany's breadbasket; under the original agreement, the Soviets were to furnish this food in return for the three-fifths of capital equipment they were allowed to remove from the Western zones. These Soviet actions led to trouble. Almost exactly a year after V-E Day, the United States announced that it was suspending all further West German reparations payments to the Soviet Union. They were not to be resumed until the Soviet Union operated its zone under the original terms of agreement. The reason for the American action was clear: if East Germany no longer furnished the food that West Germany needed, West Germany would have to increase its exports to buy food from abroad; and if it had to increase exports, it had to increase production. The British agreed. The wartime agreement to hold German industrial production down for fear that Germany would again use its heavy industry in a secret rearmament program—as it had during the years between the two world wars—was abrogated. The American and British purpose was to make Germany pay for its own needs.

But the two powers had a more important aim in mind: as Europe's economic collapse became clearer and the cold war began, it became necessary to lift Germany out of its economic stagnation and make its industry contribute to the general economic recovery of Europe. In July 1946 the United States offered to merge its zone with those of Britain and France; Germany was to be decompartmentalized to speed up its industrial recovery. The French, fearing Germany's reviving strength, at first refused to participate, but later joined. But this fusion would not by itself achieve Germany's economic recovery; it needed the willing cooperation of the Germans, too. The United States and Britain decided to let the Germans begin to take a more active part in running their own country; this, in effect, foreshadowed the eventual establishment of a West German government.

The Soviets reacted to West Germany's growing autonomy by blockading West Berlin in 1948. Berlin, like Germany, was supposed to be administered by the four occupying powers, but the growing cold war divided the city just as it did Germany. Lying deep in East German territory, surrounded by Soviet divisions, the Western half of the city was an easy and vulnerable spot for the Soviets to apply pressure on the Western powers. The issue at stake was more than the Western presence in Berlin: it was Germany itself. Berlin, as the old capital of Germany, was the symbol of the conflict. The Soviets did not want to see West Germany become a partner of the West. Germany and Russia had fought two wars in forty years. Germany had beaten Russia the first time and almost defeated it on the second occasion. Moreover, West Germany was not a *status quo* state satisfied with its postwar boundaries. Rather, it was a revisionist state; it wanted changes in Germany's eastern frontier because of German territory seized by Poland to compensate for Polish land taken by the Soviets.

The Soviet Union's fear of Germany, however, was not completely responsible for its actions in Berlin. If Soviet fear of Germany was so deep, the Soviets would have accepted an American proposal, offered by Secretary of State James Byrnes, of an alliance of twenty-five or even forty years to neutralize Germany. Moreover, although the Soviet Union had been much weaker than Germany before World War II, it emerged from that conflict far stronger—a superpower, in fact—while Germany, in spite of its potential strength, was now only a second-class power. The Soviet-German balance of power had decisively shifted in the Soviet Union's favor, and another German attack upon the Soviet Union was unlikely. In any war, whether it acted unilaterally or as an ally of the United States, Germany would be the battlefield and therefore the first country to be destroyed. Fear of this consequence was a sufficient deterrent.

But Soviet concerns were also offensive because, once the power of a revived Germany was added to that of the United States and its NATO allies, the American position in Europe obviously would be greatly strengthened. This, in turn, stood in the way of two Soviet objectives: one, the withdrawal of American forces and the neutralization of Western Europe; and two, Germany's participation in a subservient partnership. Germany's recovery, in short, would block the Soviet aims of excluding the United States from Europe and becoming the dominant power in Europe.

To forestall West Germany's revival, therefore, the Soviets resorted to a test of strength. If the Allies could be forced out of Berlin, German confidence in the United States would be undermined. The Germans would not attach themselves to a friend too weak or too fearful to protect them. Indeed, if American will power crumbled under Soviet pressure, France and Britain would also lose confidence in the United States. Had it not been met, the Berlin crisis would have destroyed the evolving American commitment in Europe (NATO was still in the future) and nullified U.S. efforts to rebuild Western Europe as a partner in the struggle against the Soviet Union. The United States had to defend its position in West Berlin because the consequences for failure were so enormous.

The method of conflict was decided at the outset by the unwillingness of either the United States or the Soviet Union to risk a total war. The Western powers ruled out any attempt to reopen the corridor to Berlin by challenging the Soviet army with troops and tanks. Instead, they decided on an airlift to supply the city with all its needs. The Soviets did not challenge this effort, for they were aware that in doing so they would leave the West no alternative but to fight a total war. Rather, the Soviets waited to see if the Western powers could take care of Berlin's 2.5 million citizens. It would take a minimum of 4,000 tons of food and fuel daily—an enormous amount of tonnage to ship in by air. After 324 days the Soviets were convinced that the Americans and the British were more than equal to the task. Although the total supplies did not immediately attain the 4,000-ton target, Western planes eventually flew in as much as 13,000 tons daily. Planes landing at three-minute intervals flew in 60 percent more than the 8,000 tons that had previously been sent each day by ground transport. By the spring of 1949, West Berliners were eating better than at the beginning of the blockade—and considerably better than the East Berliners! Faced with this colossal Allied achievement, the Soviets called off the blockade in May.

The U.S. determination to hold Western Europe and not to allow further Soviet expansion had been demonstrated. The West Germans clearly saw that they could count on America to protect them. Just as NATO had been the prerequisite for Europe's economic recovery, the Berlin airlift was the final American act that led to Germany's resurgence. The United States had laid the basis for Germany's economic recovery through Marshall Plan funds; in NATO, it had given Germany the sense of military security without which its economic reconstruction could not have been completed. For the time being, the Soviet efforts to "decouple" Western Europe from the United States ended.

Europe Moves Toward Unification

Ironically, it was renewed fear of Germany's rising strength that stimulated further efforts toward European integration. The specter of a fully revived Germany struck fear into most of Germany's neighbors. The French, with their memories of 1870, 1914, and 1940, were particularly alarmed. Germany's recovery, stimulated by America's response to the cold war, posed a serious problem for Germany's partners: How could they hold Germany in check when it was potentially the strongest nation in Europe outside of the Soviet Union? Ever since Germany's unification, France had dealt with the inherently greater strength of its aggressive and militaristic neighbor by forming alliances that could balance Germany's power. Because Britain had usually preferred to retain a free hand, and because British interests were also at times opposed to those of France, the French had relied primarily upon Continental allies. Before World War I, they discovered such an ally in Russia, and between the two wars they found partners in Poland, Czechoslovakia, Romania, and Yugoslavia. None of these alliances had saved France, however. In both world wars, British and American power (aided by the Soviets in World War II) had been the decisive factor in defeating Germany. After the war and despite the extension of Soviet power into the heart of Europe, France still saw Germany as the enemy, and in December 1944 the French signed a Treaty of Mutual Assistance with the Soviets, making an alliance they considered necessary for their security. Soviet hostility soon disillusioned the French and deprived the treaty of any meaning, however. In fact, this hostility made it necessary to add Germany's power to that of the West.

The failure of a traditional balance-of-power technique, by which an inferior power sought to balance a stronger nation, led France to seek a new way of exerting some control over Germany's growing power. French leaders found an imaginative means in European integration. It was through the creation of a supranational community, to which Germany could transfer certain sovereign rights, that German power could be controlled.

France's Initiative and Aims

France made its first move in the direction of a united Europe in May 1950, when Foreign Minister Robert Schuman proposed the European Coal and Steel Community (ECSC) composed of "Little Europe" (France, Germany, Italy, and the Benelux countries of Belgium, the Netherlands, and Luxembourg). The aim of the Schuman Plan, as it was also known, was to interweave German and French heavy industry to such an extent that it would be impossible ever to separate them. Germany would never again be able to use its coal and steel industries for nationalistic and militaristic purposes. War between Germany and France would become not only unthinkable but impossible.

But the new French technique of restraining Germany was more than an incorporation of Germany's superior strength, thereby subjecting Germany's power to a certain degree of French control. "Europeanization" was also a means for France to achieve a balance with Germany. The combination of the French and German coal and steel industries would strengthen French heavy industry and create a Franco-German equilibrium within the ECSC. Economic integration would allow France to overcome its inferior industrial strength, due primarily to its lack of energy sources. In Lorraine, France possessed Europe's largest iron ore deposits—resources that during Germany's annexation of Alsace-Lorraine from 1871 to 1918 had helped make Germany the greatest industrial power in Europe before 1914. But even when it had regained Alsace-Lorraine after World War I, France still lacked the coal to heat the furnaces. Europe's largest coal deposits lay in the Ruhr, and to a lesser extent in the Saar—that is, in Germany.

The Schuman Plan, in effect, held out a bargain to West Germany. France was to receive coal from Germany at the same price paid by German manufacturers, not at the previously higher prices that had made French products more expensive than German products. In return, France was to abandon its opposition to raising German production and prevail upon Britain and the United States to lift *all* controls from Germany's heavy industry. This would mean that Germany could compete again in the international market. Even more important for Germany, entry into the ECSC would be the first step toward nationhood. Despite its moral shame, recovering its sovereignty and strengthening its ties with its former Western enemies meant that eventually Germany could join NATO. Thus, the Schuman Plan had both an economic and a political appeal for the Germans as well as the French.

The French plan, however, was not devised only to control Germany's resurgent power or to give France a strength equal to Germany's. It had a third and more ambitious goal in mind: a united Europe under French leadership. France alone was too weak to pursue an active part in a world dominated by two superpowers. Even in the Western coalition, the most influential European nation was not France, but Britain. With Germany's recovery, it was very likely that Bonn's voice and opinions would also outweigh those of Paris in Washington. By itself, France would remain dependent upon its American protector, powerless to affect major Western policy decisions. A united Europe, with Franco-German unity at its core, was therefore France's alternative to remaining subservient to the United States and without major influence either in NATO or on the world stage. Through a united Europe France could gain an equal voice with what Charles de Gaulle was later to call the "Anglo-Saxons" in NATO, and possibly even exert independent pressure upon the Soviet Union.

These, then, were the benefits the French expected to gain from the Schuman Plan. They saw clearly that the nucleus of a united Europe would have to be a Franco-German union. The antagonism between these two states, born of their traditional enmity, would first have to be healed. Moreover, the French scheme did more than just evoke the dream of a united Europe, hoping that its vision would so fire people's imagination that they would suddenly discard their narrow nationalistic loyalties for a wider European allegiance. The new Europe could not be created by sentiment alone; the French were determined to build it on a solid foundation. They knew they would have to tie together the interests of politically powerful and economically important groups in the various nations *across* national boundaries. The removal of all trade barriers in the coal and steel sector would encourage the modernization of mines and plants, as well as the elimination of mines and plants that continued to operate inefficiently. Once producers had adjusted to the wider market and witnessed its opportunities, they would want to remove national barriers in other areas. Further, as production increased, Europe's standard of living would rise, and, as French and Italian workers received more of what they believed to be their share, labor would see that its goal of a welfare state could be achieved only at the European level.

The French showed great political astuteness in their selection of heavy industry as the first to be integrated because coal and steel form the basis of the entire industrial structure and represent a sector that cannot possibly be separated from the overall economy. The French expected that, as the benefits of the pooling of heavy industry became clear, other sectors of the economy would follow suit, eventually leading to the creation of a United States of Europe with a huge market and a mass-production system. In brief, this approach stressed supranational cooperation and institutions within a limited sphere and the creation of common interests within that particular area of activity before extending it to other fields.

French Fears of German Rearmament

The ECSC institutions, then, were the embryo of a united Europe. They were soon applied to a new area: the military forces of the different countries. The French originated this idea, too, in response to American insistence on German rearmament. To the French, the rearmament of their old enemy was distasteful and dangerous, but unavoidable because France could not supply more troops. But the French remained determined that the world would never see another *German* army, *German* general staff, *German* war ministry, or *German* ministry of armaments. The French proposed the formation of a European Defense Community (EDC). A European army, composed of army corps in which no more than two divisions could be of one nationality, would be an instrument for checking Germany's rising military power while using it for Europe's defense. The EDC treaty was signed in May 1952. NATO, of course, remained the supreme command, with a formal link to the EDC. Because all EDC members except Germany were members of NATO, this link ensured that Germany was obligated to come to NATO's defense and vice versa.

For Germany, entry into the EDC was another step toward regaining full equality with the other Western powers and asserting its political prestige. Most important, in return for providing the EDC with 500,000 men organized into twelve divisions, Germany recovered its sovereignty, with certain limitations. The Allies reserved their authority to protect the security of their forces in Germany (not only against external aggression, but also against possible attempts by the extreme left or right to subvert West Germany from within), to govern Berlin, and—to prevent any Soviet-German deal—to preserve their exclusive right to negotiate with the Soviet Union on the question of German reunification. The kind of Germany they would have liked to achieve was a unified Germany enjoying a democratic constitution—like that of the new Federal Republic, as West Germany came to be called—and integrated into the European community.

The likelihood of attaining this objective, however, was very small. Western proposals to unite Germany constantly included terms that the Soviet Union could not possibly accept. These terms included reunification via free elections in both halves of Germany and insistence upon allowing the government of this reunified Germany freedom to conduct its own foreign policy. The first part of the proposal would have meant the end of the Soviet-imposed Communist regime in East Germany, ironically called the German Democratic Republic, and the second part would have allied a unified Germany, probably headed by the pro-Western government of Konrad Adenauer, with the West. As this would bring NATO to the Polish frontier and the Eastern satellite belt, the Soviets were hardly likely to accept.

Allied terms ensured a continuation of a divided Germany, which was precisely what the Europeans wanted. France did not want to integrate with a united Germany, which the French feared would be too strong. France and Italy opposed Germany's reunification; although they, together with the United States, paid lip service to this goal to keep the West German government of Chancellor Adenauer in power. For the German people, reunification was a vital concern, and Adenauer claimed that through their alliance West Germany and the Western powers would be so strong that one day they could negotiate the Soviet Union's exit from East Germany. It ought to be noted that West Germany is a Germany without Prussia, the state whose authoritarianism and militarism had unified Germany in 1870 and whose values had deeply affected this Germany, which twice plunged the world into war in the twentieth century. The southern part of Germany had long been hostile to Protestant Prussia, and the Rhineland has been much influenced historically by Western (especially French) democratic thought. A reunified Germany might have stimulated a movement to resurrect Prussia, which had finally been destroyed by the war. It might therefore be said that, if Germany had to be divided, the present division, which cuts Prussia off from the Western part of Germany, could not have been more aptly drawn.

The Soviet Shift to Asia

It seems a cruel twist of fate that the success of American foreign policy in fortifying Western Europe should have brought about a shift in the focus of Soviet pressure from Europe to Asia, a shift that in June 1950, led to the outbreak of the Korean War. The Truman Doctrine had prevented a Soviet breakthrough into the Middle East, the Mediterranean, and the Persian Gulf. The Marshall Plan had set Europe on the path to economic recovery and health. NATO had guaranteed Europe its security. The lessons of two world wars had been absorbed, and the NATO commitment was the proof of this.

The United States had transformed a position of great weakness and vulnerability into one of relative strength. It had drawn a clear line between the American and Soviet spheres of influence and had demonstrated, in Turkey, Greece, and Berlin, that it was in Europe to stay. (The Greek crisis had passed when Yugoslavia was ejected from the Soviet bloc in 1948; the Yugoslavs no longer provided aid to the Greek guerrillas.) What all this meant was that Europe was no longer a profitable field for guerrilla warfare, *coups d'état,* subversive attempts, or military intimidation. Instead, it had become a barrier to the extension of Soviet influence. To cross the line drawn by the United States was to risk total war, and the Soviet Union was not willing to assume this risk while the United States held atomic superiority. The Soviet leaders, as George Kennan had said, did not believe in pursuing an "adventuristic" policy that gambled with the very existence of the Soviet state.

They turned their attention instead to the Far East. Here was a much more attractive field for political and military exploitation. Most countries in this area had only recently emerged from Western colonialism, and their nationalistic and anti-Western feelings were very strong. Nationalist China's collapse and the establishment of a Communist government on the mainland in late 1949 had further weakened the American position in Asia, for it had shifted the balance of power in the Far East against the United States. The United States no longer confronted only the Soviet Union; it was now faced with the challenge of the combined strength of the Sino-Soviet bloc. In addition, pressure in Europe united the Western powers, but pressure in Asia divided them, because they were split over the character and nature of the new Chinese regime. And finally, no expansionist move in the Far East would entail the risk of total war. In the American pattern of defense, Europe held strategic priority; Asia was of secondary interest. Europe was so vital to American security that any Soviet move in Western Europe ran the risk of an all-out clash with the United States; no single area in Asia was worth the cost of total war. The recovery of Europe and China's collapse, then, created a vacuum in the East and turned Soviet pressure toward Asia. It was here that the dramatic clashes of the cold war occurred during the next four years. These clashes led to a reaction within the United States against its foreign policy.

chapter four

Containment in the Far East

SUCCESS in Europe was followed by disaster in Asia. The collapse of Nationalist China, upon whose postwar support the United States had counted, was followed by the Korean War, the first limited war in U.S. experience in the twentieth century. As the war dragged on without the victory American arms traditionally had won, President Harry Truman and his administration lost popularity. These problems in Asia had serious domestic consequences. Charges of conspiracy and betrayal limited the administration's diplomatic freedom, pressured it into a policy of global anticommunism, and resulted in more than twenty years of confrontation with the new Communist China. The failure to establish normal relations with China, a country that might have been strongly attracted to a U.S.-Chinese policy of containment of the Soviet Union, was a strategic error of the first dimension, and it was one cause of the tragic U.S. involvement in Indochina. Indeed, the events in Asia in the late 1940s and early 1950s were to have a profound impact on American foreign policy for the next two decades.

The Fall of Nationalist China

During World War II the United States had a twofold purpose in the Pacific: to defeat Japan and to create a powerful and friendly China in its place. It was hoped that a strong and democratic China would play a leading role in protecting the postwar peace in the Far East. The United States took several actions to confer upon China the status of a great power. It renounced its extraterritorial rights in China, repealed the Chinese exclusion laws, established an annual Chinese immigration quota, and made it possible for legally admitted Chinese to become American citizens. At Cairo in 1943, together with Great Britain, the United States promised to return "all the territories Japan had stolen from the Chinese, such as Manchuria, Formosa, and the Pescadores." It also awarded China one of the five permanent seats on the United Nations Security Council; China was granted equal status with the Soviet Union, Great Britain, France, and the United States.

The conviction of President Franklin Roosevelt and his advisers that the mere pronouncement of China as a great power could actually convert it into one was typically American: one need only believe strongly enough in the desirability of an event for it to happen. Perhaps American policy makers also hoped that if China were considered a great power, it would behave like one. But American faith without Chinese cooperation was insufficient to accomplish the task. It would have taken a miracle to do that, and, although national leaders at times delude themselves into thinking that they can perform miracles, such things happen only in storybooks.

The first obstacle to creating a strong China was the sharp division within the country. Quite apart from the Japanese occupation of large areas of the country during the war, the Chinese were deeply split among themselves. There was not one China, but two—a Communist China and a Nationalist China. The Communists were not scattered throughout the whole population, as they were in Europe. Already in control of large segments of northwest China, the Communists extended their sphere during the war by infiltrating into north-central China. In this region, the Japanese held the cities and the major lines of communication, and the Communists organized the countryside. By 1945 they controlled 116 million people, one-fourth of China's entire population, within an area that constituted 15 percent of China's territory exclusive of Manchuria. Communist China was, in short, a nation within a nation, and the two were engaged in a bitter civil war.

If the United States wanted to create a united China, it would have to end the civil war. The American aim was to establish a coalition government in which all parties would be represented. The desirability of such a government was not questioned. What possible harm could there be in uniting the Nationalists and the Communists? The United States and the Soviet Union were cooperating against the common enemy, and most leaders and officials of the American government looked forward to friendly postwar relations. If these two nations, each representing a totally different way of life, could overcome past differences and get along together, why should the two Chinese parties not be able to settle their conflict? The United States had another, more immediate reason to end China's division as quickly as possible. A China torn apart by internal strife could not make an effective contribution to fighting the Japanese. After Pearl Harbor, the Nationalists and the Communists assumed that the United States would defeat Japan; therefore, they were fighting for control of China after the war. But the American attitude is that, once war breaks out, the total effort must be directed toward the single goal of military victory; any diversion of strength—particularly for "extraneous" political purposes—is considered unjustifiable. The war had to be won in the quickest possible time and with the minimum number of casualties. This attitude reinforced the American desire to establish a coalition government in China.

All efforts aimed at achieving this goal, both during the war and afterward, were in vain. Neither side trusted the other. Both sought a monopoly of power, and both were aware of the important role their armies played in the struggle for power: the Nationalists recognized that they would have to gain control of the Communist army to ensure their own survival; the Communists knew that they needed their army to defeat Jiang Gaishek (Chiang Kai-shek). Control of the army of a coalition government was a key obstacle to unifying the nation. At the end of the war, each side—particularly the Nationalists—believed they could defeat their opponent; compromise was believed to be unnecessary.

However, China's pro-American Nationalist government was losing popular support and disintegrating. Perhaps the Nationalists were the victims of fate. Except for the two years from 1929 to 1931, the government was constantly engaged in fighting for its very survival—against the Japanese (who attacked Manchuria in 1931, Shanghai in 1932, and China in 1937), as well as the Communists. Faced with both external and internal danger, Jiang had neither the time nor the resources to formulate and implement the political, social, and economic reforms China needed. His principal concerns were military: to stem the Japanese advance and maintain himself in power. The problem of modernizing China—above all, of meeting peasant aspirations—was strictly secondary. Moreover, Japanese successes during the war cut off an important source of Jiang's support and thereby rendered any agrarian reform impossible. By 1939 the Japanese had occupied the entire coastal area of China and had driven the Nationalists inland. This meant that Jiang's Kuomintang party, which controlled the government, had lost the main pillar of its support, the progressive commercial and financial interests in the coastal cities. Instead, it was forced to rely upon the conservative landlord class.

A government whose principal social and economic support came from the landlords was unlikely to carry out land reforms. Probably a majority of China's peasants were independent landowners, but many rented their land. Both groups were profoundly dissatisfied. Those who rented their land had to pay excessive sums; after the war, these sometimes ranged from 50 percent to 90 percent of their crops. Those who owned land were handicapped by the small size of their holdings and the lack of capital. The government's taxation policies further impoverished the peasants, who bore the main burden of the taxes. Because the peasants' crops were visible and easily appraisable, corrupt officials usually took more than the peasants could afford to spare. To survive, the peasants had to borrow from moneylenders, usually the local landlords, who charged them exceedingly high rates of interest. The result was that the peasants lived in a constant state of impoverishment and indebtedness.

The fact that the peasants constituted four-fifths of China's population meant that they provided most of the conscripts for the Nationalist army. The able-bodied and eligible sons of the rich avoided military service because their families bribed corrupt officials. In the same way, the rich tended to avoid paying taxes. Jiang, in short, seemed to be doing his best to alienate the peasants, the vast majority of China's population.

After the war, the Nationalists even managed to antagonize the business circles that formerly had supported them. As the Nationalists returned to the coastal cities, they took over all Japanese-owned industries and ran them as state enterprises. This incensed the business community. Some of the Japanese properties had belonged to Chinese, but the government simply neglected to restore such property to the owners. Even worse was the fact that private enterprise now found itself faced with the powerful competition of state industries, which were controlled by relatives and close friends of Jiang. Naturally, the American aid funds with which the government supported its enterprises provided great profits for these people.

The Nationalist position deteriorated even further because of China's unchecked inflation, which had its most devastating effect upon low-level government officials. It provided them with a massive incentive for corruption because their salaries were wholly inadequate, and they had to find a means of supplementing their incomes. Honesty in these circumstances simply did not pay, and corruption became rife throughout the government.

As Jiang's government lost popularity, it began to resort increasingly to force to hold its position. The resulting police and military measures further alienated the people. The American commander in China during the war, General Albert Wedemeyer, found this situation: "Secret police operate widely, very much as they do in Russia and as they did in Germany. People disappear. . . . No trials and no sentences. . . . Everyone lives with a feeling of fear and loses confidence in the government." This was particularly true of the intellectuals, who, together with the peasantry, have been the traditional supporters of China's governments. Professors were dismissed, even arrested, when they began to criticize the government for its policies. Students similarly inclined were also thrown into jail.

To sum up the Nationalist position: the government had alienated important segments of the politically articulate minority, especially the business community and intellectuals. The more inarticulate and passive peasants were tired of the constant fighting, high rents, and taxes. All three groups had either lost confidence in the ability of the government to take care of the problems of postwar China or felt that the government was not interested in their welfare. But only minorities in each group turned to the Communists. The majority simply disengaged themselves from the Nationalists and became indifferent to the outcome of the civil war. They did not rise up against the government in a "popular revolution." The Communists won the civil war—and the military conflict played the decisive role in determining this issue—and they did so because most Chinese were willing to give the Communists the benefit of the doubt and allow them to demonstrate that they could give China a more effective government.

Communist Strategy for Victory

One reason for the lack of hostility and suspicion toward the Communists was, of course, that they were not the Nationalists. A more positive reason was the favorable picture the Communists presented to the Chinese population. In the areas they controlled, the Communists did not destroy the traditional tenure system or eliminate the landlords and money lenders. Rather, they reduced the rents to a fixed maximum and lowered the interest rates. They permitted private enterprise and allowed all factions to participate in local government. Although they assured Communist control by retaining the power to approve all candidates, their activities nevertheless seemed to support their claim that they stood for democracy, freedom, and individual liberty. Certainly, their economic and political practices demonstrated little Marxist bias. They appeared, instead, as genuine democrats, and their pose as agrarian reformers was widely accepted—precisely because they actually carried out reforms.

If the Communists acted as if their only wish was to reform China along democratic and capitalistic lines, this was, of course, a tactical device. But the point remains that it was effective and achieved its purposes: it attracted minority support among the various strata of China's population disaffected by Nationalist policies, and it gained acquiescence among the rest of the population. As Jiang had alienated most of his popular support, the Communists, by cleverly hiding their real intentions, filled the vacuum left by the Nationalists. For their purposes, a large neutral public was almost as beneficial as positive majority support; the only thing that really mattered was that this support had been withdrawn from Jiang.

The Communist position for the final military struggle was further strengthened when, near the end of the Pacific war, the Soviet army marched into Manchuria. Once established, the Soviets did two things that hurt the Nationalists. First, they dismantled Manchuria's industry and transported the machinery back to the Soviet Union to help restore their own badly damaged industry. As a result, Manchuria, China's industrial heartland, was unable to contribute to the country's economic recovery. Second, the Soviets allowed the Chinese Communists to infiltrate the countryside and handed them large stocks of Japanese arms and ammunition. Conversely, the Soviets delayed the return of Nationalist troops, who had to launch a major offensive to establish their control over Manchuria. The government forces captured the cities, but the Communists remained in control of the countryside. The Soviet invasion of Manchuria dealt a serious blow to the Nationalists.

U.S. Role in China's Fall

The blame for these events has often been attributed to President Franklin Roosevelt and the Yalta "betrayal," which granted the Soviet Union, among other things, a continuation of the *status quo* (that is, Soviet control) in Mongolia; a restoration of the rights Russia had held in Manchuria before its defeat by Japan in 1904-1905; the lease of Port Arthur as a Soviet naval base; the internationalization of the commercial port of Talien, which, unlike the Soviet Union's own Siberian port of Vladivostok, was not icebound part of the year; and the joint Sino-Soviet operation of the Chinese-Eastern and South Manchurian railroads, which served these three cities. Joseph Stalin, in short, was seeking to regain Russia's preeminent influence, which the czarist government had lost, in Manchuria and Northern China along the Chinese-Soviet frontier.

To take the charge of betrayal seriously, however, one has to deny certain clear facts of wartime military strategy: namely, that the American military was unsure the atomic bomb would be a success; that they believed an invasion of Japan would be necessary to bring about Japan's surrender; that they expected to suffer large numbers of casualties and feared even more if the Japanese reinforced the home-island garrison with troops from Manchuria and northern China; and that, therefore, they wanted the Red Army to tackle these mainland forces before the U.S. invasion. The American government was willing to reward the Soviets if this would help save the lives of American soldiers. Moreover, the Americans were certain that the Soviets planned to restore the czarist position in Manchuria anyway by declaring war on Japan at the moment the United States seemed to be on the verge of victory. The Soviet takeover would then be a practically bloodless operation, with a minimal contribution to Japan's defeat. American officials wanted the Soviet Union to pay at least some kind of price for what it could actually take for nothing. Moreover, as noted earlier, U.S. wartime policy aimed to satisfy the Soviet Union's traditional security interests (as in Eastern Europe) and great power interests (as in northern China). The assumption was that once the Soviet Union achieved its principal goals, it would not seek further expansion and jeopardize the postwar peace.

Finally, the Americans wanted to secure a promise from the Soviets that they would sign a treaty of alliance and friendship with the Nationalist government. The purpose of this treaty was to secure the Soviet Union's support for Jiang and to isolate his Communist opponents; this would enable Jiang to consolidate his grip on China and perhaps allow him to defeat his domestic enemy. Jiang encouraged the United States in this effort because he knew how vulnerable he was domestically and he did not want Moscow to support the Chinese Communists after the war. The Soviets, in fact, signed such a treaty with the Nationalists, but violated it by aiding their Chinese comrades. Stalin, however, apparently did not believe that this help strengthened the Chinese Communists sufficiently to defeat the Nationalists. He is reported to have counseled Mao Zedong (Mao Tse-tung) to join Jiang in a coalition government, to accept Jiang's supremacy, and "bore from within." China was thought to be in America's sphere of influence (except where Soviet power had established itself), and for this reason Mao had to be very cautious. Mao is said to have nodded his assent to Stalin's advice and then disregarded it; he was more confident than Stalin of a final victory.

The Nationalists' Defeat

Throughout 1946 and 1947, the Communists limited their operations largely to raiding supply depots and communications lines, ambushing Nationalist forces, engaging in skirmishes, and attacking isolated garrisons. These local tactical successes heightened the Communist forces' confidence and morale just as they added to their opponents' demoralization. By 1948 the Communists had so increased the strength of their forces and firepower that they no longer had to rely solely upon hit-and-run tactics; they attacked the Nationalists at will, completely overwhelming them with superior masses of troops. By February 1, 1949, they controlled Manchuria.

Nationalist strength by then had declined to 1.5 million men. Up until mid-September 1948, the Nationalists had been able to replace their combat losses and maintain their army at 2.7 million. In other words, in only four and a half months, the Nationalists had lost 45 percent of their troops. Meanwhile, Communist strength had risen to 1.6 million regular troops—including defectors from the Nationalist armies. Eighty percent of the American equipment furnished to the government forces during and after the war had been lost, with an estimated 75 percent of it falling into Communist hands. General David Barr, the head of the American military mission in China, summed up the situation succinctly: "No battle has been lost since my arrival due to lack of ammunition or equipment. Their [the Nationalists'] military debacle, in my opinion, can all be attributed to the world's worst leadership and many other morale-destroying factors that led to a complete loss of the will to fight." [1] Nowhere was this more clearly demonstrated than in Jiang's failure, after his loss of northern China, even to attempt a defense of south China by making a stand along the Yangtze River. Jiang thereby forfeited the mainland. He withdrew to Taiwan (in those days also called Formosa), an island lying 100 miles off China's coast. In the fall of 1949, Mao proclaimed the People's Republic of China.

One question about Nationalist China's defeat remains: Could the United States have prevented it? The answer is "perhaps"—*if* American officers had taken over the command of the Nationalist armies, *if* the United States had been willing to commit large-scale land, air, and sea forces to fight

---

1. Department of State, *United States Relations with China* (Washington, D.C.: Government Printing Office, 1949), 358.

in China, and *if* the United States had been willing to commit even greater financial aid than the approximately $2 billion it had already given in grants and credits since V-J Day. But these conditions could not have been met. America's rapid demobilization left it with insufficient forces either for supplying the officers for the direction of the Nationalist forces or for intervention in China. The United States had only a small standing army at home. Nor were the American people in any mood to rearm and remobilize in 1947-1948, particularly to fight a war in China.

The problem of extending further economic aid to Jiang was equally vexing. His corrupt, inefficient, and reactionary government did not provide a politically effective instrument through which to carry out the social and economic reforms China needed. Aiding Jiang seemed to be "pouring money down the drain." In contrast, U.S. economic aid to Europe, the area considered most vital to American security, had a good chance of achieving its objective—the political and economic recovery of Britain and the Continent. It probably would have been unwise in these circumstances to divert a large slice of the government's not unlimited funds to attempt to restore a government that had lost the confidence of its own people. The power and wealth of the United States was, after all, not infinite; it would have to be applied selectively. Hence, those areas of vital interest in which its use would be most effective were to be the prime focus. As Secretary of State Dean Acheson stated it: "Nothing that this country did or could have done within the reasonable limits of its capabilities could have changed that result; nothing that was left undone by this country has contributed to it. It was the product of internal Chinese forces, forces which this country tried to influence but could not. A decision was arrived at within China, if only a decision by default." [2]

Reevaluation of U.S. Far East Policy

Despite Jiang's debacle and the disintegration of the Far Eastern balance of power, the U.S. government took an optimistic view of developments. Shortly after the Nationalist collapse, Acheson expressed his belief that, despite the common ideological points of view of the Chinese and Soviet regimes, they would eventually clash with one another. Acheson predicted that Russia's appetite for a sphere of influence in Manchuria and northern China would arouse Chinese nationalism. The implications of this point of view are clear. The first is that if the Chinese Communists were genuinely concerned with the preservation of China's national interest, they would resist Soviet penetration. Mao might be an independent Communist leader like

---

2. Department of State, *United States Relations with China*, xvi.

Tito. On the other hand, if Mao proved subservient to the Soviet Union, he would lose the support of the Chinese people. His regime would be identified with foreign rule because he would appear to serve the interests of another power, not of China. Given time, Acheson declared, the Chinese people would throw off this "foreign yoke." Whichever of these two developments occurred, the United States could only gain from the antithesis between communism and Chinese nationalism.

This analysis of Sino-Soviet relations indicated that the United States first had to disentangle itself from Jiang. Without this disassociation, the Chinese would link the United States with the government they had rejected. This connection would foster the growth of anti-American sentiment in China, which was just what the administration hoped to prevent. The attention of the Chinese people must remain on the Soviet Union's actions. Under no circumstances, Acheson emphasized, must America "seize the unenviable position which the Russians have carved out for themselves. We must not undertake to deflect from the Russians to ourselves the righteous anger, and the wrath, and the hatred of the Chinese population which must develop." [3] Only by disengaging itself from Jiang Gaishek could the United States exploit the alleged clash of interests between China and the Soviet Union.

Truman's first step to implement this policy was the release of a White Paper that argued that the Nationalists had lost control of the mainland despite adequate American economic and military aid. The clear implication was that Jiang was no longer worthy of U.S. support and that American recognition of Jiang's government as the official government of China should be withdrawn. Conversely, it argued that the Communists should be recognized as the official government of China. A second act was an announcement that American military forces would not be used to defend Taiwan, and that the administration would no longer provide the Nationalists with military aid or advice: "The United States Government will not pursue a course which will lead to involvement in the civil conflict in China." This opened the way for the Chinese Communists to take Taiwan—an event that was expected before the end of 1950. The Communist government would then be the only claimant to represent China, and the United States could extend it recognition. Jiang, through whom containment had been impossible because he had been not a container but a sieve, would have been eliminated; containment of the Soviet Union could then be implemented through the Chinese Communists. In short, the Truman administration wanted to do in 1950 what Richard Nixon finally did in 1972. But before this could happen, war had broken out in another area in the Far East—Korea—with the unfortunate result of a bitter twenty-two year gulf between the United States and the new China.

---

3. "Crisis in Asia—An Examination of United States Policy," *Department of State Bulletin,* January 23, 1950, 115.

Limited War in Korea

Korea had been a divided nation since the end of World War II; Soviet forces had entered Korea two days after Japan surrendered. The nearest American troops at the time were in Okinawa, 600 miles away, and in the Philippines, 1,500 to 2,000 miles away. Consequently, the two powers decided to divide the country temporarily at the thirty-eighth parallel. The Soviets would disarm the Japanese above the parallel, the United States below. With the beginning of the cold war, this division became permanent. All American attempts to negotiate an end to the division and establish a democratic and united Korea failed.

The United States took the problem to the United Nations in late 1947, calling upon that organization to sponsor a free election throughout Korea. The General Assembly established a temporary commission and charged it with the responsibility of holding and supervising such an election. The Soviets, however, refused to grant the commission access to North Korea, which had been transformed into a dictatorship, and the election was limited to South Korea. Following the election, the United States recognized South Korea as the official republic and the government of Syngman Rhee as its legitimate representative. The American government also extended to Rhee economic, technical, and military aid to bolster his non-Communist government and to help Korea establish a reasonably open society despite Rhee's increasingly arbitrary rule. Although South Korea was not an ally of the United States, there could be little doubt that the young republic was America's protégé.

Communist North Korea attacked South Korea in late June 1950, taking the American government by surprise. In fact, the Americans had worried Rhee might go north and had withheld the type of military equipment, such as heavy tanks, that would be needed for such a thrust. The South Korean army was not sufficiently armed to resist an invasion. But the main reason for the shock was that American policy makers had thought only in terms of all-out war. It was precisely this single-minded American preoccupation with total war that had accounted for Korea's being left outside the American Pacific defense perimeter, which ran from the Aleutians to Japan, through the Ryukyus (Okinawa) to the Philippines. This had made Korea militarily dispensable within the pattern of American security, for in a global war its fate would be decided in other theaters of war. A Soviet occupation of Korea would not raise Korea's strategic significance because the peninsula could be neutralized by American air and sea power. American troops therefore had been withdrawn from Korea, because in a major war they would be vulnerable to Soviet land power and would probably be trapped. The absence of the American military rendered South Korea highly vulnerable; indeed, it turned South Korea into a vacuum for Communist expansion, and on June 25 the North Korean army struck.

Far East

South Korea's Political Importance

Overnight, the survival of South Korea became identified with the security interests of the United States itself. North Korea's aggression, which in Washington's opinion could not have been launched without Soviet encouragement and support, altered the basis upon which Korea's strategic significance had been calculated. Korea's value could no longer be assessed in terms of its relative unimportance during a total war. The cold war focused attention upon the wider political and military implications for the containment policy of a North Korean military victory. If the principal purpose of containment was to prevent further Soviet expansion, American inaction in the face of Soviet aggression could only encourage future aggressive acts. The appetites of dictators were believed to be insatiable. At the very least, it had to protect South Korea.

And if containment was possible only through an alignment of U.S. power with that of allies, then failure to respond to South Korea's pleas for help must result in the disintegration of the alliance system and the isolation of the United States. If the United States stood by while South Korea fell, it would demonstrate to the world that the United States was either afraid of Soviet power or unconcerned with the safety of its friends or allies. American guarantees to help preserve their national integrity and political independence would thereafter be regarded as valueless, and this would leave nations whose security depended upon U.S. willingness to live up to its commitments with no alternative but to turn to neutralism for protection and seek some form of accommodation with the Soviet Union.

This reasoning applied particularly to Japan. With the demise of Nationalist China and the disintegration of the Far Eastern balance of power, the United States was about to turn Japan into an ally in an effort to recreate some semblance of strength in the Pacific. Japan had long regarded South Korea as critical to its security. At the turn of the century, as Russian power had penetrated first Manchuria and then Korea, Japan had proposed that Russia and Japan divide Korea at the thirty-eighth parallel. The czarist government rejected the offer, and Japan attacked Russia in 1904. The United States, as the occupying power after Japan's defeat in World War II, and responsible for Japan's security, faced a similar situation in 1950 when North Korea, close to Soviet Russia, invaded across that same parallel. Not to defend South Korea would mean that Japan would remain neutral. The same security rationale would apply in Western Europe if the United States demonstrated that it would not come to the aid of a stricken friend. The North Atlantic Treaty Organization (NATO) countries, having just signed the treaty, all recalled the U.S. retreat back to isolationism after World War I. If the United States did not rescue South Korea, the likely result would be the neutralization of Western Europe as its nations would feel that, despite its NATO pledge of protection, the United States could not be counted on to keep its word. The stakes in Korea were therefore enormous: inaction would shift the Eurasian balance toward the Soviet Union and leave the United States strategically isolated. Consequently, Washington believed it had no choice but to oppose force with force.

The aggression in Korea, however, did not fit American strategic doctrine, which was based on its ability to strike an enemy with atomic bombs. The Soviets had cleverly confronted the United States with the dilemma of either risking a total war for a limited objective or taking no action and surrendering South Korea. American policy was prepared to deal only with an all-out Soviet surprise attack upon the United States or Western Europe; such an attack would be met by the power of the Strategic Air Command. But American strategy was completely unprepared to deal with the kind of less-than-total challenge the Soviets posed in Asia. The North Korean aggression, in effect, meant that massive retaliation outside of Europe was not an effective policy because the deterrent effect of U.S. retaliatory power depended upon whether an enemy believed that the country would actually "unleash" this power in the face of aggression. The limited attack in Korea demonstrated that the Soviet leaders were not deterred by the policy of massive retaliation, despite America's far greater atomic stockpile and ability to deliver it. They did not believe that the United States would risk all-out war to save Korea. This type of challenge could be met only by local response and primarily through the commitment of American ground forces. Containment depended not just upon the capacity to deter total war with strategic air power; it required, in addition, an army to meet precisely this kind of limited incursion.

But the administration had been cutting the armed forces since the end of World War II. General George C. Marshall recalled in 1951 that the army was so small in the years preceding the Korean War that there were only one and one-third divisions in the United States. The Chiefs of Staff had so few troops at their command that they worried about obtaining enough men to guard airstrips at Fairbanks, Alaska. According to Marshall, "We had literally almost no military forces outside of our Navy and outside of an effective but not too large Air Force, except the occupation garrisons, and . . . even in Japan they were only at about 60 percent strength." [4]

For two days, June 27 and 28, the United States tried to stem the North Korean advance with air and sea forces alone. But on June 29, General Douglas MacArthur, the commander-in-chief in the Far East, reported that Korea would be lost unless ground forces were employed to halt the enemy army. The United States sent its occupation divisions from Japan to Korea, but under the aegis of the United Nations. This was done for two reasons. First, by virtue of the free election it had sponsored in South Korea, the United Nations had been intimately concerned with the birth of the young state. Second, one of the aims of American foreign policy was to associate its cold war policies with the symbolic, humanitarian values of the United Nations. Although it is traditional for nations to justify their policies in moral terms, the United States has shown a marked propensity for doing so. American depreciation of power and reluctance to recognize it as a factor in human affairs make it psychologically necessary to rationalize actions in the international arena in terms of ideological objectives and universal moral principles. American power must be "righteous" power used not for purposes

---

4. Quoted by John Spanier, *The Truman-MacArthur Controversy and the Korean War* (Cambridge, Mass.: The Belknap Press of Harvard University Press, 1959), 18.

of power politics and selfish national advantage, but for the peace and welfare of all mankind. In fact, the war was an American effort, not controlled by the United Nations.

After initial setbacks, the war went well for a while. In a daring operation on September 15, MacArthur, now UN supreme commander, landed an army at the west coast port of Inchon, 150 miles behind the North Korean lines. These forces then drove northward, trapping more than half the enemy army. The rest of the shattered Communist army was in flight. On September 30, the UN forces reached the thirty-eighth parallel. The question confronting the United States was whether to cross it. The political aims of the war were all compatible with the restoration of South Korea; this implied a return to the *status quo*. This goal was now abandoned. The military situation favored the fulfillment of an American goal of several years' standing: the unification of the whole of Korea. The U.S. government shifted its emphasis from containing the expansion of Soviet power to the forceful liberation of a Soviet satellite. The victory at Inchon, in short, transformed the whole character of the war. It also taught the United States the foolishness of changing political goals in the middle of a war in response to battlefield successes.

The Chinese Communists React

Stricken with what the Japanese, reflecting on their experience in World War II, had called the "victory disease," the U.S. government believed that it was politically safe to cross the parallel and unify Korea. The administration did not think the Chinese Communist leaders would consider the UN advance a threat to their security, because they were Chinese first and Communists second. Mao and his colleagues were already thought to be so involved in their struggle with the Soviet Union over the detachment of northern China, Manchuria, and Sinkiang that their eyes were fixed on their own northern provinces rather than on North Korea. "I should think it would be sheer madness on the part of the Chinese Communists to do that [interfere]," Acheson had said a few days before Inchon. He repeated that in northern China "a great cloud from the north, Russian penetration, is operating." And he continued: "Now I give the people in Peiping [Beijing] credit for being intelligent enough to see what is happening to them. Why should they want to further their own dismemberment and destruction by getting at cross purposes with all the free nations of the world who are inherently their friends and have always been friends of the Chinese against this imperialism coming down from the Soviet Union I cannot see."[5] In short, there was nothing to fear. The new objective of a militarily united Korea was sanctioned by a UN resolution on October 7.

But American policy makers miscalculated. The Chinese indeed viewed

---

5. "Crisis in Asia," 115.

the American march to their border as threatening, just as Washington had perceived the North Korean march southward toward Japan as threatening. So Beijing sent its armies into North Korea under the guise of "volunteers," and in late November it launched a major offensive that drove the UN forces back below the thirty-eighth parallel. Throughout December 1950 and early January 1951, there was no certainty that UN troops could hold the peninsula, but they rallied and turned back the Chinese offensives. By March they had once more advanced to the thirty-eighth parallel. The administration was again faced with a decision: whether to seek a militarily unified Korea or accept a divided Korea.

There was no doubt about what MacArthur wanted to do. War, he said, indicated that "you have exhausted all other potentialities of bringing the disagreements to an end," and once engaged, "there is no alternative than to apply every available means to bring it to a swift end. War's very objective is victory—not prolonged indecision. In war there is no substitute for victory." The very term *resisting aggression* indicated "that you can destroy the potentialities of the aggressor to continually hit you" and not "go on indefinitely, neither to win or lose." One cannot fight a "half war." The administration's policy was based upon the assumption that "when you use force, you can limit that force." This introduced a "new concept into military operations—the concept of appeasement." [6] MacArthur recommended a naval blockade of the Chinese coast; air bombardment of China's industrial complex, communication network, supply depots, and troop assembly points; reinforcement of his forces with Chinese Nationalist troops; and "diversionary action possibly leading to counter-invasion" by Jiang against the mainland.

The Truman-MacArthur Conflict

The Truman administration rejected MacArthur's proposals because they were considered too risky. It was feared that bombing China and defeating the Soviet Union's principal ally would lead to another global war. The Sino-Soviet treaty of February 1950 bound the Soviet Union to come to the aid of China if it were attacked by Japan "or any other state which should unite with Japan" (an obvious reference to the United States). Even without this treaty, China was the Soviet Union's largest and most important ally. Soviet self-interest in the Far East and the necessity for maintaining Soviet prestige in the Communist sphere would make it difficult for the Soviet Union to ignore a direct attack upon the Chinese mainland.

But even if the Soviet Union remained a spectator, the United States could not extend the war. A "war of attrition" waged by Chinese manpower in Korea would "bleed America dry" and make it impossible to build a strong military defense in Europe. A large-scale diversion of U.S. power to Asia would expose Europe to Soviet armies and might very well incite an attack at

---

6. Quoted by Spanier, *Truman-MacArthur Controversy*, 222.

a moment of maximum American weakness on the Continent. The United States had to conserve its strength to check its principal enemy, the Soviet Union; the country could not afford to dissipate its power in a peripheral area against a secondary enemy. MacArthur's strategy, in the opinion of General Omar Bradley, chairman of the Joint Chiefs of Staff, would involve the United States in the wrong war, at the wrong place, at the wrong time, and with the wrong enemy.

This view was shared by Britain and France. America's chief allies were naturally reluctant to see American power diverted to the Far East before Europe was secure against Soviet attack; and they had no desire to risk such an early outbreak of World War III for an area that was of minor strategic significance to them. If the United States decided to carry the war to China, it would have to act unilaterally. But the objective of balancing Soviet might and deterring a total war was predicated on NATO's unity and combined strength.

Finally, the Joint Chiefs of Staff rejected MacArthur's proposals because they were judged militarily ineffective. All of China's essential supplies came overland from the Soviet Union. The United States decided to concentrate its air power on the 200 miles of supply line in North Korea to interdict the Chinese logistical system. The employment of Nationalist troops was rejected because they had already demonstrated their ineffectiveness in China. Moreover, the Chinese people were unlikely to welcome Jiang back.

Inherent in the administration's rejection of MacArthur's recommendations—and his dismissal when he continued to push them—was the abandonment of its objective of a militarily unified Korea and a reassertion of the original aim of the war, the defense of South Korea. This goal remained compatible with the other political reasons for which the United States had gone to war: the defense of Japan and the preservation of the NATO alliance—that is, the protection of the eastern and western rims of Eurasia. Indeed, by the time the war ended in 1952, Japan had become a U.S. ally, and NATO had not only been preserved but strengthened by its own rearmament and the stationing of four American divisions in Europe. The wisest course was therefore to end the war where it had begun.

From Anti-Sovietism to Anticommunism

The collapse of Nationalist China and the Korean War changed U.S. foreign policy from anti-Soviet to anti-Communist. These two events constrained the flexibility of American policy and turned Washington to a more crusading and interventionist policy. It was the "loss of China" that initiated this change. Americans had regarded China as their special ward since just before the turn of the century. The original interest in China was not political but commercial—China was a potentially huge market for American products. But U.S. policy toward China had also contained a strong missionary element—a genuine interest in the welfare and Christian salvation of the Chinese people. In fact, the United States had long regarded itself as the protector of China from foreign exploitation and invasion. Through the 1899 Open Door policy—aimed at preventing Great Britain, France, Russia, Germany, and Japan from shutting American commerce out of China and at obtaining an equal opportunity to sell on the Chinese market—the United States had become politically committed to preserving the territorial integrity and political independence of China.

Because the American people had never been prepared to fight for this objective, however, the United States had failed to protect China from external pressures and invasions. The Russians had established a sphere of influence in Manchuria about 1900, and the Japanese had replaced them after the Russo-Japanese War. During and after World War I, Japan had expanded its influence and control over China, and in 1931 Japan had begun another war to further its ambition to turn China into a Japanese vassal or colony. The Open Door policy, then, had been largely verbal. Indeed, the United States had never been prepared to support this policy militarily; it was one in which diplomacy was divorced from force, and what it meant was that the United States usually disregarded its commitment whenever Russia or Japan challenged it. Even though this suggested that in reality the United States regarded its stakes in China as low, Americans, even in those days, believed that words were a substitute for an effective policy. The result was the illusion that the United States had long been China's friend, extending to the Chinese people the bountiful benefits of Western civilization and coming to their rescue during World War II.

Americans were therefore shocked by the collapse in 1949 of Jiang, who during the war had been lauded as a Chinese George Washington, and the establishment of Communist control of the Chinese mainland. Certainly, they were totally unprepared for, and deeply resentful of, the propaganda emanating from Beijing accusing the United States of being "the Chinese people's implacable enemy . . . a corrupt imperialistic nation, the world center of reaction and decadence . . . a paper tiger and entirely vulnerable to defeat." They had expected that a "loyal" and fundamentally democratic China, grateful to America for past protection and help, would emerge from World War II as a strong friend and as a powerful and reliable ally. The failure of these expectations in late 1949 came as a blow. Suddenly, the relative security achieved by the containment policies in Europe—the Truman Doctrine, the Marshall Plan, the Berlin airlift, and NATO—seemed to have disintegrated. It appeared that the United States had stemmed the Communist menace in Europe only to allow it to achieve a breakthrough in Asia.

The resulting insecurity and anxiety were further heightened by two other events about the same time. The first was the explosion of the Soviet Union's first atomic bomb, which shattered the American monopoly of the weapon widely regarded as the principal deterrent to a Soviet attack. The second was the conviction in early 1950 of Alger Hiss for perjury in connection with charges that he had delivered documents to the Soviet government in the 1930s. The Hiss case was followed shortly by the confession of British scientist Klaus Fuchs that he had passed atomic secrets to the Soviets, which suggested Soviet espionage in high places. The outbreak of the Korean War and Communist China's subsequent intervention added more fuel to the fires of discontent.

Erosion of Bipartisan Support for Foreign Policy

At the time all this was occurring, bipartisan support for U.S. policy was ending. The congressionally dominant conservative wing of the Republican party had long been restless; the party, led by liberal Republicans, had lost the presidential elections of 1940, 1944, and 1948. They wanted to win with a conservative leader in 1952. But they could not win the presidency on the Republican record on domestic issues. The Republicans were the party of President Herbert Hoover and the Great Depression. The Democrats, who had won every presidential election since 1932, were the party of Roosevelt and the New Deal. Conservative Republicans therefore needed a foreign policy issue with which to beat the Democrats, even though liberal and moderate Republicans, led by Senator Arthur Vandenberg, a former isolationist, had supported the internationalist policy of the Truman administration. But Vandenberg was dying, and, after China fell to the Communists, bipartisanship on the Far East was eroding. Foreign policy became a partisan issue as the Republicans decided to exploit the public's frustrations with the alleged failures under Democratic administrations.

Whenever the United States had been drawn into the international arena in the past, its actions had met with quick success. It had beaten the British, the Mexicans, the Spaniards, the Germans, and the Japanese. America had never been invaded, defeated, or occupied, as most other nations had been; it had, to be sure, made mistakes, but with its great power it had always been able to rectify them. To a nation in which one popular slogan expressed confidence in doing "the difficult today, the impossible tomorrow," failure was a new experience. America's history had been a witness to victories only; its unbroken string of successes seemed evidence of national omnipotence.

It was this unquestioned assumption that the United States was omnipotent that suggested to the Republicans the reason for America's failures: treason within its own government! If America was all-powerful, its setbacks must have been the result of its own policies. Ostensibly, the reason China fell was that the "pro-Communist" administrations of Franklin Roosevelt and Harry Truman either deliberately or unwittingly had "sold China down the river." This conspiracy charge articulated by Senator Joseph McCarthy, supported by Senators Robert Taft and Richard Nixon, was simplicity itself: America's China policy had ended in Communist control of the mainland; the administration leaders and the State Department were responsible for the formulation and execution of foreign policy; therefore, the government must be filled with Communists and Communist sympathizers who "tailored" American policy to advance the global aims of the Soviet Union. Low morale among the Nationalists, administrative and military ineptness, and repressive policies that had alienated mass support had nothing to do with it; nor did the superior Communist organization, direction, morale, and ability to identify with popular aspirations.

The State Department bore the brunt of the onslaught. Calls for Acheson's resignation and congressional efforts to cut funding of the department—including eliminating Acheson's salary—failed but were symbolic. With the attacks coming faster than they could be refuted, morale plummeted. Old China hands were forced out, although they were cleared of all charges against them. Those foreign service officers who stayed learned a lesson they would not forget: make no controversial recommendations because in the future they might be held against you. A report analyzing the weakness of the Nationalist government, forecasting its possible demise if it failed to reform, and recommending opening contacts with the Communists as the likely successor regime, would be read by a witch-hunting committee as a hostile attitude toward a friendly government, a desire to see it fail, and an attempt to turn China over to the Communists. It is no wonder that when Washington was considering intervention in Vietnam that few foreign service officers were willing to report on the South Vietnamese government's weaknesses and its possible defeat by the Viet Cong. Honest reporting and analysis might later condemn them as security risks and cost them their jobs and, worse, their reputations.

The political atmosphere during the 1950s, in short, often bordered on hysteria. The accusations, usually in the press, were not directed only to the State Department or government officials. Academics and others were also charged as "security risks" or "un-American." Many such individuals were fired, and others were blacklisted. For example, the Hollywood studios stopped hiring actors and writers who had been associated with radical causes during the depression years. So-called controversial books and authors were banned. (One library took *Robin Hood* off the shelf because the hero robbed from the rich to give to the poor, an obvious Communist or sympathizer!) The United States Information Agency even burned some books to avoid any accusations of left-wing disposition by eager congressional hunters for un-American activities, and a West Point debating team had to cancel a debate on the wisdom of recognizing the new China.

One significant result was to shift U.S. foreign policy from a stricter anti-Soviet orientation to a broader anti-Communist crusade. To be sure, U.S. actions in the Eastern Mediterranean and in Western Europe had been taken in the name of anticommunism, but operationally these actions had been limited to countering Soviet moves. Washington had not hesitated to support Communist Yugoslavia after its break with Moscow and for a brief moment it had even predicted the likelihood of conflict between Communist China and the Soviet Union. But the Republican attacks on the Democrats, the charges of appeasement, of being soft on communism, of losing China, and of treason, placed the Democrats in a vulnerable position. When the Korean War began, the Republicans demanded protection of the Nationalist government on Taiwan as the price for support of the war. To avoid political division, Truman sent the fleet into the Taiwan Straits, reinserting the United States into the Chinese civil war. Once U.S. troops had reached the thirty-eighth parallel in Korea, the Republicans charged that not to advance north and defeat the North Koreans would constitute appeasement. This assault on the administration probably played a part in the decision to exploit MacArthur's military victory at Inchon. After UN forces had recovered from China's intervention and driven back to the thirty-eighth, incessant Republican attacks made it impossible for Truman to end the war at that point. (Truman's successor, Dwight Eisenhower, would end the war in 1953 on virtually the same terms after considerably more casualties.) In this highly charged emotional atmosphere, it was impossible to extend official recognition to the government of mainland China.

Indeed, the aim of U.S. policy became anticommunism: the expansion of any member of the Sino-Soviet bloc, as it came to be called, was to be prevented. All Communist states were now considered enemies, regardless of whether they were large or small, strategically located or not, tied to Moscow as satellites or nationalist Communist states, which, like Yugoslavia and Communist China, were likely to pursue their own interests, even in conflict with the Soviet Union. Distinctions between America's vital and secondary interests, the importance of concentrating on the main adversary and not getting bogged down and wasting resources in conflicts with secondary enemies, and the ability to control hostile attitudes towards Communist regimes so that one could make an accurate calculation of whether their actions represented a threat to American interests—all were lost in the crusading spirit. Future Democratic administrations, trying to avoid Republican accusations of having lost some country or being soft on communism, were particularly disposed to anticommunist interventions. The Republican charges had hurt the Democrats in 1952; they lost that presidential election and were kept out of power for eight years.

American-Chinese Enmity

Anticommunism also intensified the deep rift between the United States and China. In 1950 Beijing saw that the United States not only did not recognize it but also continued to protect the rival regime; that the United States increasingly assisted the French fighting in Indochina; that it was strengthening its alliance with Japan, China's recent enemy; and that U.S. troops were marching to China's border with North Korea, despite Chinese warnings not to do so. Fearing that U.S. forces might cross the border, the Chinese government intervened in Korea.

From Washington's perspective, the Chinese intervention was unwarranted because the United States had repeatedly reassured Beijing that the border was safe. But the heavy fighting in the winter of 1950-1951, the loss of lives, and length of the war embittered Chinese-American relations. The friendly relationship the United States once thought it had with China turned into hatred. That the United States had once been China's protector and benefactor may have been an illusion, but it was widely held, and the betrayal of friendship, alleged or real, always leaves a sense of frustration and anger. The American-Chinese relationship had an emotional intensity that did not characterize the relationship between the United States and the Soviet Union. China, now seen as aggressive and militantly anti-American, was commonly called "Red China."

One can only speculate how events might have turned out during the Korean War if the United States had recognized the new Chinese government and had diplomatic representatives in Beijing. Diplomats might have alerted Washington that the Chinese were alarmed at the U.S. advance in North Korea and that the warnings to stop American forces short of China's frontier ought to be taken seriously. The American government received similar warnings from the Indian ambassador but, believing the ambassador to be pro-Chinese, the United States rejected the warnings.

The United States paid a heavy price for the breakdown of bipartisanship, for McCarthy's charges of treason, and for the crusading style that Nationalist China's collapse unleashed. But the even greater folly may have been that U.S. policy, now applying containment to the Sino-Soviet bloc, no longer considered the possibility that Mao Zedong might become a second Tito, that Mao, like Tito, drew his power from control of his party and military, not from the Soviet Union. Nor, therefore, did Washington any longer entertain the possibility that Communist China might be used to contain Soviet power. Instead, for more than two decades the United States and China were bitter enemies.

chapter five

The Strategy of 'Frontiersmanship'

T HE PRINCIPAL achievement of President Dwight Eisenhower's two terms was the completion of the walls of containment around the Sino-Soviet bloc spanning Eurasia. This was done primarily by organizing two multilateral alliances, one in the Middle East, the other in Southeast Asia, and backing them up against Soviet and Chinese encroachment with the growing nuclear capability of the Strategic Air Command (SAC). These alliances proved to be weak barriers, however, for the application of containment outside of Europe could not be superimposed upon regional rivalries, civil wars, and the powerful forces of nationalism. Moreover, the possible use of America's arsenal of nuclear power proved largely irrelevant to the specific situations that developed.

It is ironic that Eisenhower's reputation soared after America's involvement in Vietnam concluded. That misadventure made a president whose record was basically negative look good: he ended the war in Korea; he did not go to war in Indochina; he kept the United States out of the Suez War in Egypt; he did not get the United States involved in war with Communist China in its civil war with Nationalist China; and he avoided a showdown over Berlin. Democratic presidents immediately before him and after him were activists and interventionists. Ironically, it was liberal Democrats, once the chief advocates of an energetic containment policy, who praised the Republican Eisenhower during the 1970s and 1980s for his caution and avoidance of a hasty resort to military power. At the time, however, they were highly critical of the administrations's strong ideological anticommunism and rhetoric and what were seen as its inept policies. Toward the end of Eisenhower's second term, as the Soviets achieved spectacular space shots and missile tests, critics saw him presiding over a self-satisfied nation, which, while basking in affluence, was losing dynamism and its primacy to the Soviet

Union. The nation turned subsequently to a younger, more dynamic president and new generation "to get the country moving again."

Eisenhower's Promise of Liberation

During the presidential election campaign of 1952, the Republicans cleverly exploited the public's frustration with containment—a frustration grounded in the popular illusion of national omnipotence. America's great insecurity and its present involvement in the Korean War, they asserted, were the result of the "tragic blunders" that Franklin Roosevelt and Harry Truman had committed at the Tehran, Yalta, and Potsdam conferences with the Soviets. The Democratic leaders had deliberately and stealthily paved the way for communism's postwar expansion by selling out Eastern Europe and betraying Jiang Gaishek. The two presidents, according to the Republican party platform, had "flouted our peace-assuring pledges such as the Atlantic Charter, and [they] did so in favor of despots, who, it was well known, consider that murder, terror, slavery, concentration camps, and the ruthless and brutal denial of human rights are legitimate means to their desired ends. Tehran, Yalta, and Potsdam were the scenes of those tragic blunders with others to follow. The leaders of the administration acted without the knowledge or consent of Congress or the American people. They traded our overwhelming victory for a new enemy and for new oppressions and new wars which were quick to come." In other words, America's wounds were self-inflicted.

The Republicans charged that Truman's postwar foreign policy was self-defeating. It underwrote the false premise that American power was limited and committed the United States to continued coexistence and constant involvement in foreign policy. As John Foster Dulles, a lawyer who had long shown an interest in foreign affairs and been involved in Republican politics, and now the chief Republican spokesman on foreign policy, put it: "We are not working, sacrificing, and spending in order to be able to live *without* this peril—but to be able to live *with* it, presumably forever." The administration's policies were "treadmill policies, which, at best, might perhaps keep us in the same place until we drop exhausted." The failures of containment were many: it was a negative policy; it surrendered the initiative to the enemy; it merely reacted to counter the Communist danger wherever and whenever the latter chose to attack; it was so costly that it would bankrupt the country; and it aimed only at preserving the *status quo*. In short, Dulles condemned the policy of containment as "negative, futile, and immoral." [1]

The aim of American foreign policy, Dulles stressed, should not be to co-

---

1. John Foster Dulles, "A Policy of Boldness," *Life*, May 19, 1952, 146.

exist indefinitely with the Communist menace; it should be a rollback of Soviet power. The United States had only to proclaim its stand for freedom and announce that it would never be a party to any "deal" that confirmed Soviet despotism. Such a declaration would preserve the courage and hope of those living in Soviet satellites and prevent them from accepting the Soviet regime. In Dulles's words, the United States "should make it publicly known that it wants and expects liberation to occur. The mere statement of that wish and expectation would change, in an electrifying way, the mood of the captive peoples. It would probably put heavy new burdens on the jailers and create new opportunities for liberation." [2]

Never had the illusion of American omnipotence received a greater tribute. America's cause was righteous, and to be victorious it need only publicize this cause by launching a moral crusade. Right would then again prevail over might. The Republican program of action apparently envisaged Dulles, the future secretary of state, like the Old Testament Joshua, marching around the walls of the Kremlin empire, sounding the call of freedom upon his trumpet. The walls would tumble down, the enslaved peoples would be liberated, and Soviet power forced to retreat, leaving the world once more safe for democracy.

The Republicans not only promised an end to the cold war—they also pledged it at less cost. They claimed that the Democrats' foreign policy of indefinite coexistence, with its vast outlay for armaments and economic aid, undermined the nation's economy. The Republicans asserted that it was the Soviet Union's aim to destroy the United States by forcing it to spend itself into bankruptcy—an aim furthered by Democratic policy. America's defense had to be provided with a healthy economic foundation. This required a sharp cut in foreign aid and military expenditures. The Republicans promised the nation at one and the same time an offensive strategy, a balanced budget, and reduction of taxes. They pledged a curtailment of Soviet power and a simultaneous cut in the appropriations for America's defense.

The Republican Rollback to Containment

Such goals were not only incompatible; they were unattainable. The enunciation of the doctrine of liberation would not free any Soviet satellite; good intentions, unsupported by concrete political and military policies, are notoriously impotent on the international scene. But perhaps this did not really matter, because the policy of liberation was devised primarily to roll back the Democrats in the United States, not the Red Army in Eastern Europe. And for this domestic purpose, liberation was a highly effective strategy.

The country desperately wanted a more vigorous and forthright anti-Communist policy that promised an end to the cold war. At the same time, it

2. Dulles, "Policy of Boldness," 154.

was unprepared to take the risks involved, and a policy that actively sought the liberation of the satellite states would have to accept the very definite risk of all-out war with the Soviet Union. In these circumstances, the only kind of dynamism the country could afford was a verbal dynamism. And this was all the people seemed to want. It allowed them to delude themselves that the United States once again pursued a vigorous and forthright policy that would defeat its opponent. Liberation was the Republican party's therapy for a public that refused to accept the facts of America's limited power in the world and rejected any changes in its traditional approach to foreign policy.

That this policy of liberation was meant only to impress the American people was clearly demonstrated at the time of the anti-Communist revolt in East Berlin and other East German cities in June 1953, and during the national uprising in Hungary in late 1956. The Eisenhower administration failed to act—except to condemn the Soviet Union for its suppression of Germans and Hungarians and to express its sympathy for the victims. In Berlin, it substituted food packages to the East Berliners for liberation, and in Hungary, it even reassured the Soviet Union that it had no intention of intervening. The *status quo* was thereby reaffirmed. Liberation had returned to the "womb" of containment.

The Globalization of Containment and Massive Retaliation

The administration, however, carried out its promises of military and economic retrenchment. This involved three measures. The first was to end the Korean War, which allowed the administration to cut the size of the army and avoid the cost of maintaining large standing ground forces. The second was to draw a clear line of containment, or "frontier," around the entire Sino-Soviet bloc. The Democrats had already drawn such a frontier from Norway to Turkey; the Republicans expected to strengthen and extend it to the Middle East and Far East. The third measure was to preserve this global boundary around the Communist world with the deterrent power of the Strategic Air Command. The Soviets and Chinese could cross the line only at the risk of total war with the United States; the fear of total destruction was expected to deter them.

The reliance upon strategic air power was also expected to appeal to the American public. "Massive retaliation" sounded more dynamic than containment and made possible a reduction of overall military expenditures. It was obviously cheaper to concentrate military spending upon a one-weapon system than to build up and maintain large balanced forces to meet any contingency. The second appealing feature of massive retaliation was that it rejected the concept of limited war, or "half war," and reasserted the old American doctrine of either abstaining or fighting an all-out war. This return to the more traditional American approach to war was natural in 1952. The Republicans had been elected largely because of the deep popular revulsion against the Korean War; it was clear that the American people wanted no more such wars.

Basically, then, Eisenhower's policy was not very different from Truman's: the containment of communism but extending containment beyond Europe by drawing a frontier around the Sino-Soviet periphery and supporting that frontier with nuclear air power. But in one essential aspect the new administration's policy was different—and this difference was crucial. Truman and Dean Acheson had relied upon atomic striking power to deter an attack upon either the United States or America's "first line of defense" in Europe. But in Asia, once the Communists had faced them with a limited aggression, the Truman administration had met this challenge with ground troops. The Eisenhower administration also expected to deter an all-out war with the threat of massive retaliation, but its policy was not to fight local ground wars. It planned to prevent any future limited attacks by threatening to retaliate against the Soviet Union or Communist China.

This basic policy decision reflected Dulles's strong conviction that the only effective means of stopping a prospective aggressor was to give fair warning of what constituted aggression and to make clear that the punishment for an attack would far outweigh any possible military gains. Dulles believed that Korea would never have been invaded had the Communists known their attack would be met with retaliatory air strikes on Moscow. It was the absence of such a warning that had led the Communists to miscalculate. The Eisenhower administration did not intend to repeat this mistake. It meant to draw the line so clearly that the enemy could be left in no doubt of the consequences of crossing the line. The expectation was that by going to the "brink of war," the United States would be able to deter future Koreas. This policy, which later became known as "brinkmanship," was to be applied first in an attempt to bring about a cease-fire in Korea.

Ending the Korean War

Truce talks in Korea had begun in the summer of 1951, but the negotiations dragged on fruitlessly until they reached a deadlock. The war was a drain on the United States: it had to be ended. When the Eisenhower administration took office in January 1953, it decided that if its efforts to gain an armistice failed, it would bomb Chinese bases and supply sources in Manchuria and China, blockade the mainland coast, and possibly use tactical atomic weapons "to provide a tremendous beef-up in the United Nations punch." Dulles conveyed this decision to Prime Minister Jawaharlal Nehru of India in late May 1953, on the assumption that Nehru would pass the message on to the Chinese Communists.

In early June the deadlocked negotiations resumed, and in late July the armistice was signed. Whether the administration's threats were primarily responsible for the Chinese Communists' willingness to conclude the war is difficult to say. Probably other factors must be taken into account. For instance, Joseph Stalin had died in 1953, and his successors were proclaiming their belief in "peaceful coexistence" and trying hard to convince the non-Communist world that they wanted to relax international tensions. Agreement on an armistice and an end to the war would provide evidence of their earnestness. More important, they could not afford to risk increased international tensions and an enlarged war at a time when they were engaged in a struggle among themselves to succeed the late dictator. But Dulles thought his threat to unleash American air power against China had induced the Chinese Communists to end the fighting; in turn, this reinforced his faith in the utility of the advance warning coupled with the threat of heavy punishment.

The Korean War ended just where it had begun—on the thirty-eighth parallel. It had taken three years of fighting to decide that this line was to become part of the global dividing line between the Communist bloc and the non-Communist bloc. In August, the United States signed a mutual security pact with South Korea designed to deter another attack. This alliance had already been preceded by a declaration, signed by the fifteen nations that had fought in Korea, warning the Chinese Communists that, in the event of renewed aggression, it would probably be impossible to confine hostilities to Korea. They added this significant warning: the armistice must not "result in jeopardizing the restoration or the safeguarding of peace in any other part of Asia." Events in Indochina were soon to prove the meaninglessness of this statement.

The First Indochina War

After World War II, colonies that had long been ruled by European powers renewed their demands for independence. The British complied in India, Burma, and Ceylon (now Sri Lanka), but the French in Indochina did not. Returning there after its years of Japanese occupation, the French refused to grant any meaningful concessions to the government, which, under Ho Chi Minh, had proclaimed Vietnam's independence. The French, determined to reestablish sovereignty over their colony, recognized Ho's "Democratic Republic of Vietnam" as a free state within the French Union. As a part of the agreement, the French would be allowed to maintain garrisons in Vietnam for five years. Within less than a year, the Vietminh accused the French of violating the agreement. The Vietminh or Revolutionary League for the Independence of Vietnam was organized by Ho during World War II to convert Vietnam from a feudal society to a classless Communist society. After the war it emphasized nationalism rather than communism to win independence for Vietnam. Open conflict developed and soon escalated into the First Indochina War.

When France established an "independent" state of Vietnam in 1949 under Emperor Bao Dai, the Vietminh became, in effect, "rebels," but with the important difference that they were rebels identified as fighting for the independence of Vietnam. By contrast, Bao Dai, who spent much of his time on the French Riviera, was seen as a French puppet; in fact, he could not have survived one day in office without the support of French arms. Like Mao Zedong in China, Ho conducted guerrilla warfare and met with considerable success. The French, who generally held the cities, were at a disadvantage from the beginning, for in the absence of genuine independence, the Vietnamese identified themselves with the Vietminh and saw the French as colonial rulers. In the long run, France paid a very high price for the war in terms of manpower, material, and morale.

The Escalating U.S. Involvement

During the first years of the war, American public opinion was unsympathetic to France's attempt to reestablish its colonial control over Indochina. Three events led to U.S. involvement in this conflict. The first was the defeat of Jiang Gaishek. This was seen as a blow to France, because it meant that the Chinese Communists could now provide assistance to the Vietminh. The second event was the outbreak of the Korean War, with the resulting shift of containment to Asia. The third event was the change in the political climate in the United States to anticommunism. The French, who earlier were seen as trying to hold onto the vestiges of their colonial empire, now were regarded as fighters in the common struggle against communism.

The Eisenhower administration began to provide France with economic and military aid. By 1954 the United States was paying about 75 percent of the costs of the war. The French position continued to deteriorate, however, especially once the Korean armistice was signed. Despite American warnings, Communist China shifted its pressure from Korea to Indochina and increased its assistance to the Vietminh. On March 13, 1954, Vietminh forces launched an assault upon the French fortress at Dienbienphu. The French position in northern Vietnam seemed close to collapse. It became painfully clear that the French could not hold on without American intervention. What was the United States to do?

Eisenhower had already declared that the fall of Indochina "would be of a most terrible significance to the United States of America," and he had termed Southeast Asia of "transcendent importance" to American security. If Indochina fell, Thailand, Burma, Malaysia, and Indonesia were expected to collapse like a set of dominoes. The secretary of state had issued several statements that rather strongly suggested that the United States would not stand idly by while this occurred. He had warned the Chinese Communists in the same terms he had used after the armistice in Korea: any aggression—that is, open aggression—would incur "grave consequences which might not be confined to Indochina." This warning also applied to any indirect Chinese intervention, such as assistance in the form of military advisers, equipment, and training for the Vietminh forces. The strategic significance of Indochina was seen as important, not what course the Chinese chose.

Dienbienphu was the moment of decision for the administration. Eisenhower and Dulles had declared Indochina to be of strategic importance to American security and had cautioned China against direct or indirect intervention by threatening it with massive retaliation. The Chinese ignored these warnings, and the U.S. government had to "put up or shut up." It shut up; its threats turned out to be only bluffs.

The Refusal to Intervene Militarily

The reason for this inaction is fairly clear: American public opinion might be strongly anti-Communist, but Eisenhower had withdrawn from Korea because the nation had tired of the war. He was unwilling to involve the United States in another such war. Furthermore, the administration was already cutting the size of the army, and the army Chief of Staff counseled against intervention because of a lack of available troops. The administration considered two courses of action. The first was to rescue the French by attacking the Communist positions with air power alone, but this was rejected because air strikes by themselves could not halt the Communist ground advance. Air power had failed to stop the North Korean army during the opening days of that war, and this failure had necessitated the commitment of U.S. troops.

The alternative strategy was to retaliate massively against China. That would have been consistent with the administration's announced policy, but in Indochina the administration did not follow its policy. The reason is simple: it is one thing to deliver a threat of massive retaliation to an opponent, and quite another to have the opponent believe it. The Soviets had not believed it before Korea, nor did the Chinese in Indochina. Both apparently rejected the notion that the United States would risk a total war for anything less than an attack on the United States or Europe. Because the Eisenhower administration shared with the Truman administration the fear that an attack on China would precipitate Soviet intervention, the United States was faced again with the terrible dilemma of doing nothing or risking all-out war.

Truman's experience with Korea had clearly shown that containment could not be successful without the willingness and capability to fight a limited war. Reliance upon strategic air power was not a credible strategy for deterring or winning "Koreas." The United States' ability to drop atom bombs on Moscow or Beijing was less than useless when the problem was a "little" war. Ground forces were absolutely necessary if the United States was to escape either defeat or involvement in a total conflict. (Indochina should also have demonstrated—as Americans were to learn a decade later—that a limited war against guerrilla forces also required political, social, and economic measures to alleviate the popular grievances upon which the guerrillas feed.) The Eisenhower administration ignored these lessons of the Korean War. It persuaded itself that Korea had happened only because the enemy had not received a previous warning that an attack upon South Korea would bring retaliatory strikes. Although such warnings were certainly desirable to prevent enemy miscalculation, Indochina proved that warnings alone were not enough. It showed that containment was incompatible with heavy budget cutting.

The result of American inaction was the French government's decision to make the best of the situation by negotiating with the Communists directly for an end to the war. The French people were as weary of the fighting as the American public had been of Korea. Just as the Americans had elected Eisenhower to end the war, the French National Assembly had elected Pierre Mendés-France to end the Indochina hostilities. The new premier announced that he was willing to conclude the war, and on July 20, 1954, an armistice agreement was reached that divided the country at the seventeenth parallel. The Communists kept control of northern Indochina, but it seemed only a matter of time until they took the rest of the country because the collapse of the southern rump state seemed imminent. The United States prevented the takeover by supporting the new government of Ngo Dinh Diem, a staunch anti-Communist nationalist appointed by Bao Dai after Dienbienphu (Diem later ousted Bao Dai). The Eisenhower administration gave Diem economic and military aid to stabilize the situation in Vietnam, and the danger of collapse temporarily receded.

SEATO's Founding

The seventeenth parallel, like the thirty-eighth parallel in Korea, became part of the international frontier separating the Communist and non-Communist worlds. To protect this frontier, the United States, Britain, France, Australia, New Zealand, the Philippines, Pakistan, and Thailand in September 1954 signed a treaty forming the Southeast Asia Treaty Organization (SEATO) to defend the area of the South Pacific, with the exception of Hong Kong and Taiwan. A protocol to the treaty extended SEATO's protection to Vietnam, Laos, and Cambodia. It also provided for joint action to meet aggression; an attack upon any of its members would be considered a threat to all, and each would then act to meet the common danger in accordance with its constitutional processes. In case of subversion, the parties agreed to consult one another immediately and agree on common measures to meet this threat.

SEATO, unlike the North Atlantic Treaty Organization alliance, had no unified command or joint forces. Its principal force was American sea and air power. The crucial element—land power—would have to be supplied by the member nations if the occasion arose. Moreover—and again unlike NATO—SEATO did not include most of the nations in the areas it planned to protect. India, Burma, Sri Lanka, and Indonesia did not join. They had just emerged from Western colonialism and were unwilling to be tied again to the West through a military alliance. They preferred to remain neutral in the struggle between the Western powers and the Sino-Soviet bloc. The Philippines were willing to join because of its traditional ties to the United States, and Pakistan because it wished to acquire a source for arms against India. Only Thailand was genuinely concerned with Communist China's expansion. Australia and New Zealand were not really Asian powers.

SEATO was mainly a non-Asian alliance for the defense of an Asian area, a weakness that was to plague the alliance. The absence of regional concern about Communist China's expansion ensured SEATO's eventual failure. French and British membership did not prevent that result. France was unlikely to defend an area from which it had been forced to withdraw in humiliation. Britain, which had opposed U.S. intervention, saw the alliance as a means of restraining a similar act in the future. SEATO was, in reality, a U.S. guarantee for the defense of South Vietnam; it would provide a legal basis for a unilateral intervention to preserve the dividing line between the two Vietnams.

The Taiwan Straits and the Offshore Islands

U.S.-Chinese relations had turned increasingly bitter and confrontational after the United States intervened in the Chinese civil war and China intervened in Korea. Soon after the Korean War ended, China's interest turned back to eliminating its rival on the other side of the Taiwan Straits. During the summer of 1954, the Chinese Communists openly proclaimed their intention of taking Taiwan and began shelling the Nationalist-held offshore islands. Quemoy is only nine miles outside the harbor of Amoy; Matsu lies almost as close, blocking the harbor of Foochow, and the Tachen islands are 200 miles north of Taiwan. In December the United States and the Nationalists signed a Treaty of Mutual Defense, by which the United States guaranteed the security of Taiwan and the nearby Pescadores. The Nationalists pledged not to attack the mainland or reinforce their offshore garrisons without the consent of the United States.

The offshore islands were not included under the terms of the treaty. However, as the situation in the straits grew more tense in January 1955, the president requested and received from Congress the authority to employ American armed forces to protect Taiwan and the Pescadores. This authority extended to the protection of "such related positions and territories" as the president judged necessary. Although this did not specifically clarify whether the United States would defend Quemoy and Matsu, the Communists certainly thought so, and they abstained from any invasion attempts of

Quemoy and Matsu. (The Nationalists, meanwhile, had evacuated the Tachens.)

Three years later, in August 1958, any ambiguities about the American position became clear when the Communists again began to shell the offshore islands. The Seventh Fleet—with orders to retaliate if fired upon—escorted Nationalist supply ships to within three miles of the beleaguered islands and helped them break a blockade. The Nationalist air force, equipped by the United States with air-to-air missiles, defeated the Communist air force's attempt to establish air supremacy in the sky between the mainland and Quemoy.

The line remained where it had been before the two Taiwan crises—a few miles off Communist China's coast. Some months later, Dulles reaffirmed this line when he firmly rejected Jiang's calls to take back the mainland. American policy in the straits was committed to the preservation of the *status quo*. Each side should keep what it had and refrain from attacking the other. The Eisenhower administration thereby recognized what neither it nor its predecessor had been willing to admit openly before: that the Nationalist expectation of recapturing the mainland was a myth. At the same time, it tacitly acknowledged the Chinese Communist government as continental China's *de facto* government. It reconciled itself to the Communist conquest of the mainland. Containment had once more replaced liberation. The administration, moreover, resolved to back up its "disengagement" policy with force. In the straits, it could support its political position with sea and air power and the threat of using nuclear weapons to foil an invasion; ground forces were not needed.

For the moment, the situation in the Far East had been stabilized. The frontier lines between the American and Soviet/Chinese spheres had been drawn at the thirty-eighth parallel in Korea, in the Taiwan Straits, at the seventeenth parallel in Indochina, and at the line drawn by SEATO. Although it would not be clear until years later, by standing fast, the United States also helped stress Sino-Soviet differences to near the breaking point. For China, unification with Taiwan was a priority; the Soviet Union's indifference disappointed China. For the Soviet Union, however, Taiwan was not worth the risk of a war with the United States. Consequently, the tiny islands of Quemoy and Matsu had profound long-term effects. In the meantime, Soviet attention turned back to the Middle East.

The Middle East and the Suez War

In 1955 the United States completed its line around the Sino-Soviet periphery. Britain, with U.S. support, established the Middle East Treaty Organization (METO), which included Turkey, Iraq, Iran, and Pakistan. Also known as the Baghdad Pact, METO extended the NATO line from

Turkey to India. With the exception of Iraq, this "northern tier" was drawn along 3,000 miles of the Soviet Union's southern frontier and drew a sharp reaction from the Soviet Union. Although they had been rebuffed in Iran and Turkey, the Soviets had not surrendered their historic ambitions in the region. The Middle East linked Europe, Africa, and Asia. For Britain, the area— and especially the Suez Canal—had long been the lifeline to India, the crown of the old empire, and to its present Commonwealth. Of greater importance, Europe's economy was becoming increasingly dependent upon the Middle East for oil (America was still self-sufficient in oil). The power that could deny Europe oil would be able to dictate its future. In short, for the Soviet Union, the Middle East was the place to outflank and neutralize NATO. Its opportunity to attempt this came as a result of several situations: the bitter Arab-Israeli conflict, the Anglo-Egyptian quarrel, Egypt's expansionist ambitions, and the U.S. attempt to draw the line of containment just south of the Soviet Union's border.

The Beginning of the Arab-Israeli Conflict

Arab antagonism toward Israel stemmed from the Balfour Declaration of 1917, in which Britain had pledged the establishment of a "national home" for the Jewish people in Palestine, while also promising the Arabs that the civil and religious rights of non-Jews would not be prejudiced. Zionists took this pledge as a promise to convert Palestine into a Jewish state; they considered Palestine, which had become a British mandate after the disintegration of the Ottoman Empire during World War I, as their ancient and traditional homeland.

If Britain's troubles were serious after Hitler's assumption of power in Germany, they became impossible after World War II. Hitler had slaughtered 6 million Jews in his concentration camps. Few of the survivors wished to remain in Europe, with its unhappy memories, and many emigrated to Palestine. The Jews were determined to establish a Jewish state, while the Arabs feared that the Jewish immigration would crowd them out of what they also regarded as their rightful homeland. British troops were unable to keep the peace between the Arabs and Jews. Under these circumstances, Britain—already gravely weakened by the war and forced to curtail its commitments throughout the world—decided to end its burdensome mandate over Palestine.

In November 1947 the United Nations partitioned Palestine into two independent states, one Jewish and the other Arab. The Arabs refused to accept this solution. On May 10, 1948, as Britain ended its mandate, the Jews proclaimed the state of Israel, and the armies of the Arab League (Egypt, Jordan, Syria, Lebanon, and Saudi Arabia) invaded the new state. In the ensuing war, the Israeli army defeated the larger Arab armies, and the state of Israel became a fact of political life.

The Arabs, however, refused to recognize it as such. Although they signed an armistice in February 1949, they refused to conclude a peace treaty. They continued to regard the Jews as infidels who had no right to be in Israel. Moreover, they felt deeply humiliated by their defeat. The Arabs awaited their day of revenge; meanwhile, they continued to proclaim their intention to destroy Israel. They conducted constant guerrilla warfare against Israel. The Egyptians refused to allow Israeli shipping through the Suez Canal and blockaded the Gulf of Aqaba.

But Egypt, the leading Arab power, needed arms. In September 1955 Egypt stunned the West by concluding an arms deal with Czechoslovakia, acting for the Soviet Union. Under this arrangement, Egypt received a large quantity of arms, including planes and tanks. Egypt now thought that it had the means to achieve a decisive military victory over Israel. In April 1956 Egypt tightened the ring around Israel by forming a joint command with Syria, Saudi Arabia, and Yemen. In October Egypt, Jordan, and Syria announced another joint command, "the principal concern of which is the war of destruction against Israel." This, in turn, raised a critical question for Israel: Should it strike now or wait until Egypt and its allies were ready for the "second round"? As Egypt solidified the encirclement of Israel, grew increasingly aggressive, and began to absorb the Soviet arms, the Israelis decided to strike before it was too late. All that was needed was the right condition for launching their preemptive attack.

Israel's opportunity came in October and grew out of Anglo-Egyptian antagonism. Britain had controlled Egypt since 1881, when it had established a protectorate there to safeguard its passage through Suez to India. A 1936 treaty between the two countries had converted this status into an alliance. Under the treaty's terms, British troops were confined to the Suez Canal zone, and their presence was declared to be neither an occupation nor an infringement of Egyptian sovereignty. To the Egyptians, however, British soldiers on their soil represented a violation of Egyptian independence, pride, and dignity.

The Anglo-Egyptian Quarrel and Nasser's Ambitions

World War II intensified Egyptian nationalism and heightened the demand for a withdrawal of British forces. But negotiations on this question broke down, and other postwar events increased Egypt's anti-British sentiment. The Egyptians resented the Palestine partition plan, for which they blamed Britain as well as the United States. In late 1951 the Egyptian parliament abrogated the 1936 Anglo-Egyptian treaty, and in July 1952 the new military regime that took over the Egyptian government from King Farouk pressed with renewed vigor for the removal of British troops. The Eisenhower administration supported the Egyptian demand in the belief that Colonel Gamal Abdel Nasser, the real power behind the military coup, and the United States were natural allies. The military was believed to be anticolonial, progressive, and committed to improving people's lives and providing Egypt with a degree of political stability. If the United States helped Nasser to evacuate British troops from their Suez Canal base, the Egyptians might become allies in fact. Faced with U.S. opposition, and aware of its own unpopularity in Egypt, Britain signed a new Anglo-Egyptian treaty in 1954, by which it agreed to withdraw all its troops from Suez over a twenty-month period. British influence over Egyptian politics had come to an end. More important, having finished what it considered British colonial control, the new regime, which had overthrown the corrupt monarchy that it blamed for Egypt's defeat in the 1948 war, now wished to turn to its number one goal: to avenge itself by destroying Israel.

The removal of British forces from Egypt did not eliminate British power from the region. Britain shifted from Egypt to Iraq, its longtime friend, whose royalist regime needed Western protection from Egypt's new military regime. Nasser did not see the Baghdad Pact as a means of containing the Soviet Union; he saw it as an instrument to preserve Western domination throughout the area and, because Iraq had always been Egypt's traditional rival for Arab leadership, he considered the pact a personal challenge as well. The pact completed Nasser's alienation from the West, for his ambitions reached beyond eliminating Israel and expelling the British. He saw himself as a modern Saladin, the champion of the Arab cause. He promoted Pan-Arabism as a way of expanding his influence and that of his country. As the former dominant influence throughout the region, the West became Nasser's target. Setting himself up as an adversary of the West was the way for Nasser to become a hero to the Arabs.

Eisenhower's and Dulles's expectations of establishing a close relationship with Egypt were headed for disappointment. Bent upon containing international communism, they felt that U.S. policy was quite compatible with Arab nationalism and the formation of a close relationship with Egypt. There were only two obstacles to that goal: the British presence and the Arab-Israeli conflict. Once Britain had been persuaded to leave Egypt, the United States turned its attention to its Israeli policy. If the United States could show that it was not always biased toward Israel, it might enlist Arab nationalism for the containment policy. The U.S. political leadership clearly failed to understand the dynamics of Egyptian and Arab politics and rivalries, as events shortly after the formation of the Baghdad Pact demonstrated.

The pact was the instrument of its own destruction because it helped bind Egypt to the Soviet Union. Its failure testifies to the difficulties of containing Soviet expansion by drawing lines outside of Europe. In Western Europe, the states all shared a common perception of the Soviet threat and stood united against it. Outside of Europe, U.S.-Soviet competition intersected with regional rivalries, undermining the U.S. goal of containment and providing the Soviet Union with an opportunity to expand its influence. The Baghdad Pact became a target. It was in Moscow's interest to destroy the Western alliance along the Soviet Union's southern frontier; it was in Cairo's interest to gain a source of arms to destroy Israel and to put political pressure on the pro-Western regimes in the area. These overlapping interests produced the Moscow-Cairo axis. Moscow, as a result, leapfrogged over the territory of the Baghdad Pact members. For all practical purposes, the alliance was null and void. Worst of all, however, Moscow had established its influence in the Eastern Mediterranean.

Cairo received its arms, and Nasser became a hero for the Arab people. He had defied the West by turning to the East; by championing the Arab cause and winning the allegiance of the Arab masses, Nasser could make it more difficult for pro-Western Arab regimes to oppose him. If they did, he could call for their overthrow and back those elements that supported him. In the meantime, he could seek to subvert these governments. By strengthening Nasser, the Soviet Union became the Arabs' greatest friend. It had taken only one year from the signing of the Anglo-Egyptian treaty to the arms deal. But the price of the Moscow-Cairo axis was Israeli and British insecurity.

The United States further upset the West's position in the Middle East in July 1956 when it informed the Egyptian government that it would not help finance Nasser's pet project, the Aswan High Dam. The dam on the upper Nile was intended to raise Egypt's low standard of living by irrigating new land and providing electricity for industrial development. The American offer had been made shortly after the formation of the Baghdad Pact as a gesture of friendship toward Nasser. The retraction was a heavy blow to Egypt's hopes to raise itself by its own "sandalstraps" because the American loan was a prerequisite for further aid from the World Bank and Britain, and these offers, too, were withdrawn. The Eisenhower administration had several reasons for its action: Nasser had attempted to blackmail the administration into providing more money by hinting that the Soviets had offered to finance the entire project; Egypt had moved close to the Soviet Union with the arms deal and had recognized Communist China as well; Nasser had committed the funds he was supposed to provide for the dam to buy Soviet arms—which, in effect, meant that the entire cost would fall upon the United States and Britain.

Nasser regarded the American decision as a personal slap and national humiliation. A few days later, on July 26, he announced that he would nationalize the Suez Canal and use the revenues collected from it to finance the dam. Arab nationalists were ecstatic, and Nasser's stature, already great, reached new heights. The British government reacted sharply to Nasser's seizure of the canal. Prime Minister Anthony Eden did not trust the Egyptian leader, and, although Nasser guaranteed that all ships, except Israel's, could pass through the canal, Eden feared that Nasser would use the canal as an instrument of political blackmail. Moreover, if Nasser could face the West with such a major act of defiance and go unpunished, Western influence would be destroyed throughout the Middle East. Other Arab governments would expropriate Western oil interests, and all opponents of Nasser would be forced to come to terms with him. Western prestige—especially British prestige, because south of America's "northern tier" Britain was the leading Western power in the Middle East—had to be upheld. If it were not, the Cairo-Moscow axis would dominate the entire area and be in a position to strangle Europe. The British were determined to stand up to Nasser, and they insisted upon some form of international control for the canal. The Egyptians rejected all proposals to wrest their newly won control out of their hands and denounced them as "collective colonialism." All attempts to bridge this gap failed.

The United States Displaces Britain During the Suez War

On October 29, only four days after Jordan's chief of staff announced that the time had come to launch the Arab assault on Israel, the Israeli army marched into Egypt. The Israelis quickly defeated the Egyptian forces in the Sinai peninsula. The British and the French (who sought Nasser's downfall because of his aid to rebels trying to free Algeria from French control) intervened twenty-four hours later. At this point, the United States saved Nasser. Although by withdrawing the Aswan Dam offer, the administration had precipitated Nasser's seizure of the canal and the British attack, it now opposed the use of force to settle this issue.

The reason was that, despite its disapproval of Nasser's action and the pro-Soviet direction in which he was leading Egypt, the administration saw Nasser's foreign policy as purely a reaction against Israel and Western colonialism. It remained convinced that if Israel had not existed, and if the Arab states had not long been dominated by the Western powers, especially Britain, the Arabs would not be anti-Western and pro-Soviet. The administration saw the invasion of Egypt as a golden opportunity to win Arab friendship. When Israel had proclaimed itself a state, the United States had recognized the new nation within eleven minutes. Here was a chance to show the Arabs that the United States was not as pro-Jewish as they thought, and that the United States could even be pro-Arab. Because Egypt's actions were also anti-British, the United States thought it wise to oppose the British attempt to reassert control over the canal. By saving Nasser, the United States could align itself with Arab nationalism; supporting Britain, France, and Israel would leave the Soviet Union as the sole champion of Arab aspirations. American opposition to the invasion, in short, would identify the United States with the anticolonialism of the entire underdeveloped world, and particularly with the anti-Israeli and nationalistic sentiments of the Arab world. Because continued evidence of British power in the Middle East only antagonized the Arabs, the removal of this power and its replacement by American influence would be in the interest not only of the United States but of all the Western powers. In this way, the West's strategic and economic interests could be more adequately safeguarded. At least, that was the rationale for the United States humiliating its two main allies, thereby turning Nasser's military defeat into a political victory.

America's opposition to the Suez invasion was the decisive factor in stopping the fighting. Egypt had already blocked the canal, and the Syrians had cut the pipelines running across their country from Iraq, making Britain dependent upon the United States to replace its losses from the Middle East. The administration threatened to use this economic sanction if Britain did not cease the attack. Faced with this dire prospect—plus opposition to the invasion within Britain, the Commonwealth (Canada, India, and Pakistan), and the United Nations—the British government accepted a cease-fire and later withdrew its forces; France and Israel had little choice but to follow suit.

It is ironic in view of America's leading role in halting the attack on Egypt, that it should have been the Soviet Union that was to reap the benefits. After it had become clear that the United States would not support the British and French invasion, the Soviet Union threatened "to crush the aggressor." It sent notes to the British and French governments warning of possible rocket attacks on their countries and bluntly told Israel that its very existence was at stake. It even asked the United States to join forces with it to stop the war. And after the cease-fire, the Soviet Union and Communist China threatened to send "volunteer soldiers." In short, the Soviet Union risked nothing to deliver these threats, but it was the country that received most of the credit from the Arabs for saving Nasser by its threats to exterminate Israel and attack Britain and France. Losing Suez resulted in the collapse of British power in the Middle East, the strengthening of Arab nationalism, and the consolidation of Egyptian-Soviet links.

Nasser's great political victory increased his self-confidence. Supported by the Soviet Union, whose aim it was to weaken if not eliminate all Western power in the Middle East, Nasser continued his expansionist drive. Jordan abrogated the Anglo-Jordan Treaty by which Jordan had received an annual subsidy to maintain its economy; Egypt, Saudi Arabia, and Syria promised to replace the British funds, and Jordan announced that it would seek to establish a federal union with Egypt and Syria. The last two states did, in fact, join together into a union, the United Arab Republic, in early 1958. Attempts to undermine the Iraqi government continued throughout 1956, and in the spring of 1957, the Egyptians organized riots against the government in Lebanon.

The Eisenhower Doctrine

After the Suez crisis Eisenhower urged Congress to support a new commitment to resist communism in the Middle East. A joint resolution of Congress, known as the Eisenhower Doctrine, passed in the spring of 1957 and declared that the United States considered the preservation of the independence and integrity of the Middle Eastern nations vital to American security, and that it was prepared to use armed force to assist any nation or nations "*requesting* assistance against *armed* aggression from any country controlled by international Communism [italics added]." It was difficult to understand what this doctrine meant. The Soviet Union did not border on any Arab state. Iraq, to the south, was already protected by the Baghdad Pact and, through its association with Britain and Turkey, by NATO; so the doctrine could not be directed against the Soviet Union. In any event, the Soviet Union had already leapfrogged the northern tier.

The Eisenhower administration was forced to reconsider its views of Nasser in light of his continued attempts to undermine Western power in the Middle East, his vicious attacks upon all the Western nations, including the United States, and his continued flirtation with the Soviet Union. At Suez, the United States had thought it could win his trust by demonstrating its friendship. But Nasser's actions proved this expectation was ill-founded. A complete reversal of policy was in order, and this required a "reinterpretation" of the Eisenhower Doctrine. First, the term *armed aggression* was no longer to refer only to the direct attack of one nation upon another but also to attempts to overthrow pro-Western governments through subversion; and second, *any country controlled by international communism* now included nations with close ties to the Soviet Union. In short, the target became Nasser's radical Arab nationalism. The revised Eisenhower Doctrine was still based upon the same anti-Communist assumptions that had been the basis of the ill-fated Baghdad Pact; the principal difference was that it was intended to deal with a Middle East in which the Soviets had already destroyed the northern tier. Having helped eliminate British power in the hope of winning Egypt's friendship against Moscow, the administration now found itself filling the vacuum left by British power to contain what it saw as the Moscow-Cairo axis.

The doctrine was applied first in Jordan, where King Hussein's dismissal of the pro-Nasser government led to a general strike, massive street demonstrations, and riots. Jordan's days as an independent state appeared to be numbered. Hussein charged in April 1957 that international communism was responsible for the efforts to overthrow him. The same day, the United States announced that it regarded "the independence and integrity of Jordan as vital." And to prove that it meant what it said, the administration dispatched the United States Sixth Fleet to the eastern Mediterranean and extended Jordan $10 million for the support of its army and economy. The Hussein government survived.

In the summer of 1958, an even more serious crisis arose when a group of nationalist officers led by General Abdul Karim Kassem overthrew the pro-Western government of Iraq. Although the new regime did not withdraw from the Baghdad Pact until some months later, this revolt, in effect, removed the pivotal state of the alliance. The United Arab Republic immediately recognized the new government, and the two countries quickly signed an alliance. There was little the United States could do but recognize the Kassem government. Arab nationalism seemed to be sweeping everything in front of it.

Only Lebanon, Jordan, and Saudi Arabia were still outside the Nasser camp, and the first two were teetering on the verge of revolution. The whole Western position in the Middle East seemed to be on the brink of disintegration.

U.S. Action in the Middle East

The Eisenhower administration now resorted to force. Lebanon had been plagued for some time with civil war between Muslims and Christians. The Muslims wanted close relations, if not union, with the United Arab Republic, and the Christians favored a pro-Western policy and the continued independence of Lebanon. With the Iraqi revolution, men and arms for the pro-Nasser elements began to be smuggled in from Syria. In Jordan, too, the situation took a turn for the worse. The Iraqi *coup d'etat* was alarming to King Hussein, who also had his pro-Nasser masses and army officers. Jordan and Lebanon invoked the Eisenhower Doctrine and asked for military support. Now, ironically, the United States acted together with Britain. The United States sent 14,000 men into Lebanon, and the British sent paratroopers into Jordan. The large size of the American contingent seems to have been a deliberate warning to the new Iraqi government against nationalizing Western oil resources. Kassem quickly gave the assurance that he had no such intention, and possible American intervention in Iraq was thereby forestalled. Loud Soviet hints of intervention also turned out to be hollow when countered by resolute American action. Both Britain and the United States withdrew their troops in late October.

The Anglo-American action saved Lebanon and Jordan, at least temporarily. But it was also intended to have another important effect: to show Nasser and the Arabs that there were limits to Soviet willingness to come to their aid. Nasser's personal ambitions were, by themselves, important but secondary; the factors that had spelled success for Egypt's Pan-Arab policy were Soviet support and power. The Western powers, in thinking of counteraction against Egypt, could never eliminate the possibility of Soviet intervention. This, of course, further encouraged Nasser's expansionist drive. The Anglo-American action in Lebanon and Jordan disabused the Arabs of this notion. Prior to the intervention, the Soviets again had threatened to send "volunteers" to oppose the Western "imperialists" and had carried out conspicuous military maneuvers in Soviet Central Asia and Transcaucasia. The firmness of the American position and the failure of the Soviet Union to do more than denounce the intervention and call for a diplomatic settlement, made it very clear that there were limits to Soviet willingness to bail out the Arabs. This had a dampening effect on Nasser's anti-Western drive.

Another unexpected turn of events influenced this situation. The new regime in Iraq, instead of turning out to be pro-Nasser—as almost everyone, including Nasser, had expected—took the opposite position. It was not long before Kassem began to challenge the Egyptian ruler's leadership of Arab nationalism. Nasser recognized this threat of Egypt's traditional rival and attempted to overthrow the Kassem government. But the revolt by a group of pro-Nasser officers was quickly squashed. At the same time, the Soviet Union gave economic and military support to the Kassem government. Nasser's drive for Arab leadership was stalled: Jordan, Lebanon, and Saudi Arabia had remained independent; Libya and the Sudan had resisted his attempts to subvert them; Syria was restless in the United Arab Republic; and Iraq had become a rival for Arab leadership.

Nor was this situation materially changed by the events of the early 1960s: Kassem was overthrown, and Syria revolted to quit the United Arab Republic. Despite the Pan-Arab aspirations of Egypt, Syria, and Iraq, a true Arab union remained as elusive as ever. Syria and Iraq were unwilling to permit Nasser to dominate them, and Nasser was unwilling to form a union he could not control. The Egyptian leader's new emphasis on domestic reform—or what he called "Arab socialism"—therefore became crucial to his fight for Arab leadership, even though he continued his attempts to overthrow traditional pro-Western regimes and remained generally anti-Western in his policy positions.

Meanwhile, the United States had become almost a full-fledged member of the Baghdad Pact (now renamed the Central Treaty Organization) by joining its economic, military, and countersubversion committees. But south of CENTO's fragile line remained all the basic problems that had given rise to the turmoil after 1955: the conflicts among the Arab states, the Arab-Israeli quarrel, the overshadowing competition between the United States and the Soviet Union, and, above all, Arab nationalism and its xenophobia. Despite the region's vast oil wealth, the Arab masses remained very poor and suffered from illiteracy, malnutrition, and disease. Social discontent and political instability were the result. Above all, the American attempt to fill the vacuum left by the decline of British power and draw another "frontier" was unsuccessful. Ironically, it was the attempt to do this that drew the Soviet Union and Egypt together to destroy the northern tier, permitting the Soviet Union to jump over the line that was supposed to contain it.

The Soviet Shift Back to Europe

In Europe NATO had already drawn the defense line. The strength of this line on the ground depended upon supplementing NATO forces with West German troops, and the Allies had chosen the European Defense Community to achieve this goal. But in August 1954, the French National Assembly rejected the EDC by a decisive majority; fear of Germany remained too great, and French nationalists wished to maintain France's identity and honor. This decision was a real blow to the efforts toward creating a situation of strength in Europe. The whole basis of NATO strategy and European integration was suddenly imperiled.

Dulles's response was to threaten that the United States would make an "agonizing reappraisal" of its NATO commitments if the deadlock were not broken. Britain's Prime Minister Eden averted such a reappraisal by seeking a way of rearming West Germany with French approval. He found it in the forgotten Brussels Treaty. This organization was revised by the inclusion of Germany and Italy. The new alliance, which pledged all its members to come to one another's aid if attacked, was named the Western European Union (WEU). But the WEU had no forces assigned to it, and it had no responsibility for formulating a strategy to defend its members. These remained within the functions of NATO. The WEU's role was to channel West German troops into NATO, while at the same time maintaining a set of controls over West Germany similar to those included in the EDC. Furthermore, Britain agreed to keep a minimum number of troops on the Continent. Britain's pledge was a formalization of its responsibilities under the Dunkirk, Brussels, and NATO treaties. But to the French it seemed an important new commitment; they were now reassured that they would not someday be left to face German troops alone.

These commitments, embodied in the Paris Pact, came into force in May 1955. Ten years after Germany's defeat, the occupation came to an end, and the Federal Republic regained its sovereignty and entered NATO via the WEU. West Germany's military power could now be added to Western strength. Two important declarations were appended to these Paris agreements. In the first, the West German government subscribed to the principles of the United Nations, undertook "never to have recourse to force to achieve the reunification of Germany or the modification of the present boundaries of the German Federal Republic," and to resolve all disputes between itself and other states by peaceful means. In the second, the United States, Britain, and France declared that they recognized the Federal Republic as the only freely and legitimately constituted government entitled to speak for all of Germany, thereby indicating a policy of nonrecognition of the East German government. In addition, the Allies would pursue German reunification by peaceful means, which in effect meant the preservation of a divided Germany. Finally, the Western powers stated that they would continue to exercise their responsibilities with regard to the security of West Germany and West Berlin.

The Birth of the Common Market

With Germany safely enrolled as a member of NATO, the WEU members now took a momentous step toward further economic and political integration. The six states that composed Little Europe had gained increasing benefits from this movement. On June 1, 1958, they established the European Economic Community (EEC), usually referred to as the Common Market, whose objective was to join them together into an economic union. Their plan was to achieve this in a twelve- to fifteen-year period. During this time, all six states would completely eliminate the tariffs and quota systems that hampered trade among them. They would also abolish restrictions on the movement of labor, capital, and services among them, although this commitment was qualified. Agriculture was the exception. The Common Market expected to develop a policy of subsidies and price supports and eliminate discriminations among farmers within the community.

But the "Six" realized that these moves would not suffice. A government might abolish a tariff, but compensate its producers through subsidies or impose internal taxes that discriminated against foreign products. Production costs also reflected national standards for wages, hours, working conditions, and social welfare programs; producers in nations with lower standards had an obvious advantage against foreign competition. To ensure maximum free competition in the Common Market, subsidies were forbidden (except for use in developing backward areas); discriminatory taxes, price-fixing, and division of markets by cartel arrangements were not permitted; and the need to equalize hours, wages, and working conditions was recognized as urgent.

What were believed to be the chances for the development of this Common Market as it was being launched? The economic benefits were thought to guarantee it. As trade barriers were lowered and then eliminated, the increasing competition would result in the growth of efficient companies and the demise of the less efficient ones, unless they modernized or converted to new lines of production. All members were expected to gain from the capital funds. Italy would receive capital for the development of its southern area; France and its overseas territories would also receive development capital. While Germany would contribute a large share of the funds that would benefit its partners, it would in return receive access to their European and African markets. Germany was the strongest competitor among the Six. A final factor was that the community would collectively receive advantages against third parties. It was strong enough to demand reciprocal lowering of tariffs. All these advantages outweighed the burdens each nation would suffer as a result of economic dislocation and hardships, which in fact would be minimized by being extended over a period of years and by being shared among all members.

The principal advantage of the Common Market, however, was seen to be political, not economic. A common market needs common policies; only one set of rules—not six—can govern its competitive behavior. One nation cannot be allowed to pay its workers considerably lower wages than its neighbor to achieve a competitive advantage. There had to be some standardization of wages and of related items such as overtime, hours worked per week, and various welfare benefits. In the long run, the Common Market's success would lead to the adoption of common fiscal policies to control the ups and downs of the business cycle, a common currency, and a central bank. The economic "spillover"—from the original common market in coal and steel into a common market for all sectors of the economy—was expected to stimulate political unification. It was precisely the formation of a political union that had inspired the European Coal and Steel Community (ECSC).

Initiated by France and strongly supported by West German chancellor Konrad Adenauer, the European Economic Community was the culminating act of the movement to tie Germany so closely to a European community that it would never again be able to use its power for purely national ends. The formation of what came to be called the Inner Six was nothing less than the last link subjecting Germany to European restraints and responsibilities. Its success would make it impossible for Germany ever again to pursue a unilateral course.

Not surprisingly, the Soviet Union reacted quickly against the Common Market and attempted to break it up. A strong Europe, economically prosperous and politically stable, would not only prove a powerful barrier to Soviet expansionist ambitions, but also might threaten the Soviet *status quo* in Eastern Europe. The West European societies exercised a magnetic attraction for the satellite countries. West Berlin, alongside Communist East Berlin, hampered Soviet control of East Germany. Many young skilled and professional men and women left East Germany through West Berlin; it was an escape hatch that was depopulating East Germany of the very people it needed to run its society. If East Germany collapsed, Poland and the other East European states might soon follow. If the existence of West Berlin and West Germany made the Soviet Union feel insecure about the *status quo,* Soviet apprehensions about a united Europe were even greater.

The Second Berlin Crisis

The stability of the Soviet position in Central and Eastern Europe, as seen by Moscow, depended upon two factors: one, gaining Western recognition of the East German "Democratic" Republic; and two, destroying the freedom of West Berlin. To achieve these objectives, the Soviet Union announced in November 1958 that at the end of six months it intended to end the four-power occupation and hand control of East Berlin and the routes leading into West Berlin over to the East Germans. The clear implication was that in the future, free access to Berlin would require that the Western powers deal directly and officially with the East German government. The Soviets also repeated their formal proposal for the unification of Germany: that East and West Germany should join in a confederation. This, too, was a tactical device to gain the Federal Republic's recognition of East Germany. The Soviets obviously wanted to entice the West Germans to start negotiating with the East Germans on the issue of unification; at the same time, it was also clear that the Soviets were not in the least interested in any form of unification.

The Soviet proposal, in fact, was so constituted that it precluded Western acceptance. A confederation half democratic and half dictatorship was a contradiction in terms and totally unfeasible. Most industry in East Germany was owned by the government; West Germany was a booming private-enterprise state. To ensure the rejection of their terms, the Soviets also demanded that East Germany, with a population of a little more than 17 million, and West Germany, with a population of more than 53 million, should be equally represented in the confederated government. The Soviet Union naturally did not want the East Germans to be outvoted—with the possible result that East Germany would be voted out of existence—but Soviet premier Nikita Khrushchev could hardly have expected the Western powers or the Adenauer government to accept such equality.

If the Soviet proposals were meant to elicit Western recognition of East Germany, this goal remained subsidiary to the aim of strangling West Berlin. What the Soviets were actually calling for when they declared the end of the four-power occupation was an Allied withdrawal from West Berlin, turning it into a "free city." This was, in effect, a demand for the incorporation of West Berlin into East Germany. Once Western troops had left the city, the West Berliners would feel isolated and unprotected, abandoned and completely helpless. The Soviet army and the East German army and police would surround them. In these circumstances, the defenseless West Berliners would have to come to terms with the East German regime. On the other hand, if the West refused to sign a treaty turning Berlin into a "free city," the Soviet Union would then sign a separate peace treaty with East Germany, automatically abrogating the West's right to be in Berlin and making any further Western stay dependent upon the terms that could be negotiated with the now "sovereign" German Democratic Republic. This would mean that the West would remain in Berlin by the consent of East Germany, which would then gradually intensify its pressure and undermine the West's position until it became untenable.

One way or the other, the Soviets planned to remove a very troublesome thorn from their side. They would then be in a far better position to stabilize the *status quo*. The destruction of West Berlin would have accomplished not only the Soviet Union's defensive aims but also its long-standing offensive purpose of weakening its opponents, perhaps fatally. If the Soviets could drive the Western powers, especially the United States, out of Berlin, they would also be able to cut off the development of the Common Market before it gathered too much momentum and to shatter the NATO alliance. It was, above all, American power that guaranteed the freedom of the 2 million Germans living in West Berlin. If the United States were forced to abandon them, the Europeans would lose faith in America's ability to protect them. The Germans would be the first to read the lesson: because America could not guarantee their security, they would have to approach the Soviets independently.

The Soviets would certainly demand the abandonment of all Germany's political, economic, or military ties to the West. But without Germany, there could be no Common Market because Germany provided much of the capital its partners needed for their economic development. If Germany pulled out of the Atlantic alliance, the United States would have to send its troops home because it would be politically and strategically impossible to station them in France. Yet, these troops were a symbol of the American commitment to defend Europe; they were psychologically and politically indispensable. No written guarantees could be substituted for this living embodiment of America's stake in Europe.

Was America willing to defend Europe now that the United States was becoming increasingly vulnerable to a Soviet nuclear attack? This was, in the final analysis, the fundamental question posed by the Berlin crisis. The Soviet proposals had included the ultimatum that if West Berlin's status had not been "renegotiated" within six months, the East Germans would take control of the railroads and highways leading into West Berlin. If the East Germans then interfered with Western traffic and the West used force to break a blockade, Khrushchev stated that the Soviets would resist such force. The defense of West Berlin therefore raised the possibility of war. The Soviet challenge was clever: it presented the United States with a limited challenge and offered it the choice of surrendering West Berlin or fighting a total war for its preservation. It was America's will that was really at stake in Berlin.

Soviet Technological Prowess and the U.S. Response

Berlin was a major test of postwar American policy, but it was not a repeat of the 1948 situation. At that time, Joseph Stalin had acted upon two assumptions: first, that the far larger Red Army contingents would deter an Allied attempt to break through on the ground; and second, that the United States and Britain could not keep West Berlin alive. The first assumption proved to be correct, but the second was wrong. When Stalin realized this, he had to call off the blockade or shoot down Allied planes and risk a war. America's atomic monopoly favored the first solution. In 1957, however, the Soviet Union had tested the world's first intercontinental ballistic missile (ICBM), and American brinkmanship became riskier. Moreover, the ICBM test had followed a series of spectacular Soviet accomplishments in space. These Sputniks, or satellites, which flew around the world every 90 minutes, and the ICBM test were impressive symbols of Soviet technological progress. They raised serious questions in the United States about its historic technological leadership and the future of the balance of power. Khrushchev immediately began to talk of mass-producing ICBMs and asserted that the balance of nuclear or strategic power was shifting toward the Soviet Union. There was widespread public concern and anxiety in the United States about a future "missile gap," which, because ICBMs were faster than bombers, meant that U.S. deterrent forces would become vulnerable to a surprise attack and no longer be effective. To stand firm in this circumstance was risky. Yet, given the limited nature of the Soviet challenge and the all-or-nothing nature of massive retaliations, what strategy could the United States devise to prevent the Soviet Union from slowly choking West Berlin to death?

The crisis in Berlin demonstrated the weakness of massive retaliation as a defense policy. How could massive retaliation, a policy intended to deter an attack on the United States or Western Europe, be used to prevent the slow strangulation of West Berlin? Could strategic air power, upon which the Eisenhower administration depended almost exclusively to preserve the line around the Sino-Soviet periphery, successfully accomplish this task against limited challenges? The answer seemed to be that invoking the threat of an all-out nuclear war against a less-than-total challenge was gravely weakening the American ability to preserve this line. To be sure, the Soviets had to be very careful in Europe because the two superpowers confronted one another directly there, and a Soviet miscalculation could result in nuclear war. But the United States had to reduce the possibility that Moscow might make such an error. The Soviet Union had not believed that Washington would retaliate if North Korea invaded South Korea. Therefore, the American response to the Soviet challenge in Berlin was a very risky strategy. American strategic power was *so* great that it could not be used; as a reaction to a limited challenge, it was not credible.

The Berlin crisis was the most serious confrontation Washington had faced since 1948-1949. The Truman Doctrine, Marshall Plan, Berlin airlift, and NATO had made it very plain to Moscow that Western Europe was an area of vital American interest. Soviet domination over the Western edge of the Eurasian continent was no more tolerable to the United States than German control. Presumably this knowledge had deterred the Soviets in the late 1940s, and it was the fear of war that had led them to direct their challenges to Third World areas.

Now, however, ten years after the first Berlin crisis, the Soviets had once more challenged the West in Europe. Indeed, the reopening of the Berlin issue suggested that the Soviets felt a new confidence in their ability to deal with the West. That confidence seemed to reflect the Soviet claim that the strategic balance was changing in their favor. Clearly, Khrushchev was attempting to cash in on this claim, to undermine European confidence in the United States, and to drive a wedge between the European members of NATO, especially West Germany, and their trans-Atlantic protector. This would weaken, if not destroy, the strongest barrier to Soviet efforts to gain access to the Atlantic and the Mediterranean.

Indeed, the last years of the Eisenhower administration were years of gloom, expressed mainly by liberal Democrats, the authors of the containment policy. Although Eisenhower claimed there was no "deterrent gap," the succession of headlines about Soviet ICBM tests and Sputnik launchings all seemed to belie his words. American prestige and power were largely identified with technology; now the Soviets had gained a dramatic breakthrough in that area. After placing quite large weights, including a dog, in space, the Soviets derided the first American space shot. Khrushchev joked about the U.S. effort to launch "a grapefruit." More worrying was the ability of the Soviets to bring the Sputnik back to earth at a designated spot; presumably they could do the same with their ICBMs. The bombers that had provided the United States with its deterrent shield were about to become vulnerable. Suddenly, the United States lost the sense of security it had long possessed as a result of its isolationism from world politics, its atomic monopoly, and its enormous strategic superiority. Sputnik, the "missile gap," and the 1958 Berlin crisis caused a deep pessimism about the future. This pessimism was not limited to America. United States Information Agency polls in Western Europe and elsewhere showed that others shared a general sense that the United States was falling behind the Soviets, that the balance was shifting, and that perhaps the United States had lost its dynamism.

chapter six

Berlin, Cuba, and the Limits of Massive Retaliation

AMERICAN foreign policy traditionally has been based on a world view of mutually exclusive conditions: war or peace, force or diplomacy, aggressors or peace-loving states. Peace was normal, war abnormal. Force was unnecessary in the absence of conflict and hostilities; it was to be used only in wartime to destroy the source of war itself. The concept of massive retaliation fitted this American approach completely. It was an all-or-nothing strategy that could not be used short of a Soviet attack on the United States or Western Europe. At the same time, American presidents consistently rejected preventive war, both at the time of the nation's atomic monopoly and later, during the 1950s and 1960s, the period of gradually declining strategic superiority. Deterrence was the American goal; nuclear strategy was to retaliate after the opponent had struck first. If the United States were attacked, however, it would use massive retaliation, as in the two world wars, to punish and destroy the enemy in ways not conceivable until 1945.

Massive retaliation, by reducing the enemy's population centers and industries to rubble and radioactive dust, carried the American approach to war to its ultimate but logical conclusion. While some bombs were targeted on the small Soviet air force, the rapidly growing U.S. stockpile was to be used against all targets, military and economic, in one huge war-winning blow. The hydrogen bomb's megaton (equal to a million tons of TNT) explosive power, as opposed to that of the atomic bomb's kiloton (equal to a thousand tons of TNT), made that possible. In the words of a Navy captain attending an Air Force briefing on the Strategic Air Command (SAC) plans at the time, the Soviet Union was to be left "a smoking, radiating ruin at the end of two hours."

In one sense, atomic weapons and the more destructive nuclear weapons enabled the United States to pursue an old American dream in a new and gruesome way. By making nuclear war too destructive to fight, by making the distinction between victor and loser in such a conflict increasingly meaningless, the deterrent strategy aimed at eliminating war itself. This old goal had been sought through the "war to end all wars" crusade, or through international organization and cooperation, or through free trade and economic interdependence among nations. The goal could now be realized because war had become, in the popular phrase, "unthinkable."

Precisely because they were so destructive, nuclear weapons could not be an effective tool of foreign policy to deal with everyday problems and challenges. Even in the immediate postwar period, when the United States possessed an atomic monopoly, these weapons could not stop the Soviet Union from consolidating its grip on Eastern Europe, from attempting to seize a northern province of Iran, from pressuring Turkey, from permitting Yugoslavia and Bulgaria to intervene in the Greek civil war, or from urging the French Communist party to exploit France's postwar economic misery after 1947. Nor could atomic weapons deter the North Korean attack upon South Korea. The threat of massive retaliation had not prevented the Chinese Communists from helping the Vietminh or the Vietminh victory over the French in Indochina in 1954. The Soviets had only to avoid attacking the United States or an area the United States had designated as vital to its security. Short of that ultimate provocation, the Soviet Union, the strategically weaker party during the first decade of the cold war, could raise tensions and challenge the United States.

The problem for the United States was how to respond to limited challenges. As the situations in Berlin and Cuba were to show in the late 1950s and early 1960s, strategic weapons might prevent escalation of such challenges to war, but conventional forces were needed to defend U.S. interests. The chief lesson of the Korean War—that a capability for limited response was necessary to deal with less-than-total challenges, a lesson that the Eisenhower administration had rejected—could not be ignored. Indeed, as Soviet strategic strength grew during the 1950s, and the Soviet and American nuclear forces increasingly deterred one another, the requirement for conventional capability increased.

Deterrence and Challenge in the Nuclear Era

Mutual deterrence, or the "balance of terror," as Winston Churchill called it, would ensure the peace; indeed, in President Dwight Eisenhower's words, "there is no alternative to peace." His participation at the 1955 summit conference in Geneva with Soviet premier Nikolai Bulganin (Nikita Khrushchev was at that time first secretary of the Communist party of the Soviet Union) was generally recognized as testimony to this fact. War was no longer a rational instrument of national power; by simply meeting, the leaders of the two most powerful countries of the world were said to have "signed" a tacit nonaggression pact.

Strategists and foreign policy experts, however, feared that U.S. policy was handing the Soviet Union an opportunity to break this stalemate. The age of nuclear plenty increased America's strategic dilemma. The Eisenhower all-or-nothing strategy, the critics said, meant that each limited Soviet challenge confronted Washington with whether the defense of American interests was worth the destruction of most of America's cities. Faced with this prospect if it responded to the less-than-total Soviet challenges, the American government had a strong incentive to do nothing. In other words, the U.S. dilemma was one of suicide or surrender, holocaust or humiliation. Many analysts in the late 1950s thought that the nuclear stalemate might tempt Moscow to turn the balance in its favor by confronting the United States with a series of limited challenges—in Europe and outside of it—and winning them. It could thereby erode the *status quo* without ever once facing the United States with the one kind of challenge for which it was prepared. According to Henry Kissinger in 1957:

> It can be argued that the fear of all-out war is bound to be mutual, that the Soviet leaders will, therefore, share our reluctance to engage in any adventures which may involve this risk. But because each side may be equally deterred from engaging in all-out war, it makes all the difference which side can extricate itself from its dilemma *only* by initiating such a struggle. If the Soviet bloc can present its challenges in less than all-out form it may gain a crucial advantage. Every move on its part will then pose the appalling dilemma of whether we are willing to commit suicide to prevent encroachments, which do not, each in itself, seem to threaten our existence directly but which may be steps on the road to our ultimate destruction.
>
> To be sure, we shall continue to insist that we reject the notion of "peace at any price." The price of peace, however, cannot be determined in the abstract. The growth of the Soviet nuclear stockpile is certain to widen the line between what is considered "vital" and what is "peripheral" if we must weigh each objective against the destruction of New York or Detroit, of Los Angeles or Chicago.[1]

Was Berlin still a "vital" interest? Or was Berlin now a "peripheral" interest? These difficult questions confronted the United States in the late 1950s.

The Soviet challenge was underscored by the small number of conventional forces on the Continent. These North Atlantic Treaty Organization (NATO) troops had two tasks. The first was to strengthen deterrence by making the U.S. commitment to defend Europe more credible; Moscow could understand that once American soldiers were killed, SAC would be unleashed. The second, in case deterrence failed, was to implement the "forward

---

1. Henry A. Kissinger, *Nuclear Weapons and Foreign Policy* (New York: Harper & Brothers, 1957), 15-16.

strategy" by holding the Red Army at the border between East Germany and West Germany while SAC was destroying the Soviet Union. The policy of deterrence, however, dictated yet a third operational assignment for NATO forces: to conduct limited operations. It was preposterous to assume that the United States would risk suicide no matter what the level of Soviet provocation. Would the United States precipitate a total nuclear exchange if the Red Army or satellite East German troops seized all or part of West Berlin? Would it be willing to start an all-out nuclear war if the Soviets seized a small portion of West Germany? Would suicide in these instances be preferable to reacting locally? To escape this dilemma the United States and its allies needed a capacity for waging conventional warfare.

But this capacity to respond to such challenges was missing in Europe. In a large measure, this situation was a result of the Eisenhower administration's determination to "maximize air power and minimize the foot soldier." By January 1960 NATO had only seventeen or eighteen ready divisions. Moreover, the divisions were equipped with tactical nuclear weapons. This raised the same question as SAC: Would the weapons be used? Would NATO not grow increasingly reluctant to rely on these forces to respond to Soviet moves? When the original decision to equip Allied forces with nuclear battlefield weapons was made, it was believed that the Soviet Union would have few, if any, tactical nuclear weapons in the near future. The damage caused by such U.S. weapons would therefore be inflicted mainly on East Germany and Poland. The picture changed, however, when the Soviets acquired these weapons, ensuring that their use would be reciprocal. In these circumstances, the advantages that tactical nuclear arms were supposed to confer upon the West began to diminish, if not disappear.

These weapons would not protect Europe, but devastate it. Europe is densely populated. Its cities are close to one another, and civil, military, tactical, and strategic targets are all intertwined. A nuclear ground war would be a catastrophe for Europe, probably spelling the end of its civilization. NATO's capacity to fight a limited tactical nuclear war, therefore, would not allow the West to escape the dilemma of suicide or appeasement. A limited nuclear war in Europe was meaningless unless it also limited the devastation. The concentration on massive retaliation—on NATO's sword—however, had reduced the need for conventionally armed ground forces. The very appeal of nuclear weapons was that the nuclear deterrent would not require large expensive conventional forces; nuclear arms provided defense on the cheap. But in a situation of increasing nuclear stalemate, it was precisely such conventional forces that were needed to counter Soviet and East European armies. The lack of such NATO forces reinforced the need to stake the alliance's survival on each issue, no matter what the level of provocation.

Walter Lippmann had written rather critically right after the war that the bomb was the "perfect fulfillment of all wishful thinking on military matters; here is war that requires no national effort, no draft, no discipline but only money and engineering, of which we have plenty. Here is the panacea which enables us to be the greatest military power on earth—without investing in time, energy, sweat, blood and tears." [2] Lippmann was in fact describing not just the United States, but all the Western democracies.

The Berlin Retreat

The reliance upon SAC made it very difficult for the Western powers, especially the United States, to impress the Soviet Union with NATO's unity and resoluteness. The United States was determined to stay in Berlin, but after stating that it would defend Berlin by massive retaliation, it sought to escape the consequences of its own military strategy. This it could do only by granting concessions. Shortly after the presentation of the Soviet ultimatum that West Berlin must be "demilitarized" in six months, Secretary of State John Foster Dulles spoke of accepting the East Germans as "Russian agents" at the checkpoints on the route leading into Berlin. Dulles also declared that Germany could be reunified by means other than free elections. Both statements threatened a complete abandonment of the long-held American positions of nonrecognition of the East German regime and of Germany's right of self-determination. The administration, already pressured by the British, also accepted the standing Soviet call for a summit conference. But the United States insisted on the prior fulfillment of two conditions: withdrawal of the Soviet six-month ultimatum and a foreign ministers' conference to hammer out a settlement of the Berlin issue and others relating to Germany. The purpose of a "meeting at the top" was, in the administration's opinion, essentially to ratify decisions already reached at a lower level. Eisenhower rejected a meeting that would settle nothing and end in a fruitless propaganda debate.

The Soviets reluctantly accepted the precondition of a foreign ministers' conference, but denied that the six-month deadline on Berlin was an ultimatum. However, they refused to budge from their position at the foreign ministers' marathon held in Geneva in the spring and summer of 1959. Rather, the West offered concessions. First, the United States allowed an East German delegation to attend the deliberations, thereby taking a step toward *de facto* recognition of the Soviet-installed regime. The Soviet Union had made East German presence a precondition for the meeting. Second, at the first sign of Soviet opposition, the West abandoned its plan for the reunification of Germany. Third, the foreign ministers then took up the problem of an interim settlement for Berlin. In short, after years of stating that it was the Soviet division of Germany that was the cause of European in-

---

2. Quoted by Lawrence Freedman, *The Evolution of Nuclear Strategy* (New York: St. Martin's Press, 1981), 48.

stability, the United States and Britain accepted the Soviet definition of what constituted the principal sources of European tension.

The Soviets, however, refused to renew their endorsement of Allied rights in Berlin and reasserted that they would end the occupation regime. The Allies failed to obtain the Soviet guarantee they sought, but the fact that they had attempted to arrive at an interim arrangement for Berlin at all, and had been willing to grant concessions to obtain it, is eloquent testimony to the dilemma in which American strategy had placed them. In effect, the United States and Britain were willing to transform the Western position in Berlin in return for the withdrawal of the Soviet threat to the city. In an attempt to extricate themselves from the dilemma of suicide or surrender, the two countries placed themselves in the humiliating position of calling into question their well-established rights in Berlin. No wonder Khrushchev felt that all he had to do was maintain a high level of tension.

Khrushchev's bellicosity and rigidity paid handsome dividends. The more menacing he sounded and the more inflexibly he stood, the greater the number of voices in the West that called for more Western "flexibility" and "new approaches." Policies that had become almost untouchable over the years were questioned or condemned as dangerous. The controversy divided the West. The British denounced Chancellor Konrad Adenauer's "rigidity"; the Germans, in turn, accused the British of "appeasement." Franco-British relations cooled considerably. And both Adenauer and Charles de Gaulle demonstrated increasing suspicions of U.S. intentions and resolution. America's apparent willingness to discuss Berlin with the Soviets seemed to the German and French leaders to show little American conviction or courage to uphold an earlier position; to them, Eisenhower was showing far too much flexibility.

As if to prove Khrushchev's theory that his threats would have rewarding consequences, and to confirm de Gaulle's and Adenauer's apprehensions, Eisenhower invited Khrushchev to come to the United States in September 1959. His visit represented a tactical victory for the Soviets because a summit *à deux* showed Khrushchev's equality with the American president and conferred superpower status upon the Soviet Union. And, as Khrushchev knew, this summit conference could intensify the Allies' apprehension of a separate United States-Soviet agreement at their expense; conversely, it might persuade Eisenhower that the crisis was caused by the rigidity of certain Allied leaders who were opposed to the "normalization" of relations and make him more accommodating.

Khrushchev's visit to the United States had one positive result: the Soviet Union withdrew its threat to take unilateral action in Berlin in return for American willingness to negotiate on the problems of Berlin and Germany at a four-power summit meeting, which was scheduled for May 1960 in Paris. For American policy makers, this meant another postponement of the painful decision on whether Berlin was worth the cost of a total war. But if the administration believed that the crisis had ended, that from then on it could negotiate leisurely on these issues and, if the Soviets did not accept its terms, preserve the *status quo,* it was quickly disabused of this notion. Khrushchev was soon reiterating his threat to sign a separate peace with East Germany.

The U-2 Spy Plane Incident

Shortly before the Paris summit, an event took place that shattered the conference after only one session and further postponed negotiations on Berlin. On May Day, 1,300 miles within Soviet territory, the Soviets downed an American U-2 "spy plane," loaded with photographic equipment for the gathering of intelligence data. The Eisenhower administration reacted to this unexpected and unhappy turn of events with considerable diplomatic ineptitude. In response to Khrushchev's announcement that the plane had been shot down, the U.S. government claimed that it had been engaged in meteorological observation and speculated that the pilot had flown off course. When the Soviet premier revealed the flight's true mission and produced an alleged confession by the pilot, the administration reversed itself. In a move unprecedented in diplomatic history, it admitted that the U-2 pilot had been taking aerial photographs of the Soviet Union and that it had lied in its previous announcement.

Nor did the administration stop there. It claimed that similar flights had been sent into Soviet skies for several years and strongly intimated that the flights would continue. The administration justified its actions, saying that Soviet secrecy made it necessary to gather information by this means to prevent a surprise attack. It is bad enough to be caught red-handed in spying and worse for the president to admit it; it is worst of all for him to assert that the United States would continue this behavior. In effect, the United States claimed the *right* to fly over Soviet territory. One need only imagine the uproar in the United States if the Soviets announced calmly that they had the right to fly over American soil and take photographs of military installations.

The Soviets were obliged to meet this challenge. For the Soviet premier to let it pass would be like acknowledging to the world, to his people, to his domestic enemies, and to his allies that he had surrendered to the United States the right to violate Soviet territory. Khrushchev could not survive such an admission. The course he took was to strike a belligerent pose in Paris. He launched a blistering personal attack upon Eisenhower, demanding his apology for past U-2 flights, a promise that the flights would cease, and punishment of those responsible for the spying operation. Eisenhower's assurance that no more reconnaissance missions would take place during his term of office did not satisfy Khrushchev, who apparently thought this meant a temporary suspension. Khrushchev's other demands were rejected outright. Khrushchev thereupon suggested that the summit conference be postponed for six to eight months, and he bluntly told Eisenhower that he would not be welcome if he came to the Soviet Union in June. In short, Khrushchev said that he wanted nothing more to do with Eisenhower and that he would wait to ne-gotiate the Berlin problem with the next administration. A new crisis had been put off for a little while longer.

Kennedy's Berlin Crisis

It was inevitable, therefore, that the Soviets would raise the Berlin problem again once the new administration took over. Khrushchev was still convinced that the global balance was shifting in his favor, and he remained confident that he was strong enough to acquire West Berlin. President John Kennedy, fearing that Khrushchev might miscalculate, emphasized at a Vienna summit meeting America's determination to defend West Berlin; the United States would stand firm and protect the free half of the city. Khrushchev discounted these warnings. His response was characteristic: to test the president's resolution by reviving the original threat that the Berlin situation would have to be resolved within six months—that is, before the end of 1961. The Vienna summit turned out exactly opposite of what was intended: it resulted in the very type of Soviet brinkmanship against which Kennedy had sought to caution the Soviet leader.

Kennedy was confronted with a crisis over Berlin. He declared his willingness to negotiate, but also stated that he did not expect the Soviets to confront him with a ready-made treaty with East Germany. The United States was not willing to discuss merely how the West would withdraw from the beleaguered city, thereby leaving it for the Communists to swallow. The West's right to be in the city stemmed from its victory over Nazi Germany. Western presence and access to the city and the freedom of West Berlin were not negotiable. Kennedy said, "We cannot negotiate with those who say: 'What's mine is mine, and what's yours is negotiable.' " More specifically, he asked, if the West refused to meet its clear-cut commitments in Berlin, where would it meet them?

But it was also clear on August 13, 1961, when the Communists built a wall dividing the city, that they had eliminated the escape hatch for East Germans, ended West Berlin's usefulness as a "showplace for Western capitalism," and violated the quadripartite status of Berlin. The West did not knock the wall down with bulldozers for fear of military conflict with Communist—especially Soviet—forces. This passivity intensified Khru-shchev's conviction that the United States would not fight and that he could, slowly but surely, increase the pressure on NATO and drive the West out of Berlin.

This possibility, and the American fear that the Soviet leader might miscalculate Western resolve and accidentally trigger a war, accounted for the difference between Kennedy's and his predecessor's reactions to the Berlin crisis. Unlike Eisenhower, Kennedy used the tensions over Berlin to build up American military power; the new president was determined to show Khrushchev that the United States was not bluffing when it declared its intentions to defend West Berlin. Kennedy moved in two directions; indeed, he had begun to do so almost immediately after assuming office. One aim was "flexible response"; the United States needed more options than suicide or surrender. This increased flexibility was to be achieved by building larger conventional forces. In Europe, a conventional buildup meant that NATO would have a credible defense, which did not immediately depend on tactical nuclear weapons or, if these failed to stem the Soviet advance, strategic weapons. Outside of Europe, the United States would also have a capability to respond to limited challenges.

The other critical aim was to reduce SAC's vulnerability during the changeover from bombers to missiles, which had begun in the late 1950s. Bombers located at known sites were highly vulnerable to surprise attack. Even in a situation of mutual deterrence, the possibility that many of the enemy's bombers might be destroyed on the ground remained an incentive to attack. If they could be destroyed, the retaliatory attack by a crippled remnant force might not be fatal to the attacking nation. In a crisis situation, this possibility could tempt either side to launch a preemptive strike—even if the other side had no intention of striking. But solid-fuel missiles, like the air force's Minuteman, could be widely dispersed and protected, or "hardened," in underground silos instead of being concentrated on a few above-ground bases; missiles were not yet accurate enough to hit such silos. And the navy's Polaris missiles would be moved underwater so that the enemy would at no time know where to strike them.

The importance of these concealment tactics was that they deprived a surprise attack of its rationale. Obliterating the enemy's cities would benefit the aggressor very little if the enemy still retained its retaliatory capacity. Surprise, therefore, no longer conferred any significant advantage to the side that struck first. Indeed, there was no need any longer to hit preemptively because enough of the missiles would survive the first strike and be able to retaliate fully against the aggressor in a second strike. A first strike in these circumstances—which American policy makers generally conceded to the Soviets—would be completely irrational.

Invulnerable second strike forces were believed to be the basis of *stable* mutual deterrence. Mutual deterrence, according to the arms control philosophy the Kennedy administration brought in, would not guarantee that war could be avoided. If the means of delivering nuclear bombs or war heads were vulnerable to attack, they might, particularly in crisis moments, tempt one side or the other to attack. Mutual deterrence in these conditions was unstable. Stabilizing the deterrent balance was therefore a priority for the new administration. The resulting deemphasis of bombers and their replacement by hardened land-based and mobile sea-based missiles occurred over a number of years.

In the meantime, Kennedy, as cautious as Eisenhower, vacillated between his determination to stay in West Berlin and his equally strong determination to avoid conflict. Like Eisenhower, he was willing to offer concessions and negotiate with the Soviets alone if West Germany and France remained "inflexible." The meager results of these bilateral American-Soviet negotiations were due primarily to Soviet unwillingness to concede the right to any Western presence in Berlin, which, in turn, was due to Khrushchev's conviction that he need only maintain Soviet pressure to evict the Western powers from the Communist-surrounded and divided city. If, during this early period of the Kennedy administration, as during the late years of the Eisenhower era, the Soviets were unwilling to risk the final test, they had shown they were not hesitant to push the issue to a point of high tension. And although the United States had upheld the *status quo,* the manner in which it questioned its own position in Berlin and the concessions it offered in the name of flexibility demonstrated a lack of will and sense of purpose. This augured ill for the future, if: (1) the Soviet leaders could keep their challenges below the level of provocation that might arouse an American nuclear response; and (2) the Soviets confined their challenges to the periphery of Western power, especially an isolated outpost such as West Berlin. As long as they followed these two fundamental precepts, they could continue to try to exploit the dilemmas of American strategy.

It was the second rule that the Soviets failed to follow when they shifted the challenge to ninety miles from the American mainland—to Cuba—where the United States had no choice but to respond in defense of what Washington conceived to be its vital interests.

Castro and the Missile Crisis

Cuba's revolutionary government dated from January 1, 1959, when its leaders overthrew the tyrannical dictatorship of Fulgencio Batista. During his struggle against Batista, Fidel Castro had identified himself with democratic government and social and economic justice and had gained widespread popularity among the Cuban people. This public support ensured the victory of his guerrilla army against the larger government forces. The Castro revolution was essentially a social revolution. In the opening months of its rule, the new government moved to remedy the conditions of the people by instituting land reform and by building low-cost housing, schools, and clinics. But some features of this social revolution were bound to clash with the interests of the United States.

Although the United States had been instrumental in freeing Cuba from Spain in the Spanish-American War at the turn of the century, it had subsequently passed the Platt Amendment, which granted the Americans the right to intervene at any time in Cuba for the preservation of Cuban independence, for the protection of life, property, and individual liberty, and for the discharge of Cuba's treaty obligations. By 1934, when the amendment was repealed, the United States had intervened militarily three times; it also had established a naval base at Guantánamo Bay. American capital controlled 80 percent of Cuba's utilities, 90 percent of its mines and cattle ranches, nearly all of its oil, and 40 percent of its sugar. It was not surprising that the Cuban revolution directed its long-pent-up nationalism and social resentment against "Yankee imperialism." America's support of the Batista dictatorship until the moment of its collapse intensified anti-American sentiment. "Cuba, si! Yanqui, no!" became the Castro regime's rallying cry, the ceremonial burning of the American flag its ritual, and the confiscation of American property its reward.

This anti-American nationalistic feeling, deliberately fostered by Castro to increase the popularity of his regime, led to an increasing identification of his government with communism. Before long, the regime betrayed its original democratic promises and became a dictatorship with centralized control over all of the country's activities. All parties were abolished except for one—the Communist party, upon whose organizational strength Castro had become increasingly dependent. Castro also linked Cuba closely to the Communist bloc. The Soviet Union supplied Cuba with vast amounts of arms and accompanying military advisers. Cuban airmen were sent to Czechoslovakia to learn how to fly Soviet fighters, and a large number of Cuban technicians were trained in Communist countries. Cuba's armed services soon ranked second only to America's as the largest in the hemisphere. Diplomatic relations were established with all Communist countries except East Germany, and economic agreements were signed with many of the same countries, including East Germany. Cuba's economy became integrated into that of the Communist bloc; 75 percent of the island's trade was with countries behind the iron curtain. In January 1961, the United States cut off diplomatic relations with Cuba after a sequence of perceived provocations. If Castro at that point had attempted to seize the Guantánamo base, there would have been an excuse for open American intervention.

Castro was too shrewd to risk a seizure, but he also ruled out an accommodation with the United States. Castro wanted to play a major role on the world stage. He could not achieve that role as the leader of either a pro-American or neutral country of 10 million people on a small Caribbean island. He could do so only as a revolutionary leader who took on his giant neighbor as an enemy. To stand up against the United States, he would need the support of the other giant. Castro turned down all friendly overtures from the United States after he took power: a new, sympathetic American ambassador was kept waiting for weeks before being allowed to present his credentials, and offers of foreign aid were rejected.

The Bay of Pigs

As Cuban-Soviet relations consolidated, the Eisenhower administration began to plan for its overthrow. The new Kennedy administration in April

1961 launched an attempt by a small force of Cuban exiles—many of them former Castro associates who had become disillusioned by the premier's increasingly tyrannical rule, Communist sympathies, and alignment with the Soviet Union—to land in Cuba and attempt to overthrow Castro. The Central Intelligence Agency (CIA) had developed the plans for this operation and supervised their execution. The CIA assumed that, once the exiles had gained a beachhead in the Bay of Pigs, some units of Castro's army and Cuba's population would welcome the invaders as liberators. But the operation was a dramatic and appalling failure. The United States bungled because it launched a major foreign policy move, involving American prestige, on the glib assumption that a feeble beachhead operation would result in a mass uprising of Cubans against their government. The rumors and press reports, which conveyed the impression of a major invasion, made the failure appear even greater.

If nothing succeeds like success, it can also be said that nothing fails like failure. American prestige, already lowered by the Soviet Union's man-in-space achievement, sank to a new low. In Cyrus Sulzberger's pointed comment in the *New York Times,* "We looked like fools to our friends, rascals to our enemies, and incompetents to the rest." The administration had fallen victim to its own half-heartedness. The results of an unsuccessful invasion could have been predicted: an increase in Castro's domestic support, a revival of Latin American fears of "Yankee imperialism," a blunting of Kennedy's initially successful attempts to identify the United States with anticolonialism, and a loss of confidence in America's leadership by its allies.

Soviet Inroads in the Western Hemisphere

Thus, Cuba survived as a Communist base from which the Soviet Union could threaten the United States and subvert the security of the other nations in the Western Hemisphere. The importance of this cannot be underestimated. The American position in the Western Hemisphere had been preeminent. The Monroe Doctrine had announced to the world that Latin America fell within the American sphere of influence and that Europe's colonial powers were to keep their hands off. In subsequent decades the United States had intervened repeatedly, especially in the Caribbean-Central American area. While the motives for intervention varied, principal among them was the fear that a European power might establish its influence in an area that could be called America's "strategic rear," or, to use a Churchillian phrase, its "soft underbelly." During the early 1940s the concern was with German power; after that, with Soviet power. A Marxist government had come to power in Guatemala in 1954. When it received arms from Czechoslovakia, the Eisenhower administration had intervened covertly and overthrown it, thereby setting a precedent for the Bay of Pigs. In short, the United States has never tolerated Latin American governments that leaned toward Germany or the Soviet Union, at least not in the smaller countries so close to the Rio Grande and Florida.

Castro's survival after the Bay of Pigs was a significant exception and meant that the United States no longer held a monopoly of power in the Caribbean-Central American area. This change resulted from the failure of covert intervention and the unwillingness to resort to overt intervention in the belief that it might alienate the rising Latin American middle class whose support the United States thought it needed. The United States wanted to remain what it had claimed to be since Franklin Roosevelt's time—a "good neighbor." Unfortunately, the Bay of Pigs disaster incited Soviet intervention. In Moscow, where unfriendly regimes were not tolerated, but crushed, Kennedy's prestige plummeted. If it had been in the interest of the United States to eliminate Castro, then U.S. military intervention should have followed the bungled CIA attempt. A "serious" power does not tolerate its enemies so near and does not act squeamishly. It does what it has to do, regardless of international opinion. If Castro's elimination was not important enough for the United States to risk criticism, then the intervention should not have been launched in the first place. But to do so and fail suggested weak nerves and a lack of foresight. Worse, it suggested fear of the Soviet Union. Why else would the United States not intervene with its own military forces as it had many times before? Why should the Soviet Union not push a little further and see if Kennedy would tolerate a further extension of Soviet power?

The Importance of 'Not Losing' in Cuba

Once the Soviets saw that the Communist regime in Cuba was tolerated, they began to establish a missile base there. Washington had believed that the Soviet Union would not dare to do this in America's sphere of influence. In the fall of 1962, however, a U-2 spy plane suddenly discovered, to the great surprise and consternation of American policy makers, that the Soviets were building launching sites for approximately seventy medium- and intermediate-range ballistic missiles. That Khrushchev had dared to move his missiles so near the United States and apparently expected no counteraction beyond ineffective diplomatic protests, was a dangerous sign. War by miscalculation is the great danger; to prevent miscalculation is therefore an absolute necessity. But American actions had convinced the Soviet premier that the United States would not fight to protect its vital interests. Kennedy, Khrushchev told an American visitor, was "too liberal to fight."

Khrushchev had a great deal to gain. A failure to respond to his move would prove to America's NATO allies what they feared already—namely, that the United States had become vulnerable to attack and could no longer be relied upon to protect Europe. Inaction in the face of Soviet missiles so close to the American coast would have emphasized dramatically this consequence of the nuclear balance. The promised renewal of Soviet pressure on Berlin after the midterm U.S. congressional elections, together with the likelihood of an even more cautious American reaction than before, would only have reinforced this impression. Only this time, the Soviets could deliver an ultimatum to get out or else. The threat was that the Soviets could for the first time cover a large part of the North American continent with their missiles, which would come flying in over areas where there was no adequate protection against them. The early warning systems against bombers and missiles were in the north because a Soviet attack had always been expected to come in over the Arctic. Not only was the United States vulnerable to attack, but also its prestige was on the line. The sudden and unchallenged appearance of the opposing superpower in the area where the United States had long been paramount would have eroded America's authority and status and encouraged the spread of Castroism throughout Latin America. All anti-Castro forces, including the indispensable and all too few genuinely democratic reformers, would have been demoralized and perhaps paralyzed by Washington's inaction.

The political and psychological implications of Khrushchev's limited challenge, therefore, were enormous, for the global distribution of power could well be affected. But for once Khrushchev had overplayed his hand. He had pressured the United States in the wrong place, and Washington could not avoid the test. If the stakes were high for the Soviet Union, they were even higher for the United States. Khrushchev might have wanted to "win" this one, but Kennedy felt that under no circumstances could he afford to lose it. Indeed, he had warned the Soviet leader against placing offensive missiles in Cuba; therefore, Kennedy had to compel their withdrawal to preserve his credibility and America's.

If earlier American actions and inactions had convinced Khrushchev that he could "get away with it," it was imperative to set him straight about this issue. Such confidence on Khrushchev's part, Kennedy realized, stemmed from a conviction that the United States no longer possessed the will to defend its interests. Such a notion was dangerous because, if it remained uncorrected, it would lead to an even greater challenge in Berlin—as Khrushchev had already announced. If the United States then declared it would stand firm there, but the Soviet leader did not believe it, a violent clash, possibly a nuclear war, might result. Characteristically, the Soviets had not committed themselves irrevocably in Cuba. They were willing to gamble for a big payoff, but they were also willing to suffer a serious setback to avoid a catastrophic clash. The Soviets were still seeking the limits of American tolerance in its hemisphere.

Kennedy placed a blockade around Cuba to prevent any further missile shipments, and he demanded the removal of the missiles already in place. American firmness and determination left Moscow little choice. For once, the Soviets had to decide whether to fire the first shot—to break the American blockade of their missile-carrying ships—and risk a possible escalation of the conflict. The Kremlin backed down. The United States had enormous conventional, especially naval, superiority in the Caribbean, and Khrushchev was unwilling to risk a nuclear confrontation. The level of tension rapidly declined as America's determination and willingness to use its power became clear. In Secretary of State Dean Rusk's picturesque phrase, "We were eyeball to eyeball, and the other fellow just blinked."

Kennedy's critics had predicted that a Soviet humiliation in Cuba would compel Khrushchev to recoup his lost prestige by forcing the West out of Berlin (with the clear implication that the United States should let him do so or desist in Cuba). However, Khrushchev called off *both* challenges. Apparently he realized that America's superior strategic power, as demonstrated in the Caribbean, could also be marshaled in Berlin. Moreover, the missile crisis was followed by years of *détente*. But another result ought to be noted as well: the United States publicly declared that it would not invade Cuba. America had won a brilliant tactical victory, but the Soviet Union had not suffered a strategic reversal. Its base in the Caribbean remained intact.

American Strategy and Frontier Defenses

The recurrent crisis over West Berlin from 1958 to 1962, plus the Cuban missile crisis, held several lessons for the United States, if it wished to preserve the frontier line around what was then still considered a cohesive Communist world. First, despite U.S. retaliatory power, the Soviet leadership exploited opportunities to raise international tensions when it felt it could succeed and not provoke the United States. Moscow was fully aware of the dangers of nuclear war and of the need to avoid acts that would expose the Soviet Union to nuclear conflagration, but it did not allow this recognition to deter it from exploiting the West's fear of nuclear war and trying to alter the *status quo* in its favor.

To ensure that tensions would not escalate beyond control, the Soviets either left themselves a diplomatic escape hatch or were willing to make timely withdrawals. When met by a determined countermove, the Soviets did not escalate the tension. The Soviet tactic was to put a ceiling on the tension, lest it provoke an American nuclear response, and seek an end to the specific crisis. The Berlin crises in 1958 and 1961 and the Cuban missile crisis in 1962 testified to the Soviets' confidence that, short of a major provocation, which they were not willing to offer, they could challenge the United States without fearing a nuclear response. Their rapid retreat was even stronger testimony to the Soviet desire to avoid a further upward spiral of tension that might reach dangerous levels.

The second lesson was that mutual deterrence is not automatic. Advancing technology may upset the stability of the deterrent balance. It bears repetition that simply possessing the bomb is insufficient; the key to a *stable* deterrent balance is an invulnerable retaliatory force. If country A's force is vulnerable to attack by country B, A may be tempted to strike B preemptively rather than have its forces caught on the ground. Or A may lead B to strike first because B also fears a preemptive strike. In the late 1950s and early 1960s, the Soviets claimed that they were mass-producing missiles that made American bombers vulnerable. If true, this meant that the U.S. deterrent capacity would decline as Soviet first-strike capability grew. This development might affect the psychology of the policy makers in Moscow and Washington, emboldening the Russians and making the Americans more cautious.

The Soviet Union's willingness to challenge the United States in Europe, ten years after the first Berlin crisis, and the manner in which America reacted, were symptomatic of the effects of this perceived change in the balance. A Soviet claim of a shift in the nuclear balance led the Soviet Union to use "nuclear blackmail" or coercion to undermine the *status quo*. If Moscow could compel the United States to pull out of West Berlin, NATO would collapse as a barrier to Soviet expansion. Only in Cuba in 1962, after it had become clear that Khrushchev had been bluffing and that he was not mass-producing ICBMs, did Washington once more regain its confidence and react vigorously. Preserving deterrence is a continuing, never-ending task, not because some change in the balance might precipitate war, but because it might affect the risks each side is willing to take as one side challenges the other.

The third lesson is that unregulated arms competition is potentially dangerous. In the rivalry between a democratic state and a totalitarian state, the totalitarian state has a distinct advantage. The Soviet Union could easily gather information on U.S. arms, but, because the Soviet Union is a closed society, the United States could not accumulate information on the number and types of Soviet nuclear arms. After 1956, high-altitude U-2 aircraft were the principal American means of collecting information. Because these aircraft could not perform a complete daily surveillance of Soviet territory, Khrushchev could use his strategy of deception, claim that the Soviets had weapons that they did not have and a capability to destroy the U.S. deterrent bomber force that they also did not have. The United States could not be sure what was true. Earlier in the 1950s, the Soviets had flown the same few bombers around Moscow repeatedly to deceive Western military observers.

But without the type of arms control arrangements that were to become familiar after the 1950s, U.S. "worst case" assumptions about Soviet strength are understandable. When hard information on Soviet nuclear strength was lacking, the American reaction to the Soviet claims was the fear that bomber and missile "gaps" existed and that they favored the Soviet Union. The United States overreacted, for instance, by increasing the number of missiles beyond those originally planned. (Once spy satellites started in 1961 to reveal accurate information on Soviet weapons claims, the gap turned out to be decidedly in America's favor.) Meanwhile, once Moscow knew that Washington knew that it had lied, the Soviets felt compelled to compensate for its ICBM inferiority by placing in Cuba intermediate- and medium-range missiles, of which it had plenty. The subsequent missile crisis made leaders on both sides more aware of the need for arms control as a necessary complement to the unilateral acquisition of arms.

Fourth, even before the stabilization of the "balance of terror" in the 1960s, the United States refused to invoke its great strategic forces to respond to limited challenges—hence the need for conventional forces. An all-or-nothing option was no option at all. Theoretically, a series of small defeats could turn the balance of power against America, and the United States would be compelled to take a stand to prevent further deterioration of its position. But the Soviets may not believe in the firmness of this commitment because massive retaliation and the threat of mutual suicide make it less and less credible. If, however, America stood firm, the Soviet challenge would result in war by miscalculation. By its reliance on massive retaliation, the United States could in fact bring about the very war massive retaliation was supposed to deter.

Fifth, massive retaliation foreshadowed the gradual weakening of the bonds of America's foremost alliance, NATO. The European allies had joined NATO to gain the protection of the U.S. nuclear deterrent. But in an era in which the United States no longer held a nuclear monopoly, what country could truly expect the United States to risk its survival to protect an ally? Baldly stated, what would be the U.S. response to Soviet demands in Europe? Would even a Soviet invasion lead the United States to use its strategic weapons? If its threat of responding with massive retaliation were ever called, Europe might be "saved from communism" by being reduced to rubble. On the other hand—and this seemed more likely—if America were unwilling to risk its existence for issues the Europeans deemed vital, then the alliance would gradually erode. Even if NATO remained in existence as a formal organization, its bonds of cohesion would loosen.

Finally, as Berlin and Cuba demonstrated, the chief function of a military power was to draw and protect "frontiers." These frontiers were clear: along the inter-German border and through the middle of Berlin; at the thirty-eighth parallel in Korea and the seventeenth parallel in Vietnam; along the coast of China at Quemoy and Matsu; and at the "northern tier" of states from Turkey to Pakistan. Any attempt to cross these frontiers, either openly by direct attack or covertly by guerrilla warfare, risked hostilities. Admittedly, the lines drawn outside of Europe were extremely tenuous. The Central Treaty Organization (CENTO) and the Southeast Asia Treaty Organization (SEATO) were alliances in areas where nationalist forces opposed the Western-organized and Western-led alliances. They had little popular support in those regions, even in those states that were members. One result was that the Soviets might leapfrog the line, as they had in Egypt. Another result could be that the governments seeking to maintain this line would be unable, despite American help, to mobilize enough indigenous morale and support, as was to become evident in Vietnam during the 1960s.

Indeed, it might well be that the United States would have been better off had it not created what turned out to be poor replicas of NATO. That organization exists in an area in which nationalism supported containment against a clearly perceived potential external aggression; the less successful alliances were organized in non-Western areas where containment was widely perceived as an attempt to preserve Western influence and reactionary regimes. Nevertheless, because the lines drawn in Europe were clear, and neither superpower was willing to risk a clash, this delineation between their respective spheres of influence had in the 1950s shifted the attention of the superpowers increasingly toward the Third World.

c h a p t e r   s e v e n

The Third World During
the Cold War Years

POLITICAL scientist Guy Pauker wrote at the height of the cold war, "Four areas in the world are at present or potentially major power centers: the United States, the Soviet Union, Western Europe, and Communist China. In all four, productivity is on the increase, and the political system performs relatively well its integrating and decision-making functions. Despite major differences among them ... these four areas are likely to be in a position to play major roles in political, economic, and cultural international affairs in the coming decade. In contrast, the Middle East, Southeast Asia, tropical Africa, and Latin America are apt to remain power vacuums during this period, owing to their lack of unity, political instability, economic stagnation, and cultural heterogeneity. It seems highly improbable that ten years from now any of the areas mentioned above will cease to be, respectively, a power center or a power vacuum." [1]

During the 1950s and 1960s the United States saw the power vacuums in the economically less-developed countries (LDCs) as potentially dangerous. The cold war had started in Europe after World War II; the fall of Nationalist China and the Korean War had extended it to Asia after late 1949. But the birth of so many new states, as Western colonialism collapsed after 1945, underlined the importance of this new Third World. The international system was no longer divided into the First World or Western world of industrial states and the Second World, led by the Soviet Union. In 1946 the United Nations had 55 members; in 1950 the number was 60. But by 1955 there were 76 members; by 1960, 99; and by 1970, 127. In a bipolar world, the "in-between" Third World was not a center of power but an

---

1. Guy J. Pauker, "Southeast Asia as a Problem Area in the Next Decade," *World Politics*, April 1959, 325.

attraction for the two superpowers. The United States and the Soviet Union extended the cold war in their rivalry for the support, if not the allegiance, of the former colonial states, which had refused during their early years of independence, to align politically and militarily with either one. Moscow perceived the anticolonial revolt against the West as proof that the international capitalist order was disintegrating. The Soviet Union saw an opportunity for taking the LDCs into a partnership to build a new Soviet-led Communist international order.

Conversely, Washington saw the challenge of Soviet communism and Chinese communism in the Third World as stemming not from conspiracy or military takeover, but from the totalitarian model for modernization that communism offered the LDCs. The Soviet Union, discounting its rapid industrialization under the czar at the turn of the century, held itself up as a model of an LDC that had transformed itself into a modern industrial society in one generation. Said a leading U.S. scholar: "Whether most of these countries take a democratic or Communist or other totalitarian path in their development is likely to determine the course of civilization on our planet." [2] The LDCs' choice of which path to follow was seen as critical to American security and, more broadly, to an international environment safe for open societies and democratic values. The United States thought it vital to help the new countries develop, and it was a matter of basic self-interest rather than humanitarian concern for the poor.

The Revolution of Rising Expectations

The paradox was that the disintegration of Western colonialism after World War II provided the most eloquent testimony to its success. The Western powers, including the United States in the Philippines, had justified their imperial domination in terms of bringing the backward peoples of the earth the benefits of Western democracy, medical science, and technology. It was the "white man's burden," or duty, to educate the people so that one day they could govern themselves. The colonial powers apparently had taught their lesson well; they had ruled their colonies autocratically, while propagating the virtues of democracy. It was in the name of these ideals that the Western powers had come as colonizers; it was in their name, too, that the nationalist movements challenged their rulers and asked them to practice what they preached. The leaders of these nationalist movements had been educated in Europe or America, or in a Western school in their own country. They fought the European powers by using the principles of democracy and national freedom they had learned. They saw that these principles were

---

2. Eugene Stanley, *The Future of Underdeveloped Countries,* rev. ed. (New York: Praeger Publishers, 1961), 3.

incompatible with imperialism.

Once these countries became independent, however, they were left with a legacy of poverty, illiteracy, and disease. Annual per capita income in these nations rarely reached $100. To remedy the economic underdevelopment, to narrow the enormous gap between poor and rich nations, the LDCs turned to industrialization, which was to transform the LDCs' traditional agrarian societies into modern, industrial, urban welfare states. Over the years, this transformation would have great political significance. Most people in the LDCs knew only their local communities, which held their loyalty. The concept of national loyalty was new to them. Consequently, the fledgling nation had to prove it could offer its people something they could not otherwise attain. What they promised was an improvement in the standard of living. By achieving this, the nation would demonstrate that it deserved the popular support and allegiance it needed to survive and grow.

The Consequences of Population Growth

The question that confronted the new countries in the 1950s—and today—is whether they could develop themselves economically. To a large extent the answer depended upon whether their economic progress was faster than their population growth, or whether their "population explosion" ate up any increase in national income. The world population passed 5 billion in 1986. In 1830 it was 1 billion; by 1930, it had doubled. The first doubling took 100 years, but only 32 years to add the third billion. Experts predicted almost 6.5 billion people by the year 2000, with 80 percent living in the LDCs. In 1900 there was one European for every two Asians; in 2000 the ratio will probably be one to four. In the Western Hemisphere, there will be two Latin Americans for each North American.

The concern was that, despite a later slowing of the population growth rate, the LDCs might still face the problem described by the Reverend Thomas Malthus—the constant hunger and poverty that result when the population grows faster than the means of subsistence. More than 150 years ago, Malthus, who was also an economist, predicted this fate for the Western world unless the population growth were limited by either "positive checks" such as wars or epidemics, which result in a high death rate, or by "preventive checks," which result in a low birth rate.

By contrast, the West made impressive economic progress following the Industrial Revolution, despite a huge population increase. Agriculture provided plentiful food, and industry raised the standard of living to heights never before attained. The West's recent history, therefore, would appear to refute Malthus's gloomy prediction. The fact was that the conditions that faced the LDCs were quite dissimilar from the West's. One of the chief differences was that the Western countries had far smaller populations when they began industrializing, and their population increase did not outdistance the economic improvement. But India, for example, began its modernization with a population of 350 million; India's population may reach 1 billion people by 2000. Communist China, with a population of 547 million in 1950, reached 1 billion in the early 1980s. If the United States after the War of Independence had possessed a population density equivalent to that of Egypt, it would today have more than 2 billion people instead of just over 200 million. Under these circumstances, the United States would not have become a "developed" nation.

The European nations enjoyed an enormous benefit in the New World and in their colonial empires, which provided them with outlets to relieve their population pressures. About 60 million Europeans emigrated during the nineteenth and early twentieth centuries. The United States and Canada, rich in resources and fertile land, easily absorbed millions of immigrants and still increased their living standards. Australia, New Zealand, and South Africa experienced similar population and economic expansions, although on a smaller scale. From 1650 to 1950, the European population (excluding Russia) increased by approximately 300 million. By the 1950s there were about 400 million people of European descent living outside Europe. The colonies served Europe as a frontier similar to the American West, which absorbed population that might otherwise have overcrowded the Eastern seaboard; this expansion added materially to the nation's wealth. But the LDCs can find no such empty and rich spaces to absorb their surplus populations.

In Europe, moreover, the use of machinery in agriculture increased the food supply, but reduced the number of laborers needed to produce it. Unneeded farm workers went to the cities and into the factories. The ample supply of labor accelerated industrialization. Quite apart from modern technology, however, Europe was blessed with sufficient sunshine and rain. Temperate lands are more favorable to food production than tropical and monsoon areas, where many of the LDCs are found. Europe could grow sufficient food for its multiplying population; what it could not produce, it imported from the colonies and the New World in exchange for industrial products. Overseas trade enabled some European countries to support larger populations than their domestic food resources would otherwise have permitted. But the basic and critical point is that an industrial revolution must be preceded or accompanied by an agricultural revolution.

In the nonindustrialized nations, the majority of the population is still engaged in a primitive agriculture. Many of the new countries' governments, because they equate development with industrialization, have neglected to modernize agriculture. To their leaders, agriculture is the symbol of their former colonial status as producers of raw materials. Only a few countries experimented with intensive farming. Called the Green Revolution, it used high-yield seeds, more chemical fertilizer, and insecticides, and increased food production enough to keep with the population growth. But many LDCs could not feed themselves: "If our population continues to increase as rapidly as it is doing," a former president of Pakistan said, "we will soon have nothing to eat and will all become cannibals."

If his statement seems exaggerated, it dramatizes the LDCs' overpopulation problem. There are simply too many poor people. This might have been all right if the sleeping masses had not awakened—if they had continued to accept their miserable lot as natural and not become conscious that it was not a fate ordained by God but man-made, if they had not made this discovery and demanded to eat more and live better. It is this "revolution of rising expectations" that creates the problem, for it will be impossible to fulfill these expectations unless there is a reduction in birth rates. The population pressure keeps the masses living close to subsistence, and such widespread poverty makes it very difficult to accumulate enough capital to stoke industrial growth.

In the West, the birth rate declined after 1850; with industrialization and the growth of cities came the spread of literacy and knowledge of artificial birth-control techniques. Malthus was right even for the West, because preventive checks were adopted. But the Third World has not yet reached a similar level of economic development, and knowledge of birth-control methods and the willingness to use them have spread very slowly.

The Slow Pace of Modernization in the LDCs

To make any progress at all, the pace of economic development had to surpass the fast-rising rate of population growth. But many of these countries simply did not have enough capital. Internal savings in sufficient amounts could not be squeezed out of people living at subsistence level—at least, not without authoritarian controls. Another way to obtain capital was to earn it by trade. The LDCs were exporters of primary products or raw materials, such as coffee, tea, rubber, and tin. But it was precisely this fact that in the past had limited their earning capacity. Because their economies upon independence remained tied to those of their former colonial masters, their exports rose or declined with every fluctuation in Western prosperity. If a major Western recession reduced the demand and price levels of natural resources, the resulting losses of income often exceeded the Western aid extended during the same period. Furthermore, markets may become glutted with certain items because of overproduction or substitution. A nation trying to raise its income by increasing production finds its competitors doing the same, which lowers world prices further. Another problem is that the Western industrial nations, whose ever-increasing demand for raw materials was supposed to furnish the capital for economic development, no longer needed them to the degree anticipated because of the development of synthetics. The lack of stabilized international commodity prices, similar to the parity prices paid to American farmers, plus the inventiveness of modern technology (for extracting resources from the ocean's seabeds, for example) limited the prospects of financing industrialization via earnings from raw materials.

Foreign investment was the third source of capital for economic development. Private capital, however, was in the first years after independence in short supply for the kind of long-range development that the less-developed nations needed. Most private American investments outside the United States have been made by a small group of oil companies to build refineries and to discover and pump out oil fields in Latin America and the Middle East. The reasons for the lack of private Western—and especially American—capital for foreign investment are obvious. The American economy experienced a boom for most of the cold war period, and investment capital stayed mainly at home. This was true for Europe as well. European capital concentrated on rebuilding, modernization, and expansion of its industrial base. American capital that did go abroad often went to the Common Market. Private capital is drawn to investments that will return sizable and relatively speedy profits.

But perhaps the basic reason that private funds were so small for the new nations was that public funds were so small. Investors could not be expected to subsidize hospitals, ports, schools, and roads. The returns from such projects were insufficient, and, even if there were any profits, it would take too long to reap them. Optimists who felt that this first stage of economic development could be undertaken by private funds forgot that in the West the speedy economic growth of the nineteenth century, financed largely by private enterprise, rested upon an economic base developed by the mercantilist state; in brief, it was political authority, the state, that had initiated the process that transformed the underdeveloped Western economies into highly modern, industrialized economies.

Modernization, then, was the new nations' principal task, but they soon realized that it was *not* essentially an economic undertaking. More and more, modernization, of which economic development is a major ingredient, was seen as a political, social, and intellectual task. It was a revolutionary process frequently marked by political instability and violence rather than evolutionary peaceful change. One reason for instability was that most of the new nations lacked administrative and political cohesiveness. Generally, the population had no single common culture or language; tribes opposed one another; different areas fought one another. The people had no natural loyalty to the state, no tradition of cooperation except on the one overriding issue of eliminating the colonial ruler. But once the struggle for independence ended, power tended to fragment. For example, India split violently into Hindu India and Muslim Pakistan following independence, and the latter dissolved further into Pakistan and Bangladesh—with the help of India, which also may split further as Sikhs seek greater autonomy, if not independence. The Congo (now Zaire) fell apart when the Belgians withdrew. Cyprus divided into Turkish and Greek factions. Biafra broke away from Nigeria, only to lose the subsequent civil war. Even where actual disintegration has not occurred, religious, linguistic, and racial differences and antagonists tend to tear apart the fabric of these states that lack any history of nationhood. In Burundi in 1972, for example, the Tutsi tribes reportedly slaughtered 120,000 Hutus. In the late 1980s Sri Lanka, formerly Ceylon, a large island lying just south of India, was tearing itself apart between Hindu Tamils and Buddhist Sinhalese. Nation building, therefore, must be the first task.

The absence of a strong sense of national consciousness was soon reflected in the way many of the leaders of the new countries built themselves up as symbols of nationhood. It was not difficult for them to do this because, as leaders of the movements for independence, their prestige was usually high. But the task was an essential one. Just as Louis XIV had proclaimed, they also said, *"L'état, c'est moi."* They *were* the state; without their presence as its symbol, the nation would not hold together as a unit. One-party rule or military governments exist almost everywhere in the Third World. In Africa, for example, the world's last continent to be freed from colonialism, three-fourths of its 345 million people lived under single-party or military rule by the late 1960s, ten years after independence.

Such policies might seem undemocratic, but they were widely justified by native rules and believed to be necessary by most Western observers and analysts. Most people in the new nations felt less loyalty to the state than to ancestors, family, village, or tribe. Wherever the opposition represented these centrifugal forces, an American-style democracy would lead not just to a change of government but to the disintegration of the state. The alternatives facing the leaders of these countries were said to be not democracy or dictatorship but statehood or disintegration.

Another reason that modernization was seen in a political and revolutionary context is that nationalist revolutions direct their opposition not only against the colonial ruler but also against the domestic governing elite if it remained in power after independence. Many of the LDCs were split into three main groups when they gained independence. The first was the ruling minority, usually composed of the landowners and great merchants, whose vested interest lay in the preservation of the *status quo*. Their wealth and power derived from continuing, as in the old colonial days, to send their nations' crops and natural resources to the West rather than industrializing themselves and becoming economically independent. The second group, about 80 percent of the population in most LDCs, were peasants, villagers, small artisans, and shopkeepers—those whose energies have been spent largely on the struggle for day-to-day survival. This group, which had for centuries borne its hardships silently, awakened and demanded a better life. The third group, the urban intelligentsia, educated in Western ideas and committed to nationalism and modernization, voiced these resentments against the old way of life and articulated the new aspirations while it sought power to affect the political, social, and economic transformation of their societies. Change and more change was the demand of the day.

Without such social change—that is, the overthrow of the old ruling elite, modernization is inhibited. This is not a matter of "reform" but of revolution because the crucial issue relates to power. Who controls the nation—the old ruling elite committed to the preservation of the traditional, religiously oriented, preindustrial society or those who seek to secularize, modernize, and industrialize the nation? Only one thing is certain: few who rule yield their dominant political, social, and economic position without a struggle.

New Seeds of Discontent

Instability can take root even where economic development occurs, where national bonds do not disintegrate, and where the modernizing elite is in control. The cause of this instability is that a slowly rising standard of living may not create an increasingly satisfied—and therefore happy and peaceful—population. Capital for investment can be accumulated only if it is not paid to the workers; low wages militate against mass consumption and allow the reinvestment of capital into further economic expansion. Although living conditions may improve, they will not satisfy the "revolution of rising expectations." Once the population realizes that it no longer has to live in the poverty and filth of the past, that change in this world is possible, that people can create a better life here on earth through their own efforts, they become dissatisfied. The gap between their expectations and achievements is particularly aggravating when the rulers live well, even ostentatiously. Those living in poverty become frustrated. If they have been moved from the countryside to the city, the frustration comes on top of resentment and bewilderment resulting from the anonymity of the city, and anger caused by their miserable existence. Social discontent and an increasingly sullen, hostile, and more radical mood are bound to rise in the shanty towns growing on the edge of virtually every city in the Third World.

Social instability and turmoil are further promoted by the intellectual and cultural changes that accompany the transformation of a traditional, static, rural society into a modern, dynamic, urban-industrial state. Many of the old customary and religious values that helped people accept their place in society and conduct themselves throughout life simply collapse; people become disoriented, torn from their age-old moorings for which they have not yet found a substitute. Their ancestors had provided status and meaning in their lives; robbed of this, they become isolated and insecure atoms in a rapidly changing environment they neither made nor comprehend. Secular values, emphasizing materialism and progress, replace religious values that deny the importance of earthly existence and material possessions. A society in which individual effort is rewarded and people can rise socially into a higher class replaces a society with a rigid social structure in which birth determined their place and religion their mode of conduct.

Nationalism replaces local loyalty, and modern transportation and communication bring individuals to an awareness of the larger society in which they live and work. Impersonal ties to people far away in "their" country replace former face-to-face relations with neighbors, and they must learn new skills and ways of thought. In short, they must forget many of their old ways and cut long-time ties and adjust, readjust, and adjust once more. In the best of circumstances, these changes are difficult and agonizing, even if they do not arouse effective opposition from the traditional elite. The Iranians were undergoing this kind of upheaval in late 1978 and early 1979, when the religious leaders opposed the shah and his modernization, leading to his overthrow and the establishment of an Islamic republic, a theocracy, a throwback to earlier centuries. Precisely because modernization was associated with secular values, no one in the U.S. government had taken seriously the possibility of the Ayatollah Ruhollah Khomeini's succession. The idea of an old man, a religious fanatic, coming to power was so at odds with contemporary ideas of modernization that the likelihood of its occurrence was dismissed as preposterous. Yet, for the poor and the lowly in a rapidly changing society in which tradition and customs were being eroded, religion retained a strong attraction and comfort.

Domestic Instability and Superpower Involvement

It is not surprising in these circumstances that the domestic transformation of the LDCs had repercussions beyond their borders. The upheavals tended to disturb an international system largely defined by the frontiers drawn between the two superpowers' spheres of influence and by the nuclear stalemate. When the internal difficulties of the countries of the Third World spilled over into the external arena of international politics, or resulted in civil war or regional rivalries, they attracted the Soviet Union and the United States, thus leading to possible confrontation with the attendant danger of military conflict. These difficulties have attracted the two superpowers because they could either bring to power a group one superpower likes and the other dislikes or result in regional expansion and influence that could be perceived as benefiting one and hurting the other. If one superpower is unwilling to tolerate what it may consider, in terms of the overall balance of power, a local or regional setback, it will intervene; or, if it fears that if it does not intervene its opponent might, the result may be a preventive intervention. In both cases, it risks a similar move by its opponent. To quote Pauker once again: "Power vacuums are likely to disturb international relations increasingly. They are the natural targets for power centers wishing to extend their hegemony. They should be the object of anxious attention for those powers which want to strengthen the international balance." [3]

---

3. Pauker, "Southeast Asia as a Problem Area," 325.

National Disintegration: The Birth of Zaire

If a new nation disintegrates into two or more parts, those who seek to reunify their land or establish their new splinter states may appeal for help to sympathetic states that, for reasons of their own, may wish to see either a nation preserve its unity or a splinter state its independence. Such appeals were addressed especially to the Soviet Union or the United States. One of the more dramatic examples of the way the survival of a new state involved the superpowers occurred in 1960 when the Belgian Congo became independent. Patrice Lumumba, leader of the nationalist party, became the country's new premier, and Joseph Kasavubu its first president. Almost immediately, the Congo fell into disorder. First, the rich mining province of Katanga, upon whose copper and cobalt exports the Congo was largely dependent as a major source of revenue, split off into a separate state. Katanga's president, Moise Tshombe, had the support of the powerful Belgian mining interests, anxious to protect their investments. Then the army began to revolt because it resented the continued presence of its Belgian officers and wanted them replaced with native leadership. In a wild spree, the soldiers began to attack white women (including nuns) and children. The Belgian settlers' reaction was to flee. Among them were the experts the Belgians had expected to leave behind to help the Congolese in their early period of self-government. All public services now collapsed because the Congo lacked an educated native elite. The Belgians had never trained one.

In the midst of this situation, the Belgians flew in paratroopers to protect their nationals. Lumumba saw this move as a Belgian attempt to restore colonial rule, and he appealed to the United Nations to send forces to help him. It was at this point that the cold war was injected into the Congo. The UN troops, with no forces from the great powers, did not compel the Belgians to evacuate their paratroopers or agree to Lumumba's demand that they help him reestablish control over Katanga Province. Secretary-General Dag Hammarskjöld ordered that the international organization's forces were not to be involved in the internal squabbles of the Congo or employed by the contending political factions to gain power over their rivals. This, however, had the effect of underwriting the divisions of the Congo, and the country could not survive without Katanga. Lumumba turned against the United Nations, bitterly attacked the secretary-general, and accused Belgium and the Western powers, especially the United States, of conspiring against him. Lumumba's attacks grew increasingly racist. Finally, he asked the Soviet Union for help and received Soviet diplomatic backing, military supplies, and offers of troops or "volunteers." Several neutrals, especially the United Arab Republic, Guinea, and Ghana, also extended their sympathy and support.

The United States now supported President Kasavubu (who dismissed Lumumba) and his army commander, Colonel Sese Seko Mobutu, who established a caretaker government composed of the Congo's fifteen university graduates. Mobutu also infuriated the Soviet Union by driving out all Communist-bloc personnel, who had been aiding Lumumba. The Soviets insisted that Lumumba was still the Congo's legitimate ruler and demanded his restoration; so did the neutrals, who supported this demand by threatening to remove their contingents from the UN forces. This would have left the Congo in utter chaos. The United States, however, refused to budge and continued to give its support to Mobutu, in whom it saw the best means of eliminating Soviet influence in the Congo and possible Communist penetration into the heart of Africa.

Soviet-American differences now became bitter. The Soviets, thwarted in the Congo for the time being, made two demands: Hammarskjöld's resignation and a veto over the secretary-general's activities. These demands were rejected. But by early 1962, after all efforts to unify the Congo had failed, the United Nations reversed its original stand. It finally adopted the policy of forcefully squashing the opposition. Although it took many months and cost lives, the country was "unified" through the deposition of Tshombe and his Belgian advisers and foreign mercenaries. Ironically, this restoration of national order, accomplished with UN support, was a victory for Lumumba, although he did not live to see it. (The CIA reportedly had planned Lumumba's assassination, but was beaten to it.) If the central government had not received American and UN support and had been unable to reunite the Congo, it, like Lumumba, would probably have turned toward the Soviet Union for help.

Economic Stagnation and Regional Rivalries: The 1967 Middle East War

Even if a new nation does not disintegrate, the political leaders may invoke the only emotion the people ever shared to hold it together. This emotion is the nationalism fostered by the hatred of the former colonial power and is directed against both that country and, more broadly, "Western imperialism." Independence does not mean that colonialism is no longer an issue; rather, the fight against colonialism and imperialism becomes a useful tool to preserve national unity. The same technique may be used by a country with the even more common condition of a stagnant economy. The political leadership is tempted to preserve its power by finding foreign scapegoats to relieve internal stresses and strains.

It is simply easier and therefore more attractive for leaders to play a prominent and highly visible role on the international stage than to undertake the difficult task of modernization. The people can take pride in their leader's—and hence, their nation's—new status and identity in an international society that, under colonialism, had been denied importance and dignity. Kwame Nkrumah of Ghana, Sukarno of Indonesia, Muhammad Ben Bella of Algeria, and Gamal Abdel Nasser of Egypt were among the most prominent and skillful practitioners of the art of channeling domestic grievances into international strutting and adventures during the 1950s and 1960s.

Nasser provided a dramatic example of how provocative this posture can be. Just as he had done in 1956, Nasser incited a war with Israel in 1967 when he faced increasing economic hardship at home and a militant anti-Israeli Arab nationalism in Syria, which was notoriously unstable. Increasingly preoccupied with "Arab socialism" and his fight for Arab leadership, Nasser had not managed to launch Egypt on a path of self-sustaining economic growth after more than a decade of rule. Egypt was desperately short of funds to finance its development, buy food, support its sizable army, and provide enough jobs for its population. The birth-control program had failed to have any significant impact; the birth rate added 800,000 people annually to a population of more than 30 million. The pace of inflation was approximately 15 percent a year. Nasser's program of nationalization and expropriation had brought domestic investment to a near halt and discouraged foreign investment. His virulent anti-American attitude resulted in a cut-off of the American surplus food shipments. He had to buy food elsewhere and use up funds that might have been invested in development. The heavy expenditures on military equipment, probably amounting to one-third of Egypt's annual budget, also diverted funds from development.

Arab socialism, having lost its glamour, weakened Nasser's claim to Arab leadership and left him only the arena of foreign policy in which to recoup his prestige and hold on the Arab masses. But here, too, his stature had declined. He had reached the height of his self-proclaimed leadership of Arab nationalism a decade earlier when he seized the Suez Canal. Nationalism had also affected Nasser's neighbors. Iraq refused to subordinate itself to his direction, and Syria quit its short-lived union with Egypt in 1961. Nasser then resumed his verbal attacks on the traditional monarchies of Jordan and Saudi Arabia; Egyptian forces also helped the revolutionary forces who had overthrown the Yemenite monarchy supported by Saudi Arabia. Nasser was clearly seeking to extend his influence southward into the sheikdoms and sultanates of South Arabia, a British protectorate scheduled to become independent in early 1968. This would give him control over the Red Sea entrance to the Suez Canal. But the Egyptian army was unsuccessful in destroying the royalist supporters. In 1967 these intra-Arab rivalries, combined with economic failure, pressured Nasser to reassert his leadership of Arab nationalism.

The result was war. First, the Jordanians, in response to Nasser's hostility, taunted him with hiding behind the UN forces stationed between the Israeli and Egyptian forces at the close of the Suez War. Second, the Syrians, trying to displace Nasser as the leader of Pan-Arabism, openly and repeatedly called for Israel's destruction and stepped up their terrorist raids into Israel. After the Israelis retaliated, the Syrians claimed in May 1967 that the Israelis were assembling their forces for a full-scale invasion of Syria. This rumor, reportedly brought to Nasser's attention by the Soviet Union, which was seeking to exploit the Arab-Israeli-Western quarrel for its own purposes, was found to be untrue by UN observers. But Nasser, claiming to be the great hero of the Arab peoples, either felt compelled to act or saw in the invasion rumor his opportunity to regain his leadership of Arab nationalism. Whichever it was, there was bound to be trouble, particularly because, after eleven years of receiving Soviet training and arms, Nasser seemed very confident that his forces could beat Israel, which this time would be fighting by itself, without the aid of France and Britain.

The Egyptian leader took several actions. He moved reinforcements into the Sinai desert. Next, he demanded and obtained the withdrawal of the UN peace-keeping forces; Egyptian and Israeli forces now confronted each other for the first time since 1956. In addition, he blockaded the Gulf of Aqaba, through which Israel received its oil and other goods. For Israel the gulf was a vital lifeline because Nasser barred Israeli shipping from the Suez Canal. Nasser knew Israel would consider a blockade intolerable and an act of war. In short, he was deliberately provoking a military conflict. Finally, Nasser signed an alliance with Jordan. This meant that Arab armies surrounded Israel: Syria in the north, Egypt in the south, and Jordan, with its highly regarded army directed to cut Israel in two at its narrow waist. All these actions were accompanied by increasingly shrill calls for a holy "war of liberation" and the extermination of all of Israel's inhabitants.

In these circumstances, war was inevitable, unless Israel was willing to accept a major political defeat, an unlikely prospect. Whether peace could be preserved, primarily by Nasser's lifting the blockade, depended on the United States and the Soviet Union. Washington was caught in a dilemma. On the one hand, the United States had recognized Israel's right to send ships through the gulf after compelling Israel to withdraw following its 1956 victory. The United States also recognized that if Nasser did not relent, a forceful test might be necessary. Seeking support from other maritime powers, the United States found them unwilling to use force. On the other hand, it was deeply involved in Vietnam and therefore reluctant to take on a second conflict. Furthermore, a key question for American policy makers was whether such a test would precipitate a clash with the Soviet Union, which had with great fanfare sent warships into the eastern Mediterranean, fully supported the Arabs in their aims, continuously denounced Israel as an aggressive tool of American imperialism, and perhaps even spurred Nasser on with the false story of an imminent Israeli invasion of Syria.

For Moscow, the Arab-Israeli conflict, as earlier, had global implications. If Western influence could be expelled from the Middle East and if the Soviet Union could establish itself as the dominant power over this oil-rich region, Europe would be weakened and perhaps even neutralized. Soviet political support and the naval show of force undoubtedly contributed to Nasser's intransigence. Certainly it helped restore his reputation in the Arab world. Had the blockade been successful, the Soviet Union would have earned the Arabs' everlasting gratitude as the primary force behind Egypt's political victory. An effective blockade would have demonstrated the Soviet Union's ability to inhibit the American navy and would have eroded American commitments to Israel. The Soviet Union had an opportunity to replace the West as the region's leading power. For Moscow, the stakes in seeing Nasser achieve a political victory were enormous. Moscow, therefore, was unwilling to restrain Cairo's dangerous military moves and threats of war.

Because Washington was unable to arrange a diplomatic solution, the Israelis, who had not really expected one, attacked to seize the initiative in what had become an unavoidable clash. Routing the air forces of their Arab opponents in a brilliantly coordinated set of air strikes in the first hours of hostilities, they defeated the Egyptian army and reached the Suez Canal in three days—two days ahead of their 1956 record! They routed the Jordanian army and captured half of Jerusalem and the western bank of the River Jordan. Finally, they turned on the Syrian army and eliminated the bases from which Syria launched the terrorist raids and shelled Israeli settlements. Nasser's dreams of an Arab empire were shattered, despite his efforts to salvage his reputation by blaming his defeat on alleged American and British air intervention on behalf of Israel. Arab nationalism and intra-Arab quarrels once again had intensified the Arab-Israeli conflict and precipitated war. The bipolar competition for influence in the Middle East once more had exploited its problems, turning it into a "Balkans of the twentieth century," an inflammable area of political instability, regional rivalry, and great power conflict likely to explode at any moment and to cause war far beyond its borders. Domestic Arab problems only aggravated the tendency of leaders to engage in adventurism, to export internal dissatisfaction and grievances, to strike tough and inflexible poses, and to expose the world to the dangers of a superpower clash.

A World Divided into Rich and Poor Nations

The Soviet Model of Development

Washington, however, saw the new states' functional, not ideological, attraction to communism as the greatest danger to American security. Confronting an amalgam of political, social, and cultural changes (not just an economic transition), experiencing revolutionary transformations (not just evolutionary progress), the non-Western nations have no guarantee that they will successfully climb what Robert Heilbroner has termed the Great Ascent; even the attempt may well call for some sort of left-wing authoritarian rule.[4] In this context, the Soviet Union represented itself as a model of development.

---

4. Robert L. Heilbroner, *The Great Ascent* (New York: Harper Torchbook, 1963)

The Soviets could say: "In 1917 Russia was also underdeveloped but now, within the space of one generation, it has become militarily one of the two superpowers, the second largest industrial country in the world. You, too, can be industrialized quickly and live a better life." To people suffering from chronic hunger and poverty, it probably did not matter that the Soviet Union had achieved industrialization by setting up totalitarian governments that brutally squeezed the necessary sacrifices out of the people; the loss of liberty did not mean much to people who had never known it anyway, who had lived for centuries under authoritarian governments, whether domestic or foreign. Soviet totalitarianism would provide the organization and efficiency to extract the sacrifices from the masses and the discipline to hold the nation together, to speed up the pace of the cultural revolution while controlling the social tensions produced by the early stages of development, and, where necessary, to depose ruthlessly the traditional ruling class blocking the path to modernization. In short, just as capitalism was the instrument for modernization in the nineteenth century, Washington feared that Soviet communism might become a successful model for modernization in the twentieth century. (After the Sino-Soviet schism, China too promoted itself as a model for modernization, one superior to its European rival.)

Communism, therefore, was not seen primarily as a military threat in the Third World. In the newly politically aware and poorer areas of the underdeveloped world, communism was attractive because it promised a fairly rapid and disciplined way of bringing about political, social, economic, and cultural changes. The United States saw that the best way of competing with communism was to alleviate the conditions that allegedly caused it. Poverty, ignorance, hunger, and social injustice were thought to provide the breeding ground for communism; curing these conditions and giving people hope for a better life was the means to defeat it. This would be achieved once the new nations' development had gained a self-sustaining momentum. Communism's appeal to attract adherents was strong during the initial phase of modernization. During this period, in the words of W. W. Rostow, later President Lyndon Johnson's national security adviser during the Vietnam War, Communists would act as "the scavengers of the modernization process. Communism is best understood as a disease of the transition to modernization."[5] If the West offered assistance, it was optimistically believed, the LDCs would develop into Western-type, modern, urbanized, and industrial societies that would naturally look westward.

It was because of the competition of models that the United States and other Western states first offered the LDCs economic aid and technical assistance. In the final analysis, the fundamental problem was perceived to be the growing division of the world between rich nations and poor nations.

---

5. W. W. Rostow, "Guerrilla Warfare in Underdeveloped Areas," in *The Guerrilla—And How To Fight Him*, ed. T. N. Greene (New York: Praeger Publishers, 1962), 56.

Western aid was intended to close this gap, modernize the new nations without compelling them to use totalitarian methods, satisfy the revolution of rising expectations and thereby create politically and socially stable societies, and eventually promote the spread of democracy. This process, in turn, was expected to create a more peaceful world by giving developing societies a vested interest in the international order and Western values. It was clear that assistance to the Third World was justified mainly in terms of security considerations, not humanitarian reasons. A world divided into rich and poor nations was potentially explosive, for it set the majority of the poor against the privileged minority. Such a division was no more acceptable internationally than it had been within each of the Western nations 100 years earlier.

The Nineteenth Century Precedent

The two situations were believed to be so similar that the "lessons" of the earlier experience were applied to the international division of wealth. As the Industrial Revolution gathered momentum in each of the European countries and America, it created a privileged minority that owned most of the wealth and a vastly unequal distribution of income. Laborers, including women and children, worked fourteen to sixteen hours per day, six or seven days a week, earned little beyond subsistence wages (and sometimes less), and lived in overcrowded slums. The rich got richer and the poor got poorer, a fact so obvious that one of Britain's great prime ministers, Benjamin Disraeli, spoke of England not as one nation but as two.

The prevailing *laissez-faire* philosophy argued that nothing could be done to alleviate this situation. Government intervention, whether to end the worst forms of exploitation, such as child labor, or to redistribute the income to help the poor lead a decent and dignified life, was rejected as contrary to the "iron laws of economics." Any outside interference with the workings of the market would stifle the private incentive and initiative that stoked the competitive capitalistic system. These laws, which condemned a large section of the population to a hopeless and miserable existence, received even further support from Charles Darwin's theory of evolution, with its emphasis on the "struggle for survival" and the "survival of the fittest." This philosophy, called social Darwinism, argued very simply that the rich were wealthy because their success in the competitive struggle had demonstrated that they were the most fit; conversely, the poor were destitute because they were unfit. It never occurred to social Darwinists to ask themselves whether everybody had had an equal start or opportunity in this struggle.

These philosophical justifications for poverty ultimately were rejected in all Western societies. The long working hours, the unsanitary, unsafe working conditions, and the teeming slums were a blot on the West's conscience. They were also politically shortsighted and economically foolish. Politically, the division of people into "haves" and "have-nots" could lead to revolution, with the bourgeoisie being overthrown by the working class, or proletariat; or, if it surrendered its domestic beliefs and values, the bourgeoisie could perhaps retain its power by establishing an authoritarian government and crushing any proletarian protests and uprisings. Neither of these alternatives was acceptable to the ruling middle classes. Nor did this policy of squeezing the workers for maximum profit make sense economically, since the less money people have, the fewer things they can buy. Thus, social justice made sense—morally, politically, and economically.

In every Western society, government in the late nineteenth century began to intervene increasingly in the economy. Growing public awareness eventually led to the regulation of business; the passage of wage and hour legislation; the abolition of child labor and "sweatshop" working conditions; the organization of trade unions; measures to counteract the swings of the business cycle; the implementation of the progressive income tax; and the initiation, during depressions, of unemployment insurance, public-works programs, and other "pump-priming" projects to increase the purchasing power of the people, thereby stimulating renewed demand and production. These measures, especially in the United States, widened and raised the base of wealth, giving rise to the twentieth-century mass market. They also led to a discovery so simple and yet so hard to understand that Europe, particularly continental Europe, learned it only after 1945: namely, that workers are also consumers. If they are paid good wages, they will also buy the goods they produce. This is profitable all around: workers are economically satisfied and therefore gain vested interest, politically, in the social and economic order; capitalists earn handsome profits by selling volume at reasonable prices, and they retain their social status and political influence.

U.S. Indifference to Social Revolution

The same problem of inequitable distribution of wealth was now regarded in a different way. This time the problem was the widening gap *between* nations, with the rich countries becoming richer, and the poor countries growing poorer. The iron laws of economics seemed to hold for poor countries the same fate they once did for the Western working classes. Had the Marxist prophecy that the exploited proletariat would overthrow the bourgeoisie been defeated domestically only to reappear internationally to defeat the West? Modernization was expected to give the new states a stake in the international system and to help create a world in which Western values would be more secure.

Although the nature of the problem seemed clear to many policy makers, the rationale for economic aid to assist the new nations' development never attracted the degree of public support that the more easily understandable military preparations against the Soviets did. What was probably required, as many suggested, was a progressive international income tax by which all the advanced Western nations would contribute 1 percent to 2 percent of their annual national income for development. The World Bank's Pearson Commission in 1969 endorsed the 1 percent figure. But by then no Western country was giving that much. Despite the rapid economic growth of the industrial states during the 1960s, their foreign aid spending had declined. This was particularly true for American aid to Europe, which, at the time of the Marshall Plan, had been 2.75 percent of the gross national product (GNP). Aid to the less-developed countries was always less than 1 percent of GNP. In short, at a time when the American GNP had risen by hundreds of millions of dollars, the national effort was out of proportion with its increasing capacity to pay and with the growing gap between the rich and poor nations.

Indeed, the term *economic aid* was something of a misnomer. After 1950 and the eruption of the Korean War, most economic aid was, in fact, military aid. Moreover, since Western Europe's recovery, most of this aid was channeled to allied countries: Turkey, Pakistan, South Vietnam, South Korea, Jordan, and Nationalist China. Even part of the money designated for economic assistance was "defense support," which was money to sustain the economies of allies such as South Korea or South Vietnam; without this support, these countries could not maintain their standing armies. The final sum actually allocated to economic development was also concentrated in relatively few countries. Most LDCs got next to nothing.

Apart from the lack of public support for foreign aid, U.S. policy toward the LDCs suffered from three other liabilities. The first was that American dollars were all too often offered with the explicit or implicit assumption that the recipients should associate themselves with U.S. cold war policies; that even if they did not formally ally themselves with the United States, they should often thank it for its generosity, praise it for the morality of its anti-Communist stand, and certainly refrain from criticizing it. The United States was reluctant to give dollars to nations that would not join its side. After all, could any nation really be neutral in a struggle between right and wrong? Was not democracy good and communism evil? If countries wanted U.S. money, surely the least they could do was "to stand up and be counted." But in these countries, the basic aspiration was to concentrate on internal matters, to raise the standard of living and strengthen their independence, and to minimize their involvement in the cold war. Most, therefore, preferred to remain nonaligned in the struggle between the West and the Communists, avoiding all "entangling alliances." Attempts to use economic aid as a means of forcing them into an American alliance system were counterproductive, as U.S. overtures to Nasser in the early 1950s had dramatically proven.

In preferring a generally nonaligned position, the LDCs were, in a sense, following America's example. After the United States gained its independence, it, too, avoided alliances and preoccupied itself with internal developments. As a less-developed country, the United States was aware that its newly realized independence meant very little without economic and political strength. Moreover, the United States had just thrown off the shackles of colonialism; its citizens had no desire to be once more tied to the European powers. American policy makers, especially during the 1950s, forgot that it was the United States that had set this example.

The second liability that hampered U.S. policy toward the LDCs was the racial discrimination within the United States. The persistent segregationist practices and exploitation of blacks in both the South and the North were flagrant violations of the democratic principles of freedom and human dignity so often proclaimed by the United States. The peoples of the LDCs not only claimed equal status for their nations; they also sought equality as human beings. Segregation in America reminded them of their colonial days when the white man had treated them as inferiors because of the color of their skin. Conditions in the United States began to change during the Kennedy and Johnson administrations. As blacks heard Martin Luther King articulate their aspirations for a life of more dignity and full participation in American life, as the ghettos exploded after King's assassination, the government began to outlaw certain discriminatory practices against blacks and to provide greater opportunities in jobs and housing.

However, racial problems continued to haunt the United States on the foreign front. In Rhodesia (now Zimbabwe) and South Africa, minority white-controlled governments, determined to stay in power, used abhorrent methods such as apartheid and strict police surveillance. The United States, despite its often expressed disapproval of these policies, did not follow through in its actions. It imported Rhodesian chrome for years despite a UN embargo. American companies, although they provided their black workers with better working conditions and pay than local companies, lent support to South Africa through investment. America, the world's first state to articulate that all men were created equal, seemed all too often to say to the world that there was a qualifying phrase: "except blacks."

Third, U.S. relations with the developing states were hampered by the American lack of understanding of class struggle and social politics. America, "born free" as a bourgeois democratic society, had managed to avoid the kind of domestic conflicts over basic values that the countries of Europe experienced and that plagued many of the less-developed nations.[6] The United States had not experienced a genuine social revolution at its birth, for a revolution is characterized by violence; it seeks to destroy the institutions and social fabric of the old society and create a new society with new institutional and social class arrangements. Despite its self-proclaimed revolutionary character, the United States is, according to former senator William Fulbright, an unrevolutionary, conservative country.[7] Not surprisingly, therefore, America was not particularly sympathetic to revolutions and tended to associate revolutionaries with communism. Deviations from middle-class

---

6. See Chapter 1, 8.
7. J. William Fulbright, *The Arrogance of Power* (New York: Vintage Books, 1967), 72-73.

American values were likely to be condemned as "un-American" and sinful, to be rooted out so that the "American way of life" would remain pure and unadulterated.

The principal challenges to these values have indeed come not from within the system but from outside the U.S. borders, and the United States has reacted to foreign threats—German, Japanese, Soviet—in two ways. Internally, the government has hunted "subversives," a procedure that inevitably has infringed upon civil liberties and endangered the security of traditional freedoms. Externally, government policy, before the atomic bomb, was the total destruction of the hostile regime so that American principles could survive untainted.

Thus, as already noted, the real or imagined Communist threat in the early 1950s led to McCarthyism, a search for heresy in which the goal of eliminating alleged un-American attitudes and behavior justified any means, including disregard for due process of law, the basic guarantee of all civil liberties. At times, this hunt went to frightening lengths, as when the United States Information Agency actually burned "suspect" books—and, even worse, when the careers and lives of people were jeopardized and sometimes ruined. In foreign policy, the reaction to the Communist threat was to support almost any regime, no matter how reactionary, if it claimed to be "anti-Communist." As a result, the United States often associated itself with governments whose days were numbered, that had alienated the masses: Jiang Gaishek in China and Bao Dai in Indochina are but two examples that turned out badly.

This attitude was typical of American absolutism and inability to understand the deeper social struggles of Asia and the Middle East. In its attempt to contain communism—that is, to preserve the global *status quo*—the United States became committed to the domestic, social, and political *status quo* in these countries. In seeking stability, the United States was paradoxically trying to preserve freedom by supporting ramshackle autocracies that were unrepresentative of their peoples' aspirations. But this internal contradiction within the U.S. alliance system eventually had to resolve itself. American support for traditional regimes only bottled up the social and political resentment and ferment even more, thereby adding to the explosive forces that someday would burst forth and upset regional balances of power.

The Example of Latin America

Events in Latin America illustrate the way U.S. foreign policy, even when it took into account the need for development aid, became a prisoner of U.S. domestic experience. Cuba as a base for the subversion of other Latin nations was much on the minds of U.S. policy makers during the 1960s. Successful subversion constituted a threat to the United States. Conditions in

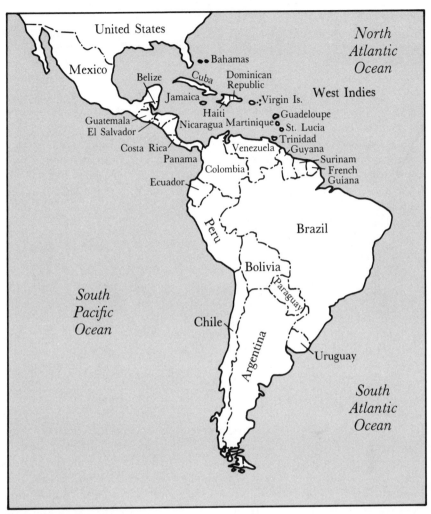

Latin America

Latin America made Castro's success a real possibility: for example, the resentment against a history of past U.S. interventions in the Caribbean and Central America; the large-scale, private U.S. capital investments and economic control of many Latin American economies; the persistent U.S. support for the privileged few who, usually closely linked to American capital, sought to preserve their position by ignoring social grievances and establishing right-wing military dictatorships; and finally, the misery, poverty, and illiteracy of the vast majority of the people, who, although they lived in the countryside, were landless.

Latin America shared two aspirations that were sweeping through all the less-developed areas: the urge for a better life for the masses and the desire of countries to determine their own national destiny. The United States has exercised its hemispheric domination indirectly, usually by alliance with the wealthy landowning governing class. Americans may believe that they are free of Europe's taint of colonialism, but that is not what Latin Americans think. The Monroe Doctrine had turned the southern part of the hemisphere into a U.S. sphere of influence; the United States did not have to resort to direct colonial rule. Invested American capital spoke louder than guns, and the U.S. government did not have to give political orders when a nation was a "banana republic." The economies of many Latin American nations remained backward, undiversified, and agrarian. They depended for a livelihood on the export of one or two raw materials or crops to the United States, their largest market. In good years, they earned money; in bad years, the ever-present unemployment, poverty, and hunger increased. Their livelihood was affected directly by the fluctuations of the business cycle, and by their sensitivity to American interests.

In these conditions, the success of Castroism was thought to depend on two elements. First, it would depend upon how the Latin American governments reacted, whether they would undertake large-scale social and economic reforms or cling to their privileges. Public pressure for change was rising, but would this change be revolutionary or evolutionary? If the ruling classes remained as hostile to reform and as irresponsible toward public welfare as in the past, Fidel Castro might well be able to export his revolution. Wherever there is social injustice, destruction of the *ancien régime* will appear as the only way of having a piece of land, enough food, or a job. Revolution and a "radical solution" become the only hope for a better life.

Second, the success of Castroism would depend on the effectiveness of U.S. policy directed toward alleviating the conditions that fostered popular resentment in Latin America. Whether the United States had the will to guide this revolution, however, was another matter. This was a task that required American acceptance of non-Communist left-wing movements and the expropriation of American property, neither of which would be easy because of the identification of reform with revolution and revolution with communism. Moreover, the United States was expected to invest billions of dollars in the Latin American economies to foster a self-sustaining rate of economic growth, to develop conditions in which private capital would be attracted to projects other than the extraction of raw materials or growth of single exportable crops, and to aid in the transformation of backward agrarian societies into modern, industrialized nations. In addition, Latin America's projected rapid increase of population lent urgency to development. In the absence of an adequate effort, the already low standard of living was expected to deteriorate further. If all these factors were taken together, the prospects of future radical revolutions might be avoidable only by an "alliance for progress."

To meet the challenge of the Latin American "revolution of rising expectations" President John Kennedy, soon after assuming office, established precisely such an alliance. He pledged $20 billion of primarily public money over the next decade to Latin America and, even more significantly, he emphasized the need for social change. Kennedy realized that, in the absence of the necessary reforms, the possibilities of economic and political development were slight. The alliance, in short, was a post-Castro attempt to abort future Castros.

Would the ruling oligarchies surrender their power, status, and prestige, and commit themselves to fundamental reforms? In the words of Herbert L. Matthews, then a veteran observer of the Latin American scene:

> In the whole of Latin America, the rich are getting richer and the poor poorer. This is the worst, the most difficult and the most dangerous feature of the area. The Alliance for Progress was created primarily to tackle this essentially social problem. . . .
>
> The most serious feature of this problem centers around agriculture and land reform. The frantic urge to industrialize that seized Latin America after the Second World War was, in part, satisfied at the expense of the agrarian sector. Yet virtually all the countries are from half to three-quarters agricultural. Latin exports are overwhelmingly agricultural and mineral.
>
> The abnormal and dangerous urbanization, caused by the flight of impoverished peasants from the rural areas to the urban centers, has led to some of the largest cities in the world and some of the worst slums. Countries with plenty of land were, and are, importing food at high cost.
>
> Most landowners are resisting the reforms that their governments and the Alliance for Progress desire. . . . Much will depend on whether the ruling classes see the need to make drastic structural reforms. Much, also, will depend on the state of the world and the world markets for raw materials, not to mention the ability of the United States to invest and to aid. . . .
>
> There are revolutions and revolutions. The fascist-military type in Latin America comes from the right; the socialistic-communistic from the left; and in between is the sort of peaceful, voluntary, gradual but genuine type of revolution which the Alliance for Progress is trying to promote.
>
> Latin America is such a dynamic area of the world that it is bound to have revolutions. The only unknown factor is: what kind? [8]

Castro's effect on the alliance was illustrated by the U.S. intervention in the Dominican Republic. The impetus for this event was the overthrow in 1961 of Rafael Trujillo, who had ruled as a dictator for thirty-one years. Following a brief period of political turmoil, Juan Bosch, a man of genuinely democratic convictions, was elected president. Seven months later, Bosch was overthrown by a military *coup d'état* whose leaders announced that they would reestablish a "rightist state." In April 1965 the pro-Bosch forces revolted against this right-wing military government. But, according to

---

8. *New York Times,* March 15, 1965.

Washington, the leadership of this revolution swung increasingly toward communism. Communists were thought to be active in the movement against the junta, and Washington feared they would gain control of the pro-Bosch forces and create a second Cuba in the hemisphere. The rebels claimed that, although some Communists might support their movement, their revolution was led by non-Communists who only sought a return to constitutional government. Before the evidence in fact was clear whether the revolution was in fact Communist-controlled, President Johnson ordered American armed intervention, even though this action once more raised the old specter of American intervention, so common in the days before Franklin Roosevelt's "Good Neighbor" policy.

The Dominican intervention demonstrated how obsessed the Alliance for Progress was with Castro. He was responsible for the alliance and for its failures. Without him, there would have been no large-scale efforts to seek the democratic development of Latin America. But the American fear that any Latin American revolution might become a Communist revolution, requiring preventive action, would not have sprung up without Castro. The overt United States intervention—the first in fifty years in Latin America—therefore undermined the Alliance for Progress, which had tried to persuade the region's ruling elites to undertake reforms if they wished to avoid revolutionary violence. Latin America's ruling classes could now relax because there was an alternative: American intervention would save them from the consequences of their own folly in holding onto an unjust way of life. American policy south of the U.S. border, as in other areas of the world, thus continued to be made in the context of the bipolar global struggle.

Was America's Third World Policy Imperialistic?

During and after the Vietnam War, it became fashionable among radical writers, often referred to as the New Left, to claim that American interventions such as those in Cuba, the Dominican Republic, and Vietnam were not accidental, nor was the failure to provide sufficient economic aid for the modernization of the new nations a mere oversight. Indeed, this argument maintains that, although these nations may have been newly formed in the sense of formal political independence, they were in reality economically controlled by the United States, the dominant economy in the "global capitalist system"; the so-called new and independent nations in fact remained in a subordinate status. *Neocolonial* was one of the terms popularly used to refer to this status. In European eighteenth- and nineteenth-century colonialism the European state had invaded a foreign land and established direct rule of the newly acquired colony. In an age of growing nationalism, American imperialism controlled its "colonial" appendages through less visible but equally binding economic chains: corporate investments, economic aid, and the needs of the Third World countries for advanced technology and for markets in which to sell their raw materials. In addition, the United States supported reactionary political and social elites who survived only with American political support that, when necessary, was supplemented with American training and arming of local police and military forces, bribes, *coups d'etat* and—ultimately—U.S. military intervention.[9]

Why all this bother about the poor countries of the world? The answer is that they are, according to the radical critique, enormously profitable. Western industry needs cheap raw materials; the LDCs constitute potentially sizable markets for Western goods; and they provide places for the investment of private capital at large returns. Capitalist economies like that of the United States, the leading Western capitalist state, constantly need profits; without them, unemployment would increase, standards of living decline, and the struggle between capitalists and the proletariat or working class resume. This struggle is muted in the capitalist countries precisely because some of the enormous profits reaped by the capitalists from exploiting the LDCs trickle down to the workers in the form of higher wages and living standards. As long as this continues, the workers' revolutionary consciousness remains weakened and they will support the capitalist system. Without this trickle, the class struggle would resume. Therefore, even with the best of intentions, America, as a capitalist society and guardian of Western capitalism, could not surrender its "neocolonial control" over the LDCs. It was structurally necessary; if capitalism was to be preserved and domestic social revolution avoided, the Third World countries had to be maintained as profitable dependencies and suppliers of raw materials. The American pursuit of counterrevolutionary and interventionist policies follows from this fundamental economic motivation driving the United States in the international arena.

Dependent, even more than *neocolonial,* has become the common term to describe these nations' standing in the global capitalist system (minus the Soviet bloc). To emphasize the character of the relationship of the United States and other capitalist states to the LDCs, the capitalist states were said to constitute the core or center of the international economy, the LDCs the peripheries. The LDCs' economies do not serve their people, nor is their purpose to improve the lives of their citizens. The cheap natural resources are sent to Western factories, where they benefit Western manufacturers and workers, and this has been an important reason for the dramatic increase in

---

9. This section, while brief, was included because U.S. policy toward the Third World in the 1960s and 1970s is often described in imperialistic terms. This important alternative explanation deserves brief mention, therefore, as does the critique of it. I relied especially upon Jerome Slater, "Is United States Foreign Policy 'Imperialistic' or 'Imperial'?" *Political Science Quarterly* (Spring 1976): 63-87; Robert W. Tucker, *The Radical Left and American Foreign Policy* (Baltimore: Johns Hopkins University Press, 1971); and Stephen D. Krasner, *Defending the National Interest* (Princeton, N.J.: Princeton University Press, 1978).

the Western standard of living over the last century. Thus, the LDCs are poor because they have been exploited, and the Western states are rich because they have been the exploiters. The international capitalist economy is unlikely to allow this relationship to change because the Western developed states benefit from it, and most LDCs remain too dependent on the capitalist states for capital, technology, and markets. The few that wish to resist and break the exploitive economic chains must use force. A successful war of "national liberation" against the pro-Western domestic ruling elite is needed to free them. Once in control of their own economy, which will be used for their people's welfare, these nations will have achieved genuine national independence.

This economically imperialist interpretation of American foreign policy from 1945 to the Vietnam years is testimony to the significance of faith and attitudes over facts. There is little evidence to support a purely economic interpretation. The survival of American capitalism and the achievement of the nation's high standard of living have not depended upon exploiting the LDCs. The vast bulk of American private investments had been made in the American economy; and of the approximately 5 percent to 6 percent of American investment that was made abroad, most, even at the height of the Vietnam War in 1968, went to Western Europe, Canada, and Japan. In short, investment in non-Western economies was insignificant for the welfare of the American economy. In trade, the pattern was identical. The United States traded primarily with the other industrial countries. They had something to sell to one another. Here, too, the Third World states were not essential to the well-being of the American economy. Indeed, until the 1970s, the prosperity of the American economy did not depend upon exports. It is primarily in the area of natural resources that the dependency argument carries a degree of plausibility, for clearly America, like other industrial countries, needed raw materials. But even here, with the possible exception of oil, the case is far from persuasive. Substitutes, alternative raw materials, and the domestic availability of a vast array of raw materials made the country less dependent upon the Third World than the imperialist interpretation would suggest. (Admittedly, the cost of materials from domestic sources may be higher than from the less-developed countries, although not necessarily higher than the prices these countries hope to get or, in the case of oil, are already receiving. Moreover, as the price of oil rose in the 1970s, alternative sources of energy or oil from deeper wells became economically more feasible.) The United States, in fact, possesses many of the raw materials it needs, including energy resources, especially coal. The United States at the time of Vietnam had the world's highest standard of living and was at the same time a net exporter of raw materials.

What is equally clear is that the imperialist interpretation suggesting that capitalist countries either exercise control of Third World economies to make a profit, or, if they relinquish control, the capitalist economies collapse, could not be more wrong. Since 1945 the Western states that have achieved the highest rates of economic growth are Japan, West Germany, and the Scandinavian states, countries that had no colonies and that exercised no "control" over non-Western countries. They bought what they needed. Imperialist control was completely unnecessary for these states with "capitalist" economies; indeed, such control was inversely related to their prosperity. The former colonial states such as Great Britain and the last colonial state of all, Portugal, fared the worst of all Western economies. Domination of the less-developed countries is not required to have access to their raw materials. Indeed, and no doubt disillusioning to radical critics who would like the Third World countries to withhold their resources to bring down American capitalism, these nations, radical or not, sell their resources to all Western countries—if the price is right.

But to return to the main point: if economic control means equal political control, one would have expected the United States to resist the increasing country-by-country expropriation of American investments and property or the shifting of majority control from American multinational corporations—the alleged instruments of U.S. imperial control—to host governments; and one would also have expected the United States to intervene militarily to reverse the Organization of Petroleum Exporting Countries' (OPEC) fourfold increase of oil prices in 1973, which led to unemployment and inflation in the American and Western economies. Yet, nationalization has been the trend in this age of nationalism, and there is little that can be done about it except to acquiesce and officially protest—with anger sometimes, but not too much—and seek some compensation for the expropriated industry.

But the United States does not send in marines or overthrow governments to save a corporation's sugar fields or banana crops or even to lower oil prices. Economic and other pressures, as well as covert operations and overt interventions, have been used only where Washington perceived the stakes to be far broader than simple expropriation—that is, not where the stakes were corporate property, but where they were perceived to be far more important than money. In Guatemala in 1954, in Cuba in 1961, in the Dominican Republic in 1965 (and later, as we shall see, in Chile in the early 1970s, and Nicaragua after 1979), the American government intervened because it saw the governments in these countries and their international orientation in the context of cold war bipolarity. All these countries seemed to be aligning themselves with the Soviet bloc. In turn, these interventions repudiate the idea of U.S. "domination." The United States, as a great power, obviously has influence in the Third World, but the degree of influence depends on the issue and country. In general, it is a declining influence as the LDCs have asserted their nationalism.

American policy in the Middle East is probably the strongest refutation of the imperialist interpretation. If corporations did indeed control Washington, it is impossible to understand why the United States since 1948 has supported Israel so strongly, alienated most Arab states, jeopardized access to the oil needed so badly by Europe and increasingly by America, and risked the nationalization of Western oil companies (almost everywhere now controlled, even if not yet totally owned, by OPEC). In fact, what this policy shows is that economic considerations, if present and important, are not necessarily dominant in the making of the nation's foreign policy.

American motivations in foreign policy must be sought elsewhere than in the economic realm. They derive primarily from security considerations and the fear of Soviet power and, after 1950, from the equation of the expansion of Soviet power and influence with the expansion of communism. It is hardly surprising that in a bipolar world the containment policy was extended to the Third World, even if at times the results were more counterproductive than beneficial to U.S. goals. The worst case of American intervention was to come in Southeast Asia where the war in Vietnam was to undermine the rationale for U.S. postwar foreign policy.

c h a p t e r   e i g h t

Vietnam and the
Collapse of Containment

THE WORLD that emerged from World War II and dominated most of the twenty years from 1945 to 1965 was bipolar. The two superpowers, the United States and the Soviet Union, plus their allies, confronted one another directly in almost every area of the globe. In a series of encounters, they drew the "frontiers" between their worlds and extended their competition to the Third World. This bipolar world was dangerous because the distribution of power in the state system between two poles was very sensitive. Both were constantly alert to the slightest shifts in power lest they upset the equilibrium to give the adversary superiority. Each side perceived a gain of power and security for one as a loss of power and security for the other. Each viewed the opponent's moves, even if alleged to be defensive, as deliberate and offensive; moves in regions of secondary importance were ranked as significant and countered because they were seen as symbolically vital. Defining the "frontiers" around their respective spheres of influence and then guarding this territorial *status quo* against encroachment, subversion, or defection became the focus of the bipolar superpower competition.

Through this competitive process the United States became what some of its critics called the "world's policeman." Others, of a more Marxist disposition, referred to America's "empire." Although, as discussed in chapter 7, it makes little sense to attribute the vast postwar expansion of power to economic motives, the term *empire* is a handy one if attributed to security motives: a great power striving to preserve the balance of power in the state system. If, as we have argued, the superpower rivalry centers on the control of the Eurasian rimlands, then the U.S. role might be defined as *imperial,* as distinguished from the economically driven *imperialistic* search for colonies to exploit their markets and raw materials. Whatever it is called, the role was arduous, constant, and, to a large degree, successful in maintaining the frontiers of containment around the Sino-Soviet bloc—until Vietnam. In going to war there to defend one specific frontier, the United States became involved in an unconventional war it did not know how to manage and lost public support not only for the continuation of the war but also for the basic containment or imperial policy of which Vietnam was merely an application. In destroying the cold war consensus, the Vietnam War was a political defeat of the first rank for the United States.

The American and Soviet Empires

By the mid-1960s the United States had signed eighty treaties with forty-two separate states. The North Atlantic Treaty Organization (NATO), the Southeast Asia Treaty Organization (SEATO), the Central Treaty Organization (CENTO), and the bilateral security treaties with Japan, South Korea, the Philippines, and Taiwan organized the rimlands around the Sino-Soviet bloc. Western Europe was protected by 300,000 U.S. soldiers, and South Korea was similarly protected. American garrisons on their soil were their best guarantee against attack. The Sixth Fleet guarded the Mediterranean, protecting southern Europe and Israel and Western oil supplies and lines; the Seventh Fleet guarded the broad ranges of the Pacific to the Gulf of Tonkin. By a process of challenge and response, U.S. commitments had extended to virtually all continents, although its interventions in Latin America and Africa were only sporadic. America's projection of its power to all corners of Eurasia, with the accompanying alliances and basing of U.S. forces, resembling that of Britain in the nineteenth century, therefore, might well be called imperial. The territorial expansion and acquisitions of the Soviet Union since 1945 can also be called imperial.

Moscow and Washington are clearly the dominant voices in their respective spheres, composed of allies and client states, which are allies in all but name, although there may be no commitment of defense involved. The magnitude of their power and the scope of their commitments defined the Soviet and American empires. A critical difference between them, however, was another characteristic, the nature of the relationships between the imperial center and the states within its empire. On this matter—the willingness of its members to be part of that empire, the independence they enjoyed as members of a larger collective association, and the manner in which alliance decisions were made—the contrast was striking.

Their Contrasting Characteristics

The Soviet empire comprised the neighboring states of Lithuania, Estonia, and Latvia, which were annexed on the eve of the war with Germany, and other neighboring states, in Eastern Europe and Outer Mongolia, that were kept obedient by Soviet-imposed Communist regimes and/or Soviet forces on their soil. These troops have been used repeatedly to prevent defection or disloyalty to Moscow. Communist regimes that came to power on their own and controlled their own armies and police forces, such as Yugoslavia and China, or where Soviet forces were withdrawn, such as Romania, have demonstrated different degrees of independence from Moscow. If Moscow considered leaders such as Tito, Mao Zedong, Imre Nagy, or Alexander Dubcek unreliable, it was even more suspicious of non-Communist rulers with whom it had signed friendship treaties, like Egypt's Anwar Sadat in the 1970s. This is why during that decade Moscow favored not only older Marxist regimes such as North Korea, Cuba, and Vietnam, but also newly self-proclaimed Marxist-Leninist regimes such as Angola, Ethiopia, Mozambique, and South Yemen.

The Soviet empire was more or less contiguous because until the 1970s the Soviets, following the czars, expanded basically around their own frontiers. Their success testified to the close relationship between territorial expansion and the strength of Soviet arms. In the Warsaw Pact area certainly, there could be no question that Soviet rule had been imposed upon helpless and unwilling nations, except perhaps Bulgaria. Although several of the East European states gained a greater degree of independence after Stalin's death in 1953, they were careful not to become too independent, especially on foreign policy issues, to avoid Moscow's wrath and its fist. Indeed, it was probably not accidental that the Soviet Union's principal friends and admirers were found far away from Moscow; states such as Ethiopia and Nicaragua became loyal supporters after the Vietnam War.

The Soviet leadership kept a tight reign on power and dissent at home. It also showed little tolerance in Communist states where, if Soviet interests required, it could enforce its edict with the Soviet army. From the Soviet perspective, different views were wrong views and disagreement was heresy. The Soviet Union was the most powerful, the oldest, and the most experienced Communist state; that gave it the right to determine policy for other Communist states.

By contrast, the American empire is an overseas empire that has emerged over time as the United States reacted to Soviet moves. For the most part, American expansion in Eurasia was by invitation of the Soviet Union's potential victims. They wanted the United States to extend its imperial protection to them in preference to becoming Moscow's satellites. American power guaranteed their national independence; Soviet power meant the end of genuine independence. In addition to its defensive nature, three other characteristics can be noted about this American empire. One, if it was not created in a "fit of absent-mindedness," as someone once said about the British Empire, it was created reluctantly, often despite U.S. preferences. After World War II the United States had sought to retreat once more to the Western Hemisphere, and the countries of Western Europe were worried that the United States would *not* help them, not that it would. The United

States only gradually extended its commitments, usually because bipolarity seemed to leave it little choice. Two, it is fair to say that the United States did not think of itself as an imperial power. Americans generally do not feel France or South Korea is "theirs." To defend or to intervene in "its" empire, the United States must advance plausible reasons. Otherwise, both abroad and at home, there will be opposition to the use of American power, even if it is justified in the name of the containment policy. Finally, the U.S. relationship with its allies was different from that of the Soviet Union and its allies.

By its sheer power the United States is in command; it is American power, especially nuclear power, that deters a Soviet invasion of Europe. Japan and the members of NATO are under U.S. protection. Their alliances with the United States are in fact unilateral American guarantees for their continued independence. As a result the United States on occasion has determined what alliance policy should be, but America's allies have rarely hesitated to express their views openly, including their differences with the United States. They consider themselves allies, not dependencies. If it wishes to do so, France can throw out U.S. bases and withdraw its forces from the integrated NATO army; Spain can refuse to renew the lease of U.S. bases unless Washington pays them more—the weaker party usually does well in these negotiations—without expecting retribution, let alone U.S. military intervention. The point is that U.S. alliances reflect the democratic character of the United States and its partners. The expression of different viewpoints is regarded as normal, and issues are usually decided by compromise. If there is no agreement, the alliance either cannot act or individual members go their own way. The United States generally does not dictate to its allies. It may lead, but, however insistent it may be, it cannot compel them to follow unless they want to, which has been obvious since the 1970s.

The United States has not always drawn the overseas frontiers wisely. Its attempt to replicate NATO outside of Europe was bound to run into trouble. The global strategy of containing communism tended to ignore the regional differences in the Third World. In Europe, NATO's members perceived a common Soviet threat; their nationalism sustained their determination to defend themselves. Outside of Europe, the new states' nationalism was directed at their former colonial masters. The new states were suspicious of the Western defense organizations, which, they felt, represented their former colonial masters. During the 1950s anticommunism made little sense to a country like Egypt, which sought Soviet help in its fight against Israel, which was supported by Western nations. Anticommunism meant little to most Asian nations; they admired the new Communist China, not the discredited Nationalist regime still backed by the United States. Unwilling to rely on the fierce sense of nationalism of the newly independent states to resist efforts to reestablish foreign domination, even by Communist states, CENTO and SEATO proved to be weak reeds upon which to rely for anti-Communist resistance.

In addition, alliances such as CENTO and SEATO stimulated regional rivalries. Pakistan, a member of both, was not interested in containing communism but in obtaining arms for its rivalry with India. The United States thereby alienated India, potentially the far stronger state and one of the Third World's few democracies, and drove it into Moscow's arms for political support and weapons. As a U.S. friend, India would have been a more effective barrier than Pakistan in the 1950s and later to Soviet probes toward the Indian subcontinent. Similarly, Iraq's membership in CENTO reinforced Egypt's anti-Western disposition because of their traditional rivalry for Arab leadership. Finally, the U.S. crusading style failed to understand that nationalism infected Communist states as much as it did non-Communist states, and, instead of exploiting conflicting national interests among members of the Sino-Soviet bloc, Washington incorrectly assumed its unity and that either Moscow or Beijing was in control of other Communist states' foreign policy.

The 'Center' and the 'Provinces'

Once this overseas empire was created, its preservation became a critical task for the United States. Pericles, Athens' ruler during its war with Sparta, told his fellow citizens the empire "you hold is, to speak frankly, a despotism; perhaps it was wrong to take it, but to let it go is unsafe." Maintenance, however, demanded continuous vigilance and effort to protect these "frontiers," across several thousand miles of ocean. Strategic deterrence has been the principal means of preventing a major incursion of Western Europe, as well as a strike against the continental United States. Limited challenges were met by a variety of means: attempted coercion in crises was countered by a mixture of military and diplomatic tactics, and actual frontier crossings by "frontier wars." Characteristically, these challenges have taken place far away from the center of power, the United States. These places are, of course, where frontiers meet and where the opponent finds it easiest to cause trouble and the defender finds it hardest to show resolution.

Because it is so distant, the frontier may not seem clearly related to security interests at the center; it is also nearer to the opponent and its defense may therefore involve great risks and expenditures. Indeed, such peripheral involvement may seem like an overextension of the center's power, which, it will be claimed, is not only dangerous but also expensive and unnecessary. Yet these frontiers have been guarded by America's armed forces, the Roman legions of our times. Occasionally in the former colonial areas of the world, the United States and the Soviet Union have agreed to allow UN forces, staffed primarily by nonaligned members, to keep the peace to avoid a superpower clash.

A key feature of the American role is the U.S. belief that the empire's maintenance depends upon its will to maintain it; the opponent must believe that the United States will honor its commitments. It follows that if commitments to maintain a particular frontier are no longer credible— no matter how distant or unimportant this frontier may seem to some—the adversary may decide that other frontiers too may be crossed with impunity. It may be true that one frontier is more vital than another, but how is the opponent to know which one? An adversary may see the failure to honor a commitment in one area as an indication that another commitment elsewhere may also not be honored and be tempted to test the defender's will. A commitment, whether eagerly sought or reluctantly accepted, therefore, becomes a matter from which it is very difficult to withdraw without dangerous consequences.

Conversely, America's allies and friends know that their defense depends upon the United States, and they are constantly alert to signs of a weakening will. Because they know that their defense may at times seem either hazardous or unimportant to their protector, they live in a continuous state of apprehension that they will be left undefended. Should that happen, they may well consider approaching the opponent and bargaining for the best terms possible. President John Kennedy observed that Soviet policy on Berlin was designed to neutralize West Germany as a first step toward the neutralization of Western Europe. If the United States did not meet its commitments in the divided city, it would mean the destruction of NATO, a dangerous situation for the whole world.

Although the "provinces" look to the center for protection, they do not see all imperial frontiers as equally important. Naturally, those in their particular area take priority. Fearful that the center's power may become overcommitted and weakened, they oppose the defense of other regional frontiers, as Europe has done repeatedly when the United States has become involved in Asia.

The last characteristic of the imperial power is that it commands and trains its foreign legions. NATO is always commanded by an American and has a highly centralized command structure and integrated forces. Only one of the provinces, France, has removed its forces, although it remains dependent upon the United States for its basic defense. When several of the provinces show concern for their self-protection by building nuclear forces, purportedly for use in situations they deem vital, but the center does not, the imperial power either tries to control these forces (Britain's) or opposes their development (France's). The provinces are not to decide when the empire will defend its interests and risk military conflict; these are for the center to decide. The United States also trains soldiers from non-Western states, some in America, some by sending military missions to these countries. Such a mission was present in South Vietnam. When the South Vietnamese army failed to deal effectively with the Communist Viet Cong guerrillas, the United States sent in its forces.

Vietnam as a 'Frontier War'

Reasons for U.S. Involvement

The United States became involved in Vietnam because to American leaders the seventeenth parallel dividing North Vietnam from South Vietnam represented a frontier between the free world and the Communist world. Just as they had decided to defend South Korea when North Korea crossed the thirty-eighth parallel, so they now decided to come to the assistance of the South Vietnamese. Like Korea, the Vietnam War was fought at a great distance from the center, in a place where the frontier was very accessible to the enemy.

But that was only the beginning of the problems for the United States. South Vietnam was a divided society; refugees from North Vietnam (approximately 1 million, about half of them Catholic) against indigenous South Vietnamese; Buddhists against Catholics; lowlanders against montagnards; and peasants against urban inhabitants. As in most new nations, loyalties were primarily local. Hostility to a central government was deeply ingrained because, as in most less-developed countries (LDCs), the government historically has been that of the colonial power, as represented by the tax collector and recruiting sergeant. Transportation and communication were primitive and industrial development nonexistent. In addition, this was a new state that had emerged from the 1954 Geneva conference that ended the First Indochina War between France and the Vietminh forces; it had no established political institutions and a precarious economy. Not surprisingly, the Vietminh expected South Vietnam to collapse. The Geneva agreement called for a general election in 1956, and Hanoi assumed that a majority of the 12 million South Vietnamese would vote for Ho Chi Minh, who had led the nationalist struggle against the French. Obviously he would have most of the North's 15 million votes, and the country would be reunited under Communist control.

Ho's popularity was the reason that neither the United States nor the new government in the South favored the election. The United States wanted the seventeenth parallel to be accepted as the new frontier, and the president of South Vietnam, Ngo Dinh Diem, a fervent Catholic and anti-Communist, wanted to stay in power. Their opposition was decisive, irrespective of whether the unsigned Geneva declaration mandating the election was politically binding. Hanoi's chances for a peaceful takeover of the South ended, and so did its stance of reasonableness and restraint. At the time of the Geneva settlement, approximately 5,000 to 6,000 local guerrillas, presumably the Vietminh's political and military elite, went underground and began to live like peasants. About 90,000 others went north; many were later infiltrated to South Vietnam. In 1959 the North Vietnamese began the armed struggle in the South. The Second Indochina War had started. The guerrillas' immediate objective was to isolate the central government from the majority of its population and substitute Viet Cong control over the peasantry by killing the government's local representatives.

This war, in short, started in a way quite different from the Korean War. Korea had begun with a clear-cut, aggressive attack, which aroused the American public and united the principal Western allies against the common threat. It had also been a conventional war in which regular Communist forces had been checked by regular South Korean, American, and UN troops. By contrast, the French defeat at Dienbienphu had been a decisive moment in contemporary history, for, it demonstrated that *guerrilla warfare* could win against a larger, stronger, conventionally equipped army of even a major power. An internal uprising of guerrillas, directed and organized by the North, was therefore a shrewder manner of "crossing" the seventeenth parallel. It would lend the resulting struggle the aura of a civil war, which would make it less likely that the United States would come to the assistance of South Vietnam because of American doubts about the morality and wisdom of becoming involved militarily in such a conflict. Diem's increasingly autocratic rule and his failure to enlist the support of his population, especially the peasantry, through political, social, and economic reforms helped prepare the ground for a successful guerrilla campaign and lent support to the view of the conflict as a civil war.

Another reason for involvement was that the war was seen in Washington as a test of its will, and meeting the test was believed to be necessary to maintain all frontiers. Until the non-Communist states of the area became more economically developed and possessed sufficient capabilities of their own, the Asian balance depended upon the United States. Commitments— and the administrations of Dwight Eisenhower, John Kennedy, and Lyndon Johnson all considered the United States to be committed to the defense of South Vietnam—were interdependent. The United States could not choose to defend West Berlin and Quemoy but not Matsu and South Korea. Washington believed that it could no more forgo the defense of the frontier in South Vietnam than in Greece and Turkey, in Western Europe and Berlin, or in Korea and Cuba. If one country fell it would, in its turn, knock down the next one and so on down the line like a row of dominoes; the political and psychological impact of an American pullout would be felt throughout the area, if not in other regions as well. As all commitments were viewed as interdependent, being unfaithful to one risked the collapse of all.

The assumptions underlying this perception were, of course, that the world was still bipolar and that the enemy was the Sino-Soviet bloc, which the United States continued to perceive as united, despite increasing evidence to the contrary. Signs of differences between the Soviet Union and China were generally explained as tactical differences on how the "Communist world" ought to wage its "war" against the United States, not as fundamental conflicts of national interests between the two powers. Even if these had been recognized, it probably would not have made much difference because "Red China" with its population approaching 1 billion and its revolutionary rhetoric denouncing "American imperialism" was viewed by Washington as far more militant and dangerous than Moscow. Ho Chi Minh and the Viet Cong were seen as puppets of China, applying Mao Zedong's guerrilla warfare tactics to destroy a non-Communist government in a country within the American sphere of influence. If they succeeded, Vietnam would be added to China's power and thus to the Sino-Soviet bloc's power; it would also be an example to other revolutionary forces in Asia and elsewhere that the United States, despite its nuclear weapons, could be defeated. Washington saw the North's war against the South as aggression similar to North Korea's against South Korea, even if North Vietnamese forces had not crossed the seventeenth parallel. Guerrilla warfare was just another variant of Communist aggression and therefore had to be defeated.

There was a double irony to this pattern of thinking. First, had the United States had diplomats in Beijing, they would have known that North Vietnam was not a puppet; that historically, China and Vietnam often had been enemies; and that in the early 1960s China was in the midst of a domestic upheaval and that the last thing Mao, who was purging all whom he considered insufficiently revolutionary, would want to do was to risk a confrontation with the United States. As with China's earlier intervention in Korea, the United States again paid a high price for not recognizing the mainland regime. Second, if the containment of China was a key goal of the U.S. intervention, U.S. policy should have let South Vietnam fall. Because Ho was a nationalist, not just a Communist, and a united Communist and nationalistic Vietnam would have proven a stronger barrier to any possible Chinese ambitions of hegemony in Southeast Asia than a non-Communist South Vietnam governed by an unpopular regime.

Instead, the Vietnam War, undertaken in the name of containment, undermined containment. It involved the United States against an enemy in an area of only secondary interest in a war that lasted eight years and wasted enormous resources. The beneficiary of this effort was the Soviet Union, the United States' primary enemy, which focused *its* resources on first catching up and then surpassing the United States in missiles. Because of the popular backlash to the war and to military spending, the United States fell behind in the strategic buildup during the 1970s. Indeed, South Vietnam was not the key domino that fell; that was American public opinion.

The Incremental Intervention

Yet, in a way, the U.S. intervention in Vietnam was by 1965 inevitable, and from the administration of Harry Truman to that of Richard Nixon, every president deepened the involvement in Vietnam. Although Truman at first opposed France's postwar efforts to restore its colonial rule, he changed his position to overcome French resistance to the American plan for the revival of Germany, especially its rearmament. After the Korean War erupted, the French war in Indochina became part of the global struggle against communism. At the time of France's defeat at Dienbienphu in 1954, Eisenhower, although deciding not to intervene militarily, backed the new government in South Vietnam, organized after France's defeat and withdrawal, with economic assistance and military training for its armed forces. This training was in orthodox warfare, not in the unorthodox or guerrilla warfare that had already been observed in Vietnam. SEATO was supposed to be the new state's security guarantee. Kennedy escalated this commitment by sending in 16,500 military advisers to help the South Vietnamese army; starting in the spring of 1965, Johnson raised this number and changed the nature of the commitment by sending in 500,000 American troops.

Particularly significant during the years of piecemeal commitments was that at no point did policy makers in Washington ever ask themselves some fundamental questions about Vietnam: Was it vital to American security interests and, if so, how vital? Could the situation in South Vietnam be saved militarily, given the nature of the Saigon government and its seeming lack of popular support? If American forces should be sent, in what numbers? And how could they be effectively used in an unorthodox type of war? What cost, if any, was South Vietnam "worth"? As incremental commitments were made whenever conditions in South Vietnam appeared ominous, these questions were never really debated at the highest levels of the government. American commitments and credibility virtually foreclosed any debate except how, when, and how much force was needed to save South Vietnam.

During the Kennedy period, military advisers managed to prevent total collapse, but by 1965 Johnson—who, since Kennedy's assassination, had concentrated on passing a major domestic reform program and getting reelected—could no longer operate on this basis and avoid the central question of what the United States ought to do. South Vietnam was about to be cut in two, and the Viet Cong would then be in a position to mop up first one part, then the other. In the face of this reality, Johnson sent in 200,000 troops that year, extending U.S. involvement and turning an incremental policy into a long-term commitment. After years and years of neglect and procrastination and with the situation growing worse daily, Washington had neither the time nor the inclination to make a carefully calculated basic decision; when the crucial decision was made, it was made by Johnson, a new president—whose primary interests, experience, and skill were domestic—on the advice of the Kennedy staff and cabinet he had inherited. Long-range policy had become the prisoner of a number of earlier short-range decisions that had been made to tackle crises. Johnson's misfortune was that he could not procrastinate or make more piecemeal moves. He was stuck with the decision whether to escalate to prevent the defeat of the South Vietnamese army or be, as he phrased it, the first president in U.S. history "to lose a war." Each president had done just enough to prevent this defeat. Johnson's escalation was the logical culmination of his predecessor's decisions.

One critical problem that also made the U.S. commitment inevitable was domestic politics. The Democrats, having been accused of losing China, were not about to risk losing Indochina. Until Kennedy's election, they had been out of power for eight years and wanted to stay in control of the White House. But more was at stake than control of the presidency. The earlier charges of being "soft on communism" and "selling China down the river" had undermined Truman's foreign policy and domestic agenda even before he left office. Johnson did not want to jeopardize his foreign agenda and, even more important to him, the Great Society domestic reform program, by being embroiled in a vicious partisan dispute over "who lost Indochina." The Democrats' sensitivity to such accusations and their determination to avoid them was obviously strong. Even Eisenhower, a conservative Republican president and the victorious general who had led the Western Allies to victory over Germany—a man who could not be accused of disloyalty—had felt sufficiently threatened by the Republican right that in 1954 he did not pull the United States out of Vietnam. He kept America in Vietnam by supporting the new South Vietnamese government. Each president thought each step in the growing involvement in Indochina to be less costly than doing nothing and disengaging from Vietnam. In the context of U.S. politics, defeat was believed to be unacceptable. The costs of nonintervention in terms of the loss of public and congressional support were calculated to be much higher than the costs of intervention.

The Misconduct of Counterguerrilla Warfare

The United States virtually ignored the political structure of South Vietnam, which was the key to the successful use of American arms. For years the United States had supported Diem, a devout Catholic, whose increasingly authoritarian rule and aloofness from the mainly Buddhist population had alienated most of it. By the time the military overthrew and murdered Diem, with Kennedy's knowledge and tacit blessing, the Viet Cong already controlled much of South Vietnam; the social, political, and economic reforms needed to win the war had been neglected too long. That the United States had acquiesced in the coup against Diem should have alerted future administrations; that Kennedy had said Diem had "gotten out of touch with the people" testified to the political bankruptcy in Saigon, as well as to the questionable wisdom of having begun the military intervention in the first place. Even with Diem gone, South Vietnam's governments were unable to rally popular support for a vigorous prosecution of the war against the Viet Cong. But Saigon's succession of corrupt, reactionary, and repressive regimes apparently never reawakened thoughts in the minds of U.S. policy makers of Jiang Gaishek and his Nationalist government in postwar China.

At the time of China's fall the Truman administration had decided China could not be saved, except perhaps—and it was only *perhaps*—with enormous military and economic costs, which it felt the American public would not be willing to pay. In addition, these costs would have diverted the nation's resources and efforts from its area of primary interest in Europe where American security was at stake. In Secretary of State Dean Acheson's words, as noted before: "Nothing that this country did or could have done within the *reasonable* limits of its capabilities" could have changed the result in the conflict between Mao Zedong and Jiang Gaishek.[1] In short, containment could not be achieved through a sieve. By attempting containment in South Vietnam, Truman's successors in Democratic administrations risked major domestic discontent. They also risked a public questioning of the fundamental assumptions of American postwar foreign policy that had led to the war.

Guerrillas and Social Strategy

Certainly, the possibility of achieving a quick victory over the Viet Cong was remote, for a guerrilla war is totally different from traditional Western warfare. The militarily weaker side resorts to guerrilla tactics because it has no other options. The aim of a guerrilla war is to capture the government from within and to do so by eroding the morale of the army and by undermining popular confidence in the government. To achieve this objective, it is not necessary to inflict a complete defeat on the government's forces or to compel them to surrender unconditionally. Indeed, until the final stage of the war, guerrillas do not even meet these forces openly, and then they do so only to apply the *coup de grâce*. Guerrilla war is therefore a protracted conflict in which the guerrillas use hit-and-run tactics—here, there, everywhere—and engage only those smaller and weaker government forces they can defeat. To cope with this strategy, year in and year out, the government troops must be dispersed to guard every town, every hamlet, and every bridge against possible attack. Unable to come to real grips with the enemy and defeat it in battle, and suffering one small loss after another, the army becomes demoralized and its mood defensive.

Although such tactics gradually weaken the military strength of the army, the guerrillas' main effort is directed at the civilian population. As the weaker side, the guerrillas aim to wrest the allegiance of the population from the government, and, without popular support, the government simply collapses. The guerrillas do this in two ways. First, by increasing their control of the countryside, where most of the people live, and by winning battles with government forces, they demonstrate to the peasants that the government cannot protect them. The execution of the village headmen, who are generally

---

1. Department of State, *United States Relations with China* (Washington, D.C.: Government Printing Office, 1949), xvi. Italics added.

government representatives, or of other people who may have helped the government forces proves this most vividly. Second, and even more important, the guerrillas exploit any existing popular grievances. Communist guerrillas do not pose as Communists, and they do not usually receive support because they are Communists. The populace supports them because it believes the guerrillas will oust the government with which it is dissatisfied and that a new government will meet its aspirations.

Mao said that guerrillas need the people as fish need water; without popular support, the guerrillas would not receive recruits, food, shelter, and information on the government forces' disposition. Unlike conventional warfare, in which each army seeks the destruction of the other's military forces, guerrillas seek the support of the people. A government that has the allegiance of its population does not provide fertile soil for guerrillas; where social dissatisfaction exists, however, guerrillas find an opening. The guerrillas gain the support of the peasantry because they successfully represent themselves as the liberators from colonialism or foreign rule, native despotic governments, economic deprivation, or social injustice. In this way, they isolate the government in its own country.

Counterguerrilla war is therefore not a purely military war but a political war as well. Although the government under attack must try to defeat the guerrillas in the field, its principal task is to tackle the political, social, and economic conditions that bred the support for the guerrillas. Fundamentally, counterguerrilla warfare is an extremely difficult and sophisticated form of war to wage—far more so than the traditional clash of armies—because the war cannot be won without thoroughgoing reforms. Yet these reforms have to be carried out in the midst of battle. Such a war is also likely to take years; five to ten years is not at all unusual. And finally, it takes approximately fifteen counterguerrilla fighters to one guerrilla—in short, a sizable army, and one trained in counterguerrilla tactics.

What all this means is that the United States finds such a war extremely difficult to fight. America likes its wars "strictly military." A war that is concerned primarily with social and political reforms runs completely counter to the American approach. The war's length would also cause great frustration, because the United States likes to get its "boys home by Christmas." If this new kind of warfare did not yield swift and successful results, the American temptation would be either to pull out or to seek a shortcut to victory by purely military action.

The Military Battlefield: Vietnam

American policy makers misplaced their confidence in the nation's military prowess and its ability to change the guerrillas' "rules of the game." In 1965 the illusion of American omnipotence had not yet died. Had not the United States successfully confronted the Soviet Union in Cuba and compelled it to back down? Could there really be much doubt that its well-trained generals in command of armies equipped with the newest and latest weapons from America's industry and under the leadership of that most efficient Pentagon manager, Secretary of Defense Robert McNamara, could beat a few thousand "peasants in black pajamas"? With its sizable forces and its superior mobility and firepower, could not America find the enemy's troops and destroy them, compelling that enemy to desist from taking over South Vietnam? Characteristically, then, the emphasis was strictly military.

In Vietnam, the war required forces to secure villages and to stay in them to root out the Viet Cong cells and show the villagers that Saigon did care about them. Instead, the military carried out massive search-and-destroy operations. The guerrillas, even if driven away from the villages, returned after the helicopters had left and continued to control the countryside. Because such large-scale operations could not be launched without preparation at the base camp and were usually preceded by airstrikes and artillery bombardments of the area in which the troops would land, the Viet Cong often disappeared and the whole operation ended in frustration.

American military men clearly did not understand the political nature of counterguerrilla war. They had been trained for conventional battle, and their strategy was to use maximum firepower to wear the enemy down in a war of attrition. The military was confident it could do this because its helicopters provided superior mobility and modern technology gave it the necessary firepower. The measure of success became the daily body count of Communist dead. The war was also extended by air to the North. The purpose of bombing the North was clearly not military, although the United States claimed its purpose was to stem the flow of men and supplies coming south. Guerrillas can live off the land and capture many of their weapons from their enemies; in any case, the sustained American attacks on Chinese supply lines in North Korea during the Korean War had shown that air power alone was unable to stop the flow of supplies to the fighting zone. The aim of the attacks was political—to persuade North Vietnam to stop the war. The gradual extension of these attacks was intended to stress that the United States meant to protect South Vietnam and would not withdraw, that the price Hanoi might have to pay for victory would be disproportionately costly, and therefore that it had better desist.

But the bombing did not weaken Hanoi's will to prosecute the war, nor did it cut the supplies sufficiently to hamper the fighting in the South or greatly reduce troop infiltration. Hanoi's persistence, in turn, led to increased military and political calls for more air strikes and new targets. Those who advocated increasing the air war did not acknowledge that air power could not by itself win the war; rather, they insisted that it could, if it were used with maximum efficiency. Air power, in short, came to be seen by some as an immaculate way of fighting the guerrillas, of efficiently inflicting great destruction on them, throttling their supply lines, breaking their morale, and finally compelling them to end the conflict at little cost in lives.

This objective, however, remained unattainable. Even the more stable military regime of Nguyen Van Thieu and Nguyen Cao Ky, which sought to legitimate itself in the election of 1967, failed to implement a program of social and economic reform. It was particularly remiss in not carrying out a necessary redistribution of land from the usually absentee landlord to the peasant. Without such reforms, the Viet Cong grew stronger. Militarily, every increase of American forces was met by increased infiltrations of both guerrillas and conventional troops from the North to the South. Nevertheless, the U.S. government issued optimistic battle reports and forecasts of victory on a regular basis.

The 1968 Tet (or Vietnamese New Year) offensive was the Johnson administration's Dienbienphu. Tet showed once and for all—and Americans could see it nightly on their television sets—that, despite the repeated optimistic predictions, the enemy had again been badly underestimated. It had launched a major countrywide offensive and attacked Saigon, Hué, and every other provincial capital; a Viet Cong squad had even penetrated the American Embassy compound, thereby scoring a significant symbolic victory. Above all, the Viet Cong had clearly demonstrated that neither an American army of a half-million men nor the far larger South Vietnamese army could give the people living in the urban areas security—and the Communists already controlled much of the countryside.

The Political Battlefield: The United States

American power and its effectiveness in unorthodox warfare were shown to be greatly exaggerated. Tactically, American forces had seized and retained the offensive, claiming the destruction of large numbers of enemy soldiers. But strategically the Viet Cong had maintained the upper hand, and the Americans were on the defensive. And by using about 80 percent of their forces to find and destroy North Vietnamese troops in the relatively unpopulated central highlands and frontier regions, they were unable to secure *and* protect the 90 percent of the population living in the Mekong Delta and coastal plains. The pursuit of victory through physical attrition could not be transformed into military or political advantages. Indeed, in question was not just America's protective capacity but also its wisdom. Having left the cities unprotected, except for elements of the South Vietnamese army (Tet dramatically revealed Saigon's impotence), allied forces then had to fight their way back into the hearts of the various cities and towns the Viet Cong had infiltrated. If, after almost three years of American help, South Vietnam was still that insecure and the enemy that strong, the wisdom of continuing the war, let alone sending further American reinforcements, was bound to be intensely debated.

This was particularly so because so many Americans perceived the war to be morally ambiguous, if not downright immoral. There had never been a clear-cut crossing of the seventeenth parallel dividing North Vietnam and

South Vietnam, which made less believable the accusation that Hanoi was an aggressor. The undemocratic nature of Saigon's government and its apparent lack of popularity gave credence to the view of the war as a rebellion or civil war against Saigon's repression. (Interestingly, in 1950, the South Korean government had a similar autocratic reputation, but the attack across the thirty-eighth parallel focused attention on North Korean ambitions and justified the American intervention. No one in the United States raised questions about defending a "corrupt dictatorship.") The massive, sometimes indiscriminate, use of American firepower, leading to widespread destruction of civilian life and property; the creation of thousands of refugees; and, reportedly, the hostility of the peasants, upon whose support military success depended, had already pricked the conscience of many Americans concerned with their nation's historic image as a compassionate and humane country. The tanks rumbling into cities after Tet, the divebombing of apartment houses, the civilian suffering and personal tragedies left television viewers asking themselves if there was any point in "destroying a country in order to defend it."

Within the United States, the Tet offensive coalesced the opposition that had been growing throughout 1967 as the war continued, seemingly without end. Johnson's initial support eroded on both the right and the left, with the right demanding an end to the war through escalation and the left through deescalation, if not withdrawal. (Sometimes, in fact, the same people held both views.) The articulate opposition to the conflict by a number of liberal and moderate Republican and Democratic senators, especially the chairman of the Senate Foreign Relations Committee, J. William Fulbright, made the opposition of many politicians, professors, students, journalists, editorial writers, and television commentators respectable instead of "un-American." Indeed, after Tet, Fulbright and his committee became an alternative source of interpretation and policy recommendations to the president. Although the Viet Cong was virtually destroyed during the Tet fighting, so that the North Vietnamese army took over the fighting almost completely, the United States suffered a political defeat. The guerrilla strategy of *psychologically exhausting* the opponent had been successful. The American strategy of *physical attrition* was the wrong strategy. The military won all the battles, but lost the war as the public grew tired of it.

The Vietnam War involved two battlefields. The first, in Vietnam, was bloody but inconclusive. The second, in the United States, was not bloody, but it was decisive. As the war dragged on, the nation's will to continue it declined. In a total war like the two world wars, when the United States sensed its security, if not its survival, was at stake, all issues were subordinated to the prosecution of the war. In a limited war, important issues may be at stake, but the security threat to the United States may not be apparent. How could the loss of South Korea or South Vietnam diminish U.S. security? Neither North Korea nor North Vietnam could invade the United States. During hostilities, politics go on as usual, with most domestic interest groups pursuing their interests and preferences; butter is not automatically subordinated to guns. But, as the costs of the conflict rise in terms of lives, inflation, and taxes, public disaffection also grows.

The guerrillas were well aware of the two battlefields and of which one was more important. North Vietnam's General Vo Nguyen Giap, the strategist behind its victories against France and the United States, spoke of the impatience of democracies at war. He saw that a strategy in which the war seemed never to end, in which the minimum purpose was simply not to lose, would eventually erode the opponents' will to continue. As the war dragged on, as the casualties and costs mounted, the democracies would throw in the towel. It was their "home fronts" that were decisive, where the "real battle" would be won. The Tet offensive was deliberately launched as the 1968 political primaries were about to begin in the United States, where opposition to the war had become widespread.

Disagreement over the war led two senators from the president's party, Eugene McCarthy and Robert Kennedy, to contest Johnson's renomination as the Democratic standard-bearer. Running as "peace candidates," they provided a rallying point for the growing numbers of Americans disenchanted with the war. Then, in March 1968, at the end of the speech that laid the basis for the Paris peace talks, the president announced that he would not run for a second term. Lyndon Johnson's tragedy was that he had come into office seeking a great society in America; instead the war destroyed him. The changing American mood was evident in the 1968 campaign. Vice President Hubert Humphrey, nominated in Chicago after bloody clashes between police and antiwar students (many of them McCarthy supporters) and bitter disagreement among the delegates over the Vietnam platform, was mercilessly heckled during most of the campaign. As a member of the administration, he found it difficult to disavow the war; when he took his own "risk for peace," it was very late in the campaign.

In these circumstances of Democratic disunity, former vice president Nixon, a long-time hawk, found it inexpedient to charge the Democrats with a "no-win" policy; instead he softened his views on the war. Indeed, in his speeches the menace abroad suddenly ran a poor second to the "moral decay" at home. Generally, both candidates fell over themselves in their eagerness to abandon both anti-Communist slogans and the war, offering instead hopes for an "honorable" peace in Vietnam and for "law and order" at home. Halting Communist aggression was abandoned as an issue; stopping further costly foreign adventure—"no more Vietnams"—became the issue. In Vietnam, the only question was when to get out and on what terms. By not losing, the North Vietnamese had won; by not winning, the United States had indeed lost.

A New Mood of Withdrawal

The United States was weary, disillusioned, and ready to retreat from its imperial role. This mood manifested itself in the attempt to curb presidential power in foreign policy, especially the power as commander-in-chief to commit American forces to battle. Under the Constitution, the president is chiefly responsible for the conduct of foreign policy, which made the office the target of those opposed to these policies. During the 1950s the conservatives had wished to limit presidential authority because the president was, in their minds, not anti-Communist enough and might, acting on the advice of the "pro-Communists" in the State Department, sell the country down the river. Starting in the late 1960s the liberals sought to restrain the president's authority because, in their opinion, the president, the military-industrial complex, and the Central Intelligence Agency (CIA) supporting him were too anti-Communist and were intent on involving the country in too many costly adventures abroad.

Conservative or liberal, the remedy for the "imperial presidency's" alleged abuse of its authority and its virtually solo determination of foreign policy was identical: to reassert the control of Congress in the formulation of external policy and to restore the constitutional balance that purportedly had been upset. The president presumably would be restrained so that, for conservatives, he would no longer be able to "appease" America's enemies or, for liberals, be able to act in an interventionist, warlike manner. The abuse of power by Nixon, a conservative president who resigned his office rather than be impeached, reinforced the liberal sentiment to curb presidential powers and compel a more restrained and moderate policy.

A second symptom of the new mood was that priority should be paid to the nation's domestic problems. These problems became apparent when in the 1960s the affluent society began to reveal its seamier and more violent sides, such as urban slums, air and water pollution, and the dissatisfaction of the poor, who were primarily those discriminated against by society—blacks, Puerto Ricans, Indians, Chicanos, and Orientals. Critics of the war wanted to spend money to improve the quality of life for all American citizens and prevent the fabric of their society from being torn apart. Instead of crusading for democracy abroad, they argued, the United States should start crusading to make *America* safe for democracy. Liberal critics of the war in Vietnam quoted Edmund Burke to the effect that "example is the school of mankind, and they will learn at no other." The example should be one of a free society enjoying its freedom fully.

These blessings could not be fully realized in a nation whose excessive preoccupation with foreign affairs drained its powers and resources, both human and material. A "strong" foreign policy was unlikely to bring with it any lasting greatness, prestige, and security; rather, the constant expenditure of energy in foreign adventures would ruin the domestic base. The cold war preoccupation was corrupting the nature of American society. Institutional imbalance was eroding constitutional processes, particularly when powerful and energetic presidents, in the name of national security, not only committed the nation to war but also appeared to sanction plots to assassinate foreign leaders such as Fidel Castro (with Mafia help), lied to the American people and Congress about what they were doing or why they were doing it (intervention in Vietnam), acted covertly (bombing Cambodia secretly for years), and in various ways violated the constitutional rights of some American citizens. And the large-scale devotion of the country's financial and intellectual resources to its external commitments meant a corresponding neglect of domestic issues. Extensive involvement in the world, in short, was tainting the American promise and vision; the priority of foreign over domestic policy had to be ended. This idea had always been at the heart of the old isolationism: America could only take care of its own needs, serve as an example for mankind, and remain pure in a morally wicked world if it stayed out of or minimized its political involvement in it. The consequence of assuming an active role internationally was to endanger American democracy, instead of protecting it.

Perhaps the most revealing symptom of America's reaction to Vietnam was the reassertion of the deep-seated attitude toward the exercise of power internationally as immoral and corrupting. Once power politics could no longer be justified in moral terms of democracy versus dictatorship, as in the two world wars, the sense of guilt over using power returned. Vietnam seemed to prove that in the exercise of power the nation had forsaken its moral traditions and violated its own democratic and liberal ideals. Not surprisingly, sensitive people deeply committed to human values—and daily watching the exercise of power in the form of violence in history's first televised war—repented their former support of containment-through-power as if in giving that support they had been unwitting sinners. Fulbright, who had been a leading advocate of postwar foreign policy while it could be disguised as a moral conflict, now attacked America's global role as evidence of an "arrogance of power."[2] He did not merely assert that the United States had overextended itself and that its commitments needed to be cut down to its capacities. Nor did he say that Vietnam had been an unwise commitment, although the basic policy of containment had been a correct one. He stated something far more fundamental: that all great powers seem to have a need to demonstrate that they are bigger, better, and stronger than other nations and that it was this arrogance of power, from which the United States now suffered, which was the real cause of international conflict and war.

In brief, it was the exercise of power *per se* that, regardless of a nation's intentions, made it arrogant. Power itself is a corrupting factor; even if justified in moral terms, its use is immoral except in clear unambiguous cases

---

2. J. William Fulbright, *The Arrogance of Power* (New York: Vintage Books, 1967).

of self-defense. No idea could have been more characteristically American. Power is evil and its exercise is tantamount to the abuse of power; abstention from power politics, providing an example to the world of a truly just and democratic society, is a more moral policy. America should be loved for its principles and for practicing what it professes, rather than feared for its might. Democracy and power politics were simply incompatible.

The questioning of the imperial center's role manifested itself in other ways and in other places. In both NATO and the Sino-Soviet alliance the key issue was the center's dominant position and the manner in which it exercised authority. Vietnam disillusioned many Europeans with U.S. leadership of NATO at a time when the Europeans were asserting their right to play a more equitable role within the alliance. The resulting conflicts reflected not so much that the United States did not want to share power, but that the Europeans, although unwilling to accept a subordinate status, had not decided what their political aims should be beyond ensuring the commitment of American power to their defense. After two world wars and the loss of their colonies, they felt vulnerable and preferred to focus their energies on domestic affairs and economic growth. They rejected taking the primary responsibility for their own defense, an issue that was to become especially important and divisive from the 1970s on.

Nevertheless, while quarrelling, the alliance did manage to hold together. The Communist alliance did not. Mainland China, unified, led by a new vigorous leadership that was both highly nationalistic as well as Communist, was in a more assertive mood and determined to play an important political role in Asia and a key role in the Communist world. But as the Communist "Rome," the leading state and interpretor of Marxist-Leninist doctrine, Moscow was unwilling to share its authority. The result was the gradual erosion of the Sino-Soviet bloc.

The European-American Conflict

Having committed its wealth and manpower to their defense, the United States considered the states of Europe, particularly the continental states, ungrateful, because during the 1960s they increasingly questioned America's authority to speak for the alliance. But the NATO partners had good reason for doing so. The European nations had recovered and had become economic competitors; their rapid progress toward integration still held the possibility that someday Europe would emerge as a superpower. To be sure, this union might not turn out to be the federation originally envisaged; it was becoming clear that the establishment of a United States of Europe would not emerge automatically. During the 1960s, President Charles de Gaulle of France opposed a union in which the Six would lose their individual identities. He sought instead a "Europe of Fatherlands" in which each country would retain its power, but all would coordinate their political policies through regular meetings of the heads of state and other ministers. But whichever Europe might emerge, it was no longer the weak, divided, and demoralized continent of 1945.

Europe had been almost powerless when NATO was formed. The imbalance of power within the alliance resulting from Europe's virtually exclusive reliance upon the United States for its defense had placed Europe in a subordinate position. Washington's voice had been the voice of the alliance. For example, West Germany was rearmed over the objections of the French, although some accommodations were made to assure French security. Britain and France were obliged to give up their interests at Suez because the United States opposed them. Final decisions were made in Washington and were based on what the United States defined as the West's vital interests. But once the Europeans had recovered economically, they wanted a greater voice in the determination of NATO's political and strategic policies; they no longer accepted their subordinate status.

European Fears

Much of their concern revolved around their fear of abandonment. As the United States became more vulnerable to Soviet attack, the Europeans wondered if they could continue to rely on American protection. Without sufficiently large and credible nuclear forces of their own, their national security was entirely in American hands. But, as Soviet intercontinental missile forces grew, what would happen if the Soviets made demands considered vital by the Europeans but not by Washington? Could the small British or French strategic force be relied upon to deter the Soviet Union?

The U.S. management of the Berlin crises from 1958 to 1962 had not re-assured them—especially France and West Germany—of Washington's steadfastness as its risks and costs of defending the alliance rose. At the same time, they were well aware of their weaknesses and vulnerability and dependence on the United States. De Gaulle was especially vigorous in articulating the need for Western Europe to define its own interests and sustain them. His theme was that Europe must learn to stand on its own feet once again. He proposed the French-German alliance as the core of the new Europe.

The fact was that the Western alliance also reflected the different geographic position of the partners and historical roles played by the United States and Europe in the postwar period. Since 1945 each of the major European countries, including Great Britain, had relinquished or been divested of its colonies until, by 1960—with only a few relatively minor exceptions—their role outside of Europe had come to an end. By contrast, during this same period the United States had become a global power. At a time when its allies were looking inward, concentrating on their economic growth and groping toward a larger political organization and identity, the

United States found that it had to deal with those areas of the world in which the European powers had previously played the key roles. During the Korean War, Britain, France, Turkey, and the Netherlands had sent forces to show their solidarity with the United States; the United States fought in Vietnam without its allies. Britain's declining role in the eastern Mediterranean and the Middle East had compelled the United States to play an increasingly greater role there, a role that grew after Britain withdrew from "east of Suez" in the early 1970s. As former great powers, the Europeans naturally resented their rapid postwar decline in prestige and status and their dependence upon a vigorous, self-confident and, in their eyes, youthful and often impetuous newcomer who might disregard their counsel—advice that, the Europeans felt, was based upon greater experience and wisdom.

But if a sense of dependence and the fear of abandonment were driving U.S. allies in Europe, they also feared entrapment. The Europeans were deeply concerned over the diversion of U.S. resources and attention away from them during the Korean and Vietnamese wars. They also worried that the United States, in its new global role, might involve them in an all-out war resulting from a confrontation, such as the Cuban missile crisis, or from an escalation of a limited conflict, such as the Vietnam War. While the Europeans worried about U.S. recklessness, the United States resented their lack of political sympathy and support for its ventures outside of Europe. This feeling deepened U.S. disappointment over the failure of the Europeans to play a far greater role in their own defense.

The European 'Revolt'

The European "revolt" against American hegemony revolved largely around the issue of nuclear weapons, which have played a triple role within NATO: as the symbol of great power status; as a means of influencing U.S. policy by contributing to American strategy, so heavily dependent on nuclear weaponry; and as a means of defense. But the United States was not willing to surrender its primacy in nuclear weapons. Washington's concern was that the diffusion of these weapons would increase the opportunities for accidents and miscalculations and might trigger a nuclear war. For almost two decades the United States had possessed the power to determine an issue on which Europeans might have to die; but now that France, for example, could make a similar decision for Americans, the United States balked.

What this meant was that the issue of more than "one finger on the trigger" became central in the American-European partnership. The internal cohesion of NATO's "entangling alliance," and the external security the alliance provided for its members, were thus weakening under the pressure of this ominous question: How does an alliance preserve its unity when each major crisis poses the risk that actions by one member may precipitate a nuclear holocaust for an issue that the other members may not consider worth so high a price?

Washington, particularly during the Kennedy years, had insisted on maintaining its nuclear superiority and with it the key to war and peace. One of the principal ways it sought to do so was by supporting Britain's bid to join the new Europe. British membership, it was hoped, would mean that one of the leaders of the resurgent Europe would be the United States' close friend and would act as the spokesperson for the American point of view. This would result in a more harmonious American-European relationship. Britain had already built a nuclear deterrent and, unlike France, whose atomic development was vigorously opposed by the United States, Britain had received extensive U.S. help. Britain's reasons for developing a deterrent were exactly the same as those stated by France, namely, to gain prestige, security, and particularly a political voice in Washington. Indeed, the "special relationship" between a nuclear Washington and a nuclear London was one reason why France wanted these weapons.

But continental Europe no longer recognized Britain's leadership. Throughout the 1950s—before de Gaulle—it had been somewhat suspicious of the intentions of America's junior partner. Since the end of World War II, Britain had stayed out of all European integration schemes for two main reasons: first, because it considered its close ties with the Commonwealth and, more generally, its global interests to be incompatible with integration into Europe; and second, to preserve its special position as America's closest ally. The only European organizations Britain had joined were those that committed America to Europe.

Britain's status, however, continued to deteriorate. The Commonwealth, traditionally an economic outlet for British goods and, in this respect, Britain's common market, was buying less and less from Britain. It either manufactured what it needed or bought more cheaply from the United States or Common Market countries. Also, by the early 1960s, after its searing experience in Suez, Britain had begun to realize the advantages of a European political union. Increasingly, in the scale of world powers, London's voice would be heard less and less in comparison to those of Washington, Moscow, Brussels (the new Europe's "capital"), and Beijing; nations would pay principal attention to these centers of power, not to a comparatively feeble London. But when Britain sought entry into Europe, de Gaulle and German chancellor Konrad Adenauer were suspicious. They feared that if Britain maintained its special relationship with the United States, continental Europe would remain subordinate in an Anglo-American dominated alliance.

The crucial task for Britain, therefore, was to prove its loyalty to the Europe it had shunned at the founding of the European Coal and Steel Community (ECSC), the European Defense Community (EDC), and the European Economic Community (EEC). This is exactly what Britain failed to do. Confronted by a choice between the Commonwealth and Europe, Britain preferred the Commonwealth. And when forced to choose between

Europe and the United States, it chose the latter when offered U.S. Polaris missiles for its nuclear submarines and warheads. De Gaulle vetoed Britain's entry in January 1963.

Thus, by the mid-1960s, the members of NATO had arrived at a critical point in their relationship. On the one hand, the United States retained its preeminent position in the alliance, reflecting its superior conventional power, its overwhelming nuclear strength, and, starting in the 1960s, its economic influence in Europe. American business, with its immense amounts of capital and technical and marketing skills, wished to profit from the Common Market by establishing industries behind its tariff barrier. The United States had a technological lead in computers, electronics, space, and rocketry. Although in later years American-owned industries in Europe accounted for no more than 5 percent of the total business activity in any one country, they were concentrated in a few highly technological sectors, such as chemicals and oil, that not only shaped the contemporary economy but also tended to reshape the environment of the future.

On the other hand, in the mid-1960s the Europeans were seeking a more egalitarian relationship. Even the British government, which reapplied for Common Market membership in 1967, only to be turned down again by de Gaulle, had by then become more "European." Although a majority of the British public was opposed, the conservative government finally took the island-nation into the Europe whose division it had historically exploited to assure its own security. Together with Ireland and Denmark (Norway voted to stay out), Britain's 1973 entry changed the Europe of Six into the Europe of Nine. Whether this enlarged community would give new impetus to the movement for a political union remained to be seen; that was also true for whether it would result in a closer relationship with the United States or a more intense political competition and economic and financial rivalry. What was clear was that only a united Europe, economically vital and politically able to establish a European foreign policy and the military strength to support it, could balance American power in NATO, define European interests, and play a major role again in the world.

The alliance faced a dilemma. The United States did not oppose a more equal relationship per se; indeed, NATO's original purpose had been to protect Europe for twenty years to give it time to recover so that it could defend itself. During the 1940s and 1950s the United States was the producer of security; the Europeans, the consumers. America's European partners were less allies than wards. The dominance of the United States was a reflection of Europe's postwar weakness. As its global responsibilities grew, however, the United States wanted its allies to play a larger role in the defense of Europe and other parts of the world. During the Kennedy-Johnson years, the sought-after goal was an Atlantic community, composed of a genuine and equitable partnership between the United States and Europe.

Although they wanted more influence in the alliance, the Europeans remained opposed to playing a larger role, especially of relieving the United States of the main burden of Europe's defense. Western Europe's growing economic and financial strength had not yet been translated into political and military terms that looked much beyond Europe. Political unification, even cooperation on forming a joint European foreign policy, still seemed far off. The European countries remained preoccupied with their individual affairs. They had lost their empires, but not yet found a new role in the world. A relaxation of cold war tensions—a *détente*—was their preference.

The Sino-Soviet Conflict

Although *détente* did not blossom until 1972, it came about largely because of imaginative American statesmanship exploiting conflicts within the Communist bloc. Of these, the most important one was the dispute between the Soviet Union and China. This stemmed from the tendency of China, first, to assert its equality with the Soviet Union, and second, to take independent actions in foreign policy. That this assertion of China's independence might lead to a break with the Soviet Union became more likely as China began to take different stands on international issues with increasing frequency. For instance, in late 1959 and 1960, the Chinese acted in opposition to Soviet wishes. First, the Chinese crushed a revolt against their rule in Tibet. Perhaps because the Soviets remembered China's support in Hungary in 1956, they remained silent on Tibet. But they openly criticized China's dispute with India. The quarrel with India, which involved minor military skirmishes, concerned the precise location of the Sino-Indian frontier in the Himalayan mountains. This was a clear test of strength, and the Chinese were determined to press their point of view as a way of damaging the prestige of their main Asian rival. China's aggressiveness was a shock to Asia and hurt the Communist cause there. No one realized this more keenly than Nikita Khrushchev, and he made no attempt to hide his annoyance. Few things could have mattered less to him than a few square miles this way or that on the Indian-Chinese frontier. Compared with the need to make a favorable impression on the less-developed countries, this matter was picayune. The issue at stake was a triumph of communism throughout the formerly colonial world and a shift away from the West in the global balance of power.

The Chinese did not disagree; they just thought that the Communist victory must be won in a different way. The Soviet Union and China differed with increasing vehemence on this central issue of the proper strategy with which to win the global victory, and their "debate" focused on the two interrelated issues of war and peace and policy toward the leaders—the so-called national bourgeoisie—of the LDCs. The Soviet position was that in a nuclear war the Soviet Union would not only destroy its enemies, but also be destroyed; therefore, it wanted to avoid unnecessary risks by fostering cooperation between the superpowers on arms control.

Consequently, the main line of the Soviet attack upon the West had shifted to the Third World. The aim was obvious: the establishment of friendly political relations with the nationalist regimes, whose emotional dispositions were generally anti-Western. The Soviet Union tended to encourage their nonalignment (often a pro-Soviet nonalignment in fact, as, for example, Gamal Abdel Nasser's Egypt) in the cold war. This was clearly a tactical device. If the Soviet Union tried too hard to recruit them, the new nations might become alienated. An attitude of "if you're not with us, then you must be against us," an attitude Joseph Stalin and John Foster Dulles frequently had expressed, might drive these states back into the capitalist camp. If their neutrality were supported, however, their separation from the West might be widened, and world capitalism would be further weakened.

The Chinese Communists had a somewhat different point of view. They seemed more willing to risk war, perhaps because of their gigantic population. China could afford to lose 400 million to 500 million people, and still have a population of 200 million or more. No other country could survive such mammoth losses. "On the debris of a dead imperialism," Beijing had pronounced, "the victorious people would create very swiftly a civilization thousands of times higher than the capitalist system and a truly beautiful future for themselves." Moreover, unlike the Soviet Union, China did not have a large industrial establishment. China had less to lose in a total war.

At the same time, the Chinese had grown increasingly skeptical of aiding nationalist governments. Though often anti-Western, these governments were also bourgeois and, by nature, anti-Communist. Economic aid and technical assistance served to build up nations whose true colors would sooner or later come out. Consequently, the Chinese preferred to encourage local Communist parties to seize power. In any case, they held that the Soviet Union should channel its aid exclusively or primarily to Communist countries, especially to China.

These disagreements over tactics, however, exaggerated the differences between the two Communist powers. Beijing might speak of several hundred million Chinese surviving a nuclear attack, but it was also aware that such a war would endanger Communist control of the country. The Chinese might talk of constructing a superior postnuclear civilization, but they had also tried to avoid any major clash with the United States. In Korea, they had warned the United States several times not to advance to their frontier, and they finally intervened only for defensive reasons. In the Taiwan Straits, they had not invaded the offshore islands when the United States openly supported the Nationalist troops there. For all the Chinese leaders' militant talk, they had acted with great caution. And for all his talk of peaceful coexistence, it was Khrushchev who had threatened to attack London and Paris during Suez, who had precipitated the Berlin crisis, who had broken a moratorium on nuclear testing, and who had installed missiles in Cuba.

The real difference between the Soviets and the Chinese was not that one favored peace and the other desired war. Rather, the key issue that divided them was how much pressure should be exerted against the United States, how far Washington could be pushed before it would react. The answer determined both the opportunities that could be exploited and the consequences that might have to be suffered. If not much pressure were applied because of the high risks, then the gains would be small, if any, and this is why the Chinese charged the Soviets with a cowardice that led them to "kowtow" to the United States. If a great deal of pressure were exerted, the "profit" might also be far higher, but so were the risks, which was why the Soviets accused the Chinese of a recklessness that could end in suicide.

The issue of strategy toward the West and the LDCs, however, was closely related to the issue of leadership of the Communist bloc. The Soviets dominated the Communist world. As the capital of the first Communist-controlled nation, Moscow had since the early 1920s controlled the international Communist movement and formulated its policies. After World War II, it had established control over the states of Eastern Europe. Of these states, only Yugoslavia was not controlled by Moscow, but by its indigenous Communist party. When Yugoslavia resisted Stalin's efforts to impose control, it was ejected from Stalin's empire. Communist China's birth—another state controlled by the indigenous party—therefore represented a real problem for the Soviets. Potentially far more powerful than Yugoslavia, China was determined to be the Soviet Union's equal, not its subordinate, in the Communist bloc.

Beijing therefore had sought to share Moscow's authority to formulate bloc policies. But Khrushchev would have none of this. Moscow, like Washington, too long had defined the policies for its followers and had become a poor alliance manager. Instead of sharing authority with Beijing, Khrushchev acted as Stalin had—and ironically, he did so first on the issue of de-Stalinization! He had decided to de-Stalinize at home and within the bloc and expected China to adopt the same policy. Although the Chinese agreed with the policies, they were offended that Khrushchev pronounced policy for the entire Communist bloc without even bothering to consult them.

The debate over authority, then, was a key issue in the growing Sino-Soviet conflict. To this extent it was comparable to the conflict in the West, especially the Franco-American conflict. It was totally different in another respect: the Chinese and Soviets conducted their struggle in ideological terms. Because of this, the struggle held more ominous implications for the Communist bloc. Paradoxically, the very ideology that bound them together also divided them. On the one hand, Moscow and Beijing interpreted the world through the same ideological framework: communism provided them with a *Weltanshauung*. Both held the same view of man, society, and history. They saw world conflict in terms of class struggle and the final triumph of communism, and they defined capitalism as their common enemy.

On the other hand, precisely because of the intimate relationship between ideology and action, ideology, which defines the general purposes of the movement and provides the framework through which events in the world are analyzed, became a divisive factor. Moscow had long been the Communist "Rome," and the ruler in Moscow therefore became the Communist "pope" when he assumed power. If an ideology claimed to represent the truth, there could only be one correct interpretation and application of the doctrine. No ideological-theological movement can tolerate two popes. A schism—and a fight for the leadership of the movement—was inevitable. Hence, Moscow denounced Mao for having deserted Marxism-Leninism and, by fragmenting what had been a united Communist front against the United States, for having aided the devil's cause, imperialism. Denouncing the actions of the Soviet Communist party as "Khrushchevism without Khrushchev" after his overthrow, the Chinese charged that the party had been seized from within by "revisionists" who were in fact capitalists, cooperating with Washington to contain China! Beijing called for the overthrow of the Soviet leaders.

Mao attributed the caution of the Soviets toward the United States and their hostility toward China to the *embourgeoisement* of the Soviet leadership. He launched his Cultural Revolution in the mid-1960s to purify his nation and keep it loyal to the true Marxist-Leninist faith. Persons suspected of "taking the road back to capitalism," no matter what their position or function, were to be rooted out. Purges—especially by mobs of youths called Red Guards—were carried out against the army, government, industry, agriculture, even the party itself. The president of China and the general secretary of the party were among those deposed as the conflict raged on for several months.

The Sino-Soviet schism was, by the late 1960s, dramatically clear. The epithets hurled between Beijing and Moscow reached a ferocity unknown since the early days of the American-Soviet cold war. The Soviets called Mao "Hitler" and compared the Chinese with the Mongol hordes who overran Russia a millennium earlier; and the Chinese talked about the "Soviet revisionist clique" as a "dictatorship of the German fascist type," and quoted Karl Marx as saying that Russia's aim had been, and always would be, world hegemony. As the struggle against the Soviet Union intensified, Mao and his followers were more careful to avoid conflict with the United States. During Vietnam, for example, China continuously counseled Hanoi that revolutions had to be self-sufficient; it repeatedly stated that only an American attack on China would precipitate Beijing's intervention. In brief, North Vietnam should not and could not count on active Chinese help to help defeat American forces in South Vietnam. Rhetorically, Mao's policy was militantly anti-American, but it was restrained in fact. (U.S. policy makers never realized this however, and, thinking of the Korean War analogy, did not dare send U.S. forces into North Vietnam, the organizer of the war in the South.)

Even after Mao's death a complete Sino-Soviet reconciliation was impossible for, quite apart from any ideological issue, these two powers remained divided by the same issues that divided NATO: differences of power and of geographic position; different evaluations of international problems; and the obvious conflict between a power with global interests and an ally whose capabilities were essentially regional. The Soviet Union and China also had a long history of conflict that antedated their becoming Communist states and still affected the intensity of their antagonism. The Soviets held lands seized by the czars when China was a weak state, exploited by all the major Western powers, especially Russia. China wanted Moscow to acknowledge that these lands had been seized unfairly, but Moscow considered them Soviet, regardless of how or when they had been acquired. The two also had a number of clashes along their 4,500-mile border, the longest in the world. Both had heavily reinforced their troop strengths; the Soviet army, larger than the one in Eastern Europe, reportedly had large quantities of tactical nuclear weapons.

The Soviets even had to bargain with the East European "people's democracies" because, partly as a result of the Sino-Soviet conflict, these increasingly nationalistic states gained a degree of independence from Moscow in return for their support of Moscow against Beijing. Indeed, it was doubtful that most could any longer be called satellites. Their conflict with the Soviet Union, moreover, took on a dynamic of its own. Romania was the most defiant of the people's democracies, but, in 1968 Czechoslovakia was also moving rapidly toward greater independence. Soviet fears that Prague's domestic reforms would jeopardize the survival of communism in a country bordering on West Germany (Romania, which does not share a frontier with West Germany, is also, internally, a quite orthodox Communist regime) led to the Soviet army's intervention. Although this intervention reminded the East European nations of the limits of Soviet tolerance, they retained a greater degree of independence than they had during Stalin's reign. All have gained a measure of maneuverability, although the Soviet Union considers as final and nonnegotiable that Eastern Europe is in its sphere of control. However, the countries of Eastern Europe increasingly looked westward for economic-technological assistance. Concomitantly, they needed a relaxation of international tensions; a return of the cold war would reduce their links to the West and bring back greater Soviet control and intervention in their affairs. On the whole, therefore, they approved of the changing nature of American-Soviet relations from cold war to *détente,* which had started slowly after the Cuban missile crisis and which was to become more dramatically visible with the advent of the Nixon administration.

Toward *Détente*

After 1962 the United States and the Soviet Union sought a relaxation of tensions, and both had clear motives for doing so. For the United States, the two chief reasons were the assassination of President Kennedy and the country's increasing involvement and preoccupation with Vietnam. Johnson focused his attention on domestic problems. He did this in part because of the shock of the assassination and the need to calm the nation and provide continuity in the government. Domestic affairs also were a natural choice for him. A Texan, a devoted disciple of President Franklin Roosevelt, Johnson was determined to create what he called a Great Society for white and black Americans alike and, in the process, outdo Roosevelt in the achievement of social reforms. He had little experience or interest in foreign policy. His main interest in being elected to a full term was to have the opportunity to carry out his social program. Starting in 1964, however, the rapidly deteriorating situation in Vietnam began to compete for his attention and energy. As the U.S. intervention deepened and the protests against the war mounted, the conduct of the war became Washington's focus. Domestic politics were subordinated to foreign policy, which was more and more affected by public opinion as the war dragged on with no end in sight.

The Soviet Union also needed the cooling of American-Soviet relations. The humiliating withdrawal from Cuba in 1962 had been a major factor in the overthrow of Khrushchev by his disciple, Leonid Brezhnev, two years later. Brezhnev needed time to consolidate power and decide on the direction of Soviet domestic and foreign policies. More important, the Soviet leadership blamed its defeat in Cuba on the strategic superiority of the United States. The Soviets could not have risked escalating the conflict in Cuba by defying the ban on further missile shipments or even by making their missiles operational. With only 150 bombers of doubtful quality and 50 missiles against 1,300 U.S. bombers fully supported by air-refueling aircraft plus more than 200 missiles, Moscow would risk the Soviet Union's total destruction. Therefore, the principal task of the Brezhnev regime was a massive military buildup, which would last into the 1980s and include both strategic and conventional forces. When Brezhnev took over the reins of government, the Soviets possessed about 200 ICBMs. By the time Nixon assumed office in 1969, the Soviets had overtaken the United States in numbers of land- and sea-based missiles by 1,900 to 1,710; and, by the time of the first Strategic Arms Limitation Talks agreement (SALT I) in 1972, the figures stood at 2,350 and 1,710, respectively.

One of the first signs of the changing relationship between the superpowers, in fact, was the beginning of arms control talks. After the missile crisis, both sides were determined not to have another such incident. Among their first agreements were the limited test-ban treaty and the establishment of the hot line, which made it easier for the two powers to communicate at times of great tension and thereby reduce the possibilities of miscalculations. Johnson had also proposed that the superpowers talk to one another about their strategic forces. These SALT talks were scheduled to begin in 1968 but were postponed by the United States to protest the Soviet Union's invasion of Czechoslovakia.

But it is fair to add that the 1960s, which for the United States had started with a major victory in Cuba, ended in disaster with Vietnam. The Eisenhower administration, so stodgy in its appearance and apparently not very concerned by Soviet missile and space achievements (or with achieving racial equality in the United States), had seemed to many—especially Americans of liberal persuasion—to be a reason for pessimism. Kennedy's youthfulness and his attractive family had signaled a change of mood. In his famous inaugural address, the new president, characterizing his ascendancy to the office as a shift to a younger and more energetic generation, had called upon his fellow citizens to place the nation ahead of themselves—to ask what they could do for their country, not what the government could do for them. And he had promised that his generation, committed to freedom as strongly as previous generations, would "pay any price, bear any burden, meet any hardship, support any friend, oppose any foe to assure the survival and success of liberty."

The first years of the Kennedy administration were years of optimism and activism. America stood triumphant after the missile crisis. But the triumph changed quickly as a result of defeat in Vietnam; the Soviet strategic buildup; the murder of a beloved president who had style, grace, and a sense of humor; and the ugliness of racial violence that attended the integration of American society. U.S. foreign policy in the 1970s was to find itself essentially on the defensive as Moscow claimed what it called the "correlation of forces" shifted toward the Soviet Union. By correlation of forces, the Soviets included not only the military balance but also other components of power such as will-power, national unity, and economic vitality. Marxism emphasizes the social and economic basis of political and military power. America's lack of will and unity was obvious after Vietnam; the decline of the economy came about after the shock of the quadrupling of oil prices after 1973.

chapter nine

From Cold War to *Détente*

THE WAR in Vietnam left the United States disillusioned with anticommunism as a rationale for American global involvement. The war had been justified in the name of anticommunism, but Americans thought the price was too high. Before Vietnam, the nation could be mobilized to stop Communist aggression; after Vietnam, the concern became avoiding engagement in further adventures overseas. Even more basically, anticommunism had been weakened by the increasing pluralism of the formerly cohesive Sino-Soviet bloc.

In the bipolar world, it had been relatively easy to moralize about power politics precisely because the bipolarity had been one of power *and* ideologies. Globalism, which had made sense as long as any Communist expansion meant an addition to Soviet strength, could be explained in terms very understandable to Americans; that is, democracy versus dictatorship. But it was one thing to "fight communism" as long as there was only one communism to fight; when communism became fragmented, which sort were they to fight? Were all Communist states, because they were Communist, enemies of the United States? Or did the United States now have to distinguish among them, determining which was hostile, which friendly, which neutral—in short, which posed a true threat. More specifically, in these new circumstances, what changes in the distribution of power could America safely allow, and where, if anywhere, and against whom did it still have to draw "frontiers"? These questions were more difficult to answer than during the simple days of bipolarity because each situation would now confront policy makers with alternative policies, thereby arousing great debate and intense controversy. Anticommunism also would no longer be very useful as a means of eliciting popular support because the United States might well be supporting one Communist state against another.

From *Idealpolitik* to *Realpolitik*

One crucial question this posed for the future conduct of American foreign policy, therefore, was whether, in the absence of anticommunism, the United States would "dirty" its hands by playing straight and unadorned power politics. When *Realpolitik* was synonymous with *Idealpolitik*, it had been easy to be a leader and organize various coalitions whose basic task was to push back when pushed. The state system's requirement to maintain the balance of power could be performed by the United States government so long as it could disguise from its own people what it was doing and pretend it was engaged in a noble task. But could a nation that historically has condemned power politics adapt its outlook and style to a world in which justifying foreign policy in terms of ideological crusades was outmoded; could it "play the game by no other name" in an increasingly multipolar world? More specifically, how could the United States, disabused of anticommunism and disenchanted with a world in which the forces of good could no longer crusade against the forces of evil, mobilize congressional and popular support for the continued conduct of its foreign policy? Or would America, no longer believing it had an ideological mission to perform, sway from occasional fits of moral passion and crusadism to moralistic isolationism—or, if that were no longer possible in the late twentieth century—to a major withdrawal from the world? Would the country, having enjoyed its drug of anticommunism and the resulting "high" of global responsibility and exercise of world power, now swing to the "low" state of reaction and withdrawal?

The incoming administration of Richard Nixon in January 1969—which, after the president's resignation in 1974 because of the Watergate scandal would become the Nixon-Ford administration—confronted a novel postwar situation: how to conduct foreign policy without a consensus. The administration thought it could substitute a policy based on the traditional logic of the state system. This dramatic shift away from a style that stemmed from the nation's domestic values and experiences to a balance-of-power rationale was somewhat surprising because Nixon, as representative, senator, and vice president, had been an exponent of virulent anticommunism, of the "illusion of American omnipotence," and of an inflexible moralism that rejected having anything to do with Communists lest one be tainted with an "un-American" virus. But as president, he and his national security assistant Henry Kissinger, a German-born Jewish immigrant and Harvard professor, who became secretary of state in Nixon's second administration, rejected the traditional American justification for participating in foreign affairs. Indeed, the Nixon-Ford years might well be called the Kissinger era. Kissinger articulated and justified the Republican approach to foreign policy; personally carried out much of its private as well as public diplomacy; and provided an element of continuity amid the transfer of power from a disgraced president to his unelected, or appointed, successor. Kissinger so dominated these eight years that one wag even said of him that he was the only national security assistant and secretary of state ever served by two presidents. His diplomatic exploits earned him widespread admiration and popularity; he was frequently pictured in cartoons as "Super-Kraut," a pudgy figure decked out with a cape as he flew through the sky from one set of negotiations to another. His successors in Jimmy Carter's administration continued to feel his presence, if only because national security assistant Zbigniew Brzezinski, a Columbia University professor and one-time Harvard colleague of Kissinger, and Secretary of State Cyrus Vance, were constantly being compared with Kissinger—usually unfavorably.

The Kissinger Philosophy

The philosophy underlying American foreign policy during the Kissinger years from 1969 to 1977 began with the assumption that international politics was not a fight between the good side and the bad side. All states, Communist or non-Communist, had the right to exist and possessed legitimate interests. A nation, therefore, did not launch crusades against an adversary on the assumption that differences of interests represented a conflict of virtue and evil. The better part of wisdom was to learn to live with other states, to defend one's interests if encroached upon, but also to attempt to resolve differences and build on shared interests. International politics was not just conflict, but cooperation as well. Differences, admittedly, would not be easily or quickly reconciled; states' views of their interests were usually deeply held and not easily relinquished. Summit meetings were important as part of a negotiating process, but one summit could not solve all problems, and to raise false hopes that it would was to produce the cynicism and disillusionment that would endanger diplomacy itself. Good personal relations among leaders might smooth this process, but they were not a substitute for hard bargaining, and accords basically reflect the ratio of power between the nations the leaders represent.

How should the United States deal with a Communist dictatorship whose values and practices were abhorrent to it? The most the United States could expect was to influence its international behavior in a responsible direction; American power was too limited to transform another nation's domestic behavior and to make agreements dependent upon such a transformation would be counterproductive and raise tensions. American demands would be resisted, and this, in turn, would jeopardize accords on international issues that might otherwise have been resolvable. The United States was not omnipotent and had to abandon its habit of crusading to democratize adversaries. Negotiating with a Communist regime, such as that of the Soviet Union, was a matter of dealing with a powerful state with which the United States had to discuss issues if peace and security were to be preserved. The key, of course, was the balance of power, but within the parameters of that balance it was necessary to try and accommodate the legitimate needs of the principal disturber of that peace. Power neutralizes countervailing power, and satisfying the interests of other Great Powers would be more likely to produce acceptance of the present international system than continued frustration and hostility to an international system in which they had little vested interest. No state could be completely satisfied, but it could be relatively satisfied.

Kissinger's view, then, concentrated on the powerful actors. Although the rhetoric and style of American foreign policy were to be different and were to reflect more candidly and publicly the operational norms of the international system, there was to be an essential continuity in policy. The Soviet-American balance remained the preoccupation; it was still the Soviet Union, as a great power, whose influence needed to be contained and behavior moderated. This unity of rhetoric and action—the explanation of U.S. policy in terms of power, balances, spheres of influence, prestige, national interests, and the limits of American power, as well as the specific rejection of ideological justifications and crusades—represented the socialization of American foreign policy by the state system. The United States now explained its actions on the international scene in the same terms as all Great Powers before it in terms of the logic of the balance of power.

During its first two years, the Carter administration did not always share Kissinger's preoccupation with the balance of power and American-Soviet rivalry. Its concern was to lower America's profile in the world, to ensure that there would be "no more Vietnams," which it attributed to the global containment policy. Carter questioned whether this policy had not resulted from an exaggerated fear of the Soviet Union and, therefore, had been an overreaction. He asserted that his administration would not be driven by "an inordinate fear of communism." Indeed, even more fundamentally, the Carter approach to foreign policy questioned the entire postwar policy of his predecessors, both Democratic and Republican. He saw the war in Vietnam as the end product of not only containment but also of the whole "realist" approach. Was not the critical problem not the immoral—or at best, amoral— "power politics" philosophy upon which operational, as distinct from declaratory, American foreign policy since World War II had been based?

Indeed, Carter for a brief time embraced a new vision of a more "interdependent" world, which emphasized not security issues, but economic or welfare issues; not superpower competition, but closing the gulf between the rich and poor nations. He emphasized cooperation among nations seeking to advance the collective human interests, not an international hierarchy based upon power and the use of force, not conflict in which each nation acts primarily in terms of its national interest. But before he could change American foreign policy, he needed to continue *détente* to keep international tensions low and achieve a series of arms control agreements. Therefore, even before the collapse of *détente* that followed the Soviet invasion of Afghanistan, the Carter administration's focus remained largely on the Soviet Union.

The Need for *Détente*

The Nixon, Ford, and Carter administrations all pursued *détente* because of changes in the United States and the state system that made a re-laxation of tensions necessary. Within the United States the change was that the nation had become weary of its foreign policy burdens. This mood, often portrayed in this post-Vietnam era as neo-isolationist and anti-national security, was illustrated by the attacks on the "imperial presidency," by the 1973 War Powers Resolution, and by restrictions on Central Intelligence Agency (CIA) covert operations. The president was to be restrained by a more assertive and watchful Congress; the freedom to use the instruments of overt and covert intervention abroad were to be limited. In the pre-Vietnam era of containment, Congress had rarely questioned the president's authority to use the armed forces or CIA to carry out U.S. policy. But after Vietnam, the criticisms of America's "global policeman" role were widespread, and emphasis was placed on the nation's "limited power," suggesting a more restricted role in what was popularly regarded as the post-cold war era. Indeed, the Carter administration, coming to power shortly after the collapse of Vietnam in 1975, thought the cold war was finished. Nixon and Gerald Ford were constrained by the public mood of neo-isolationism, but Carter represented that mood until 1979. For Nixon and Ford, *détente* was therefore necessary until the nation could "recover its nerve" and once more play the leading role they felt was required to protect U.S. interests against Soviet expansion; for Carter, it was necessary because the United States was living in a more complex post-cold war era in which an activist anti-Soviet policy would needlessly rekindle the superpower conflict.

Another change, around 1970, was in the balance of power, a longer-term reason for *détente*. This change occurred because the Soviet Union had attained strategic parity. The balance between the two superpowers had long been between the U.S. Strategic Air Command (SAC), later supplemented by the navy's nuclear submarines, and the Red Army. The American bombers and missiles deterred the Soviet Union by threatening to destroy its cities. The Soviet Union gained its intercontinental capability and capacity to destroy the United States from its massive buildup that began after 1964. From the 1950s to the late 1960s, however, America's strategic power was balanced not by Moscow's bomber and missile force, which was small in comparison with the United States, but by the Red Army. The powerful Soviet army, it was believed, could overrun Western Europe and quickly defeat North Atlantic Treaty Organization (NATO) forces.

The American-Soviet balance had been asymmetric: the United States had held strategic superiority and an intercontinental reach; the Soviet Union, conventional superiority and a regional reach. But by 1969 the balance had become symmetrical; the Soviet Union's strategic power had caught up with that of the United States, and the Soviets could now hold America's population, as well as Western Europe's, hostage. Moreover, this Soviet buildup showed no sign of slowing down, not even after the number of Soviet intercontinental ballistic missiles (ICBMs) had surpassed the number of American land-based missiles.

Even during the period of U.S. strategic superiority, Moscow had been willing to risk limited challenges, such as in Berlin and Cuba, but it had remained cautious during confrontations; if there was resistance, it could retreat and call the challenge off. U.S. power had set limits to how far the Soviets felt they could push. But in a period in which the strategic balance was shifting and the Soviet leaders had at the very least achieved parity, a continuation of the containment policy by means of threats of force would become more risky and costly. The Soviet leaders had gained a new sense of confidence in their power. Their country was at last truly an equal of the United States. In 1945 the Soviet Union did not have the atomic bomb; much of the country lay in ruins. Even after the American atomic monopoly had been broken, the United States retained a decisive strategic superiority. As late as 1962, the Soviet Union was not strong enough to resist when the United States compelled it to pull its missiles out of Cuba. But only a quarter of a century after World War II, it had caught up. The Soviet Union now belonged to a club of two, the most exclusive in the world. The potential danger of this development was clarified when the Soviet foreign minister informed the world that no important issue anywhere could be resolved without the Soviet Union. In brief, the Soviet leaders might be more willing to challenge the United States; with their new power, they might perhaps even expect the Americans to back down first in a Cuba-in-reverse situation. It became important, therefore, to reduce international tensions and try to slow down the arms competition, if it could not be stopped.

The last and most important change was the Soviet Union's emergence as a global power. Although its leaders' ambitions might be worldwide—the Soviet Union saw itself as the nucleus of a new and more humane postcapitalist world, as well as a great power—its reach had been limited to Eurasia, and attempts to extend its power beyond Eurasia had been largely unsuccessful. The Congo and Cuba were painful reminders that the Soviet Union was not, like the United States, a country with a worldwide capacity to project its power. The Soviet Union had concluded from its experience in Cuba that strategic power paid off politically because it could be used not only to deter but also to intimidate and compel the adversary to retreat.

In addition, within the context of this growing strategic power, the Soviet Union had also engaged in a parallel massive conventional buildup, particularly of a modern surface navy and airlift capability. This meant that as its ability to neutralize America's nuclear force grew, its capacity to project its conventional power beyond Eurasia also grew. The Soviet naval buildup, which by the late 1970s had produced a navy that exceeded the U.S. Navy in numbers of combat ships (although it did not yet have large U.S.-type aircraft carriers) was not needed for defense. Soviet allies were contiguous, not overseas as were those of the United States; nor was the Soviet Union dependent upon imports of oil and other natural resources, as were all the Western allies. Would the Soviet Union, in these new circumstances, be content to expand its influence only on land and in nearby areas? Or would it, as a result of its new might, feel a confidence that had been absent before, act more boldly, take greater risks, and reopen old issues and challenge the United States in new areas farther away from the Soviet Union? Would the United States, by contrast, now that it had lost its strategic superiority, be more cautious and hesitant to react?

Kissinger compared the Soviet Union's emergence as a world power to Germany's development at the turn of the century. In both cases, the challengers were land powers. The symbols of their aspiration and determination to expand were the navies they built; nothing could have been more symbolic to Great Britain and the United States, the two greatest naval powers in their respective times. Germany's emergence and desire to be a world power with its overseas colonies resulted in World War I. How could the Soviet Union's newly gained power and its determination to pursue a *Weltpolitik,* or global policy, and achieve its "place in the sun," as the Germans had called it, be managed peacefully and not threaten American security interests? Clearly, as a badge of its newly achieved equal status, Moscow also sought its overseas "colonies," basically Marxist-Leninist states that would become members of the Soviet "empire." As they had been for Germany, these colonies, usually of limited strategic value and needing to be subsidized economically, were geopolitically important as a symbol. Thus, the question of the Soviet Union's massive military buildup raised questions not just about the military balance and its stability but, more fundamentally, about its ultimate intentions and whether the emergence of a true "structure of peace," to use Nixon's phrase, was possible.

Managing the New Relationship

Détente, therefore, was first adopted as a political strategy for managing the superpowers' adversary relationship. This strategy would seek to secure American interests at a lower level of tension and cost than those required by the policy of cold war confrontation and frequent crises. The American-Soviet balance would still be bipolar, but it would be somewhat more complex and fluid than in the earlier, cold war era. But the way in which foreign policy was explained was different: Nixon's predecessors, while also pursuing a balance-of-power policy, felt compelled to justify their policy in terms of the past crusading style. From President Harry Truman on, they had frequently been trapped by their anti-Communist rhetoric and felt forced to be more inflexible and interventionist than perhaps they would have been. For twenty years they had been unable to abandon the fiction that Taiwan was China and to establish a formal diplomatic relationship with the real China on the mainland. The Nixon-Kissinger balance eventually included Communist China. As Moscow's bitter rival, Beijing could be used to provide the Soviets with an incentive to act with restraint and a greater willingness to compromise if it wished to avoid closer Sino-American relations and cooperation against the Soviet Union. The Nixon tripolarity was a tactic devised in order to make the superpower bipolarity work more smoothly and securely.

Furthermore, this balance was to be supplemented by a network of agreements and a set of rules of mutual restraint beneficial to both powers. Cold war bipolarity had been based on the fundamental assumption that what benefited one side would hurt the other and, therefore, had to be prevented by counteraction. This kind of bipolar competition was now to be supplemented by agreements and rules profiting both, thereby presumably enhancing each country's stake in cooperation with the other. The key Kissinger word was *linkage*. If a series of agreements and understandings on matters such as arms control and trade could be arrived at, the more expansionist-minded Soviet Union, because of the benefits of these agreements and understandings, would gain a vested interest in good relations with the United States. While the Soviet Union was to be faced, as before, with a con-tinued balance and a strong American military that would provide an inducement for restraint in foreign policy, this "stick" was to be supplemented with enough "carrots" to make the restraint more appealing. Indeed, because employing military sanctions to contain the Soviet Union at a time of strategic parity was becoming riskier for the United States, the offer of economic rewards for Soviet restraint or self-containment was particularly appealing.

There was another meaning to linkage. It referred to the fact that the various issues would be linked together diplomatically. Progress on one front would be tied to progress on another; the Kremlin could not expect to make gains on one issue that interested it but refuse to meet American interests on other issues. If it did so, there would presumably be a penalty exacted in the form of nonprogress on issues of interest to the Soviet Union or the withholding of benefits Moscow was seeking. During the Nixon-Ford years linkage was often explicitly declared to exist; it was officially denied by the Carter administration (although it was on occasion pointed out that certain Soviet actions could not but affect American public opinion or congressional support for administration policies). Cooperation and mutual concessions were obviously preferable. The adversary part of the relationship was to be balanced by the partnership element in a new adversary-partnership. The overall purposes were to lower tensions between the superpowers, to confront fewer crises, and to encourage diplomatic negotiations; the new policy did not mean an end of American-Soviet conflict and competition. A *détente* was not an *entente cordiale*.

For Kissinger (as for Brzezinski later, if not always for Carter and Vance), then, *détente* was not only a strategy selected to secure American interests at a lower level of tensions and costs. It was also a continuation of containment at a time when the United States had lost its strategic superiority and its extensive role in world affairs was widely questioned by its citizens. *Détente* was to achieve its purpose by exploiting the Sino-Soviet split and by using American technology and food as nonmilitary "weapons." It should be noted that this political-diplomatic strategy was not utopian; it did not assume that the Soviet Union had become a benign power or that the cold war was over. *Détente* was intended to be a realistic strategy for a time when, because of neo-isolationism at home, the United States was no longer in a position to compete as vigorously with the Soviet Union as in the days before the Vietnam War. *Détente* was the continuation of containment by other means.

Disengagement from Vietnam

Before the relationships among the United States, the Soviet Union, and China could be reshaped, the United States had to unburden itself of the Vietnam War. Vietnam was an albatross around the Nixon administration's neck. But Nixon's and Kissinger's perceptions of great power relationships heavily influenced their thinking about acceptable terms for withdrawal. One course open to Nixon, which would have brought him popular acclaim, was to pull out all American forces immediately on the grounds that the United States had fulfilled long enough its obligations to defend Saigon. But in the president's view the central issue was not getting out of Vietnam, but *how* to get out. If the United States withdrew quickly and if South Vietnam collapsed, the credibility of American commitments and power would be gravely weakened.

The Nixon administration was determined not to accept any settlement that was tantamount to a defeat, namely, a coalition government in Saigon controlled by the Communists. Nixon believed that establishing *détentes* with the Soviet Union and China would not be feasible if America's prestige— reputation for power—was badly tattered. The president wanted to modify U.S. relations with the two largest Communist states, especially the Soviet Union, the more powerful of the two. Why should the Soviet Union, rapidly building up its strategic power, settle for parity and mutually acceptable peaceful coexistence if it sensed that America was weak and could be pushed around? Why should China tone down its revolutionary rhetoric and conduct a more traditional state-to-state diplomacy, and indeed move closer to the United States, if it could not count on American strength and determination to resist what it saw as Soviet attempts at hegemony in Asia? In short, the country had to "hang tough" in Vietnam to normalize relations with the Soviet Union and China.

Nixon and Kissinger, therefore, devised a twofold strategy. First, American ground troops were to be gradually withdrawn to cut the costs of the war and make further hostilities tolerable for the "silent majority," which Nixon felt was loyal, although fatigued, and would support him in an "honorable" ending of the war. But in addition to silencing his domestic critics, Nixon hoped the continued involvement of U.S. forces, especially in the air would provide an incentive for Hanoi to negotiate an end to the war. This incentive would presumably be all the stronger if the president's strategy worked at home, for he would then remove Vietnam as a principal issue in the next election and be reelected. Hanoi, confronted with the prospect that the war could last longer than four more years, would have a reason to settle the war diplomatically. The second part of the president's policy was the "Vietnamization" of the war. South Vietnam's forces were to be trained better and supplied with modern arms so that they could bit by bit take over the ground fighting. This would counter the criticisms and pressures that had multiplied in Congress, on campuses, and elsewhere for faster troop withdrawals and for the abandonment of Saigon.

The danger inherent in the president's strategy was that the North Vietnamese would attack during the time that American troops were withdrawn, but before the South Vietnamese were ready to meet the enemy in battle. In March 1970 Cambodia's Prince Norodom Sihanouk, who had long tolerated the Communist troops and supply lines in his country, was overthrown by a military regime that wanted Communist troops out of Cambodia. The Communists moved toward the Cambodian capital to unseat the new government. Nixon decided to intervene, which reignited domestic dissension. After four demonstrating students at Kent State University were shot to death by the Ohio National Guard, many campuses erupted, and a number of colleges and universities were completely shut down. Protesters once again turned out for peaceful mass demonstrations in Washington and in other cities. The reaction to Cambodia made it clear that it would be foolhardy for the president to repeat such an action.

Saigon's army unfortunately remained the key to the success of the president's strategy. In the spring of 1972, with the U.S. army withdrawn from the battlefield, North Vietnam launched an unexpected large-scale attack across the demilitarized zone between North Vietnam and South Vietnam. The South Vietnamese army performed poorly and only American air support staved off even worse losses.

Nixon was therefore in a quandary on the eve of a summit conference in Moscow to advance *détente*. The Soviet Union had supplied Hanoi with modern arms and, whether it knew the date of the North Vietnamese offensive, Nixon thought it should have restrained its ally. As a great power, the Soviet Union must have known that a major South Vietnamese defeat would be humiliating to its adversary on the eve of vital negotiations from which Moscow had as much to gain as Washington. The president was unwilling to negotiate under the shadow of defeat.

With Vietnamization in danger, Nixon "re-Americanized" the war by ordering extensive bombing of the North and blockading North Vietnam's ports with mines. The aim was to stop Soviet and Chinese supplies for the North Vietnamese. Because the war was now a conventional one, dependent on oil and heavy weapons and large amounts of ammunition, air power might be more effective in halting them than it was during guerrilla operations. Simultaneously, Nixon also offered Hanoi just about all it could reasonably expect to be given: the complete withdrawal of all American forces from Vietnam within four months if all prisoners of war were returned and an internationally supervised cease-fire were arranged. The Communists could keep their forces in the South, a significant concession previously offered only in secret talks. Equally important, the president did not insist on the survival of Nguyen Van Thieu's government. He specifically said that the United States' withdrawal "would allow negotiations and a political settlement between the Vietnamese themselves." This new set of proposals provided a concrete and serious basis for negotiations. But Hanoi rejected the offer. It appeared to want the president to do the one thing he refused to do—guarantee Communist control in Saigon. His proposal, in fact, had seemed to suggest that the North Vietnamese do this job for themselves, if they could.

The North Vietnamese also faced a dilemma. Despite the heavy bombing and blockade, the Soviet Union had gone ahead with the summit meeting. Communist China no longer opposed a negotiated settlement of the war. Moscow and Beijing both gave priority to their relationships with Washington. Hanoi was politically isolated. Yet the North Vietnamese leaders had sought their goal of a unified Vietnam for so long, paid such a high price for it, and been so often cheated out of the fulfillment of their dream by their adversaries that they were suspicious of Nixon's offer and resentful of the declining Soviet and Chinese support.

But a month before the U.S. presidential election, Hanoi, probably fearing Nixon's reelection and that he might be less accommodating after the election, signaled its willingness to accept something less than a total victory. By late October Hanoi had negotiated a tentative Indochina settlement. The terms included an internationally supervised cease-fire that would halt all American bombing and mining and bring about withdrawal of all U.S. forces within two months; separate future cease-fires were expected in Laos and Cambodia. Prisoners of war would be exchanged. A series of mixed political commissions, composed of elements from the Viet Cong, the Saigon government, and neutralists, would then be established to work out a new South Vietnamese political order leading to a new constitution and the election of a new government.

The Nixon administration felt it had achieved an "honorable peace." The North Vietnamese, after having declared for years that the Thieu government would have to go as a precondition for a cease-fire, now accepted Thieu as the leader of the government faction. Thieu remained in control of a sizable army and large police forces with which he administered most of the country and all the urban centers, leaving only minor areas and a small percentage of the population under the control of the Viet Cong and the approximately 145,000 North Vietnamese troops. The Thieu faction therefore seemed to have a good chance to compete politically and militarily with the Communists after the fighting ended. Thieu stalled against this tentative October 1972 settlement because the United States had accepted the presence of North Vietnam's troops in areas of the South from which U.S. and South Vietnamese troops had been unable to dislodge them. While Thieu could object, he held no veto. The end of the Second Indochina War for the United States came in January 1973. The administration could now focus its primary attention on improving relations with China and the Soviet Union.

Détente with China

When the Nixon administration came into office in January 1969, the United States had no official relationship with Communist China. The Chinese Communists were opposed to resuming relations with the United States as long as Washington defended the Nationalist regime, a rival to legitimate power over China, on Taiwan, Chinese territory. But Nixon recognized the changing circumstances and considered it vital to bring mainland China into the diplomatic constellation. Calling the regime by its chosen name, the People's Republic of China, ending regular patrolling of the Taiwan Straits by the Seventh Fleet, lifting trade and visitation restrictions against China, Nixon opened the way for a personal visit to China. This visit served in part to symbolize to the American public and Congress, long hostile to dealing with Beijing, the dramatic shift of American policy and in part to begin clearing away mutual misperceptions and defining the real nature of some of the more outstanding issues and problems impeding improved Sino-American relations.

Therefore, it would be a mistake to speak of *détente* only in terms of the relationship between the United States and the Soviet Union. There were two *détentes*, one with the Soviet Union and one with China. Indeed, it may be argued that *détente* with China was the greater U.S. achievement because of the tremendous hostility that had existed between the two countries since 1950. At least with the Soviet Union, the earlier period of high tension, confrontation, and recurring crises, particularly since the Cuban missile crisis, had been balanced by an increasing degree of cooperation in the area of arms control. In any event, there can be little doubt that *détente* with China was a prerequisite to *détente* with the Soviet Union because it was expected to increase the Soviet Union's incentive to improve relations with the United States.

U.S. Chance to Outflank the Soviets

For the United States, then, the Sino-Soviet split provided an opportunity to bring pressure to bear on the Soviet Union; the clearly implied message to the Soviet leadership was that their obstinacy would compel Washington to align itself more closely with Beijing. To the Soviets, already fearful of China, such an alignment and the encouragement it would give China to be more hostile, as well as renewed tension on the Soviet Union's other front in Europe, had to be a nightmare. Similarly, Beijing had for years complained loudly about alleged American-Soviet collusion to isolate and contain China. But as the Soviet Union began to move huge numbers of troops eastward to defend its frontier with China, and on occasion let a rumor slip about the possibility of an attack on China, Beijing—apparently convinced that Nixon was pulling out of Vietnam—was interested in detaching Washington from any possible cooperation with Moscow against China. Even more important, better relations with the United States would presumably restrain the Soviet Union from attacking China, for the Kremlin could not be sure that Washington in such a contingency would not support Beijing.

In the Shanghai communiqué released at the end of Nixon's historic visit, the United States and China declared their opposition to the hegemony of any power in Asia; it was clear that the power they meant was the Soviet Union. Thus Sino-American relations began despite Taiwan. The Communist position long had been that Beijing would not establish any relationship with Washington before the official ties with Taiwan were cut. U.S. ties with the rival claimant to power over all of China was, Beijing claimed, interference in a domestic matter. That the People's Republic signed the Shanghai communiqué constituted evidence of its fear of the Soviet Union; so was Nixon's signature on a statement in which the United States declared that it would gradually remove all its forces and installations from Taiwan and not interfere in a "peaceful settlement" between the Communists and Nationalists of their differences, including the future of Taiwan, which the administration acknowledged to be a "part of China."

President Nixon's trip to Beijing in 1972 symbolized a dramatic change in Sino-American relations and once and for all ended the irrationality of a situation in which the United States for almost a quarter-century had ignored the existence of the world's most populous country, a nation with great potential power, a significant stake in Asia's future, and an ideological rival of the Soviet Union. And just as Washington, during the 1950s, had feared the Sino-Soviet coalition, and Beijing, during the 1960s, had frequently pointed to an alleged Soviet-American collusion to isolate China, so Moscow now became apprehensive of closer Sino-American relations because it gave the United States a persuasive lever—if skillfully used—in its negotiations with the Kremlin. The American shift of policy from Taiwan to Beijing was long overdue. Domestic politics had too long blocked a rational adjustment and exploitation of the Sino-Soviet conflict, a conflict in which tensions may rise or fall from time to time, but one that is likely to continue despite changes of leaders in both countries. Their quarrels reflect differences of interest more profound than merely differences of personalities.

Indeed, the succession struggle in China and the change in the presidency in the United States did not stop progress toward full normalization. On Janaury 1, 1979, the People's Republic of China and the United States exchanged diplomatic recognition and ambassadors. This was followed almost immediately by an official visit in Washington by China's apparent strong man, Deputy Premier Deng Xiao-ping. The timing of this last step toward normalization had come from Beijing, which confronted large modern Soviet forces along its 4,500-mile northern frontier with increasingly obsolete weapons. At the same time, it looked to the West to help it modernize everything from building hotel chains and steel mills to exploring China's enormous estimated oil reserves. For the United States, the final shift from Taiwan to Beijing meant ending diplomatic recognition of Nationalist China and the mutual security pact, as well as the last withdrawal of American military personnel. In return, Beijing appeared to accept the American position that this problem be resolved peacefully, although it expressed anger at the United States for continuing to supply the Nationalists with weapons to defend themselves against a possible Communist invasion.

The likelihood of invasion was not great anyway. For one thing, Beijing lacked the air and naval capacity to cross 100 miles of water to launch such an attack. More important, however, Beijing, having turned primarily to the United States and Japan to help it modernize, would not risk taking an action that would alienate both of these countries, especially the United States, which it also needed to balance Soviet power. That an invasion of Taiwan would be politically counterproductive was further underlined by the fact that Tokyo (which had recognized Beijing earlier than Washington) maintained very close and profitable commercial relations with Taiwan, and the United States expected to do the same. However, nothing prevented the United States, after it had long insisted on a peaceful resolution of Communist-Nationalist differences, from resorting to force and defending Taiwan should Beijing some day change its mind and violate the understanding about the peaceful resolution of this problem.

With recognition of the mainland came new directions in trade. Although the United States at first did not sell arms to Beijing in order not to provoke Moscow, it was willing to let its European allies sell China arms, such as jet fighters and antiaircraft and antitank missiles. The United States limited its own sales to dual-purpose equipment such as radar, trucks, and transport planes, which could be put either to civilian or military use. Ronald Reagan's administration, in an effort to forge stronger links with China against the Soviet Union, offered to sell Beijing arms. As China had limited

funds to buy arms on a large scale, the significance of this move was more political than military. It signaled to the Soviets that the Chinese-American
alliance they feared was a little closer to being realized. The United States
and China were already cooperating in jointly operating an electronic
intelligence-gathering station in China to monitor Soviet missile tests.

Implications of Sino-American Relations

For the United States, hostility between the two largest Communist
states was preferable to a united Sino-Soviet bloc. A strong China, dividing
the Soviet Union's attention between East and West, was a benefit for
NATO. Washington, therefore, had a vested interest in supporting the new
post-Mao Chinese leadership, which opposed Moscow and looked toward the
West and Japan. Fundamentally, the United States was taking advantage of
its adversaries' dilemma and resorting to the time-honored tactic of "divide
and rule." In the past, America always had to choose between China and Japan: when the United States was friendly to China before World War II, Japan became the adversary; and when Nationalist China collapsed, the United
States became an ally of Japan and enemy of the new China. Now the
possibility of closer Washington-Beijing-Tokyo cooperation appeared increasingly possible. The new China connection, however, was not without risk.
The danger was that the United States would align itself too closely with
China and that such an alignment would be regarded as unfriendly and
provocative by Moscow. The same would be true for Beijing, if, in seeking to
improve its relationship of *détente* with the Soviet Union, Washington pulled
too close to the Kremlin.

One dramatic example of this dilemma occurred shortly after the United
States had officially recognized the People's Republic of China and its deputy
prime minister had toured America vehemently denouncing Moscow. Beijing,
concerned with what it saw as increasing Soviet-Vietnamese collaboration to
the south—which it interpreted to be part of a growing Soviet influence and
attempt to encircle China—struck at Vietnam. Angered by Vietnam's
expulsion of almost 200,000 ethnic Chinese, by border conflicts between the
two countries, and especially by Hanoi's signing of a friendship treaty with
the Soviets in late 1977, followed by its invasion of China's friend, Cambodia,
China decided to "teach Vietnam a lesson" by crossing the border and
inflicting heavy casualties. The resulting border war demonstrated once again
that a common ideology was not enough to prevent conflict and that
nationalism was as divisive a force within the Communist sphere as in the rest
of the world. The danger for the United States was the possibility of a Soviet
military reaction. An attempt "to teach China a lesson," if it was more than a
limited incursion into China, could affect American interests and would draw
the United States more deeply into the Sino-Soviet quarrel. Moscow already
saw Washington's normalization of its relationship with Beijing as collusion
and tacit support of China's military action, although Carter explicitly

opposed this invasion of Vietnam, as he had opposed Hanoi's earlier invasion of Cambodia. Thus, the possible advantages for the United States of "playing the China card" against Moscow were matched by the dangers of China's "playing its American card"; and the possibility of Moscow's someday "playing its China card" against America could not be completely excluded. Yet on the whole, the United States and the People's Republic of China were driven together by their respective security interests and shared fear of rapidly growing Soviet power. Geopolitics prevailed over ideology.

Arms Control as the Centerpiece of *Détente*

Arms control over the years has gained increasing importance in relations between the United States and the Soviet Union, and for very good reasons. The two powers have been rivals since the closing days of World War II, and their rivalry has reached almost every region of the world. As a result, profound distrust and mutual fear, if not hatred, characterize their relationship. The arms race is an expression of their deep political differences. The danger is that the arms race, fueled by continuing conflict may at some point spill over into a nuclear war. One way each side has tried to avoid such a cataclysmic end is to build up its nuclear forces as a defense; the other is to meet and negotiate agreements that reduce the chances of war breaking out. But, as the basic conflict probably cannot be resolved and nuclear weapons are unlikely to be abolished, the next best tactic is to "manage" the nuclear arms balance by instituting arms control.

During the 1960s arms control had dealt largely with issues such as the establishment of a "hot line" between the Kremlin and the White House for quick communication in a crisis, a limited ban on testing nuclear devices, and, through the United Nations, an agreement on the nonproliferation of nuclear weapons. In the 1970s these negotiations shifted to each side's strategic forces. Indeed, the Strategic Arms Limitation Talks (SALT) stood at the center of *détente*. More specifically, SALT had four objectives. The first was to make the arms race more predictable by establishing the numbers of strategic weapons for each side. It was hoped that such knowledge would reduce the anxiety of the arms race; uncertainty and the fear that the opponent might be gaining superiority in military strength fueled competition. The Soviets had begun a steady, large-scale military buildup in strategic and conventional weapons after the Cuban missile crisis. By the time Nixon became president, the Soviets had overtaken the United States in numbers of deployed missiles, and the missile production continued. A new arms race therefore was likely unless mutually accepted ceilings on missiles could be negotiated. Indeed, given the antimilitary mood in the United States following the Vietnam War and congressional hostility to increased defense spending, the pressure on the Nixon administration to negotiate an agreement was intense. The alternative would be a huge missile gap in favor of the Soviet Union.

SALT's second aim was to ensure parity. The assumption was that if the two sides had approximately the same number of warheads and bombs, neither side could launch a crippling strike against the other. More specifically, parity was a condition in which no matter who struck first, the attacked side would still have the capability to retaliate and destroy the aggressor. When each power possessed missiles with single warheads, even with reasonably accurate warheads, a two-to-one superiority was needed to launch a devastating first strike. Short of such a superiority, the United States and the Soviet Union would each retain a sufficient retaliatory capability to assure the continuation of deterrence.

The third purpose of arms control was to reduce threats to each side's deterrent forces. By the early 1970s, the deterrent balance was threatened not only by the continuing Soviet quantitative strategic growth but also by technological innovations that were widely believed in the United States to be undermining the stability of American-Soviet deterrence. One matter of concern was the development of a new defensive weapon. The Soviets had deployed antiballistic missiles (ABMs) around Moscow and were thought to be working on a second-generation ABM for possible nationwide deployment. If ABMs could shoot down enough incoming American ICBMs and reduce the destruction inflicted on the Soviet Union to an "acceptable" level of a few million casualties, the ABMs would undermine U.S. deterrence, which depended upon its capacity to impose "assured destruction."

In turn, this defensive weapon stimulated the United States to improve its offensive technology, specifically, the development of the multiple independently targeted reentry vehicle (MIRV). MIRV is an ICBM with multiple warheads that can separate in flight, change trajectory, and fly independently to assigned and dispersed targets. The advantage of MIRV was that the large numbers of warheads would be able to overcome any ABM defense, meaning that the United States would still be able to destroy Soviet society in a retaliatory blow.

But MIRVs also threatened to destabilize the deterrent balance. It is one thing for the United States and Soviet Union to possess missiles with single warheads, even if these warheads are reasonably accurate. If side A has 1,000 missiles and side B 1,400, B still does not have the two-to-one superiority it was assumed necessary to destroy A's missiles. But if both possessed the same number of missiles—let us say, 1,000—but A's missiles could carry ten warheads and B's could carry only three, the ratio of warheads would be greater than three to one. This would permit A with only 200 missiles to launch a first strike to disarm the latter. Multiplying the warheads and providing them with greater accuracy thus undermined the stability of the nuclear balance because it placed a premium on attack. Whichever side got in the first blow was likely to win because it might be able to prevent any major retaliation.

This was a potentially dangerous situation. When both sides possessed such counterforce weapons, their mutual fear of a preventive war, and especially of a preemptive strike during a crisis, would make both jittery. Each would fear that if the other struck first, it would be unable to retaliate with sufficient force to destroy the other; the very vulnerability of the opponent's forces, therefore, provided an incentive to attack first. Each would feel it had to "use them or lose them."

The fourth reason for SALT was that it was necessary for *détente*. On the one hand, a failure to arrive at an agreement or at least to continue the SALT dialogue was bound to have a deteriorating effect on their overall political relationship. On the other hand, only a relaxation of tensions could provide the diplomatic atmosphere that would enable the two nuclear giants to arrive at an arms agreement that would leave them feeling more secure, sanctify the strategic parity between them, and avoid new costly offensive and defensive arms races. SALT, in brief, became a symbol of *détente*. With it, *détente* seemed to blossom; without it, *détente* seemed to fade. Success or failure to achieve a SALT agreement became the barometer of *détente*.

The first set of agreements, known as SALT I, was signed by President Nixon and Soviet Communist party leader Leonid Brezhnev in May 1972. SALT I had taken two and a half years to negotiate and incorporated two agreements. The first, a treaty, limited each nation's ABMs to 200 launchers, later to be reduced to 100 each (the United States built none because such a small number of ABMs could not prevent a catastrophic strike). For all practical purposes, by eliminating the ABM, the two powers ensured that their deterrent retaliatory forces would be able to retaliate while also avoiding a renewed offensive arms race in response to large-scale defensive deployments.

The second agreement, a five-year interim agreement, essentially froze offensive missiles at the number each side possessed at the time. This meant 2,358 ICBMs and SLBMs (submarine-launched ballistic missiles) for the Soviet Union (of which 300 were very large missiles, the SS-9s) and 1,710 ICBMs and SLBMs for the United States. Bombers, in which the United States had in 1972 a numerical superiority over the Soviet Union of three to one, were not included in the accords. Given the American lead in MIRVs, the accord on offensive weapons meant that the larger number of Soviet missile launchers was matched with the large number of U.S. bombers plus the technological superiority of American missiles and their greater number of warheads. Each side retained the right to improve its weapons within the overall quantitative agreement, thus preserving parity (or, officially, *sufficiency*). Although no on-site inspection to check for violations was agreed on, both sides pledged not to interfere with each other's reconnaissance or spy satellites, which would be the principal means to check compliance with both accords. What the freeze meant was that neither side could launch a crippling first strike against the other.

Basically, SALT I was a trade-off: a freeze on Soviet missiles against low numbers of ABMs. The United States wanted to stop the ever growing number of Soviet ICBMs; the Soviets, fearful that the American ABM would be technologically far superior and more effective than their own, wanted to halt a U.S. deployment before it started. Moscow at first offered only an ABM agreement, but Nixon resisted; he would not sign a defensive arms agreement without an offensive arms agreement. How could he limit the numbers of ABMs the United States would deploy without knowing how many ICBMs the Soviet Union intended to produce? The defensive and offensive arms race were inextricably intertwined. There could be no missile ceilings without an accompanying ceiling on defensive weapons.

Finally, the two powers agreed to hold further negotiations to formulate a final, overall strategic arms treaty. The offensive freeze was intended to give them time to negotiate a more lasting agreement. SALT I was to be the beginning of a process, a continuing dialogue and effort to control the arms competition. The two nuclear giants appeared to recognize their special obligation for the preservation of peace by complementing SALT I with certain standards of behavior. They pledged to avoid confrontations, to exercise mutual restraint, and to reject efforts to gain unilateral advantages.

SALT II was therefore regarded as critical to a long-term effort to stabilize mutual deterrence. President Ford, after Nixon's resignation, arrived at the guidelines for SALT II with Brezhnev at a 1974 meeting in Vladivostok. This time each side would have an equal number of strategic weapons: 2,400 missiles and bombers, 1,320 of these delivery systems could have MIRVs. Despite this broad agreement, it was seven years after SALT I that Brezhnev and Carter signed SALT II. It was a complex series of agreements, carefully balancing off the varying interests and different force structures of the two powers. Not surprisingly, SALT II became controversial in the United States.

Proponents pointed to the fact that it provided for some reduction of strategic launchers from the Vladivostok ceiling of 2,400 to 2,250. This change meant that the Soviets would have to reduce their force levels by about 150 older missiles. This set a precedent for SALT III, whose main purpose was to be a major reduction of strategic forces. Critics, however, noted that the SALT II ceilings were so high that it was the very opposite of any reasonable interpretation of the words *arms control;* other critics asserted that, despite the equal numbers provided for both sides, the treaty would give the Soviet Union strategic superiority because Soviet missiles were considerably larger, could carry more and bigger warheads, and were more accurate. The Soviets, therefore, would acquire a sizable first-strike force that by the mid-1980s would be capable of destroying up to 90 percent of America's ICBMs. A "window of vulnerability" was opening over the American deterrent.

Defenders of SALT II argued that it could not be expected to undo what technology and earlier political decisions had done. For example, having developed MIRV to overcome possible extensive Soviet ABM deployment, the United States continued with MIRV, even after Moscow had agreed to the virtual elimination of ABM. That decision came back to haunt the United States. The Soviet Union's 1,400 land-based missiles would not be a threat to the 1,000 Minuteman force if each Soviet missile possessed only one warhead. U.S. vulnerability stemmed from the combination of big Soviet missile launchers with the large number of warheads they could carry. At best, SALT could reduce the consequence of this development, and it attempted to do so by limiting the number of Soviet land-based MIRVs and the number of warheads they could carry, especially the SS-18 (the successor to the SS-9), which could carry upwards of thirty warheads. Still, both liberal and conservative critics scored points—liberals, because SALT II was not a step toward major reductions, conservatives because the 300 SS-18 missiles with ten warheads per missile and the more than 300 SS-19 missiles with six warheads per missile *each* carried potentially more warheads and total megatonnage than the *total* American ICBM force. Each therefore posed a potentially formidable threat to Minuteman's survivability and America's deterrent capability.

SALT II's supporters asserted that the treaty in fact would permit the United States to undertake programs that would both reduce the vulnerability of American deterrence and strengthen it. The treaty allowed the United States to deploy 200 new land-based MX missiles which, because of their planned mobility, decreased the likelihood of their being destroyed in a Soviet first strike. Also because it was larger than the Minuteman and could carry ten large, accurate warheads, the MX gave the United States a counterforce capability. Additionally, it could deploy twenty extremely accurate, long-range, subsonic, air-launched cruise missiles (ALCMs) on some B-52s at a time when the Soviets did not have a comparable ALCM. Finally, the United States also could proceed with the replacement of its older Polaris submarines with the new Trident submarines, each with twenty-four missile tubes (as opposed to sixteen on the older submarines); the Trident I missile, with a range of more than 4,000 miles, would be placed in some Poseidon submarines as well, thus giving U.S. nuclear missile submarines a far vaster range of ocean in which to hide from detection. In the meantime, testing of the more accurate Trident II, with a range of more than 6,000 miles, could proceed.

The primary debate about SALT II was between the administration and its conservative critics and revolved around two main issues. The first was whether the real vulnerability of U.S. ICBMs was as great as the 90 percent theoretical vulnerability the critics claimed. An attack upon the U.S. deterrent force would have to hit simultaneously the ICBMs, SLBMs, and bombers that compose the American triad. Even if all ICBMs were destroyed, they represented only about 25 percent of U.S. strategic power. The two other elements had an enormous retaliatory capability of their own, which was growing. Would any Kremlin leader take the chance of launching a first strike, gambling that Soviet forces could destroy a sufficient number of U.S. deterrent forces so that they would no longer be able to inflict overwhelming losses on the Soviet population? Would the Soviets, as Carter's defense secretary, Harold Brown, said, gamble on this "cosmic roll of the dice"?

The administration said no, but the critics feared the worst. The Soviets, they claimed, were driving for strategic superiority and rejecting parity. Their force development testified to their commitment to a first-strike capability, not a second-strike or retaliatory capability. The Soviets, they asserted, not only rejected the belief that nuclear war was unthinkable but also articulated a strategy of fighting a nuclear war and winning it. In the final analysis, the defenders and critics of SALT II differed most about how aggressive and ruthless the Soviets were. Proponents pointed to the unwillingness of the Soviet leadership to take great risks, precisely to avoid a possible clash with the United States. Conservative critics minimized the past record, insisting that the Soviets were ruthless, determined to achieve global domination, and that for the first time they had the power with which to pressure the Western powers and even risk an attack upon the United States, whose deterrent forces the critics maintained were vulnerable.

The second issue was the Soviet Union itself. If the Soviets had not invaded Afghanistan, Carter might have gained the Senate's consent for SALT II. A majority of the American people and senators favored the treaty, but not the two-thirds of the Senate required for ratification of a treaty. The invasion led the president temporarily to withdraw the treaty from Senate consideration. For several years, Carter had argued that SALT was so important that the negotiations ought to continue and that, when concluded, SALT II should be ratified despite repeated Soviet efforts to expand their influence. But the brazenness of the Soviet use of force in Afghanistan led the president to resort to Kissinger-like linkage he had consistently rejected and that his conservative critics had long demanded. In the final analysis, Soviet behavior—the continued military buildup and the meddling in the Third World—killed the treaty. Concern about this behavior had reinforced the more specific fears about a Soviet first strike. The growing American disillusionment with *détente* also led to the collapse of Kissinger's other weapon, the economic one. From the Soviet perspective, the failure of *détente* to yield arms control and trade benefits reinforced their determination to seek unilateral advantages. This was a recipe for cold war II.

Trade and Technology as Incentives for Soviet Self-Containment

In the early days of *détente* American policy makers were willing to fortify the incentives for Soviet political and military restraint with economic help. The Soviet economy as it entered the 1970s was in serious trouble. After rapid advancement in the 1950s and early 1960s, its growth rate headed down to 2 percent by the early 1980s. The economic decline was particularly notable in those branches of industry associated with the Second Industrial Revolution: computers, microelectronics, and petrochemicals. In short, the Soviet Union was behind and falling further behind the West in those industries that were most important for economic growth. The implications of this decline could not be ignored; it damaged the Soviet Union's appeal as a Socialist state and hampered its ability to compete with the United States.

Even in agriculture the growth in production had fallen sharply below expectations and official plans. Workers on the land, like workers in the factory, were far behind their American counterparts in per capita production. The Soviet Union's continued inability to provide a balanced diet— indeed, in some years just to avoid widespread hunger—was not just the result of poor weather, but of the ideologically determined organization of an agrarian economy administered by a rigid bureaucracy. By contrast, the small private plots that peasants were allowed to own produced much of the Soviet Union's poultry, pork, vegetables, and other staples. Just as the regime was failing to live up to its promise of more consumer goods, it was falling short of its goal of a more nutritious and varied diet, including more meat. During the 1970s, the Soviet workplace was characterized by high absenteeism, drunkenness, corruption, and shoddy production. The Soviet Union was also the only industrial society in which the peacetime life expectancy of males was declining and infant mortality rising.

Brezhnev could not forget that Nikita Khrushchev's promises of a higher standard of living had played a large part in his fall from power. He had raised popular expectations and then failed to meet them, which helped precipitate his fall; the same thing could happen to Brezhnev. In a system in which the leadership is determined to maintain a monopoly on political power and control, it seeks popular approval—legitimacy—by providing multiple social benefits at low costs: jobs, housing, health care, retirement benefits, and similar social services. The Soviet standard of living may not be high by Western standards, but as long as it improves gradually over past levels, the regime can claim to be fulfilling its aim of ameliorating the lives of its citizens. Conversely, a decline has serious implications. The Kremlin had to look no farther than Poland. In 1970 the poor state of the Polish economy and worker dissatisfaction with food shortages and a lack of consumer goods had led to riots in several cities and the collapse of the government which, even in a Communist-controlled state, had to be replaced. (Similar unrest occurred in 1980-1981.)

Soviet concern about falling behind in the scientific-technological revolution led the Kremlin to look toward the West for a "technological fix" to help stimulate their economy. In the absence of basic structural reforms of their highly centralized and bureaucratic system, Western technology, machinery, food, and the credit to buy them were the only recourse. Structural reform was unlikely because it would run into the regime's basic ideological hostility to capitalist ideas such as private property, the profit motive, and free market, as well as into the deeply vested interests of the economic bureaucracies committed to central planning and self-preservation. Decentralization of authority—devolving authority to factory and farm managers and their work forces—was above all a risky business because it might threaten the party's total control of political power. Importation of Western goods and food was the best alternative to such fundamental reforms; trade with the United States, with its scale of production, high technology that the Soviets envied, and agricultural abundance, was especially desirable to Moscow. In return, since it had little to sell the United States, it offered to let Americans develop and exploit the huge Soviet deposits of raw materials, especially in Siberia; the American capital to help finance this extraction would presumably be repaid in oil, natural gas, and other mineral resources in the future. The Soviets also looked to the United States for food in years of shortages, which occurred more and more frequently.

The Nixon-Ford administration believed these economic problems would give the United States leverage. Trade obviously was profitable for American industry and agriculture, but the main reason for permitting it was political. American productivity, it was hoped, would provide a powerful material reinforcement for a Soviet foreign policy of restraint and accommodation made necessary by the desire to prevent closer Sino-American "collusion," to achieve strategic arms agreements to stabilize mutual deterrence, and to gain American recognition of Soviet parity and equal status with the United States. Kissinger put it negatively: "Economic relations cannot be separated from the political context. Clearly, we cannot be asked to reward hostile conduct with economic benefits even if in the process we deny ourselves commercially profitable opportunities." But Kissinger's idea of using economic means to achieve political purposes was undermined by the Senate, which approved offering the Soviets trade and credits but on the condition, specified in an amendment offered by Sen. Henry Jackson and Rep. Charles Vanik, that Moscow would allow more Soviet Jews to emigrate. Considering the amendment an intervention in its domestic affairs, the Soviet Union rejected the trade agreement. No great power—let alone the Soviet Union, which claimed to be a nation in which class distinctions and religious and other forms of prejudice no longer existed—would publicly admit that it mistreated part of its population and allow itself to be placed on probation by a foreign nation in return for trade. As a result, the Soviet Union conducted its business with Western Europe instead of the United States, and a potentially powerful American weapon remained largely useless. And to the extent that the Soviets' primary motive for *détente* was economic, as many observers thought, the lack of payoff reduced their incentives for maintaining *détente*.

Détente: Real Change or Political Tactic?

The Jackson-Vanik amendment was an early indication of a growing American skepticism about *détente*. High expectations had been generated by the 1972 summit conference at which Nixon and Brezhnev had signed SALT I and the 1973 summit at which they had set down the principles to govern the superpower relationship. But then a number of events took place that raised questions about Soviet sincerity. Was their more moderate behavior in foreign policy genuine or was *détente* a tactical adaptation to a new international environment but still part of an expansionist policy? Did it reflect a Soviet willingness to live and let live with the West on the basis of strategic parity, acceptance of the *status quo* and mutual restraint? Or, having learned from experience that a hard line and iron fist tended to arouse and unite the West, were the Soviets using *détente* with its summits and smiles as a way of relaxing the West's guard and shifting the balance? Were they using *détente* to gain a superiority of power by lowering Western defense budgets, weakening NATO, and acquiring Western technology and economic assistance? Was *détente* anything but a "selective *détente*" in which the Soviet Union reaped general benefits from the lowering of tensions while unilaterally exploiting opportunities that increased its influence?

Middle East War of 1973

The situation that first and most dramatically raised these questions was the 1973 war in the Middle East. Only a few months after the second summit, which had reaffirmed the general rules of conduct between the two superpowers, Egypt and Syria attacked Israel on Yom Kippur, the highest of all Jewish religious holidays, the Day of Atonement. What shocked Washington and other Western capitals was the Soviet role. Egypt was ruled by Anwar Sadat, an Egyptian nationalist who had succeeded Gamal Abdel Nasser. Egypt had become increasingly frustrated by Israel's continued occupation of Egyptian territory up to the east bank of the Suez Canal. This territory, captured by Israel in the Six-Day War in 1967, looked as if it might remain in Israeli hands for a long time because Israel had no incentives to surrender it. The Arab states continued to be hostile to its existence. Even after losing the war of 1967, they refused to sit down with Israel and negotiate a settlement; Israel's victory therefore did not bring peace, only another ceasefire.

But Israel thought it was a peace of sorts. Israel was militarily superior and not likely to be attacked. The American-Soviet *détente* also benefited Israel because the United States did not press it to give up the captured Egyptian and Syrian territories. The Soviet Union, having improved its relations with Washington, was not about to permit Cairo to jeopardize these relations. Indeed, having once risked U.S.-Soviet relations by supplying arms to North Vietnam, Moscow made sure that the offensive arms Cairo wanted for an attack on Israel were not delivered. Only Egypt's defenses were bolstered, and the territorial *status quo* became frozen.

But Sadat was unwilling to live with this *status quo*. He was subject to strong external pressures from other Arab states and domestic pressures to seek revenge against Israel. An unknown figure succeeding the much loved and charismatic Nasser, Sadat was in danger of being overthrown, particularly by pro-Soviet Egyptian leaders, whom he had alienated by his attempts to reduce, if not eliminate, their influence. Sadat was also under fire for trying to attract foreign, including American, private capital to rescue Egypt's stagnant Socialist economy. Above all, Sadat realized that Moscow would be no help in persuading Israel to give up the Arab territory captured in 1967. Only the United States, Israel's friend, could help him achieve this goal; implicit in this emphasis on the return of the 1967 territory was a reciprocal willingness to recognize Israel's existence. But Israel, skeptical after its bitter experiences with the Arabs, did nothing; to Israel, Sadat was merely talking, wanting the return of territory that, once returned, would only strengthen him for yet another war. The United States, too, did nothing, even after Sadat in 1972 threw out some Soviet military advisers in an effort to entice Washington to take the initiative in seeking a peace agreement.

Sadat, frustrated, his power endangered, therefore launched the Yom Kippur War, taking Israel by surprise. The Arab armies achieved initial success in crossing the Suez Canal and driving into the Sinai desert, which they could not have done without large amounts of Soviet arms and equipment. Although it seems relatively clear that the Soviet Union did not wish to risk *détente* by helping to precipitate another Arab-Israeli war as it had done in 1967, it is also obvious that, once informed of the Egyptian-Syrian determination to go to war, it was unwilling to risk losing influence in the Arab world by opposing them. Instead Moscow stepped up its delivery of offensive arms, including ground-to-air missiles and highly accurate antitank missiles.

When indeed, the Egyptian and Syrian armies proved successful in the opening round of fighting, the Soviet Union began a huge airlift of war material and opposed any cease-fire calls that were not linked to a pullback by Israel to the 1967 frontiers. Moscow also called upon other Arab governments to join the war and approved the Organization of Petroleum Exporting Countries' (OPEC) oil embargo against the United States. And when the United States finally began its massive airlift of military supplies (because the Soviet Union refused to match the American restraint) in the face of enormous Israeli fighter plane and tank losses, Soviet denunciations of the United States were stepped up. In the United States, this Soviet behavior was seen as incompatible with *détente*.

Once Israel had recovered from its shock and had driven the Syrians back from the Golan Heights, its forces concentrated on Egypt, crossed the Suez Canal to the west bank, and moved to cut off supplies to the Egyptian forces on the east bank and to encircle them. At this point, the United States and the Soviet Union agreed upon a cease-fire resolution in the UN Security Council. The United States took this step because it felt that no peace could be arranged if Egypt were again humiliated in war—indeed, the psychological boost derived from its initial successes had to be preserved if Egypt was to make any concessions in a peace settlement. Moreover, the Soviet Union might be compelled to enter the war to rescue its client state. But the shooting continued, and the Israelis drove to encircle and destroy the Egyptian army on the eastern side of the Suez Canal. Sadat now asked the United States and the Soviet Union to use their own forces to impose their cease-fire resolution. The United States declined to intervene with its forces, but the Soviet Union threatened to do so unilaterally. The two superpowers now confronted one another, as American military forces were placed on a worldwide alert. However, Moscow backed off, and the United States, also anxious to avoid an escalation, pressured Israel to end its military advance. These moves assured the cease-fire.

Civil War in Angola

The second example of selective *détente* came in 1975 in Angola, a country rich in oil and mineral resources and geographically dividing "white supremacist" Africa—Rhodesia and South Africa, which controlled South-West Africa or Namibia—from black Africa. As a Portuguese colony, it had helped protect the two racist states from black liberation movements. But as Portuguese colonialism came to an end, Angola's interim government, which was composed of three factions based on tribal allegiances, underwent a power struggle. This rivalry continued after Angola became independent, and the different factions attracted outside support. Some claim that the large-scale, decisive Cuban military intervention occurred after repeated South African military strikes into Angola, as well as intervention from Zaire (formerly the Congo, now governed by a pro-Western leader) on behalf of two of the rival factions. But the Ford administration did not see what took place as a rescue effort of this "national liberation" movement from probable military defeat. The Soviets first shipped in military supplies and Cuban advisers, which were followed later by Soviet jet fighters, mortars, rockets, armored cars, ground-to-air missiles, military advisers, and a Cuban military force of more than 12,000 men to help the pro-Soviet faction. Rather, the administration viewed the Cubans as proxies acting on behalf of the Soviet Union, and the attempt to influence the outcome of the conflict in Angola as an expression of "Soviet colonialism."

The result was to reintroduce a measure of great power rivalry and possible confrontation into southern Africa. While rejecting any military reaction, Washington denounced the Soviet and Cuban acts but limited itself to covert arms aid, purportedly to strengthen the two rival factions, make it impossible for the Soviet-backed movement to win, and to compel a negotiated

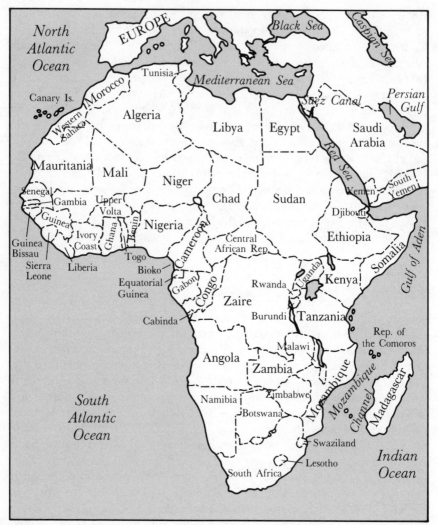

Africa

settlement in which power would be shared. But this effort not only did not match that of the Soviet Union but was cut off by the Senate, fearful of another Vietnam in an area that did not constitute a vital American interest. Rejecting the contention that Angola might become another Vietnam, Ford and Kissinger conceded that Angola was not a significant American interest. They emphasized, however, that Soviet behavior could not for that reason be ignored. Angola might be far away, but, in their view, it was a test case of the superpower relationship. Soviet actions were simply incompatible with *détente;* it was another case of their selective *détente,* of the Kremlin's seeking unilateral advantage from the general relaxation of tensions. The secretary of state asserted that the United States could not be indifferent to the Soviet Union's attempt so far from home and so distant from traditional Soviet concerns to impose a government favorable to Soviet interests.

Angola was probably a turning point in *détente*. The Soviets had been allies of the Egyptians since 1955; it was understandable that they would not wish to risk a two-decade investment of political prestige, economic aid, and military assistance by not shipping Egypt offensive weapons or by informing Washington of the impending attack in 1973. But to Kissinger, Angola was far beyond any Soviet sphere of influence, and the Soviet action constituted a military intervention to impose a regime of Soviet choice. The Soviet Union's response was to defend its behavior by asserting that support of national liberation movements, including armed intervention, was not incompatible with *détente*. *Détente* did not mean the end of the struggle against imperialism. "What's mine is mine, what's yours is negotiable," President Kennedy had once said in summing the essence of Soviet foreign policy. Had things really changed, *détente* notwithstanding?

The Carter administration's answer was more ambiguous than that of its predecessor. The administration was divided between the "global-ists" and the "regionalists." For globalists, the prime concern was Soviet-American rivalry; a gain of influence for the Soviets was a loss of influence for the United States. For regionalists, these types of quarrels among indigenous states in an area were local in origin and had to be resolved locally by addressing the causes that had given rise to them. The globalists maintained that Soviet-Cuban intervention added the element of a super-power competition, which could be ignored only at great cost to Ameri-can prestige and the credibility of American power, as well as strategic position. The regionalists countered that these conflicts, which had eth-nic, racial, regional, or nationalist origins, should be resolved on their merit, depriving the Soviets of opportunities to meddle. For the United States to intervene with military assistance and advisers on the anti-Communist side, which often did not have sufficient popular backing, would be to escalate the conflict, needlessly embroil a local problem in a global contest, and, in this way, to follow the pattern of Vietnam and risk another long, and losing, war. Political problems, they asserted, could not be solved by the use of force.

Vietnam haunted the Carter administration. Some of the senior officials, including the secretaries of state and defense, had participated in the decisions leading to the U.S. intervention and had since declared that they had been mistaken; they felt a deep moral responsibility for their past roles. At the as-sistant secretary level were a number of officials, some former foreign service officers, who had resigned over the war and supported the Democratic presidential candidate, Senator George McGovern, in 1972. All shared the sense that the United States had given too much priority to the East-West conflict, and they held the containment policy responsible for the nation's past overcommitments and follies in foreign policy.

Soviet Involvement in Ethiopia

Moscow's next move in Africa came in 1977 as Somalia, the Soviet Union's closest African ally, a country in which it had a naval base at Berbera and which it had supplied with arms, supported the Western Somali Liberation Front in the Ogaden region of Ethiopia (Somali troops had invaded Ethiopia to fight alongside the Front). Somalia had long claimed that this area, populated by people of Somali origin, was part of Somalia. Ethiopia, already facing disintegration as it confronted other rebellions and secessionist attempts, especially the attempt by Eritrea to establish itself as an independent state, rejected the claim. Like other African and Third World nations, it recognized the borders existing at the time of independence—that is, borders drawn by the colonial powers—as its legal national boundaries. Because Ethiopia is about ten times as large as Somalia with its population of just over 3 million, the Soviet Union supported Ethiopia with an estimated $1 billion of military supplies, military advisers, and 20,000 Cuban advisers and troops to squash the Ogaden rebellion. It was willing to risk alienating Somalia and the loss of its naval base and some air facilities facing the Indian Ocean because the stakes were even greater in Ethiopa than in Angola.

There was irony in a Soviet-supported Marxist regime attacking another Soviet-supported Marxist regime, which the Ethiopian government had become after the overthrow of Emperor Haile Selassie. But, as Soviet relations with Washington worsened, Moscow saw its opportunity to enhance its influence in the strategic Horn of Africa, the eastern tip of the African continent. Across the Gulf of Aden lay Saudi Arabia. Washington's fear was that the Soviet Union might gain control of the southern entrance to the Red Sea, which led to the Suez Canal and Israel, and that it would pose a threat to the important oil routes from the Persian Gulf to the West.

The Carter administration's reaction was schizophrenic. Brzezinski, like Kissinger, tended to see the Soviet-Cuban activities in Africa in the context of the American-Soviet rivalry. So did the Defense Department, which wanted to send military aid to Somalia to displace Soviet influence. Among the states urging American help for Somalia, a Muslim country, were Saudi Arabia, the Sudan, and Egypt, all worried by the expansion of Soviet influence and the need to protect the oil routes through the Suez Canal or around the Cape of Good Hope.

Secretary of State Vance and the State Department's African desk, however, tended to see the problem as essentially an indigenous one in which American intervention would be counterproductive and lead to deeper involvement, which would be costly and tarnish America's reputation. In a continent where national boundaries lacked geographic and ethnic logic and where virtually every state had its tribes with separatist hopes, the United

States—which in the early 1960s had supported the UN effort to prevent Katanga (now Shaba Province) from splitting away from the Congo (now Zaire)—could not intervene to help Somalia without alienating most African states. Short of preventing Cuban and Ethiopian troops from crossing over into Somalia after recapturing the Ogaden, the United States could do little. The situation, as it existed, simply favored Moscow. Moreover, the Ethiopian government had specifically asked for its help, as numerous governments in the past had asked for U.S. help. In the long run, it was contended, Soviet efforts to establish a foothold in this region would fail because of the strength of African nationalism, even in Marxist-oriented countries. Egypt and other countries in which the Soviets once had exerted influence, only to be ejected later, were cited as proof.

The Carter administration's division between the globalists and regionalists continued in the following years and the president alternated between them. Sometimes he would denounce Moscow and Cuba and declare, as Kissinger had, that the Soviet Union could not benefit from and exploit *détente* simultaneously. Linkages existed, Carter would declare, as he pointed out that the chances for Senate approval of SALT II would be endangered if the Soviet Union continued its African adventures (indeed, Brzezinski would later say that SALT II was buried in the sands of Somalia). After Cuba's alleged involvement with old Katanganese rebels, who had invaded Shaba Province from Angola in 1978, Carter ordered the U.S. air force to help airlift Belgian and French troops to the area. The basic administration position, however, remained that African problems were indigenous and that the American response should be to encourage solutions based on each situation, particularly with the help of other African states.

Carter's Reaction to Afghanistan

The split in the Carter administration ended with the Soviet invasion of Afghanistan. The 1978 coup in Afghanistan by pro-Soviet elements had been overlooked, but 85,000 Soviet troops, which were sent in during the last week in December 1979, were hard to ignore. The Soviets had acted because fierce resistance by Muslim tribesmen to radical and antireligious reforms had created a situation in which it looked as if the Soviet-supported regime might fall. Perhaps the Soviets feared that the Islamic fundamentalism then sweeping Iran and Pakistan might also engulf Afghanistan, which lay between these two countries, creating an insecure situation on the Soviets' southern border where it might affect the approximately 50 million Soviet Muslims living in the area. In any event, Moscow invoked the Brezhnev Doctrine, that once a nation had become Socialist, it was not again to be surrendered to counterrevolution (as the Soviets defined these terms). The march of history toward socialism was inevitable and irreversible. But this doctrine previously had been asserted only in Eastern Europe—in Hungary in 1956 and Czechoslovakia in 1968. Now the Red Army was to ensure history's progress outside of the Soviet sphere in a Third World country.

The Soviets probably expected no more of an American response than in Angola or Ethiopia; that is, words condemning Soviet action as deplorable, but no action. Clearly, they believed vital security interests to be at stake and did not give much thought to American reactions. In truth, there was little to lose. *Détente* hardly survived. SALT II was dying in the Senate; Carter, to rescue the treaty, had promised to increase defense spending and to build the new MX missile, and he was intent on matching Soviet intermediate-range ballistic missiles (IRBMs) aimed at Western Europe with U.S. IRBMs in Western Europe (where, to Soviet consternation, they could reach the Soviet Union). The Soviet Union had received little of the trade, technology, and credits it had expected, and it was denied the most-favored nation commercial status, which China had received. Nevertheless, such a disregard for American reaction, implying contempt for American power, was rather new.

For Carter and Vance, who had pinned so much of their hope in *détente* on SALT II and restrained themselves from countering Soviet behavior in the Third World in order not to further jeopardize American-Soviet relations, the Soviet invasion was a shock. Carter publicly confessed his earlier optimistic views when he said that the Soviet action had "made a more dramatic change in my opinion of what the Soviets' ultimate goals are than anything they've done in the previous time I've been in office." No president in the postwar era has more dramatically testified to his naiveté. Brzezinski, for whom this type of Soviet behavior held no surprise, but who until then had little influence on Carter's policy toward the Soviet Union, began to gain influence; Vance's star, once bright, faded quickly and he resigned a few months later.

The president, swinging with events, now became a "hard-liner." He halted high-technology sales, embargoed feed grain shipments, and imposed a U.S. boycott on the Olympic Games scheduled for Moscow in the summer of 1980. Most important of all, in the context of growing Soviet influence in the Horn of Africa and the collapse of pro-Western shah in Iran and his replacement by a militant anti-American regime (see chapter 10), Carter announced his own doctrine. Even if Soviet motivations for the invasion of Afghanistan had been basically defensive, the consequence was nevertheless a major advance of Soviet military power toward the vital Persian Gulf-Indian Ocean oil line to the West. After three years of nonresistance to Soviet moves in Ethiopia and after coups in 1978 in both Yemen (on the Arabian peninsula) and Afghanistan, the president suddenly became fearful of a Soviet pincer movement on Saudi Arabia and the other oil kingdoms on the Gulf. Having previously denounced those still primarily concerned with the East-West conflict as globalists and cold warriors, Carter shifted gears toward the end of his term and embraced the approach he had previously rejected.

Détente thus came to an end. Carter undoubtedly had been correct that not all regional conflicts were tests of superpower strength and credibility; but events had demonstrated that some became so because of Soviet intervention.

In fact, few purely regional quarrels existed. Ironically, then, *détente* collapsed because of a series of regional conflicts that the administration had tried to isolate from the American-Soviet rivalry—only to find that it could not do so. Soviet activities in the Third World were evidence that the Soviet Union did not consider this rivalry over. Quite the opposite: it sought to exploit the United States' post-Vietnam reluctance to act and the illusion that Third World problems could be separated from the superpower competition.

The Erosion of U.S. Alliances

The whole concept of *détente* was bound to pose several problems for the United States. Alliances are normally drawn together by common perceptions of an overriding external threat. But what cements the bonds of such relationships when that threat is no longer seen as great—indeed, as vastly reduced—by the principal members of the coalition? Is it not inevitable that the strands of such entangling alliances become untangled? In Europe, among America's most important allies, that appeared to be the situation.

In the days when all members of the alliance had seen the Soviet threat as serious, NATO had been a reasonably cohesive organization. To be sure, the alliance had become strained because its European members, although still dependent on the United States for their security, had recovered from the war and wanted a greater voice in the alliance. The common perception of external danger had sufficed to keep the bonds of the alliance close.

In the era of *détente,* however, the various nations were no longer so willing to give priority to alliance interests. Washington, for example, now negotiated directly with the Kremlin on key issues, as relations with Moscow became in some respects more important than those with NATO members. Not surprisingly, the European states also went their own way, and economic issues proved especially divisive within the Atlantic community. During the immediate postwar era economic policies such as the Marshall Plan had been consistent with and supported American political-military policy, but now economic relations were at odds with the other strands of policy.

NATO Develops Cracks

The Common Market emerging in the 1970s was an increasingly powerful economic competitor. During the cold war, the United States had been a leading proponent of European union; a strong United States of Europe would be a significant contribution to the U.S. balance with the Soviet Union. The competitiveness of an economically unified Europe was thought to be worth the risk. In a period of *détente,* however, as the European unification movement stalled, and differences between the United States and Europe grew (especially as Europe's heavily subsidized agriculture became productive and exportable, which reduced U.S. agricultural exports to Europe and competed with it elsewhere), past policy often appeared counterproductive because of the economic losses it entailed.

In addition, by the late 1970s, as the United States was increasingly disillusioned with *détente*, the allies were intent on preserving it. Western Europe had greatly expanded its economic relations with the Eastern bloc, especially the Soviet Union. As European industry became increasingly less competitive in the international market, Western Europe viewed Eastern Europe and the Soviet Union as an economically complementary unit. Western Europe had the industrial goods and high technology; the Soviet bloc had natural resources. Each needed the other. Western Europe's economic stake in *détente*, therefore, was larger than that of the United States, whose trade with the Soviet Union had sharply declined.

Politically, too, the Europeans were content with *détente*, in contrast to the Americans, who had become more and more concerned with the growth of Soviet military power and the expansion of its political influence in the Third World. The Europeans virtually ignored Soviet activities outside of their continent, as if relieved that Soviet energies were directed away from Europe. Compared with the confrontations and frequent Berlin crises of the cold war, the decade of the 1970s had been a period of peace and calm in Europe. For West Germany especially, the period had seen the stabilization of the European territorial *status quo*, the four-power settlement of the Berlin issue, and the mutual recognition between West Germany and East Germany, with increasing trade and person-to-person contact across their boundary. The West Germans saw this situation as the nearest thing to reunification they were likely to achieve. Thus, while the United States wanted less *détente*, Europe wanted more. The Europeans sought to maintain a *détente* separate from U.S. policy, to preserve *détente* with the Soviet Union, but still have America's military protection. They did so by distancing themselves from the new harder-line, anti-Soviet rhetoric and actions emerging from Washington.

Carter's economic boycott of the Soviet Union after the Soviet invasion of Afghanistan, therefore, received little enthusiasm or support; nor did the rather painless boycott of the summer Olympic Games in Moscow. During the Cuban missile crisis, America's allies had rallied to its side despite differences of policy over the issue of West Berlin and the continuing Soviet threat to that city; in contrast, after Afghanistan the French and German leaders journeyed eastward to salvage a separate European-Soviet *détente*. As the Soviets achieved strategic parity and Soviet power in Eastern Europe grew, Western Europe appeared to become more accommodating. Europeans, many of whom had become deeply disillusioned with the United States because of Vietnam, now feared the possibility of U.S.-Soviet confrontation outside of Europe even more than before because it might escalate and engulf Europe in a nuclear war. Increasingly, it was American behavior that was seen as reckless and dangerous because it might provoke Moscow.

Indeed, the fundamental question raised in the post-Vietnam period was whether Western Europe, with a population of well over 300 million, highly developed industry, and a long military tradition, had the will to defend itself. Or had it become too used to being defended by the United States? The mood of accommodation was strong, and pacifism and neutralism were gaining respectability. The British Labour party, out of power and under the strong influence of its left wing, favored unilateral nuclear disarmament and declared its opposition to American nuclear bases in Britain; it almost came out for Britain's withdrawal from NATO. On the Continent, governments— with the major exception of France—were also sensitive to public opinion. In West Germany the Social Democrats, formerly strong supporters of NATO, swung, like the Labour party, to the left.

Symbolic of this trend, European defense budgets did not usually even meet the 3 percent of gross national product (GNP) the alliance members had agreed to spend in response to the extensive Soviet military buildup in Eastern Europe. As reasons for not doing more in their self-defense, the Europeans cited the economic problems of inflation and unemployment that resulted from higher oil prices. They also interpreted Soviet intentions as more benign than did Washington. They had to see Moscow in this light, for to admit that the Soviet Union was more than an occasional bad neighbor would have required higher defense spending and the cutback of extensive domestic welfare systems. Instead, the Europeans blamed the United States for raising international tensions and tried to separate themselves politically and psychologically from American policies. But depending upon the United States for their defense while simultaneously being more conciliatory toward Moscow were not feasible long-run policies; they were bound to erode the bonds of the alliance. The unanswered question was, if the United States faltered or did not exist, would the Europeans do what had to be done to enhance their security or would they become vassals of the Soviet Union?

Besides Afghanistan, events outside of Europe were also divisive, especially in the Middle East and Persian Gulf area. The Yom Kippur War of 1973 nearly brought the alliance to the breaking point. The Europeans, almost totally dependent upon Arab oil for their well-being, were reluctant to antagonize the Arabs and risk an oil embargo. Therefore, although the Syrians and Egyptians had started the war, there was little backing for the United States in its support of Israel. While Europe supported American efforts to seek a comprehensive peace between Israel and its neighbors after the 1973 war, the deadlock on the Palestinian issue, as well as others, led the Common Market countries to take an independent stand.

The Europeans' sensitivity and vulnerability on the question of oil supplies was also in evidence during the period following the seizure of the American hostages in Iran (chapter 10). In several key areas of the world, therefore, Western Europe did not follow the lead of the United States except reluctantly and only when unavoidable. Some sanctions, such as against Iran, were invoked largely for symbolic purposes, not because of any painful effect they might have. They were intended primarily to assuage the United States, which felt that Soviet actions in Afghanistan and the humiliation of America in Iran demanded more than verbal protests as a response. The key point was that the Europeans sought above all to restrain the United States from doing anything that they perceived as rash and dangerous. As these events unfolded, *détente's* relaxation of tension led Greece and Turkey to a military clash over the island of Cyprus. This disintegration of NATO's flank in the eastern Mediterranean was made even worse when Congress, pushed by the Greek-American lobby, cut off all military assistance to Turkey even though Greece had precipitated the conflict.

SEATO and CENTO Dissolve

While the Western allies were having their difficulties, the Southeast Asia Treaty Organization (SEATO) collapsed completely. It formally dissolved in 1975 after the fall of South Vietnam and its takeover by the North. All expectations had been that Hanoi would make its big push for victory in 1976 during the American presidential campaign. But a rather routine fight turned into a rout as President Thieu of South Vietnam, allegedly short of military equipment as a result of congressional cutbacks of funds for South Vietnam, sought to withdraw troops from the northern part of South Vietnam and concentrate them in the more populated areas. Hanoi, undoubtedly as surprised as Washington at the sudden collapse of Saigon's army, quickly sent its troops southward to keep up with the retreating South Vietnamese. Thieu had made his decision to pull back in mid-March; Saigon fell April 30. South Vietnam's leaders now reaped their reward: having inherited France's colonial legacy, they had been overly concerned with their own power and had relied too much on American assistance and forces instead of developing a social strategy to boost the morale and mobilize the support of their people.

The war was finally over. Despite a show of force when the Cambodians seized the American merchantman, *Mayaguez,* and the recovery of the ship and its crew, there was no way to halt the erosion of American influence in Southeast Asia. Shortly after its victory, Hanoi announced plans for the early unification of Vietnam. Communist troops also won in Cambodia, and the Communists gained political power shortly thereafter in Laos. Everywhere in Southeast Asia the result of what was seen as an American defeat in Vietnam was anxiety and nervousness. In these circumstances SEATO did the only thing it could do—bury itself. No one wept at the funeral. SEATO had been an alliance that, unlike NATO, lacked the principal indigenous nations as its members and was organized against a threat that the countries of the area did not recognize. Its principal members were Western and white, two of whom had been colonial powers in the area. At best, SEATO had provided the United States with the justification for unilateral intervention, but the treaty forming the alliance had hardly proved itself to be what Secretary John

Foster Dulles had once called it, the Monroe Doctrine for Asia. It had been another exercise in overstatement, so characteristic of the rhetoric of crusadism; unfortunately, it had also led the country into a disastrous war.

The Central Treaty Organization (CENTO) died more slowly. First, with the splitting off of Bangladesh from Pakistan, which had also been a SEATO member, India emerged as the dominant power on the subcontinent. Pakistan, which had joined both alliances primarily to receive U.S. arms for its adversary relationship with India, no longer had much interest in either alliance. In the meantime, it had moved close to Communist China, a regional rival of India. Turkey, at the other end of the alliance's geographical area, was still nursing its wounds after the arms embargo and suffering from increasing domestic instability. In between, Iran was now the only reliable friend of the West in the area of Southwest Asia.

After Britain had withdrawn from "east of Suez," Iran had become America's local policeman in the Persian Gulf, because the United States, given its own isolationist mood, was incapable of filling the vacuum left by the disappearance of British power (as it had done shortly after World War II in Turkey and Greece). The shah, whose throne had been restored to him in 1954 by the CIA, was a strong supporter of U.S. policy. He had, among other things, sent oil to Israel during the 1973 war, backed Egypt's efforts to make peace with Israel, and not embargoed oil shipments to the United States in 1973-1974. In return, the Nixon-Ford administration had supplied him with all the weapons he requested for building up large and modern Iranian armed forces. But the shah, who, as an absolute ruler, seemed so safe as the guardian of Western interests in the region, lost his power at the end of 1978. Traditional Muslim religious leaders inspired their flock to protest against the shah's rapid modernization and the accompanying westernization, which was destroying the traditional religious society, as well as eroding their own status and influence. They, together with secular left-wing and constitutional forces, protested the shah's despotic rule and pro-Western policy. The shah was widely perceived by Iranians as a tool of the United States, doing its bidding. And so he fell, and his "foreign" regime was replaced by a more orthodox Islamic republic. Iran quit SEATO, to be followed shortly by Muslim Pakistan.

The collapse of the shah was a tremendous strategic loss for the United States, but whether it could have done anything to prevent his fall remains controversial. The shah's concentration of all political power in his own hands forced the opposition, especially the Western-educated middle class seeking a more democratic Iran in which it would play a large political role, to join together with the more traditional opposition led by the clergy. At the same time, the Carter administration was paralyzed by internal disagreement. On one side Brzezinski kept Iran's strategic position and role foremost in his mind, urging that the shah be told that the United States would support him fully, even if he used the army to suppress the crowds in the streets. On the other side the State Department was largely hostile to the shah, repelled by his human rights record; it also believed that a successor regime would be made up of those seeking democracy in Iran and that if the Ayatollah Ruhollah Khomeini came to power, he would be a figurehead only. Khomeini was a religious figure, too old and without the necessary experience in government to play an active, let alone dominant, role. The State Department, almost looking forward to the shah's collapse, advised against support- ing him; if he fell, the United States would be rid of an embarrassing supporter and could replace him with pro-Western, prodemocratic forces. It was a risk-free policy that would presumably strengthen the U.S. position in the Gulf.

The president, who had stressed human rights in his election campaign and pointed to the shah, among others, as an example of his predecessor's amoral, if not immoral, policy, was caught between these conflicting views. The disagreements in Washington were such that the subsequent fall of the shah and Khomeini's triumph were greeted with relief. As happened so often before—for instance, in the Eisenhower administration's analysis of Nasser— the Carter administration's understanding of Khomeini was superficial, consistent with its own hopes of what it hoped would happen. Perhaps Carter's misapprehension is forgivable, for, after all, who in Washington or any other Western capital, would in this secular age have given serious consideration to the strength of a religious movement and the possibility that it would transform Iran into a medieval theocracy? Modernization after all, if it meant anything, meant secularization, an emphasis on life here on earth. Western scholarship's explanations of the "stages of economic growth" through which the less-developed countries (LDCs) would have to pass, emphasized only that traditional society was an obstacle to progress. The possible emergence of an Iran dominated by the clergy was so alien to all Western thinking that it was not taken seriously; there was no precedent for such a reaction to efforts at modernization.

The result, in any case, was that the whole area was suddenly in crisis. The overthrow of the shah and his replacement by a fundamentalist Islamic, anti-American regime; the increasing insecurity felt by the Saudis, who had watched the United States stand by helplessly as another monarchy fell; the spread of Soviet influence in Ethiopia and South Yemen on the Arabian peninsula, as well as the Soviet invasion of Afghanistan, amounted to a collapsing American position throughout the area and a greatly increased danger to the vital oil supplies upon which the United States and its allies de- pended. Thus, in the irony of ironies, Carter found himself forced to declare that the United States would fight to guard these oil resources. The United States under the Carter Doctrine was now committed to the defense of the Persian Gulf countries.

The United States could learn two lessons about its role in the world: first, no local power, especially if it is suffering from internal weaknesses, can substitute for American power, and second, no matter how strong its preference to play a less prominent role in the world, the United States as a superpower has extensive interests that it cannot run away from. The world will not sit still while the United States decides whether it wants to play international politics or not. These lessons had to be learned again in the post-Vietnam era in which the United States was left with only one major alliance in Eurasia—NATO—and NATO's power and resolve to act collectively in the common interest were questionable.

Disillusionment with *Détente*

Any evaluation of *détente* reflects expectations. In the context of America's national style, it is not surprising that views of *détente* swung from euphoria in 1972 to increasing disillusionment as early as 1973 or 1974. The national mood wavered between opposite and mutually exclusive categories: isolationism or intervention, peace or war, diplomacy or force, harmony or strife, optimism that the United States can reform the world or cynicism about an evil world that resists reform and, in the process, corrupts the reformer—all of which suggested withdrawal from the world as a solution. Thus, *détente* was widely believed to be the opposite of cold war.

The Nixon administration's overselling of *détente* and slogans like "negotiation, not confrontation" reinforced the expectation that the cold war was over and that the two superpowers had put their conflicts and crises and the danger of war behind them. Raising people's hopes too high is bound to lead to disillusionment when subsequent events do not live up to expectations. The problem is that each administration tends to package its foreign policy in slogans that emphasize how its policy differs from that of its predecessors; and, anticipating the next election, it wants to make that policy look appealing and successful. Despite the high degree of continuity of American foreign policy, the United States has rhetorically indulged in containment, liberation, frontiersmanship, and *détente*.

In addition, *détente* as a state of existence that combined both conflict and cooperation was more difficult than the cold war for people to understand. It is easier to explain a relationship that is essentially one of confrontation or cooperation. The cold war aroused people; *détente* relaxed them, as if *détente* were the same thing as *entente*, meaning friendship. In fact, *détente* meant a reduction of tensions, not an absence of tensions or superpower rivalry. To regard it as if it were such an absence was bound to produce disillusionment.

Indeed, in its conception, *détente* was intended as another form of containment for a period of domestic neo-isolationism, superpower parity, and Sino-Soviet schism. The cold war stick was to be supplemented by the carrot of *détente*, and issues were to be linked, explicitly or otherwise. The

Soviet Union was to be constrained from foreign adventures with force, or the threat of force, plus the withholding of agreements it desired. The United States hoped that Moscow, enticed by Western goods, technology, and credits, would restrain itself to avoid the loss of such benefits and of agreements such as SALT. In other words, Moscow would be given the incentives to practice self-containment!

But this U.S.-Soviet adversary-partnership was not static; the mix of these two elements varied according to circumstance. In 1972 the Soviets wanted Western, especially American, trade, technology, and credits, a slowdown of the American-Chinese rapprochement, a strategic arms agreement, plus millions of tons of American wheat. But in 1973 the Soviet harvest was good; SALT I had been signed, but there had been little progress toward SALT II; the Senate had not yet decided what terms of trade and credit to offer the Soviet Union; and, perhaps most important, Nixon's authority was rapidly eroding as the Watergate scandal unraveled. Whereas in 1972 Moscow withheld the offensive arms Sadat wanted and, as a result, suffered the humiliation of having its advisers thrown out of Egypt, in 1973 the Soviet Union did not need the United States for food and was still waiting for the economic payoff of *détente*. The Soviet Union may also have been unsure whether it should still sign any arms agreements with Nixon and felt that he might be unable to react to any challenges; therefore, Egypt received not only the arms with which to launch its war against Israel but also the Kremlin's hearty political endorsement. In short, *détente* is not one thing that stays the same year after year. It changes with conditions.

As emphasized earlier, one of the basic reasons why the United States first adopted *détente* as a diplomatic strategy was the country's pervasive mood of withdrawal after the Vietnam War. This attitude made containment of the Soviet Union very difficult at the exact time it had become a global power. *Détente*, however, was not a set of self-denying rules. If the Soviet Union is faced with favorable situations to exploit, should it shun these opportunities just because the United States is in no mood to resist? Self-restraint as a policy is asking a great deal of any major power. Nixon and Ford felt largely restrained by public and congressional forces, although Nixon opposed the potential Soviet intervention in the Yom Kippur War, and Ford attempted to resist Soviet-Cuban moves in Angola. The Jackson-Vanik amendment also made it more difficult to wield the economic "weapon." The Watergate scandal and Nixon's resignation were critical in weakening the presidency as an institution. The passage, over Nixon's veto so soon after his landslide reelection, of the War Powers Act, which restricts the president's ability to use force, was symbolic of the shifting of power from the executive to the legislative branch, whose mood was to restrain the United States's role in international affairs. The nation had had a "bellyful" of an interventionist foreign policy. It wanted a rest, a *détente*. Carter shared the mood and attitudes of the middle 1970s: that the United States had overextended itself in the world; that it had incorrectly estimated the Communist danger and overreacted; that American power had, especially in Vietnam, been misused; that the cold war had ended, and it was time to play a less prominent role in the world.

As the 1970s were passing, Americans were increasingly reluctant to use American power because of their sense of guilt about its uses in the past. It was as if the exercise of *American* power, not the expansionist efforts of the Soviet Union, were the main problem. If the United States acted in a more restrained manner, it was said, the world would become a more peaceful place; the Soviets would then follow our example. The Carter administration's constant refrain was "the limits of American power." The phrase made good sense if it was intended to say the obvious, that the United States was not omnipotent and could not indiscriminately commit itself everywhere. It made less sense if it meant—as it often appeared to—that the United States was virtually impotent and could not, therefore, influence events or resist adverse trends. Deeply embedded in the administration's attitude was the old American feeling of shame about the use of power in a morally ambiguous world, as if using it had made Americans wicked. Vietnam seemed to be obvious evidence of evil.

Apart from the collapse of the cold war consensus, another issue was whether the American political system was suitable for the conduct of a policy of cooperation and confrontation that relies upon an ever-changing mixture of sanctions and incentives. Could it be considered suitable when the Senate attached a provision about Jewish emigration to a commercial agreement with the Soviet Union or cut off funds for arms being sent to the anti-Communist factions in Angola? How can it be so when the president refuses to use wheat as leverage because he is unwilling to alienate the vote of farmers who prefer cool cash to cold war (or if he does use it, as Carter did after Afghanistan, it is only to find strong farmer resistance); or the president does not want to link arms control to other issues but there is strong congressional pressure for him to do so (or vice versa)?

The built-in executive-legislative conflict resulting from separate institutions sharing power has always made it difficult to formulate foreign policy. The United States' first experience after a century of isolationism, World War I, ended in a peace treaty that the Senate defeated. It was the strong opposition in Congress that led President Franklin Roosevelt to resort increasingly to executive agreements in his conduct of foreign policy from 1939 to 1941. During the cold war, the shared presidential and congressional perception of great external threat plus agreement on America's foreign policy aims had generally toned down the conflict between the two branches and increased the president's influence with Congress. But in the absence of a clear-cut and overwhelming perception of danger during the *détente* years and the presence of intense disagreements about the roles and purposes of America in the world after the war in Vietnam, the president and Congress often pulled in different directions. Given the lack of access to U.S. industrial technology and the failure to achieve a significant arms control agreement, even after years of difficult negotiations and America's signature on SALT II, a Soviet leader might well ask why the Soviet Union should restrain itself. This was especially so at a time when the United States appeared to be in no mood to risk confrontation, when almost every policy became caught in a bitter dispute between Congress and the president, and the Soviet Union had the opportunities to expand its influence with impunity.

Probably any great power rival would have behaved as the Soviet Union did. The United States, after all, during the heyday of *détente,* had bombed Moscow's ally, North Vietnam. After the Yom Kippur War, the United States had promoted a Middle East peace settlement by making itself the arbiter between Israel and the Arabs and excluding the Soviet Union from playing a key role in the area. But Moscow was especially likely to exploit America's paralysis of will and any opportunities to enhance Soviet influence. The Soviet Union believed itself to be engaged in an irreconcilable struggle with international capitalism led by the United States. For the Soviet Union, *détente* did not mean an end of the competition; it only meant competing at a lower level of tension so that the rivalry would not erupt in nuclear war. But, as the Soviets frequently reminded listeners, *détente* meant a continuation, if not an intensification, of the competition at that lower level. It was not their fault if Americans did not want to hear their message that the "class struggle" or "ideological struggle" would go on, that Moscow would give its blessings to "national liberation" movements in the Third World. The Soviet leaders had no intention of betraying their historical obligation to assist the inevitable struggle of peoples for freedom from Western neocolonial controls.

Indeed, *détente* was a particularly favorable situation in which to promote this struggle. *Détente,* to the Soviets, was the product of the new strategic parity in nuclear weapons. Before parity, U.S. strategic superiority had allowed Washington to intervene all over the world and to intimidate Moscow and compel it to be very cautious. But now that U.S. nuclear forces had been neutralized and deterrence had become truly mutual in terms of the reciprocal capability to destroy one another's society, the United States had to act more cautiously. In fact, that is why Washington pursued *détente.* Note the cause and effect carefully: it was the growth of Soviet nuclear forces that induced the United States to behave with greater self-restraint. And the obvious corollary: the greater the military power the Soviet Union acquires, the better; American compromises and concessions in negotiations were offered *only* because of Soviet strength. This perception of American behavior was nothing less than a rationale for a continuing arms buildup. The implications of this became so clear that the Carter administration began the U.S. rearmament effort; the continued Soviet military buildup after SALT I was a major factor disillusioning American opinion with *détente.*

Now that the Soviet Union was less likely to be opposed by the United

States and Moscow had in its own eyes achieved equality with Washington, the world was a safer place for Soviet expansion, which was another reason why the United States was disillusioned with *détente*. The achievement of strategic parity and the acquisition of new Soviet "colonies" in the Third World were directly linked. They were the product of the Kremlin's new *Weltpolitik*. Like the Soviet navy, they represented for Moscow—as colonies and a navy had once for Germany—the geopolitical status symbols of the Soviet Union's new standing in international politics.

The Search for Consensus and Human Rights

A major problem to emerge from *détente* was how the United States could conduct its foreign policy without a domestic consensus. In the absence of external threat, the United States has wanted only to be left to its own devices; when provoked, however, the country has been easily mobilized and united for its foreign policy crusade. As the cold war anti-Communist consensus had disintegrated in Vietnam and the country had tired of being the world's policeman, Kissinger's abandonment of the missionary style and the moralistic justification for foreign policy seemed very much in order. His emphasis on states and their legitimate interests, instead of moral causes and the division of the world into saints and devils, assumed a clear-cut distinction between a nation's foreign and domestic policies. The United States had an obligation to itself to defend its interests and, in doing so against another great power, it could use a range of diplomatic, military, and economic tools. It could seek to restrain an adversary with carrots or sticks or a mixture of both.

But the United States should abandon ideological goals because they spill over into crusades and hinder the diplomatic process by making the recognition of, or compromise with, allegedly immoral states virtually impossible. To make changes in the adversary's domestic structure and ideals a part of the negotiating process and perhaps a prerequisite for other agreements is bound to be unproductive—indeed, counterproductive, because it may well harden the opponent's positions and raise tensions. A Soviet leader, Kissinger contended, may make concessions in private diplomacy (as Brezhnev did when he arranged with Kissinger to allow a large number of Soviet Jews to emigrate), but to try to compel a Kremlin leader to change the way he governs the Soviet Union, a sovereign nation, will expose him to accusations of "coddling capitalism" and selling out "Socialist interests" and may even endanger his tenure.

Yet, in asking for the abandonment of America's traditional national style, which had allowed the country to play its foreign policy roles in the past, what was Kissinger substituting? The answer was basically the balance of power, which was not a new or exciting idea that would arouse Congress and the public. It was difficult to sustain support for a policy that involved elements of conflict and cooperation with the Soviet Union and that tried to use rewards and sanctions in an ever-changing mix as conditions changed. Personal charisma and diplomatic successes gained public attention and support (for SALT, the opening to China, and the attempts to move the Middle East toward peace). But the increasing public cynicism about *détente,* the Watergate scandal, Kissinger's own reported involvements with wiretaps, and the succession of an unelected president (and vice president) eroded support for *détente* and led to increasing attacks on its architect. "Superkraut" had been shot down, and American foreign policy continued to operate without a consensus.

Carter sought a consensus in America's self-proclaimed historical role as the defender of democracy and individual liberty. "Human rights" became the platform on which he expected to mobilize popular support; the liberal tradition, which Kissinger was accused of having abandoned in favor of his amoral geopolitics, had been reunited with American foreign policy. The nation, it was now proclaimed, once more stood for something, having reclaimed its democratic heritage and a moral basis for its foreign policy. Jimmy Carter, the born-again Christian, had become the redeemer of the American tradition.

Carter's policy ran into trouble abroad almost immediately. The Soviets, as Kissinger had predicted, did not care for Carter's emphasis on human rights, which they felt was specifically directed against them. Moreover, they interpreted political opposition, freedom of assembly, and free speech—all tenets of human rights—as dangerous to their system and "counterrevolutionary." The president's policy and his support for Soviet dissidents was viewed in Moscow as a fundamental attempt to undermine the Soviet system. Predictably, it led to a stiffening of Soviet diplomacy on SALT, postponement of a final agreement from the time when its approval by the Senate might have been relatively easy, a sizable reduction of Jewish emigration from the days when Kissinger had handled this problem privately, and a greater crackdown on dissidents.

Similarly, when Carter first took office and announced the withdrawal of all U.S. ground forces from South Korea, a move heavily influenced by its government's poor human rights record, Japan, the chief U.S. ally in Asia, felt much less secure; Japan regarded the American army in South Korea as the principal deterrent to a North Korean attack. In addition, the withdrawal, if it had been carried out, would not have improved South Korea's respect for human rights. Indeed, it might have had the opposite effect because that government, feeling abandoned by its protector, would have been more concerned with censorship and arresting its critics as its sense of insecurity rose. Thus, for American security and the human rights of individuals living under despotic regimes, the wisdom of the Carter administration's policy could be questioned.

Indeed, some critics suggested that because the United States could apply sanctions for the violation of human rights more easily to its friends and allies than its adversaries, the policy was applied more frequently to friendly countries that were generally aligned with the United States on foreign policy. This may be an admirable policy when American efforts make such countries more democratic and respectful of elementary human rights. But in Iran, as we have seen, the human rights abuse led the U.S. government to give the shah what at best was only half-hearted support while in effect expecting that his overthrow would result in a regime led by westward-looking democrats. Instead, the result was an Islamic theocracy that was not only militantly anti-American but also proved as brutal as the shah's secret police. The ousted dictator was replaced by an even crueler and more repressive despot. It had happened earlier in Vietnam, after South Vietnam collapsed and Hanoi took over, and in Cambodia, where the Communists slaughtered 2 million people out of a population of 8 million.

Even if one ignored the consequences for American security, could one say that respect for human rights had been improved by these political changes, or, for that matter, by Castro's overthrow of Batista or the shift to the Sandinistas from Somoza? A human rights policy may, then, lead the United States on occasion to topple friendly dictators by not supporting them if they are particularly vile or under siege. But such a choice may also endanger U.S. strategic interests if this policy is pursued regardless of consequences. There can never be certainty about who will be part of the successor's regime or what policies it will pursue. Moreover, it should now be clear that U.S. leverage to shape other regimes is rather limited.

A further result of the emphasis on human rights was to expose America's double standard of judgment, if not its hypocrisy. How could President Carter square his human rights stand with his strategic interest in normalizing American relations with China? Or that when he needed to complete the SALT II negotiations, the president toned down his denunciations of Soviet infringements of human rights? The same doubt about Carter's sincerity was also raised by his pre-1979 support and praise for the shah of Iran; the United States depended on the shah to help stabilize the Persian Gulf area, although it was known that he ruled his country with an iron fist. Furthermore, despite his earlier criticism, the president visited South Korea. Clearly, in all these instances the problem for the administration was one of deciding priorities; failure to decide whether to give priority to human rights or security where these values clashed meant that the pursuit of both enhanced neither.

It is no accident that it was the two realists, Nixon and Kissinger, who were not given to publicly condemning other regimes for their domestic practices, who gained the greatest concessions from Moscow on human rights, including emigration from the Soviet Union for dissidents and Jews. It may give enormous self-satisfaction and moral self-righteousness to denounce a nation's government for its inhumane policies, but private talks, pressures, and negotiations, which do not hold up the offending regime to public condemnation, are more likely to produce practical results. Normally, short of overthrowing a regime, not much can be done about its disregard for human rights. All too often, it is at the heart of its policies. There are, 'sad to say, too many governments that care little for what they see as "Western niceties." Often the best that can be done is to alleviate the plight only of specific individuals or perhaps small groups. This is most true for a country like the Soviet Union where suppression of political rights is at the heart of the system.

In fact, the human rights emphasis of the Carter period suggested a kind of cultural arrogance based on the assumption that the American concept of civil and political values was the appropriate standard for all other societies. The human rights concern, in short, was a revival of the old crusading instinct, and perhaps its timing was not accidental. For its most vocal proponents were also the chief critics of pre-Vietnam America's "global policeman" role. One crusade was simply being substituted for another. This is not to downgrade human rights in U.S. policy. That, indeed, could not be done because such rights express the profound commitment of the nation to the values upon which it was founded. Such values must be as much a part of U.S. policy as power. But they cannot be pursued regardless of consequences; they ought to support U.S. interests.

Thus, neither Kissinger nor Carter could find a new basis for a consensus underlying U.S. foreign policy. The balance of power as a justification remained alien to the American tradition, and Carter's human rights policy was unworkable. Yet Carter was not that far off the mark, at least traditionally. The United States historically has explained its international involvements in terms of the defense of democracy or human rights against the onslaught of undemocratic and antidemocratic regimes. Indeed, during cold war I, the anticommunism inherent in the containment policy, was legitimated by the liberal Democratic administrations of Truman, Kennedy, and Johnson by their human rights concerns. Liberals were concerned about civil rights and social justice at home; rights and justice also had to be advanced and protected abroad from the Soviet Union and its allies.

Ironically, it was after Carter that a conservative president reunited anticommunism and human rights, at first in support of right-wing regimes that ignored human rights, but then to help transform a number of them into democracies. In the meantime, Carter tried to divorce human rights from the American-Soviet conflict and marry them to his concern for the lot of people living in the less-developed countries. Here is where the majority of humanity lived, and, in the new emerging interdependent world, Carter's focus was to be on the relationship between the Western industrial democracies and the poorer Third World in the creation of a more peaceful and more decent "world order."

chapter ten

Conflict with—and in— the Third World

THE LESS-DEVELOPED countries (LDCs) benefited from the cold war, although many of them criticized the superpowers for their preoccupation with the conflict between them and their neglect of the poorer nations of the world. Far from neglecting them, in fact, the United States and the Soviet Union had given attention and resources to the LDCs that were wholly disproportionate to the Third World's power. The reason, as we know, was the bipolar distribution of power, which conferred upon these new nations, most of whom were not only poor but also weak, a greater leverage than their own strength and influence warranted. Confronted by two nations competing for their allegiance and loyalty, the Third World countries could lean first toward the East, thus attracting Western economic and military aid and political support, and then toward the West, thereby attracting similar assistance from the East. The replacement of bipolar competition by the newer adversary-partnership in the early 1970s meant that their bargaining capacity declined. Nonalignment also became more acceptable to the United States in these circumstances.

If the change in the superpower relationship was the fundamental reason for the decreased American attention and aid to the Third World, attitudes based on the results of past aid reinforced "donor's fatigue." It had become clear after two decades that the optimistic expectations of "instant development" had underestimated the difficulties and complexities of modernization. Aid seemed never-ending. Moreover, aid had not even been particularly successful in winning friends and gaining influence. In the absence of traditional means of control, the friendship of countries receiving aid was unreliable and inconstant. American aid, as a consequence of all these changes, had not only been reduced to its lowest point—less than half of 1 percent of the gross national product (GNP)—but the emphasis had shifted from capital development to technical assistance and an increasing role for private enterprise, meaning basically the multinational corporations. In 1979 U.S. aid was only 0.2 percent of the GNP, behind the aid given by Sweden, Norway, the Netherlands, France, Britain, and West Germany.

As the 1970s began, the lot of the LDCs appeared grim. With a few exceptions, they were still far from developed. The optimism had faded that foreign aid would stoke their modernization, or later, that "trade, not aid" would permit them largely to earn their own way and finance their own development. Food shortages in Africa and Asia were stark reminders of the LDCs' fate. After years of trying to lift themselves up by their own sandal-straps, they still faced formidable problems in their attempts to modernize. The hopes of the 1950s and early 1960s had turned into disappointment, even despair, as many of these countries remained mired in backwardness. The expectation of the former colonial states that they could realize their dream of a better and more rewarding life for their peoples was unfulfilled. Poverty, illiteracy, ill-health, and overpopulation, among other problems, continued to coexist with dreams of national dignity and material welfare.

The New International Economic Order and Nonalignment

The Western states might point out that the causes of the persistent poverty of so many of the LDCs were of their own making: the fragility of nationhood; the low priority given to agriculture, resulting in hunger; the high birth rate, which defeated the most valiant efforts of economic growth; the large amounts of money spent on arms; and, all too frequently, widespread inefficiency and corruption. The LDCs, however, rejected the argument that the responsibility for their failure to modernize was internal. They pointed to the external system, the nature of the international economy. In this economy they were the sources of raw material for Western industry. When demand declined, or several non-Western suppliers competed with one another for the same markets, or Western industries found substitutes or synthetics, the prices of their resources went down. As prices declined, so did the LDCs' capacity to earn foreign exchange with which to buy Western industrial products, which have tended to rise in price. In short, their earnings declined while the cost of Western-made goods rose. In addition, when these countries developed some industry and exported to the West, they often ran into protective tariff barriers. In short, even if they worked harder, it was of little help. The structure of the international economy was against them and kept them in a subordinate position, as suppliers of cheap raw material for the rich Western states. Thus, the Third World countries seemed condemned to poverty.

As they saw it, they were dependencies. They may have gained political independence, but in reality they remained economically chained to the Western, industrialized economies. Their status remained neocolonial because their economies were geared not to the needs of their own markets, but the needs of the developed countries' markets. As exporters of raw materials, they were dependent upon Western demand and access to Western markets; therefore, they were the victims of Western economic policies, obviously made in the interests of the Western countries who were favored by the law of supply and demand. The international market was stacked against the weak and poor and favored the strong and rich. That is why, they claimed, that after decades of working hard and despite foreign aid they remained less developed. For Western nations, the Third World's status as suppliers of relatively cheap raw materials was a matter of self-interest. Why should the industrialized world favor their development? Their dependency status in an international economic and political order dominated by the West, as the Third World nations perceived it, limited their ability to grow economically; their integration into the global economy has benefited the dominant Western nations with a high standard of living and left the LDCs poor.

The LDCs, it ought to be emphasized, were not just arguing that the Western-controlled international economic order gave an advantage to the strong over the weak. Their main point was that they were poor because they had been exploited by the West. They had been plundered during the colonial days, and this plunder continued as they sold their resources cheaply on the international market. In this context, their demand for a new international economic order was a claim for a redress of past wrongs. Having allegedly used their power unfairly to take from the poor countries what rightfully belonged to them, the rich nations were obligated to make restitutions in the name of social justice and decency. The transfer of wealth from the West to the Third World was a moral debt, or conscience money. Whatever the real mix of internal and external reasons, then, for the slow development of the Third World, the "revolution of rising expectations" had become the "revolution of rising frustration." This was the reason for the increasingly strident demand for a new order, which was essentially a demand for a redistribution of wealth from the rich nations to the poor nations.

It was in this context that during the 1973 war in the Middle East the Organization of Petroleum Exporting Countries (OPEC) raised oil prices fourfold from $3 to $12 a barrel and that its Arab members for a while embargoed shipments of oil to the United States and the Netherlands, both supporters of Israel. The oil companies, which, according to the imperialist interpretation, were supposed to be such powerful multinational corporations that they dominated the economies and countries in which they operated, were shown to be without much power. They were at the mercy of the governments of the countries in which they operated. The so-called imperialist states, whose governments were presumably controlled and directed by the capitalists, did not mobilize to squash the governments that were allegedly their puppet regimes. Confronting a vital threat to their well-being and security from countries that had no military power to speak of, the industrial democracies did not even debate the issue of military intervention. Had this event occurred a few decades earlier, they would not have hesitated to resort to force rather than face the possibility of being destroyed economically. In 1973 they talked of accommodation and acquiesced.

OPEC's action was widely viewed in the Third World as symbolic of a general protest by LDCs against their lot. OPEC was regarded as a kind of "vanguard of the (world's) proletariat," or poorer nations. This mood of anger, resentment, and revolt was clearly directed against the West. Ironically, the effects of the quadrupling of oil prices were felt most keenly by other non-Western nations. The sharp increase in oil prices threatened their plans to industrialize and handicapped their efforts to grow more food with technologically intensive, oil-based, agricultural techniques. But whatever fears they had about the future, the LDCs stood united with OPEC. Materially and rationally, they should have aligned themselves with the First World, the Western industrialized nations, to compel OPEC to lower its prices to a more acceptable level.

Despite their increased suffering, the Third World countries did not form a coalition with the United States, Western Europe, and Japan to force lower oil prices. This can be partly explained by their fear of irritating OPEC, partly by their hope for promised but largely undelivered OPEC economic help (most went to fellow Muslim nations, where it was spent on arms), and partly by their desire to imitate OPEC. But the basic reason was that the Third World identified emotionally with OPEC. The organization's action was widely perceived by these countries as "getting even" for past exploitation. It gave them a good feeling that for once the weak had turned the tables and made the strong suffer. The German word *Schadenfreude* says it best: pleasure received from seeing someone who deserves it really suffer, or "get his." The sight of the rich and privileged nations who had so long ruled them as the "lesser breeds" being humiliated and quaking before their old co-lonial slaves was just too delicious. While OPEC gained quick immense wealth, the rest of the Third World received an enormously satisfying "psychic income." That was why OPEC's action inspired so much hope. The suppliers, instead of competing against one another and keeping prices low, organized themselves into a producer-cartel to control access to the oil and its price. Perhaps OPEC had provided the example to the other LDCs of how they could raise their commodity prices and earn the funds they needed.

Among the LDCs demands were higher and more stable commodity prices, indexing those prices to Western inflation rates, more foreign aid, and preferential tariffs so that they could sell their products on Western markets. They felt they had the resources Western industry needed, and, without them, Western industry and society would be in serious trouble. The rich nations appeared vulnerable, and the poor nations seemed to have gained real leverage. Increasingly, observers noted the new First World-Third World confrontation and asserted that it was becoming at least as important as the conflict between the Soviet bloc and the Western allies.

This coalition held into the 1980s, even after oil prices had by early that decade hit $32 a barrel after the collapse of Shah Mohammed Reza Pahlavi of Iran, the subsequent decline of Iranian oil production (some of which was made up by other Persian Gulf countries), and the resulting tighter supplies in a world with an ever-expanding demand. Bitterness at the West intensified, and, as the LDCs' frustration and anger grew, their nonalignment increasingly appeared to be changing into alignment with the Soviet Union and its ideological friends. The Soviets had charged all along that the poverty and misery of the non-Western world were the results of Western capitalism and imperialism. Still, it seemed odd to find Vietnam, Afghanistan, North Korea, and Cuba accepted as nonaligned nations and odder still that their 1979 conference was held in Havana. It seems oddest of all that, when Vietnam was cruelly driving its Chinese population out of the country, usually in boats that would not survive long ocean journeys, its behavior was not condemned as racist, and that neither Vietnam's invasion of Cambodia nor the earlier genocide of the Cambodian people was condemned as aggression or a crime against humanity. The Soviets and the LDCs would not have hesitated to use such phrases had the United States acted in similar ways. Nevertheless, this coalition between the Soviet Union and the non-aligned nations was by and large tactical. The nonaligned countries were nationalistic, and they had not fought for national independence only to lose it to Soviet imperialism. Yet it was a sign of the times that this coalition existed and that only a small number of Third World governments criticized the direction of the nonaligned movement and defended American policies.

Oil as a 'Weapon'

The sharp rise of prices in the wake of the shah's collapse left no country untouched. In the United States and among its principal industrial allies, high oil prices stoked inflation; brought on unemployment; created a stagflation (a simultaneous inflation and recession); slowed down economic growth; lowered standards of living; brought about the largest redistribution of wealth in history from the West to the OPEC nations; created large Western imbalances of trade; and sharply lowered the value of the dollar. The "energy crisis" of the 1970s did not merely cause occasional inconveniences such as long lines of cars waiting to buy gas or higher prices to be paid at the gasoline pump. It profoundly upset entire economies and changed ways of life, as evidenced by smaller cars and lower speed limits in the United States. Moreover, the energy crisis raised the questions of how the Western states, which had paid for welfare programs by means of rapidly growing economies, could still afford such programs and whether to do so, they would have to reduce defense expenditures. Or would they be able to maintain strong defenses only by cutting social expenditures? Plenty of "guns" and "butter" no longer appeared affordable.

OPEC's Success and Third World Expectations

Mao Zedong once said that "power grows out of a barrel." What he had in mind, of course, was the barrel of a gun. But he would have been equally correct had he meant a barrel of oil. By organizing themselves into a producer-cartel, the petroleum-exporting countries were rejecting the open market that the LDCs had been claiming favored the consumers and not the producers. In the past, each producer, seeking to enhance sales, maximized production, which caused an excess of supply and kept prices low. The cartel gained power by seeking to control both the levels of supply and prices. If it could control enough of the world's supply of oil, so that outside suppliers could not make up for a cutback in the cartel's total production or meet the expanding needs of consumer countries, it would hold the bargaining chips. A second condition was also important, namely, that the resource the cartel controlled was of such importance to the consuming nations that they could not do without it. The demand, in brief, was intense, and it was less painful to accept higher prices than to tell OPEC "to drink its oil." These conditions gave power to the producer of a barrel of oil.

Oil is a vital commodity and is irreplaceable. It cannot be recycled. It takes large-scale capital investments and many years to explore, find, and drill for new oil. Similarly, new technologies to exploit solar energy or shale oil also require enormous investments of time and money. Finally, other sources of energy such as nuclear power are considered unsafe or, as with coal as well, to have undesirable environmental effects. No short-run substitute is readily available for economies that have long depended on relatively cheap oil and have neglected research and development.

No wonder that the developing countries were delighted and held high hopes in the wake of the 1973 price hikes. OPEC's actions gave rise to two expectations: one, that OPEC would use its leverage to raise the prices of natural resources from the other Third World countries; and two, that the other producers of resources could follow OPEC's example by organizing their own producer-cartels, limiting supplies and raising prices. Maybe, finally, the LDCs could acquire the large-scale funds for investment in modernization that foreign aid and free trade had not raised.

The expectation of a resource coalition against the West did not emerge, and First World–Third World negotiations on changes in the economic rules of the game were not very fruitful. The fact is that if we use the rather oversimplified distinction of rich and poor nations, in the 1970s the rich were becoming the "declining rich," while OPEC and a few other Third World countries were becoming the *nouveaux riches.* The latter's fundamental interest lay basically with the richer nations, not the poorer. Even more radical states such as Libya, Algeria, Iraq, and Iran, all of them "price hawks," have not withheld oil at their nation's cost to advance the collective welfare of all Third World states, although all were generally hostile to U.S. policies.

Conversely, OPEC has not refrained from raising its prices because of any social conscience and concern about the devastating impact these raises have on other LDCs. OPEC's foreign aid for some LDCs remained puny in comparison with what the rising prices have extracted from these nations; this is money that could no longer be invested in their own development. Third World unity, in fact, was fragile, if it existed at all. It was a handy term to describe countries characterized by certain social and economic conditions and by common emotions and attitudes about past colonialism and modernization, and which often vote together in the United Nations. But on material issues that affect each of them differently, there was division. The OPEC countries followed their national interests, even if the cost was great injury to the other LDCs.

Nor has OPEC's example been of much relevance for most of the LDCs with other resources. Nonoil mineral resources exerted less leverage: there were more readily available substitutes; industrial scraps could be recycled; conservation, stockpiling, and new sources of minerals, including beds under the sea, were available options. Furthermore, there are barriers to setting up producer-cartels. First, in many areas producing raw materials there are a larger number of producers than in OPEC, which could complicate the task of organizing a united front. Second, the LDCs that would benefit from a cartel were those already better off because they had a product in demand; the poorer nations, less blessed by nature, would not benefit and, given the higher commodity prices that they had to pay, would be worse off. Third, the most difficult barrier was the fact that the role of the LDCs as the suppliers of raw materials for the industrial world is in part a myth.

Western countries produce most of the world's resources. The ironic fact is that most LDCs are net importers of raw materials! Of the nonfood, nonfuel commodities, the Western industrial nations in the mid-1970s supplied 60 percent, the Communist states 20 percent, and the less-developed countries 30 percent. And most of the world's food exports, as shown by repeated Soviet imports of wheat and the threats of starvation in certain areas of Africa and Asia during the 1970s, are from the rich countries, especially the United States. Therefore, there would not be a straight transfer of wealth from the rich to poor. It was not only unlikely that the West would soon confront a series of commodity cartels, but also unlikely that such cartels could do much to help lessen Third World poverty.

Economics and Political Pressure

These conclusions, however, were not of much comfort in the West while OPEC retained its key position as an oil producer. The economic effects of rising prices was not the only matter of concern; the possibility that a political price might be exacted by the oil producers was also worrisome. Would Saudi Arabia maintain high oil production and restrain prices to some extent if the United States could not fashion a solution of the Palestinian problem satisfactory to the Arab states and obtain Israeli withdrawal from Arab lands captured in 1967? If the United States supported South African domestic and foreign policies towards its neighbors, would Nigeria—second only to Saudi Arabia as an exporter of oil to the United States in the 1970s—refrain from exploiting its oil weapon? Indeed, had not America's more even-handed policy in the Middle East since 1973 been partly the result of the fear of the Arab OPEC's use of another oil embargo? Were the West European countries not influenced by the possibility of an oil cut-off when many of them received Yasir Arafat, head of the Palestinian Liberation Organization (PLO), as if he were already a head of state, thereby conferring upon the PLO a degree of legitimacy?

Economics is not a new instrument of state policy. Indeed, during the cold war, economics had become a well-known means of advancing American interests, especially the Marshall Plan and the various foreign aid programs for the LDCs. The United States had on other occasions resorted to embargoes, such as cutting off Cuba's U.S. sugar quota to punish Fidel Castro in his early days in power for moving closer to the Soviet bloc. In Chile, the United States cut off loans from international agencies and prevailed upon American banks not to support Marxist president Salvador Allende, and, after the Iranian seizure of U.S. hostages and the Soviet invasion of Afghanistan, it attempted to use economic coercion either to change the targeted nation's behavior or to exact a price for that behavior.

But economic means are usually of limited effect in gaining short-range or medium-range goals. Foreign aid has won few reliable friends; cutting off access to American markets or embargoing food is not helpful if other markets or other sources of supplies are available. Castro, finding his American market cut off, found a market for Cuban sugar in the Soviet bloc; after Afghanistan, the Soviets bought much of the grain they needed from other countries once the U.S. embargo took effect. In addition, publicly announced sanctions such as these usually have the opposite effect: they unite the targeted nation, mobilize popular support for its regime, and provide a scapegoat for the regime's failures.

But if OPEC provided the world with a clear demonstration of how devastating and influential economic instruments can be in international politics, it is striking that in the United States the intellectual impact of OPEC's actions was the suggestion that world politics were in a state of change. The oil embargo and quadrupling of prices was not viewed as reinforcing traditional interstate relations because of oil's potentially coercive effect. Rather, these events produced an image, widely shared in academia, government, and the mass media, of a more interdependent world, dedicated to enhancing the material welfare of its peoples. The shock of the energy crisis was seen as fundamentally beneficial. Interdependence among nations would transform the very nature of international politics.

Interdependence: Global Transformation or Escape from 'Power Politics'?

In one sense, the interdependence of nations—if it meant mutual impact or vulnerability—was obvious. The multiple and profound effects on the West of OPEC's actions have already been mentioned. This interdependence involved the non-OPEC nations of the Third World as well. Recession in the West reduced the demand for raw materials, which lowered their prices, which in turn produced less foreign aid and raised the prices of Western machinery and other goods. With smaller earnings of foreign exchange, the ability of these countries to import high-priced oil declined too, unless they borrowed heavily from Western banks. Another consequence of this interdependence was that national planning by itself could not lead to full economic recovery, that the actions of other countries had a profound impact. For example, U.S. attempts to cope with stagflation depended on the stability of OPEC's oil prices rises and production. The price shocks of 1973 and 1979 taught that lesson in the most painful way.

The OPEC countries were also deeply enmeshed in this interdependent world. Without the industrial countries, they could not sell their oil, so that ruining the Western states was presumably not in their self-interest. If they wished to modernize they needed Western assistance, for the West had the industry and technology. The West could also supply a country such as Saudi Arabia, which believed it had a major security problem, with the most modern weapons and the men to train its forces. In addition, American political support for the Saudi government was desirable because the regime was conservative and concerned with political stability. The government was staunchly anti-Communist and always worried about radical Arab regimes that leaned toward Moscow.

In a rather obvious sense, then, the nations of the world had become more interdependent. Price rises, production cuts, inflationary forces, and recession all reached across national frontiers. No nation was any longer "an island unto itself." In an interdependent world, nations obviously could hurt one another. But why were broader conclusions drawn, suggesting that the entire nature of international politics and the historical pattern of state behavior would be replaced by a new world politics whose characteristics would be quite the opposite of the old "power politics"? Why were so many observers, mainly American, so optimistic about this growing international interdependence? Why did interdependence become the new wisdom during the 1970s and have such wide appeal among President Jimmy Carter's policy makers and among American news commentators and academics?

The Appeal of Interdependence

The attractiveness of interdependence was its promise of a more peaceful and harmonious world consistent with American values and an escape from the more troublesome world of power politics. Moreover, transnational economic and technological forces made this more humanitarian planet "inevitable." The assumptions underlying interdependence as a model of the future were both multiple and interesting. First, it is asserted that in an ironic paradox, nuclear weapons have ensured the peace. The superpowers' strategic nuclear arms are weapons of denial and deterrence, and their existence makes the use of conventional arms less likely because of the danger of escalation of hostilities. The likelihood of major war between them, even among their allies and friends, is therefore not great. When wars occur, however, as in the case of Vietnam, the conflict may last a long time and be expensive to wage in terms of lives lost, money, and social divisions—in short, the costs may be excessive in relation to the goals.

Second, as a result, attention has turned from security to economic or welfare issues. These issues have become increasingly salient not only because security seems more assured but also because the democratic societies of the West have become more and more preoccupied with economic growth rates, consumerism, and ever-higher standards of living, and the LDCs are bent on modernizing and on satisfying their own people's expectations for a better life. The key issues are economic and social rather than military and involve values such as social justice and human dignity rather than violence and destruction.

Third, nations cannot fulfill their socioeconomic goals by themselves. Western societies, for example, run largely on imported oil. The non-Western countries, in their turn, seek Western technology and food. No nation any longer completely governs its own destiny, and no government by itself can meet the aspirations and needs of its people for a better life. Worldwide cooperation is not just desirable but a necessity if goals such as peace, political stability, human welfare, and individual dignity are to be achieved on earth.

Fourth, on the traditional issues of security, the state system assumes the separation of states and conflict among them, but on these bread-and-butter or welfare issues only cooperation will enhance each nation's prosperity. Whereas in international politics one nation's increase in power and security is seen by its adversary as a loss of power and security for itself, on economic issues each country's welfare was perceived to depend on the existence of prosperity in other countries. Economically, they gained or lost together; one did not gain at the other's expense. Precisely because in an interdependent system nations are vulnerable to one another, they need to work out problems together. Such cooperation requires a greater willingness to resolve disputes peacefully and a higher degree of mutual understanding and international harmony. Unlike cold war security issues, which were bilateral, the issues of oil or other resources or population or environment require multilateral negotiations. Many nations are affected—indeed, usually different nations on different issues. By "the logic of interdependence," they have to find collective solutions to their common problems.

Fifth, and very important, force and the threat of force are said to play a minimal role on these welfare issues, again in strong contrast to the primary role they play on security issues. The downgrading of force is largely attributable to the fact that countries with whom the United States would negotiate on these issues are allies and friends. Even if the threat or application of force were effective once or twice, invoking or applying it frequently could only alienate countries that are needed on these social and economic issues. Although many of the nations with which the United States must deal on these prosperity issues are comparatively weak militarily, they are not helpless or without leverage of their own. They have commodities that, if production were shut off, would hurt the consuming nations. Militarily weak states such as the major oil-exporting nations therefore have formidable bargaining power, which the traditional way of calculating power, by adding manpower, industrial capacity, military strength, and other factors, would not reveal. The old hierarchy of states based upon military strength was therefore more and more irrelevant, and the new emerging world order would be a genuinely more egalitarian one.

At least, power politics would be less relevant. The emphasis would be on cooperation among nations and their common interests, and the prime values to be sought would be human welfare and dignity. Nations clearly continue to exist, but their military fangs are to be drawn and their aggressiveness subordinated to the task of building a better future for all peoples. The national interest could be satisfied by serving the human interest. Interdependence, in brief, supposedly restrains national egotism and enmeshes nations in a web of interlocking relationships that compels them to cooperate for the "good of mankind."

Interdependence is unquestionably in part a description of current reality, but it is *also*—usually implicitly—a cry to move "beyond the nation-state" to a "world without borders" by dissolving, so to speak, power politics in welfare politics and "planetary humanism." Without denying the reality of existing economic problems of Third World poverty and hunger, the emphasis on interdependence is to some degree an attempt to escape from the structure of the present state system with its inherent conflicts and dangers. It is a plea for mankind to cooperate despite national differences to make "spaceship earth" a truly decent and fit place for all people to live and enjoy life free from oppression and want.

Indeed, what could be more characteristic of America's national style than interdependence, with (1) its distinction between economics, which is thought of as good because it is identified with social harmony and material benefit, and politics, which is equated with conflict, destruction, and death;

and (2) the normative commitment to a better future for humanity, to be achieved by a rational response to the allegedly inexorable forces of economics and technology? At one time, free trade was thought to be the answer to war and a unifier of nations because commerce would benefit all of them and presumably give them a vested interest in peace. Then economic development was advocated as the key. Is interdependence not just another idea in search of a more peaceful and harmonious world, because the earlier proposals have *not* done away with power politics?

Interdependence and American Guilt

Moreover, is the timing of the idea of interdependence not coincidental with, as well as a reaction to, Vietnam and the profound moral revulsion of many policy makers and analysts to that war and "realism" as a way of understanding and conducting American foreign policy? There is a certain irony to advocating interdependence. Vietnam created a strong reaction to globalism, which was dismissed as an overreaction of the cold war. Yet, under the guise of interdependence, globalism has been resurrected as the best way for nations to coexist and resolve not security issues but welfare or prosperity issues—population, resource depletion, energy, food, and the maldistribution of wealth.

It is not surprising that this new philosophy of global change strongly influenced the Carter administration's policy. Carter came to power just after South Vietnam's final collapse, when the United States was sick and tired of the war and the power politics that allegedly had been responsible for the country's involvement. Many of the administration's top officials, who as leaders or members of the bureaucracy under Lyndon Johnson or Richard Nixon had participated in the decision making about the war, shared the widely felt sense of shame about the war. They felt guilt about this abuse of American power, as well as other misuses (such as covert political interventions). Henry Kissinger's balance-of-power approach, therefore, was dismissed as dated; the world had moved beyond the days when this allegedly older or "European approach" seemed relevant. The incoming administration claimed that it would be more sensitive to the "new" realities of a more complex world and no longer a prisoner of the old cold war myth of superpower competition and confrontation, which in the past had received strategic priority and had led the United States to support right-wing dictatorships in the name of freedom. The administration, therefore, would move beyond the balance-of-power politics of East-West relations to "world-order" politics and a focus on North-South relations (between developed and less-developed countries).

East-West matters, then, were no longer regarded as of central concern except in the sense of working together for arms control to reduce the superpowers' nuclear arsenals and prevent the outbreak of a catastrophic war, as well as to reduce the spread of nuclear weapons to nations that did not yet possess them. *Détente* remained a necessary prerequisite for doing "good works" in the less-developed areas of the world.

This image of the post-Vietnam War world with its distaste for national egotism and use of power and the reassertion of an older and allegedly more moral American approach to foreign policy—nicely disguised as interdependence and a transformation of world politics—testified to the strength of that approach and its set of attitudes and ways of perceiving the world. Yet the emergence of interdependence as the new intellectual fashion together with the disutility of force as the new wisdom came at the very moment when the Soviet Union became a global power, American strategic superiority vanished, and the "imperial presidency" was weakened. Thus, at the same time that the new administration wished to deemphasize the East-West balance-of-power conflict and to focus on North-South world-order cooperation, the Soviet Union saw opportunities to exploit and expand its influence militarily in the Third World.

The East-West struggle was not just an old and bad memory. It was still very much alive, even if the United States preferred not to compete actively and told itself that containment no longer seemed wise or relevant because history, the nationalism of the new nations, and the shift in emphasis from national security to global welfare, would limit and defeat such old-fashioned expansionism. The Soviets showed that they shared neither the belief that the nature of international politics had changed nor the view that force had become an increasingly inept, if not irrelevant, instrument of policy. At the time, the Soviet Union was estimated to be outspending the United States on its military forces by at least 25 percent, perhaps by as much as 50 percent. Given an economic base about half that of the United States, this very heavy emphasis on "guns" at the cost of "butter" for the Soviet people suggested that these forces were intended for more than just defense. With its simultaneously increasing political-military involvement in the Third World, the Soviets taught the United States once more that there was no escape from the world of great power conflict.

Undoubtedly, the United States, on occasion, has made mistakes by giving too much emphasis to East-West relations; some of them, particularly with regard to China, were costly mistakes. But experience has also shown that ignoring or downplaying these relations also led to grave errors. It is one thing to learn from the past and correct errors; it is quite another to reject the very nature of international politics, whose chief characteristic, one might argue, was its strong sense of continuity. Soviet behavior—the continuing growth of Soviet military power, interventions in the Third World by proxies (Cubans especially), and the outright use of the Red Army in Afghanistan— made one question inevitable: Had Kissinger and preceding administrations been so wrong in granting priority to American-Soviet competition and placing a strong emphasis on military power or in thinking that the East-West struggle sometimes intersected with North-South issues?

From Globalism to Regionalism and Back Again

The Carter administration's emphasis on the creation of a "new world order," with its central focus on the relationship between the Western industrial world and the LDCs, left no doubt of its answer to that question, namely that it was precisely this preoccupation with American-Soviet competition that had led to U.S. involvement in Vietnam. By applying the superpower struggle to regional and even domestic rivalries, the United States in the past had become needlessly embroiled in situations it should have stayed out of and had become identified as a reactionary power supporting the *status quo* rather than needed changes. The Carter administration cited two examples from the Nixon era to support its contention that regional issues should be seen as such and solved in terms of the local forces that had given rise to them. According to the new administration, the United States would be better off not upgrading quarrels from regional to global if it wished to avoid aligning itself with the sides opposing democratic values and nationalism in the Third World.

Pakistan

The first example was Pakistan's breakup in 1971. A nation divided into two parts with 1,000 miles of India lying between them, Pakistan had split off from India in a burst of communal hatreds in which hundreds of thousands of Hindus and Muslims slaughtered one another. It confronted the issue of survival only twenty-four years after its birth, during a period in which India (already hated for its seizure of Kashmir) had tried on several occasions to humiliate Pakistan and destroy it as a possible military threat.

Pakistan's breakup began when, after years of military rule, it held a free election. A majority in East Pakistan voted for autonomy, because under the West Pakistan-dominated government the East had received less than what it considered a fair share of the national wealth (such as it was) and felt itself treated like a colonial appendage. West Pakistan attempted to crush the movement for autonomy with great brutality. The army killed and raped at will, burning village after village; almost 10 million refugees streamed across the border into India to escape. The result was the growth of a full-fledged armed independence movement for the establishment of a Bengali nation, or Bangladesh.

The United States during this period did not utter a single official word of public condemnation against the brutal behavior of its Southeast Asia Treaty Organization (SEATO) partner. America's silence and continued shipment of arms to Pakistan was partly the result of Pakistan's help in opening new relations between Washington and Beijing, a close friend of Pakistan and rival to India. Alone, India supplied arms to the East Pakistan forces and provided sanctuaries for the rebels. India also turned for support to the Soviet Union and received it in the form of a twenty-year friendship treaty intended to deter a Pakistani attack.

India's move away from its historic policy of nonalignment was also presumably intended to deter American support for Pakistan and give India the confidence to move against Pakistan. While denying that the new treaty represented a departure from nonalignment, India did have a good short-term reason for wanting to go to war, quite aside from the longer-range aim of once and for all eliminating Pakistan as a rival on the Indian subcontinent. This more immediate objective was to end the burden of the millions of refugees, a cost sufficiently great to slow down India's rate of economic growth. In a real sense, a war was cheaper than continuing to support the refugees.

Thus, under circumstances in which both sides claimed the other shot first, war erupted. Pakistan lost its eastern half, and Bangladesh attained statehood. India's policy of dismemberment succeeded; the Soviet Union reaped the rewards of India's victory, and Soviet influence on the subcontinent reached new heights. The United States—and to some extent China—lost prestige by siding with Pakistan, the weaker, military-ruled nation, whose soldiers' brutality had undermined the legitimacy of its cause all over the world.

Chile

The second example was Chile. In Latin America, American policy showed a strong continuity with a policy that historically had regarded South America to be within America's sphere of influence. Although Washington had gradually become more accommodating to the nationalism of its Latin neighbors, it remained very sensitive to what it perceived to be radical left-wing revolutions and regimes that might bring Soviet influence close to America's shores. When in 1970 Chile elected the Marxist Allende to the presidency, the Nixon administration, while behaving with diplomatic correctness, sought first to prevent Allende from becoming president and, after that failed, to make life difficult for him and encourage a military *coup d'état*. In a less overt way than John Kennedy at the Bay of Pigs or Lyndon Johnson in the Dominican Republic, the new Republican administration used the Central Intelligence Agency (CIA) for the same anti-Communist reason as preceding administrations. Yet the reasons for the Chilean coup, when it came, stemmed essentially from Allende's own actions and the domestic reactions these precipitated. The CIA may have helped shorten the time until the coup occurred, but the causes of the crisis were internal; by 1973 Allende's end was merely a matter of time. Indeed, Chile provided a most persuasive example of why the United States should *not* intervene in this type of situation.

It is important to stress this point because Allende has become something of a martyr, frequently portrayed as a revolutionary who was fairly elected to seek reforms and better the lot of the poor and underprivileged, only to be blocked and finally overthrown by a fascist conspiracy on behalf of a reactionary ruling class in league with capitalist America. Had he lived, Allende's reputation would have been stained by the failure of his political leadership; his suicide at the time of the coup elevated his reputation to a level he could never have achieved as leader of Chile's "road to socialism."

Allende came to power with 36 percent of the vote, only two points ahead of his next competitor in a three-way race. In the runoff vote in the Congress, he received the support of the centrist Christian Democratic party. At the start of his rule the opposition supported much of his program, including the nationalization of the American-owned copper mines, banks, and major industries and land reform. While it should have thus been possible for him to work within Chile's constitutional norms with a democratic consensus, Allende believed in class struggle. He deliberately pursued a policy of polarizing Chileans, which did more to consolidate the professional middle and lower-middle classes in opposition to him than to broaden his worker-peasant base of support.

As he pursued his program, his vow to maintain constitutional rule fell by the wayside. Representing a sizable minority, but hardly "the people," he could have governed only if he had gained the majority support in the Congress, which he did not have. He survived by increasingly bypassing the Congress and the courts. The Christian Democrats joined the rightist opposition, and class polarity was then matched by executive-legislative polarity. Allende had eliminated the middle ground of Chilean politics and emasculated the spirit of the constitution.

The nucleus of Allende's opposition came from the lower-middle class, which was hurt by an inflation rate of more than 300 percent by 1973, shortages of all kinds in the shops, and worries that their small businesses might be wiped out by inflation or government takeovers. In 1972 and 1973, small truckers, those who owned only one or two trucks, went on strike and were joined by shopkeepers, doctors, lawyers, engineers, bus and taxi drivers, and airline pilots. Between the strikes even the workers in the largest copper mine struck.

The military during this period became increasingly politicized. Asked by Allende at several points to participate in his cabinet to reassure those worried about law and order in the midst of strikes, street marches, and illegal seizures of land by the president's followers, the military at first served Allende as it had his predecessors. What precipitated the military's intervention was the rapid growth of paramilitary forces among Allende's extreme left-wing followers, who had always believed in armed confrontation with "reaction," and the call for an insurrection in the navy by a close Allende friend and party leader; both events apparently occurred with Allende's complicity. The country was on the verge of civil war when the military struck. It did not need American urging.

Not that the United States had not been hostile to Allende from the start. After the expropriation of American property without compensation, Washington cut off American credit and pressured international financial institutions to follow suit. But Allende more than made up his American losses with credits from Communist states, other Latin American countries, and West European countries. Chile also had rich copper mines. Had Allende imitated Gamal Abdel Nasser, he would have survived U.S. pressure and hostility by arousing his people's nationalist ardor. But that was why Allende did not survive; he declared himself to be president of only some Chileans—against other Chileans. Such polarization of society, a galloping inflation, and increasingly unconstitutional rule were hardly recipes for political success. Had the CIA practiced abstinence, responsibility for the Chilean coup would properly have fallen on Allende; he destroyed himself politically. The CIA's meddling drew attention from this and reaped the blame for Allende's difficulties and fall for the United States. Whatever it says for or against American intervention in its sphere of influence—if such a sphere can still be considered important and relevant in areas far beyond the nearer Caribbean-Central American area in this intercontinental age—Chile, like the earlier Bay of Pigs, makes a persuasive case for nonintervention.

Americans, perhaps because of the democratic nature of their society, on the whole seem rather clumsy at covert intervention and feel morally uneasy about it. Perhaps most reprehensible and in some ways symbolic were the several attempts to assassinate Castro, involving the Kennedy administration, the CIA, and Mafia figures—certainly an immoral alliance for murder in the name of national security. And, unlike in a television play, this unholy alliance failed in all of its attempts. In Chile, a country as far away from the United States as the Middle East, the question is surely whether the United States had the right to try to upset the constitutional election of any political figure, either in the name of American national security or for the broader consideration of the preservation of democratic values—values Washington did not later insist on in Chile or in other parts of a largely nondemocratic globe. One major result has been that the United States reaped widespread condemnation for its intervention and that Chile became for many liberal people a *cause célèbre,* just as the Spanish civil war before World War II had become a symbol of the conflict between fascist and progressive forces in the world.

The Panama Canal

The Carter administration had no wish to emulate these efforts. These were local problems that could have been handled more appropriately on a local basis. This meant above all support for those domestic or regional forces that were identified with nationalist aspiration. Symbolic of the new attitude was the acceptance of a change in the status of the Panama Canal Zone. Negotiations had begun in the 1960s, were carried on throughout the Nixon-Ford administration, and finally concluded under Carter. For Latin America, the disposition of this issue was critical. This was not a strictly American-

Panamanian issue; all of the Latin American states—left, centrist, and right—supported Panama in its determination to assert its control over a piece of territory that America treated as if it were its own. Would the United States try to keep its control of the zone, which would lead to violence between the American forces there and the Panamanians, or would it accommodate itself to the nationalism of Panama and of all the states to its south?

Theodore Roosevelt had created Panama in order to build the canal for the growing American navy at the turn of the century; the 1903 treaty between the two countries had granted the United States "in perpetuity the use, occupation, and control" of a ten-mile-wide zone to build, run, and protect the canal, although the sovereignty of this territory was to remain vested in Panama. The result was a virtual colonial situation. The American role in that small country became dominant. The Canal Zone cut Panama in two and was run by the U.S. Army. Panamanians in the zone were subject to American law administered by American courts. All business enterprises were operated by the United States; Panamanians were denied the opportunity to compete. And the American government held large tracts of land and water needed by Panama's rapidly growing population. What all this amounted to is that the United States acted as if it were sovereign in the zone when in fact it only possessed certain treaty rights over a piece of Panamanian territory.

The Panamanians also felt that they had received rather scanty economic benefits from the canal; fair or not, the contrast between the standards of living of those living in the zone and those living outside was grating and humiliating. Political discontent had become so high in 1964 that nationalist frustrations burst into riots when Panamanian students tried to fly their country's flag next to the American one at the zone high school. American students resisted, and twenty-one Panamanian and three American students were killed in the subsequent brawl. The confrontation was a symbol of what faced the United States should it seek to preserve its control "in perpetuity."

By the middle 1970s the canal's economic benefits to the United States were declining with shifting world trade patterns and the increasing use of supertankers and container ships too large to pass through the canal. Even its military value was being reduced by a two-ocean navy with huge aircraft carriers, which could not go through the canal, and nuclear submarines, which would have to surface to pass from one ocean to the other (providing intelligence to the Soviets of their whereabouts.) The Canal Zone issue, like the flag issue, had become primarily symbolic. American liberals recognized the need for change to meet Panama's aspirations for territorial integrity and real instead of nominal sovereign control; if denied, Panama might become "another Vietnam." But American conservatives, very strong in Congress, bitterly resisted a new treaty, which would restore the zone to Panama by the end of the twentieth century while ensuring America's right to continued use of and protection for the waterway. According to conservatives, the "American Canal in Panama" would become "another Suez," an indication of a retreat of American power, another instance of a once-powerful America groveling before a tiny country. Common sense prevailed in the end, but not without a struggle in Washington.

The canal obviously could be better protected with the Panamanians' consent than without it. Should the Panamanians actively work against protection with sabotage and violence, the United States would be compelled to send large military forces to protect the zone from "the natives." Stories of American troops shooting Panamanians would make ugly headlines, as would the public confrontation in the United Nations. In the world organization, the United States would stand virtually alone against a solid bloc of less-developed nations. The symbolism of the issue was domestic and international. While for many Americans, and not just some in Congress, the Canal Zone was "American," anything less than eventual Panamanian control over its own territory was unthinkable. A new treaty would demonstrate a change in American attitudes toward the nationalist aspirations of its southern neighbors and show that the United States had reassessed its formerly dominant position in its hemisphere. Already Peru, Venezuela, Bolivia, and Argentina had asserted themselves strongly against the United States, and American influence throughout Latin America was clearly on the wane. The real stake in Panama, in brief, was America's new global image and role. In April 1978, by only one vote more than the two-thirds required for a treaty, the Senate ended thirteen years of negotiations and a lengthy national and Senate debate by voting to turn the canal over to Panama by the year 2000.

This became part of a new pattern in Latin America. President Johnson had intervened in the Dominican Republic to stop left-wing forces from taking over the government, but Carter pressured the Dominican generals to stop their opposition to the election of a left-wing president. In Nicaragua, Carter opposed the dictatorship of Anastasio Somoza, which collapsed in 1979; his predecessors frequently had supported despotic regimes like Somoza's. Carter thus ended up favoring the Sandinistas, who during Somoza's days were domestically supported by such elements as the Catholic church and the business community, even though they were externally supported by Cuba.

These policies were characteristic of the administration's attempt to be sensitive to the nationalism of Third World countries in its pursuit of world-order politics, with the primary emphasis on the North-South relationship. The administration accepted the risk that the new regimes might turn toward Cuba and the Soviet Union for friendship and eventually repress all domestic opposition forces, including those working for genuine democracy. But supporting right-wing dictatorships, it felt, certainly would doom U.S. interests. Popular resentment and anger eventually would lead to their overthrow; American identification with the *status quo* would alienate the new rulers. Unlike Vietnam, the argument went, the United States had to place itself on the "right side" of historical development. Thus, the new administration favored social and political change and tried to identify U.S. policy with such change rather than oppose it.

Southern Africa

In Africa, this attitude meant that U.S. policy moved away from identification with the white supremacy regimes of Rhodesia and South Africa and toward a closer alignment with the black states of the continent. Fear of the Soviet Union was admittedly present, for the United States worried that if the guerrilla wars in South West Africa (Namibia) and Rhodesia (Zimbabwe) could not be ended by political settlements, the Soviets and Cubans might not only provide arms and training for the guerrillas but also send Soviet advisers and Cuban troops to help. The West would then be at a definite disadvantage because it would be identified with white racist regimes. But the fundamental purpose was to align U.S. policy with the prevailing African sentiments that were strongly opposed to the white-dominated governments.

The United States therefore sought to promote South West Africa's independence from South Africa, which had governed the former German colony since World War I, and to bring about a cease-fire in its guerrilla war and majority rule under U.S.-supervised elections. Rhodesia, however, was the more critical area. Its leader was Ian Smith, who had separated Rhodesia from the British Commonwealth in order to maintain the rule of 300,000 whites over almost 7 million blacks. After years of resisting any change, Smith was compelled by the increasing cost and drain on manpower imposed on Rhodesia by the black nationalist guerrilla war, as well as by economic sanctions, to shift his position. Proclaiming his willingness to accept "majority rule," Smith said free elections would be held. As a token of his intent, he formed a transitional government, which included several moderate black leaders who were believed to have popular appeal. Smith hoped that the "internal settlement" would end the war by attracting black support at home and isolating the guerrillas in their bases in neighboring Mozambique. Presumably, such a settlement would also gain American and British approval and lead to a lifting of economic sanctions.

The externally based Patriotic Front rejected the internal settlement as a fraud, asserting that it was a clever device to preserve white privilege and power. Virtually all black African states backed the Patriotic Front, led by Joshua Nkomo and the more militant, Marxist-oriented Robert Mugabe. In these circumstances, the Carter administration argued that Anglo-American support for the internal settlement and lifting of economic sanctions would be disastrous and would end the attempts to arrange for talks among all Rhodesian leaders, including the guerrillas. But sentiment for the internal settlement was growing in Britain and in the United States. It appeared to be a solution to the civil war without risking the possibility that the guerrilla leaders would capture power.

The newly elected Conservative government in Britain, however, decided to make one final effort to reach an overall settlement. Despite the widespread belief that a conference including black domestic and guerrilla leaders, as well as the white representatives, would fail, the British succeeded in bringing the various factions to agree to forgo a military solution and abide by the results of a free election. More surprises were in store. The election was won by the more radical Mugabe and not, as expected in London and Washington, by Nkomo. Mugabe at first showed himself to be a pragmatist and did not dispossess the white farmers and businessmen, whom the newly named Zimbabwe needed to remain prosperous. These results meant that the Carter administration had been saved by the British from choosing to alienate either the black states of Africa or the U.S. Senate, which had voted to lift economic sanctions. (In 1984, however, Mugabe declared that Zimbabwe would become a one-party, Marxist-Leninist state.)

One problem remained: the Soviet Union was determined to exploit Third World situations to expand its influence. For Moscow, the less-developed world was a natural place to enhance its power. "National liberation" meant the erosion and overthrow of pro-Western regimes. This was all part of the continuing "ideological struggle" that the Soviet Union had never promised to stop during the era of *détente*. The class struggle to free the poor and exploited was ordained historically. Thus, as the Soviets saw it, seizing opportunities for undermining the Western position throughout the less-developed world was a legitimate, low-risk endeavor that would simultaneously serve the cause of social justice and bring Moscow high political returns.

In a way, it was an old pattern. During the cold war the problems of the Third World had affected the superpowers and led to several conflicts. Soviet political strategy after Joseph Stalin's death had been to support the first generation of nationalist but non-Communist leaders of the newly independent countries. They might be bourgeois but their nationalism was directed against the West. In this way, a coalition could be forged to weaken the West. But by the early 1970s many of these leaders had either died or they or their successors had turned against the Soviets, who had made enormous political, economic, and military investments in the Third World. Moscow lost positions of influence in the Sudan and Egypt, which turned toward the West; earlier, it had watched in dismay as President Sukarno of Indonesia had turned from the Soviet Union to China before he was overthrown and Indonesia turned to the West.

Although the Soviets did not abandon the policy of support for anti-Western nationalist regimes, they limited it to where it could still be pursued, as in Iraq and Syria, for example. The Soviets increasingly turned to helping Marxist or pro-Communist factions gain power and then defending them. They helped the North Vietnamese with arms supplies during the last phase of the Vietnam War; helped their friends capture power in Angola; assisted

Marxist officers to seize power in Ethiopia; helped bring pro-Moscow Marxist regimes into power in Afghanistan and South Yemen; and, by extending a treaty of friendship and cooperation to Hanoi, allowed North Vietnam to invade Communist Cambodia and replace the pro-Beijing regime there with a pro-Soviet government. In the mid-1960s only Cuba, North Korea, and North Vietnam identified themselves as Marxist-Leninist states in the Third World. By the late 1970s there were six more: Afghanistan, Angola, Ethiopia, Mozambique, Nicaragua, and the People's Democratic Republic. Moreover, North Vietnam had expanded and controlled all of Vietnam, as well as Cambodia.

These pro-Soviet regimes may not necessarily enhance Soviet influence in the long term. Communist states, like non-Communist states, increasingly have been divided by nationalism, a force even stronger than communism—witness, in Asia, the conflicts between the Soviet Union and China, China and Vietnam, and, until it invaded Cambodia, Vietnam and Cambodia. In the meantime, however, Soviet intervention had two disturbing effects. The first was a rise of regional tensions. In Southeast Asia, the Vietnamese conquest of Cambodia and imposition of a Hanoi-controlled government led to China's punitive invasion of Vietnam, which, had it advanced toward Hanoi or lasted longer, might have led the Soviet Union to punish China by a similar limited border crossing. The dangers were—and are—obvious, as is the danger of Vietnam's expansion and dominance throughout Indochina and other Southeast Asian countries.

In Southwest Asia, in the area from the Horn of Africa to India, the combination of domestic instability, regional conflicts, and growing Soviet influence had created another dangerous and unstable situation. Zbigniew Brzezinski called the area an "arc of instability." Soviet-Cuban influence in Ethiopia and South Yemen on the Arabian peninsula especially worried the Saudis. Their anxiety about Soviet influence, moreover, was paralleled by anxiety about their internal stability. They saw that the shah of Iran, who, like them, had been using his enormous oil funds to modernize rapidly, was overthrown by a clergy upholding traditional Islamic society and opposed to westernization. The Soviet invasion of Afghanistan only enhanced this anxiety.

Fear in the area was widespread. Pro-Soviet Iraq, seeking to take advantage of Iran's weakness and domestic preoccupation, attacked Iran, in an attempt to replace it as the primary Persian Gulf power. Iraq also sought to become the preeminent Arab state and to strengthen its role as spokesman for the Arab cause now that Egypt, traditionally the leading Arab power, was isolated as a traitor to that cause. But the war divided the Arabs, with Syria and Libya supporting Iran and Jordan supporting Iraq; this division increased the rivalries in the area. Saudi Arabia and the other oil kingdoms became fearful of possible air strikes against their oil fields because they too supported Iraq. And Pakistan, which sent troops to Saudi Arabia to help defend the royal regime, worried over what the Soviets might do as 2 million Afghan refugees fled into Pakistan, many of whom returned to their homeland to fight with weapons bought and supplied by the CIA.

Always fearful of India, the Pakistanis were rumored to be developing a nuclear bomb to match India's. Iraq also appeared to be seeking the bomb, a matter of great worry to the Israelis, who presumably already possessed a number of them. The Israelis had watched the Iraqis organize the Baghdad front, which rejected Arab peace negotiations with Israel, and noted the Iraqi leader's attempt to become the new Nasser. The Middle East seemed even more of a tinderbox than before. And because of its close relationship with Israel and even more because of its dependence on Middle Eastern oil, the United States could not avoid involvement as the superpowers' rivalry was superimposed upon these regional problems. The Carter Doctrine was simply open recognition of the vital interests at stake for the United States in this critical region.

The second effect of Soviet intervention was the impact on *détente* itself. The Soviet Union continued to fish in the troubled Third World waters because the potential gains were high and the costs virtually zero. The problems in Africa or Asia might well be regional, but Soviet-Cuban military interventions in Angola and Ethiopia and pro-Soviet coups in Afghanistan and South Yemen had transformed these local disturbances into aspects of the wider Soviet-American competition for influence. Yet before the invasion of Afghanistan in 1979, no penalties were imposed, and so long as the Soviet Union believed that the United States was paralyzed by memories of Vietnam, Moscow had no reason to desist. The Carter administration abandoned the virtually automatic response to Soviet involvement in the less-developed areas that had characterized American foreign policy during the earlier, bipolar, cold war days and first few years of *détente*. But the lack of understanding of the consequences of Soviet-Cuban interventions for American interests and of the world's perception of American power and will as weak were very harmful. Increasing sensitivity to the nationalism of the Third World and sympathy for the social struggles and causes involved, while clearly desirable, appeared therefore to be an insufficient response. The East-West context continued to intrude. Nowhere was this more vividly demonstrated than in the Middle East, the region that had within a few years become critically important to U.S. security and prosperity.

The Middle Eastern Linchpin

By the 1970s the Middle East, with its unstable governments, militancy, high emotions, and its ability to suck the superpowers into its regional quarrels, more and more resembled the Balkans at the turn of the century. Even before Carter, the Nixon, and later the Ford, administration resolved to

Middle East

avoid the past pattern in which the Israelis won a military victory but were unable to translate it into a political settlement. The Israeli victories had left the Arabs humiliated and resentful, more determined than ever not to accept the right of Israel to exist and willing only to prepare for another round in the struggle. In the American evaluation, the 1973 war had shown a number of things: the fact that Israel could be caught by surprise, the ability of Arab armies to learn how to use modern weapons effectively, the intolerable cost in manpower losses to Israel of a war lasting longer than a few days, the grave difficulties for the Israeli economy when much of its manpower is mobilized, and the political isolation of Israel in a world in which even the Europeans (except the Dutch) feared the Arab oil weapons and cowered before people they had once governed. All this spelled further trouble for Israel, whose only friend in the world was now the United States. But in the face of oil embargoes and higher energy costs, would the United States continue to support Israel, which was still holding the territories it had captured in 1967?

For Kissinger, the urgency of attempting to reach a Middle East settlement was obvious, and the time seemed favorable. Anwar Sadat had declared his willingness to accept the existence of Israel and make peace with it on the basis of the 1967 frontiers. The Arab armies for the first time had shown bravery and skill and recovered some self-esteem; diplomatic concessions in these circumstances might be easier. Their earlier defeats had led only to inflexibility. An Arab-Israeli peace would have other desirable consequences as well. One was avoiding an American-Soviet confrontation that could escalate into a superpower war. Each of the Arab-Israeli wars had held the possibility of such a confrontation, and in 1973 that possibility had come frighteningly close. Would another Arab-Israeli war prove to be the incendiary device setting off World War III? Another consequence was the reduction of Soviet influence in the area and its replacement by American influence. American support for Israel had been a principal reason for this Soviet influence. Playing a more even-handed role and arranging for peace, which would achieve security for Israel as well as satisfy Arab territorial and political purposes, would enhance America's position in the area. Peace would also secure a reliable source of oil, which was particularly critical at a time when the United States was becoming an oil importer.

Two Approaches to Middle East Peace

Kissinger's strategy for peace was a step-by-step approach. There were many issues to be settled; to attempt to solve them at one time with all the parties present would be impossible. In a public conference at Geneva, co-chaired by the United States and the Soviet Union, the most extreme Arabs would set the pace; to take a moderate position in this atmosphere would seem a betrayal of the Arab cause. The presence of the Soviet Union was likely to lend support to the militants, because it profited from continued turmoil in the area. And such a conference would openly bring out Israeli-American differences. A step-by-step approach would start with the easier issues and proceed to the more difficult.

The first task was the disengagement of the Israeli forces and the Egyptian and Syrian forces after the war. Next would be a further Israeli withdrawal from the Sinai and then the Golan Heights. The two issues that would be the hardest and most emotional were the establishment of a Palestinian state, a cause espoused by the terrorist Palestine Liberation Organization, with whom the Israelis would not talk directly, and control of the old city of Jerusalem. By successfully resolving the initial issues, a momentum would be established to help resolve the other matters; and success would divide the moderates from the more militant regimes, strengthening the former and weakening the latter.

Kissinger was successful in achieving two unprecedented interim agreements—first the disengagement of the hostile forces on the Egyptian Sinai and Syrian Golan fronts, and later a further withdrawal by the Israelis from two strategic passes and an oil well in the Sinai. Throughout the process the Soviets denounced Kissinger. Becoming cooler toward the Egyptians, who expected the Americans to pressure the Israelis to leave, the Soviets threw their support behind the more militant Syrians and the PLO. By its agreement, Egypt, as the Syrians saw it, had left them to face Israel all by themselves; Egypt had agreed to let Israeli-bound cargo on non-Israeli ships pass through the reopened Suez Canal, and it had given general pledges to use diplomacy, not force, in the settlement of Egyptian and, more broadly, Arab-Israeli differences. To the Syrians and many other Arabs, these acts were tantamount of a "sell-out" of the Arab cause. Egypt was isolated in the Arab world.

The Carter administration, coming into power, viewed this situation with alarm. Carter and Brzezinski believed that the step-by-step approach had reached its end. It had, in their view, some fundamental liabilities. One, Israel was required in each step to give up territory for promises that, when all steps had been taken, it and its neighbors would sign a peace treaty and Israel would be accorded legitimacy. But by then, it would no longer have any bargaining chips. Two, the incremental approach avoided the central problem of the Palestinians, whose grievances would have to be met if a genuine peace were ever to be established. The Kissinger way of trying to deal with the easy problems first in the hope of gaining sufficient momentum and trust among the negotiating parties to resolve the difficult issues later, frittered away precious time and might thereby jeopardize the possibility of peace. The greatest danger was that if the key differences between Israel and the Arabs were not resolved, Sadat would either be outflanked by more militant Arabs; be overthrown within his own country; or, to survive politically, if not physically, be forced to play the role of the new Nasser. Time, in brief, was not on the side of the United States.

An Egyptian-Israeli Breakthrough

The Carter administration proposed that all parties resume negotiations at Geneva. Kissinger had fashioned his strategy to exclude the Soviets; only at the final conference would the Soviet Union attend as the co-chairman. Carter decided to approach the Soviets and enlist their cooperation. Moscow had influence with the more militant Syrians and the PLO, and it therefore had the capacity to cause a lot of trouble and block negotiations. If, on the other hand, Moscow participated in the peace negotiations, it would retain a degree of influence in the Arab world if and when a peace treaty was signed, reduce the possibility of a superpower clash, and help strengthen *détente* with the United States.

Neither Jerusalem nor Cairo was happy with the Soviet-American accord in late 1977. Israel did not want to face all its enemies simultaneously, and Egypt had already broken with Moscow, which now favored Syria, Egypt's rival. Israel and Egypt decided to bypass Moscow and Washington and negotiate directly. In a dramatic and internationally televised visit to Jerusalem in November 1977, during which he addressed the Israeli Parliament, Sadat, the leader of the Arab world's strongest nation, in effect extended recognition to the Arabs' archenemy. He expressed his hope that there would be no more war. The impact was euphoric as a comprehensive peace—a peace with all of Israel's Arab enemies—seemed near.

Begin and the Settlements Policy

The mood did not last long. Sadat apparently believed peace was easily and quickly achievable because he had taken the significant psychological step to reassure the Israelis that his peace offer was genuine, not a trick. Israel would withdraw to its 1967 frontiers from the Sinai, the West Bank, Syria's Golan Heights, and Jordan's East Jerusalem and would recognize the Palestinians' legitimate rights; and, in return for their land, the Arabs would sign a peace treaty and Israel would gain the legitimacy and peace with security it had sought since birth. The Israelis had always asserted that if only the Arabs would negotiate with them directly, implying recognition, they would be willing to return the territories taken in 1967. Israel had specifically disclaimed annexationist ambitions. The Labor government after the 1967 war had accepted UN Resolution 242 committing Israel to the withdrawal from the captured land (or, given some adjustments for security reasons, from almost all).

But Israel's new coalition government was led by Prime Minister Menachem Begin, who had spent his parliamentary life in opposition, and he had other ideas. He proposed to withdraw from the Sinai desert, but offered the Palestinians on the West Bank and in the Gaza Strip only autonomy, or self-rule, not self-determination. Begin referred to the West Bank by its ancient Hebrew names, Judea and Samaria; he claimed that they were not occupied territory to be returned but liberated territory to be kept as a part of the Greater Israel of which Begin had long dreamed. He left no doubt that he expected to establish Israeli sovereignty over both the West Bank and Gaza, each of which contained several hundred thousand Arabs. In the meantime, the Israeli government announced that Jewish settlements in the Sinai and West Bank would remain and encouraged more settlements.

To Sadat, Begin's plan for the West Bank and Gaza meant the perpetuation of Israeli military occupation under the guise of autonomy. And without a settlement of the Palestinian issue satisfactory to the Palestinians and the withdrawal of Israel from the conquered Arab territories, he could not sign a separate peace with Israel. Should he do so, he would be branded a traitor. Indeed, after his trip to Jerusalem, Syria, Libya, Iraq, Algeria, South Yemen, and the PLO had already condemned Sadat and formed a "rejection-ist front." Sadat, in turn, had broken diplomatic relations with the five states. But there were limits to his freedom of maneuver.

Bilateral negotiations therefore broke down. The fear of what might happen next brought the United States back into the negotiating process. American interests were clear. First, the United States was committed to the security of Israel. But from the American point of view, another war would be even more costly in lives for Israel than the 1973 war, and, as before, Israeli victory would not bring with it a favorable political settlement, but more Arab humiliation and resentment. Second, and of even greater concern, was the fear that it might also bring about a Soviet-American clash, as had almost happened in 1973. Third, the United States, Western Europe, and Japan needed oil to preserve the political, social, and economic viability of their societies. If no Arab-Israeli peace accord could be reached, and if a fifth war should erupt, another and longer oil embargo was expected to be very damaging even if an American-Soviet military clash were avoided.

But war or no war, if Sadat, who had turned away from Moscow toward Washington, failed to achieve a peace that the Arabs considered fair and just, other pro-American, moderate Arab states such as Jordan and Saudi Arabia would feel compelled to distance themselves from the United States. In such circumstances, Saudi Arabia might not be able to hold out if the other Arab states decided to confront Israel once more. Access to oil and the price of oil clearly would then become a weapon in this struggle, particularly because its successful use in 1973 had demonstrated how vulnerable the West was and how much it feared the use of oil as a means of pressuring it. Not only did the Carter administration, therefore, feel that another war was to be avoided but also that progress toward a settlement was imperative.

The effect of U.S. mediation in the stalled Israeli-Egyptian negotiations, however, was to bring into the open what Kissinger, without complete success during the second interim agreement, had expected to avoid with his step-by-step approach—namely, American-Israeli differences on how to achieve peace. Carter, like Kissinger, felt that Sadat was offering Israel the security and peace it had so long sought, and if this opportunity was not seized the result would be disastrous for Israel and the West. Israel was already basically isolated diplomatically. The United States had become Israel's sole source of diplomatic support internationally, providing sophisticated military equipment, especially fighters, and economic aid.

Upon coming into office, the Carter administration had quickly made known what it thought were the ingredients of a solution in the Middle East. First, UN Resolution 242 meant the return of most of the Arab territory Israel had captured in 1967. Only minor adjustments for security reasons could be allowed. Second, (and in this respect the administration went far beyond any of its predecessors) it boldly asserted that the key to peace was the Palestinian issue. More specifically, it said that the Palestinians had the right to participate in the peace-making process, and Carter himself soon publicly declared that the Palestinians had a right to a "homeland," a deliberately vague term that nevertheless carried great symbolic weight. Third, in return for such Israeli concessions, the Arab states had to commit themselves not only to ending their state of hostilities with Israel but also to signing a peace treaty followed by diplomatic exchanges and trade and tourism agreements. The Israelis had been insistent upon this point, but the Arabs were balking at such normalization, declaring that it would take a whole generation for this to occur after so much bitterness and anger.

Begin was at odds with the first two positions. He had reinterpreted UN Resolution 242, accepted by his predecessors, to mean that Israel was not required to withdraw from the West Bank and Gaza. He was also opposed to a Palestinian state which he, and indeed most Israelis, felt would constitute a danger to the existence of Israel. The issue that most clearly symbolized U.S.-Israeli differences was the policy on Israeli settlements in the occupied lands. Ever since 1967, the United States had consistently opposed these settlements as illegal. The Carter administration repeated this while it watched with disbelief as the Israeli government actively encouraged new settlements on the land the Arabs were reclaiming. It appeared as if Israel was deliberately setting out to destroy the one chance it had ever had to gain legitimacy and peace; it certainly impressed Washington and Cairo as an act of bad faith to begin new settlements in the midst of peace negotiations. Secretary of State Cyrus Vance, a diplomat's diplomat who was careful in his choice of words lest he offend, expressed the administration's anger when he declared that Israeli settlements were not only illegal but an "obstacle to peace."

Repeated American efforts to halt this policy and encourage the Israelis to hold out more hope to the Arabs for the eventual recovery of the West Bank and Gaza were all in vain. By contrast, Sadat appeared reasonable and conciliatory. He had with great courage provided the psychological breakthrough with his trip to Jerusalem. He had shown characteristic sensitivity to Israel's security needs by being willing to listen to various ideas for demilitarizing or thinning out forces in certain areas, and he had been willing to accept Israel's demands for a peace treaty and the subsequent normalization of relations not after twenty-five years, or even five years, but immediately.

The Camp David Accords

Nevertheless, the stalemate continued. As the three-year, second interim Sinai agreement was about to run out in October 1978, Sadat began to sound more pessimistic about a settlement. Carter therefore gambled and invited Begin and Sadat to meet with him at Camp David. The invitation was a gamble because had this summit meeting produced no results, the president's prestige, already low, would have been even more seriously impaired, American mediating attempts would have run their course, and Israeli-American relations would have been set back even further. But the president, perhaps for the first time in his administration, showed persistence and skill and emerged after twelve days of patient negotiations with a series of agreements, including a commitment by the two men to sign a peace treaty within three months.

Sadat made most of the concessions. He did not gain a commitment to an eventual Israeli withdrawal from the West Bank and Gaza Strip, or full Palestinian self-determination. The Israelis, however, promised to recognize "the legitimate rights of the Palestinians," to permit West Bank and Gaza Palestinians to participate in future negotiations on these areas and ratify or reject a final agreement, and to halt temporarily new Israeli settlements on the West Bank. But Israel vetoed the participation of the PLO leaders in such negotiations or the establishment of a Palestinian state; on these issues Israel's position remained intact. Yet Israel gained a separate peace treaty with the strongest of its Arab neighbors; without Egypt the others could not by themselves take on Israel. Thus, for a seemingly small investment Israel had gained the enormous dividend of a real sense of security, because Jordan or Syria alone or together were too weak to wage war against it. That was why, in fact, Syria had opposed Sadat's journey to Jerusalem and the subsequent bilateral negotiations. Once the threat of war with Egypt had ended, there would be no reason why Israel should return the Golan Heights to Syria.

Sadat, however, had taken a chance. Rather than selling out, he appears to have felt that a peace agreement would start a momentum for further agreements with Israel. The first Arab reaction to Camp David, however, was negative. Jordan and even Saudi Arabia joined the rejectionist group of Syria, Iraq, Libya, and Algeria in condemning Sadat, who became more isolated than ever. Under these circumstances, Carter's courageous personal intervention—his trip to Egypt and Israel—produced the necessary diplomatic breakthroughs and brought peace between these two long-term enemies. Yet the subsequent treaty did not bring a stable peace to the area. On the eve of the Israeli-Egyptian peace treaty in March 1979, Begin in a defiant mood told his parliament—and therefore the world—that Israel would never withdraw to its 1967 borders, Jerusalem would remain Israel's "eternal capital," and that there would never be a Palestinian state on the West Bank and Gaza. The prospect for regional peace remained somber because stable, long-term peace could be created only if the process continued after Israel and Egypt signed a treaty. If, on the other hand, Israel, with Egypt now neutralized, was unwilling to accommodate the grievances and aspirations of the Palestinians, Jordanians, and Syrians, the peace treaty would be subjected to great strain. As it was, Egypt's fellow Arab states, including Saudi Arabia, punished Egypt for signing by suspending Egypt's membership in the Arab League and instituting an economic boycott; most of them broke diplomatic relations with Egypt.

The ink on the Israeli-Egyptian peace treaty was hardly dry when Israel announced the formation of new settlements on the West Bank. Israel was ensuring that the West Bank would belong to Israel. Not long afterward, the Israelis began to dispossess the Arabs of their land. Because this policy enhanced pro-PLO sentiment, the military occupation became increasingly repressive and the censorship tightened. Ironically, as Israel appeared bent on annexing Arab land with a sizable Arab population, the high Arab birthrate became an internal threat to Israel as a Jewish state.

American policy often appeared to be the prisoner of Israeli policy, although Israel was the dependent state. The United States still supported Israel almost without reservation; it was also committed to Israel's defense. American policy was intended to help Israel achieve peace and security. But Israeli policy often seemed self-defeating, short-sighted, and annexationist. Yet America exerted no pressure on Israel to be more accommodating; instead it continued to finance and militarily support an increasingly untenable political situation.

The Arabs, of course, held the United States responsible for a peace treaty that omitted resolving the key Palestinian problem and for an Israeli policy that was calculated to make a comprehensive peace impossible. Symbolic was the unilateral Israeli decision to incorporate East Jerusalem into Jerusalem and declare that the city would never again be divided. The action aroused great anger throughout the Arab countries. The Arabs blamed Israeli policy on American acquiescence. American efforts to be more evenhanded after 1973 appeared in the eyes of the Arabs to have ended in a return to the pre-1973, one-sided support of Israel, regardless of how provocative Israeli actions were. Did the United States not know its own interests? This question was particularly asked in Saudi Arabia, upon whose oil the United States now greatly depended and whose position in the Arab world had been endangered by Washington's stance.

Saudi Arabia, strongly traditional and conservative, as well as pro-Western and anti-Communist, was also pro-American as it sought U.S. help for its modernization and defense. Small in population, it could not by itself continue to support Sadat's peace efforts after the failure of the Camp David agreement to tackle what the Arabs saw as the central problem of Palestinian self-determination. The Saudi royal family feared for its security, threatened, among other enemies by the millions of foreign workers, many of them Palestinians and other Arabs, whom Saudi Arabia needed in its drive to create a more modern society. The Saudis did not like the position in which they were placed by American Middle East policy: a separation from Egypt, which, under Sadat, was also a moderate, pro-Western, and anti-Communist state; a "distancing" from the United States in order to avoid too close an identification with it; and a fear that if the peace negotiations stalled, Soviet and radical Arab influences would again rise while the influence of the United States would decline once more.

Thus, while the Saudis were being asked to raise oil production to meet American needs and restrain the "price hawks" among the oil producers, their confidence in the wisdom of U.S. policy and American leadership declined. This lack of confidence was reinforced by the perception of an increasing lack of credibility of American power as the shah of Iran was overthrown; the Soviets, whose influence was already established in Ethiopia and neighboring South Yemen, invaded Afghanistan; and the Saudis, along with the rest of the world, watched the new Islamic Republic of Iran humiliate the United States by seizing American diplomats in their embassy in Tehran. For fourteen months following the seizure, the United States appeared impotent and incompetent to deal with the situation.

Iran and the End of the Vietnam Syndrome

The year 1979 witnessed, as noted earlier, the crumbling of U.S. positions in Southwest Asia. Deterioration began in Iran, second only to Saudi Arabia in non-Communist world oil production, with the overthrow of the shah. Iran's oil production fell off sharply, and the resulting tightening of world oil supplies led to a huge escalation of oil prices to approximately $34 a barrel (more than $40 in some markets), with devastating effects on inflation and unemployment in the industrial world, especially in the United States. Most important of all, however, was the spectacle of a disintegrating American position in an area of absolutely vital importance for the United States.

The low level to which American resolution and power had fallen was symbolized by the invasion of the American Embassy in Tehran in November 1979 by a mob of militant students, who seized American personnel. This outrage occurred after the deposed shah, suffering from cancer, had been admitted to the United States for medical treatment. (He died a few months later in Egypt.) The revolutionary authorities gave the unprecedented action—not even Hitler or Stalin had tried to seize enemy diplomats—their blessing and support. The subsequent efforts by the Carter administration to gain the safe release of the Americans became high public drama. Under the watchful eyes of the cameras of the three major U.S. television networks, the American public was repeatedly exposed to pictures of crowds, like well-rehearsed choruses, chanting their hatred of America, the "Great Satan," as it was called by the Ayatollah Ruhollah Khomeini, Iran's chief religious leader. "Death to America," the crowds screamed constantly. In frequent interviews Khomeini and other Iranian leaders lectured the American public for America's support of the shah and spoke mockingly of the U.S. naval power gathering in the Indian Ocean. They virtually dared the president to use it.

In the 444 days following the taking of the hostages, the world watched as the Carter administration tried one means after another to gain their release: appeals to the United Nations and the International Court of Justice, both of which were ignored by Iran, and a series of economic sanctions, which were largely ineffective because Japan and Western Europe needed Iran's oil more than the United States did. All was in vain: the holding of the hostages was a symbolic act of defiance and revenge for the shah who was portrayed by the new regime as an American puppet who had cruelly exploited Iranians on behalf of U.S. interests. As the administration's patience wore thin, it attempted a rescue mission in the spring of 1980. The mission was called off when three of the eight helicopters malfunctioned, leaving the operation short of the six considered necessary to proceed. One helicopter collided on the ground with the refueling aircraft for the flight out of Iran, killing eight servicemen and injuring five others. The mission's failure dramatically symbolized the humiliation and apparent helplessness, clumsiness, and impotence of the United States, as well as the low level of readiness, competence, and reliability of its armed forces.

Two events helped gain the hostages' release on January 20, 1981. The first was the Iraqi attack on Iran in the fall of 1980. The war suddenly made the U.S. economic sanctions, especially the freeze on Iranian money in U.S. banks, painful for Iran because its military forces were largely American equipped; the need for spare parts and the cash to buy them and other goods grew as oil production in Iran fell to almost nothing. The second event was the November victory of Ronald Reagan, the former governor of California, as the next president. Because he had run on a tough foreign policy platform and denounced the Iranians as "barbarians" and "kidnappers," the Iranians expected harsher measures from Reagan, including military action. In these circumstances, diplomacy finally proved successful, and symbolically, the actual release of the fifty-two diplomats and marines occurred just after Reagan's inauguration. A humiliating chapter in American history had ended. In the exuberance of the welcome that the ex-hostages received upon their return to America one could almost hear the refrain "never again," for in a real sense, America itself and the U.S. government had been taken captive and held hostage.

Until the war in Vietnam, the United States had been extensively involved in the world, and it had justified its role as anti-Communist. As in the two wars against Germany, the cold war was a moral cause: democracy versus dictatorship. After Vietnam, the reaction had set in, illustrating the usual American pattern of swings from isolationism to crusading and back again. The mood of disillusionment and disengagement from the burdens of more than two decades of American-Soviet conflict—plus the accompanying sense of shame and guilt about the uses to which American power had been put—found their outlet in the Carter administration's rejection of the "inordinate fear of communism"; the emphasis on America's "limited power" and restraint in its exercise; the avoidance of force or covert intervention in the domestic affairs of other states; a preference for North-South cooperation to erase poverty and broaden human rights—or, at least, reduce the worst abuses of them; a distaste for East-West relations, except for arms control; and a repudiation of old-fashioned power politics in favor of reorienting U.S. policy toward the forces said to be transforming world politics.

Interdependence as a theory fitted the temper of the 1970s like a glove. If balance-of-power considerations were indeed becoming less critical and economic forces and global welfare more important, there was little reason to worry about the Soviet Union despite its steadily growing military power. The reasons advanced for not worrying were many: the Soviets were just catching up with the United States; they had to worry over China as well as the North Atlantic Treaty Organization; and, given the frequency of past invasions, they were insecure. But, it was forecast, once they had achieved parity with the United States, they would stop. When they did not stop, new explanations said it did not really matter: nuclear weapons were suicidal and conventional ones too costly to use; the Soviets were just wasting their money; the Soviet leaders were clearly in need of education for thinking that past patterns of behavior would be as useful in the future as in the past.

In any event, whatever the level of Soviet military capability, there was little need to worry about Soviet intentions. By the middle 1970s, it was commonplace to regard the cold war as over. The Soviet Union was said to be a *status quo* power; it might still mouth ideological slogans and revolutionary global aims, but these had about the same practical effect on Soviet policy as most Western churchgoers' Christian beliefs had on their everyday behavior. At worst, Soviet Russia—like czarist Russia—might still harbor imperial ambitions like those of other great powers throughout history, but these were of a limited nature, not at all comparable to the universal goals of revolutionary powers. The Soviet Union in the 1970s was no longer considered a revolutionary power. Nationalism in the Third World, the determination of the ex-colonial countries to assert their identity and interests, would ensure that they would not become Soviet colonies.

The upshot was predictable of this unwillingness to face fully the "real world," to explain away continued superpower competition, to minimize concern for the results of this competition while it remained largely one-sided, and the reluctance to assert American power. The Soviets sensed that they could defy the United States with impunity. Perhaps indicative of this state of affairs was Carter's handling of the issue of the Soviet combat brigade that U.S. intelligence had discovered in Cuba in the summer of 1979. Although the brigade had probably been there for years and Brzezinski recommended against demanding its withdrawal, the president, pushed on the issue by domestic politics, took a hard-line position. He first declared that this "*status quo* was not acceptable." When Moscow said that the troops were there merely to train Cubans, Carter accepted this reassurance and accepted the very *status quo* he had a few days earlier found unacceptable. Moscow refused to budge on this issue, even though it might—and did—hurt the chances of SALT II's passage through the Senate. But, rather than risk a confrontation or a delay of SALT II, Carter changed his mind. The issue was undoubtedly publicly overblown and not comparable in its importance to Soviet moves in Africa and elsewhere, but Carter's ineptness and impotence seemed to symbolize post-Vietnam America. Is it any wonder that shortly thereafter, having seen the United States frequently change its mind, hesitate, or remain passive since Angola in 1975, the Soviet Union felt it could invade Afghanistan without fear of U.S. retaliation? Or that Iran thought it could seize American diplomatic personnel with impunity and that the sizable U.S. naval forces gathered in the Indian Ocean after the seizure were only a bluff?

Yet, the capture of the hostages and invasion of Afghanistan dispelled much of the post-Vietnam atmosphere and led to a demand for a more vigorous policy. Khomeini and Leonid Brezhnev may have done the United States a favor, just as it had taken a German submarine attack on U.S. ships (World War I), a Japanese attack on Pearl Harbor (World War II), and a Soviet coup in Czechoslovakia (cold war), to mobilize the nation when the public mood was one of disengagement and relaxation. After years of neo-isolationism, the two successive slaps in the face in November and December of 1979, may have been necessary to demonstrate that impotence can result only in national shame. Carter sensed this shift of mood as he took a harder line toward the Soviets. But it was Reagan who received the full measure of the benefit of this shift of mood. He had long taken a hard line toward the Soviet Union, and, although inflation and the weak state of the U.S. economy may have been the primary factors for Reagan's election, the fact remains that because of OPEC and the collapse of the shah, the domestic economic issue was inseparable from American foreign policy and the U.S. position in the world. As on earlier occasions when America had felt provoked, its reaction was predictable. The pendulum of public opinion swung back part of the way to a recognition of the continuation of American-Soviet rivalry and a more vigorous reassertion of American interests and power.

Reagan and Cold War II: Reviving U.S. Military and Economic Capabilities

B<small>Y</small> THE time Ronald Reagan came into office, the national disillusionment with *détente* was widespread and the term *cold war II* was heard more and more frequently. The president's long-term hostility toward communism in general and more specifically toward the Soviet Union as the strongest of the Communist states fitted the new *postdétente* mood. The Soviet threat became the centerpiece for the Reagan administration. No more was heard about "world-order politics," the priority of North-South issues over East-West issues, or the limits of American power. Quite the opposite: the president often sounded like an old-fashioned evangelist rather than a born-again Christian. Reagan never indicated that he thought the United States had abused its power or that it should feel ashamed or guilty about the past exercise of power. Vietnam had been an "honorable" war. He denounced Soviet communism as "the focus of evil in the modern world." He said, "There is sin and evil in the world, and we're enjoined by Scripture and the Lord Jesus to oppose it with all our might." [1] Opposition to the Soviet Union, therefore, was a religious as well as a political imperative. In his first years in office, Reagan sounded like a crusader, even if in practice he was cautious and avoided confrontations.

Clearly, Reagan thought of the American-Soviet conflict not only as the critical struggle in the world but also as a struggle between good and evil, and he was probably more of an ideologue than any of his predecessors. In that respect, Reagan most resembled President Dwight Eisenhower's secretary of state, John Foster Dulles. Reagan spoke of the march of freedom and democracy leaving "Marxism-Leninism on the ashheap of history," of the

---

1. Remarks to the National Association of Evangelicals, March 8, 1983, in *The Russians and Reagan*, by Strobe Talbott (New York: Vintage Books, 1984), 113.

"great revolutionary crisis" of the Soviet political-economic system, and the "decay of the Soviet experiment." Of Eastern Europe he said, "Regimes planted by bayonets do not take roots"—that is, the Communist regimes had no legitimacy. He stated that the United States could not accept the "permanent subjugation of the people of Eastern Europe"; that the Yalta conference had not divided Europe into Soviet and American spheres of influence (which was true because the Soviets had promised free elections in the countries of Eastern Europe and then placed Communist regimes in power at bayonet point).[2] In making the point that democracy and freedom were the waves of the future, the president was giving the Soviets a dose of their own medicine, as the Soviets constantly denounced the United States and forecast the "inevitable end" of Western capitalism. More important, he was questioning the legitimacy and longevity of communism as a social and political system, not only in Eastern Europe but also in the Soviet Union. The Soviet leaders, surprisingly thin-skinned, were greatly irritated.

Korean Airline Downing and Anti-Sovietism

Admittedly, the president was not always diplomatic, as shown by his comment that Soviet leaders would lie, steal, cheat, and do anything else to advance their goals.[3] When critics questioned this and other blanket condemnations, arguing that the United States and the Soviet Union had to live together in the world and that the president's denunciations of Moscow would make productive arms negotiations less likely and nuclear war more so, the Soviets did something to make the president's characterization of them look almost moderate. In September 1983 they shot down a South Korean Boeing 747 airliner, killing 269 people.

The incident was an extraordinary commentary on Soviet behavior for two reasons. First, the Soviets lied about it for a week, at first disclaiming any knowledge of the affair. Then they said that a Soviet fighter had intercepted the airliner, but that the South Korean plane had flown out of the Soviet airspace into which it had strayed. Then they admitted that the fighter had shot tracers to warn the airliner, after which it had flown away; and finally they confessed that the intruding airplane had been "downed." Second, the Soviets blamed the United States for their act, claiming that the Central Intelligence Agency (CIA) had used the South Korean plane as a spy plane. In fact, the Soviets later admitted that they had believed that the civilian airliner was an American reconnaissance plane, a Boeing 707, a smaller plane with a silhouette that is very different from a 747. The lying, the shifting of

---

2. Address to Members of Parliament, June 8, 1982, in Talbott, *The Russians and Reagan*, 89-104.
3. *New York Times*, January 30, 1981.

responsibility, the refusal to admit that they had made a serious mistake, the fact that the Soviets would shoot down an unarmed plane at all, regardless of what it was, instead of escorting it out of Soviet airspace or forcing it to land on Soviet soil, aroused an enormous furor in the West.

The president, calling the Soviet act the "Korean airline massacre," denounced it as a "crime against humanity," which must "never be forgotten" and for which there was "absolutely no justification, either legal or moral." Reagan related it to other Soviet acts:

> It was an act of barbarism, both of a society which wantonly disregards individual rights and the value of human life and seeks constantly to expand and dominate other nations.
>
> Memories come back of Czechoslovakia, Hungary, Poland, the gassing of villages in Afghanistan. If the massacre and the subsequent conduct are intended to intimidate, they have failed in their purpose. From every corner of the globe the word is defiance in the face of this unspeakable act and defiance of the system which excuses it and tries to cover it up.[4]

The president's words clearly reveal that he saw Soviet behavior as a confirmation of his view of the Soviet regime as brutal and uncivilized. He also raised the issue of the wisdom of doing business with a regime that endlessly talks about brotherhood, peace, and disarmament, but acts in a savage manner. Could there be legitimate discourse and negotiations with such a government?

Responding to the president's words and reasserting that the plane had been sent on a spy mission by the United States, Yuri Andropov used some of the harshest language that any Soviet leader had used in a long time.

> In their striving to justify in some way their dangerous, inhuman policies, the same people pile heaps of slander on the Soviet Union, on socialism as a social system, with the tone being set by the President of the United States himself. One must say bluntly—it is an unattractive sight when, with a view to smearing the Soviet people, leaders of such a country as the United States resort to what almost amounts to obscenities alternating with hypocritical preaching about morals and humanism.[5]

The intensity of the verbal denunciations and insults matched the chill of American-Soviet relations in the early 1980s. Not surprisingly, the Soviet Union boycotted the Olympics held in Los Angeles in 1984; the Soviets were seeking revenge for America's withdrawal from the 1980 Olympics, which Moscow had intended to exploit as a glorification of Soviet socialism and superpower status. That it did so in a presidential election year was deliberate; the Soviet Union intended to underline the message that Reagan's

---

4. "President Reagan: Korean Airline Massacre," U.S. Department of State, Bureau of Public Affairs, *Current Policy*, September 5, 1983.
5. Statement by Yuri Andropov, September 28, 1983, in Talbott, *The Russians and Reagan*, 121.

anticommunism and militarism were the sole source of the new superpower chill.

The Korean airline incident could not have created this chill all by itself had American-Soviet relations not been so shaky to start with; the airliner was, after all, not American-owned, and it *was* flying over Soviet territory. For the president, however, this incident, coming on top of Soviet expansion in the 1970s, the invasion of Afghanistan, and the increasing repression of dissidents in the Soviet Union, strengthened his view that the Soviet Union was a wicked power. He almost seemed to be suggesting that it was wrong to have good relations with such an evil country. Not *détente* but confrontation and containment were a more appropriate relationship.

Reasons Behind the Rhetoric

The harsh denunciations of the Soviet Union, undiplomatic perhaps but not totally inaccurate, were not just the president's statement of his personal ideology. They served at least two specific purposes. First, they were intended to remobilize American public opinion after the years of *détente*. To be sure, Reagan's election was itself a sign of the public's growing cynicism about *détente* and anger at America's recent humiliations in foreign policy. The stronger anti-Soviet rhetoric and more assertive post-Vietnam role, in fact, had started with President Jimmy Carter. But Carter was more strongly identified with the seizure of hostages in Iran and his confession of error about misunderstanding Soviet intentions until the Soviet invasion of Afghanistan. Reagan, to whom *détente* all along had been an illusion based upon the unwarranted belief that the Soviets had changed their character, sought to arouse American opinion for the longer term. The angry mood would pass; the public during the 1970s, after all, had shared the hopes that the cold war was dead. The conflict with the Soviet Union was long-term. The nation's attention needed to be refocused on the Kremlin's leaders.

The second function of the president's war of words was to send the Soviet leaders a message, especially at a time the Soviet Union was having a severe geriatric problem. First, Leonid Brezhnev died in late 1982; his successor, Andropov, died just over a year later in early 1984; and his successor, Konstantin Chernenko, in ill-health when he took over, died just over a year later in 1985. Mikhail Gorbachev, who had risen rapidly to the top of the Soviet party hierarchy, partly as a result of being close to key leaders, especially Andropov, who had served as head of the KGB, now became the Soviet Union's fourth leader since Reagan had assumed office. Gorbachev's early career spanned the years of growing Soviet military strength, expansion of influence beyond Eurasia, and America's declining appetite for an activist global role. Reagan's blunt declarations sent the new Soviet leadership the signal that the Vietnam syndrome was a thing of the past, that America's will to resist Soviet expansion was back. The president's purpose was to avoid confrontations and possible military clashes. The signals were perhaps intentionally sharp so that the Soviet Union would not act, as it had during the 1970s, in the belief that America would not react. In that sense, the tough words were a substitute for deeds.

In fact, the Reagan years, particularly the early years, were characterized by *rhetorical* confrontations, but no real encounters. In policy terms these were quiet years; there were no crises. Despite his reputation among some Americans and Europeans as a rather wild cowboy, operationally the president was very cautious and careful. Reagan's foreign policy was a return to the classical containment policy of the post-World War II years. The primary emphasis was on East-West relations, on the Soviet Union as a Communist expansionist state, and on the need to contain that expansion, including in the Third World, by force, if necessary. Like his predecessors, Reagan had a "doctrine," but with his own twist. From the Truman Doctrine until the war in Vietnam, the basic purpose of U.S. foreign policy had been to prevent or limit the further expansion of Soviet power. The Reagan Doctrine was a response to Soviet gains in the post-Vietnam period. The doctrine's aim was to undo these gains by supporting insurgencies in some of the countries to which Soviet power had been extended in the 1970s. It expected thereby to legitimate the insurgents' challenge to these nations' pro-Soviet regimes. In a sense, the Reagan Doctrine was an American version of Nikita Khrushchev's "national liberation" strategy. Supporting "freedom fighters" became a centerpiece of the Reagan version of containment.

An Old Policy Revived

Despite his strong anti-Communist ideology and rhetoric, then, Reagan's foreign policy moved the United States back to its anti-Soviet position. Relations with China clearly illustrate both the president's personal anticommunism and his administration's strategic sense. The reconciliation of the United States with China in the 1970s had been motivated in part by the Soviet Union's growing power; that is, the reason for the United States and China moving closer together from positions of mutual dislike and hostility was strategic. The president's ideological sympathies, however, were with the Nationalist Chinese on Taiwan. His administration at first appeared to downgrade Communist China's military strength and political influence, even though China held down about fifty Soviet divisions along its long frontier with the Soviet Union. Moreover, by pursuing a tough anti-Soviet policy, the president offered Beijing few reasons to be more accommodating toward Washington. Why should China offer concessions to the United States when its president was so hostile to the Soviet Union? Chinese concessions would be far more likely if Washington were also negotiating meaningfully with Moscow and Beijing wished to prevent the establishment of closer relations between the two superpowers.

During the Richard Nixon-Gerald Ford years the United States had gained leverage with the Soviet Union and China when it negotiated with both and each wished to prevent the other's gaining greater influence in Washington and benefits from its "American connection." Nixon had positioned himself between the Soviet Union and China to try and play the "China card" against the Kremlin. Reagan's hard line against Moscow allowed China to place itself in the middle; it encouraged China to distance itself somewhat from Washington, to play its "American card" and achieve a *détente* of its own with Moscow. Admittedly, there were limits to how far such a *détente* could go because the Soviet Union was unwilling to meet China's basic demands. Moreover, China could not go too far in breaking with the United States lest the Soviet preeminence that had originally driven China toward America be reestablished. Reagan's anticommunism made it unnecessary for Beijing to be more accommodating toward Washington, as the president discovered on his journey there when his hosts censored his anti-Soviet remarks on television.

The United States could not afford to break with Beijing either and to face once more, as during cold war I, an alliance of the two Communist states. The president was faced with a problem. Clearly, Reagan's "heart" lay with the defunct Nationalist regime on Taiwan. At one time he even talked of upgrading the United States mission there to a full-fledged embassy, even though the United States had officially recognized the People's Republic in 1979 and transferred its embassy to Beijing from Taiwan. Reagan's policy bordered on the old "two Chinas" solution, despite the 1972 Shanghai communiqué issued at the end of Nixon's visit that stated there was only "one China." After the Chinese several times expressed irritation over American arms sales to the Nationalists, the Reagan administration signed an agreement in 1982 in which the United States for the first time agreed to cap the quality and quantity of arms sales to Taiwan and eventually to phase them out. Beijing, in turn, restated that its basic policy was to seek peaceful reunification with Taiwan, not to take it by force.

Ideology and pragmatism thus struggled with each other in the Reagan administration, strongly reflecting the president's own inner conflicts. Taiwan almost became an obstacle to maintaining the more important strategic relationship between the United States and the People's Republic of China, but the president's visit to China in the spring of 1984 was a concession to strategic reality, as well as a bid for reelection. Given his lack of any dramatic foreign policy successes during his first term and great public concern that he might get the United States into a war somewhere—in Central America, if not with the Soviet Union—the president needed a successful trip to China to show he was a peacemaker and superpower leader. In this instance, Reagan's domestic needs dovetailed with the country's strategic needs. Indeed, the upcoming election had already moderated Reagan's language concerning the Soviet Union; it had even led him to endorse arms control negotiations, something he had denounced while he was concentrating on a U.S. arms buildup.

For Unilateral Rearmament

By 1981 any president would have been concerned about Soviet intentions as well as the growth of Soviet military power. Carter's defense secretary, Harold Brown, had said: "As our defense budgets have risen, the Soviets have increased their defense budgets. As our defense budgets have gone down, their defense budgets have increased again." Reagan had once asked, "What arms race? We stopped, they raced." During the 1970s American defense expenditures had fallen to the 1950 (pre-Korean War) low of 5 percent of the nation's gross national product (GNP) at a time when the Soviet Union, despite having an economy only half the size of that of the United States, was spending substantially more than the United States on defense. From 1950 to 1969 congressional cuts in defense budget requests had averaged only $1.7 billion annually, compared with $9.2 billion in cuts for nondefense programs. The six Nixon-Ford defense requests were cut by an average of $6 billion annually, while the nondefense budget was increased by an average of $4.7 billion. The 1970s were the days of antimilitary sentiment, neo-isolationist hopes, and cries for "domestic priorities" and for reductions of the defense budget; they witnessed "the most substantial reduction in American military capabilities relative to those of the Soviet Union in the entire postwar period." [6] Any administration coming into power after a decade and a half of Soviet efforts to exploit America's post-Vietnam mood of withdrawal from the world and the weakening of the American presidency would have been concerned with the Soviet Union's growing first-strike capability against an increasingly vulnerable U.S. deterrent force, the shifting military balance as the buildup continued in Soviet strategic and conventional forces, as well as the increasing Soviet capability to project power beyond Eurasia. It was in the context of Soviet perceptions of a changing "correlation of forces" that the Soviets had exploited Third World situations to increase their influence by means of military advisers and arms, proxies such as the Vietnamese in Cambodia and the Cubans in Africa, and, of course, their own troops in Afghanistan.

It appeared to the administration in 1981 that the Soviet Union continued to view its relationship with the United States as a rivalry in which any Soviet gains were losses for the United States and vice versa; that, although the reasons for Soviet actions in Africa, Southeast Asia, and Southwest Asia might have differed, there was an increasing emphasis on the use of military power as the primary instrument of Soviet policy; and that Soviet respect for American interests and power was declining. Indeed, the Soviet emphasis on military strength seemed in part to be a reflection of its lack of attractive alternatives, such as economic aid; but it also suggested that

---

6. John Lewis Gaddis, *Strategy of Containment* (New York: Oxford University Press, 1972), 320-322.

Moscow saw greater political opportunities to use the threat of force as a means of intimidation. U.S. strategic superiority in the past had placed limits on how far the Soviets could safely escalate a challenge; they were prudent to act with restraint. Parity, however, provided the Soviets greater opportunities and fewer risks because for the United States the costs of opposing a Soviet move had risen.

The Utility of Force

The Reagan administration rejected an assumption that had become widely accepted during the decade of *détente:* that force no longer had much utility in international politics. The enormous growth of Soviet military power and Moscow's willingness to use it to support its diplomacy suggested otherwise. Force was a useful instrument of policy, whether it was applied, threatened, or just provided the background for diplomatic negotiations. The widespread belief in the disutility of force appeared to the new administration to result from two decades of deterrence by strategically superior U.S. forces. Ironically, this view had come into vogue in the United States at the very moment when the deterrent balance was shifting and force seemed once more to have political and military utility. It was time to abandon this myth. The lesson of the 1970s, as the administration read it, was the wisdom of the old-fashioned adage that unwillingness to invoke the threat of force or to actually use it in defense of national interests encourages an opponent to try to expand its influence, because any risks or penalties for this behavior are eliminated. The advantage then goes to the party willing to threaten or actually use violence. But if the threat were met by the possibility of military opposition and thereby given an incentive for restraint, the belligerent nation might moderate its aims. The administration used force several times to make this point: in Grenada in 1983, and against Libya in 1981 and 1986. Typical of Reagan, however, while he used harsh language to denounce the Soviet Union, he used force only against minor opponents. Carefully avoiding clashes with Soviet forces, he nevertheless sought to impress Moscow with U.S. readiness to defend its interests by using its military power against Moscow's smaller friends.

The administration was especially worried about the state of America's deterrent forces. Their basic rationale had always been that if the enemy knew that after launching an attack it would be destroyed, the enemy would not strike. For example, once the United States had enough missiles to absorb a Soviet first strike and a sufficient number left to hit the Soviet Union's major cities and destroy most of its urban population and industries, no more missiles would be needed. Any more would be "overkill" and unnecessary. This logic had provided the rationale for some of the lack of concern about the Soviet strategic forces as they surpassed those of the United States in numbers of intercontinental ballistic missiles (ICBMs) and submarine-launched ballistic missiles (SLBMs), megatonnage (the total amount of explosive force they could carry), and the number and size of ICBM warheads. Tight post-Vietnam defense budgets had made this rationale even more acceptable.

But once it was believed that Soviet ICBMs might strike at U.S. deterrent forces, it became a key task to do something about the vulnerable Minuteman land-based ICBMs and the aging B-52 bombers and Polaris submarines (all weapons systems built in the 1950s and early-middle 1960s). American strategic forces needed to be modernized to ensure their continued deterrent capability. The Reagan administration therefore gave priority to this task, although it also sought to strengthen the nation's conventional power which, at least for missions outside of Europe, had been neglected as part of the "no more Vietnams" mood of the 1970s. A 600-ship navy, including 15 (instead of 12) carrier battle groups, plus several restored World War II vintage battleships, were particularly high on the administration's list of conventional military goals.

MX and Nuclear War Fighting

At the center of the administration's early rearmament program, however, was the MX (missile experimental) ICBM, a missile as large as the Soviet SS-19 and carrying ten warheads like the even larger Soviet SS-18. The MX aroused enormous controversy for two reasons. First, the administration rejected Carter's method for deploying the MX missiles in a mobile fashion so that they would not be vulnerable to a Soviet first strike, as were the stationary Minuteman missiles, the backbone of the U.S. land-based deterrent. The reasons for this rejection were the high cost of mobile deployment and that Utah and Nevada, the two states Carter had selected for basing the MX, had voted Republican in 1980 and neither wanted it.

But in deciding to deploy the MX in Minuteman silos, the administration negated a major reason for wanting it: to make the ICBM component of the deterrent less vulnerable. In addition, according to the critics, the MX's accurate warheads were capable of hitting Soviet silos. This meant that if the MX were deployed in vulnerable Minuteman silos, it would be particularly attractive to a preemptive Soviet strike, especially during a crisis in which the Soviets might expect an American first strike. The United States would either have to "use them or lose them." The danger was that the MX would create a mutual hair trigger situation which, in turn, could lead to a nuclear war that neither side wanted. Each would feel that it had to take that risk because if it failed to strike first, its ICBMs would be destroyed.

The second and even more critical reason why MX aroused enormous controversy was the administration's talk of *limited nuclear options, protracted nuclear war,* and *nuclear war fighting.* These phrases did not mean that the United States was no longer committed to deterrence. It was. But what if deterrence failed? The reason why the United States had to think of this possibility, according to administration spokesmen (and, it must be added in fairness, according to the secretaries of defense in the Nixon-Ford and

Carter administrations) followed from the Soviet deployment of large numbers of accurate warheads on its big missiles. What if, in a crisis, the Soviets attacked only or primarily American ICBMs? Was not the retaliatory capability of American submarines and bombers still so enormous that the Soviets would not dare a first strike? Would not the second-strike threat still prevent a first strike? The administration feared it would not.

Why not? A Soviet first strike aimed at ICBMs, generally deployed far away from large cities, would leave the vast majority of Americans alive and most cities still standing. An American retaliatory blow with the remnants of the U.S. deterrent forces—bombers and SLBMs—however, would destroy much of the Soviet Union's population and many of its cities because these were largely imprecise weapons, usable mainly against urban-industrial areas. Only ICBMs were sufficiently accurate to be used to strike back at Soviet military targets, especially its remaining ICBMs. So? Why did it matter if the United States struck back at cities or at missiles? The key question was what would happen if the Soviets, after their initial blow, announced that they had carried out their attack with 30 percent to 40 percent of their strategic forces and that, if the United States retaliated against Soviet cities, they had enough missiles left to strike again against American cities they had deliberately avoided attacking before? In short, would a Soviet threat of a *third* strike not deter the American *second* strike? Would a president order a second strike, knowing that if he did so he would be signing the death warrant of most of America's population? Or would he, faced with that possibility, do nothing?

No one could say. He might retaliate regardless of the consequences. But the real issue is whether any president should be confronted with this awful choice. This choice would occur even in the absence of an actual Soviet attack because, in a crisis involving the vital interests of both sides, a president would understand that the Soviets possessed sufficiently accurate warheads and the United States did not. Moscow could stand firm, increase its pressure if needed, while Washington would have to retreat in future "Cubas-in-reverse." Indeed, this possibility of nuclear blackmail was thought far more likely than a Soviet attack.

MX was the way to avoid having to cope with such a situation. Should deterrence of a "limited nuclear attack" fail, then the United States could respond in kind to punish the Soviet Union in equal measure, prevent further escalation, and compel it to desist. Most of all, it was expected that the existence of the MX would deter the possibility of such a limited strike, thereby avoiding future crisis confrontations in which Moscow could intimidate Washington. MX would provide extra insurance in case Soviet leaders thought that they could threaten a first strike or actually attack. MX—first thought of during the Nixon-Ford administration and first proposed for deployment by the Carter administration—was intended to strengthen deterrence.

Critics, however, thought the whole scenario either bizarre or improbable. Given the past record of Soviet caution and unwillingness to risk the survival of their homeland, the Soviets were unlikely to risk a limited nuclear strike. And critics further pointed out that nuclear weapons were far too destructive to be used discriminately against military targets only. In any event, the momentum of an initial nuclear exchange would inevitably escalate to a full-scale war. What was truly frightening about Reagan's (and before him, Carter's) limited nuclear war scenario, they said, was the possibility that the policy makers might really believe that such a war could be waged and that society, suffering "only" a few million casualties, would survive; if they thought this they might be tempted to resort to a nuclear war. The likelihood that this might occur was increased by the fact that not only was MX basically a first-strike weapon but also part of a larger buildup of strategic weapons that could hit Soviet military targets with great accuracy. Among these weapons were the new B-1 bomber, the Trident II submarine missile (scheduled for deployment in the 1990s), and a variety of cruise missiles. The critics saw these weapon acquisitions as part of a larger U.S. effort to regain strategic superiority and shift to a war-fighting or counterforce strategy, which would intensify the arms race.

Instead, they argued that mutual assured destruction (MAD) was unavoidable and therefore MX was unnecessary. In the final analysis, they contended, plans for a limited nuclear war and MX were based upon the claim that Minuteman had become 95 percent vulnerable to destruction. But this figure was based on simulated computerized war games; in a real-life operation, the Soviets could not achieve such a high kill rate and therefore count on an absence of American retaliation, including retaliation by U.S. ICBMs. Neither the Soviets nor the Americans had any experience in nuclear war, which would involve coordinating hundreds of missiles and thousands of warheads and targeting them with split-second timing and accuracy on the opponent's multiple and widely dispersed nuclear forces. If either side launched a first strike, it was unlikely to be carried out with the efficiency and effectiveness of a war plan; such a plan would be degraded by what professional soldiers knew as the "friction" of war (or, what many Americans refer to as Murphy's Law: If something can go wrong, it will). Therefore, according to the critics, much of the Reagan strategic buildup was not only unnecessary, but downright dangerous.

Against Bilateral Arms Control

After the disillusionment with *détente,* whose centerpiece had been arms control, it is doubtful that there would have been any strategic arms control agreement in the early 1980s, even if Carter had been reelected. Given the extensive Soviet arms buildup during the decade of *détente,* it was not surprising that unilateral rearmament received priority over bilateral arms control; indeed, this rearmament program had begun under Carter. Reagan, however, expanded it.

Nevertheless, despite considerable public support, the administration's initial $1-trillion, five-year rearmament program stimulated enormous controversy (from 1980-1987, the total was $1.9 trillion). This was so even though much of defense spending went for personnel and for weapons that were needed: conventional weapons to modernize the nation's nonnuclear forces and strategic weapons to supplement or replace increasingly obsolete delivery systems with newer systems at a time when almost all of the Soviet Union's strategic forces were less than ten years old. In other words, the U.S. forces had been deployed since SALT I in 1972. But the administration's harsh anti-Soviet rhetoric, its seemingly reckless talk of limited nuclear war—which appeared to suggest that U.S. policy was shifting from deterring nuclear war to getting ready to fight one—its absolute determination to increase defense spending over that already scheduled, all intensified the impression that it relied too much on military strength and looked for military solutions to political problems. It seemed that the United States was largely responsible for the "arms race." The momentum of the Soviet Union's program of arms acquisition across the board and its impact on the balance of nuclear and conventional balances often appeared to be forgotten.

The Peace Movement Gathers Strength

Ironically, therefore, Reagan inspired a widespread "peace movement" in the early 1980s. Its adherents ranged from academia to religious institutions, especially the Catholic and Methodist bishops, who questioned the morality of nuclear deterrence, a policy based on the threat to use nuclear weapons in order to prevent their use. Both sets of bishops opposed the *use* of nuclear weapons. But if such weapons could not be used even in retaliation, how could deterrence be made credible? Was the goal of peace moral but the means of preserving it so immoral that it was preferable to submit to enemy demands? Would a nonnuclear deterrence be moral, even if it failed to prevent war? And would one side's renunciation of nuclear weapons mean that the other side would not use them? This was unclear. The bishops certainly did not advocate large-scale conventional rearmament as an alternative to a nuclear defense. In the meantime, antinuclear books and films became popular.

Besides the immorality of nuclear deterrence, the second major theme of the peace movement was that nuclear war would mean the end of civilization, the "last epidemic," as a doctor's organization phrased it. This theme was given strong support by new scientific arguments that the smoke produced by the many fires resulting from nuclear attacks would shut out sunlight, plunging the world into darkness for several months, and causing a prolonged freeze or "nuclear winter," leading to the extinction of most plant and animal life. Even if the attacker had successfully eliminated most of the opponent's retaliatory capability, climactic catastrophe would follow and spread over the globe. The aggressor might be a winner—but for two weeks only. In brief most of these antinuclear writings and films, emphasized "the day after," and some concluded that if humans were to survive, nuclear weapons not only had to be eliminated but also, if possible, a world government established that would end national rivalries. The public mood, which had initially favored the Reagan rearmament program, had shifted.

Yet there was really little that was novel about these antinuclear books and films. By 1980 the horror of nuclear war had been common knowledge for thirty-five years. That was, after all, why the United States had adopted a deterrent strategy. And it was the suicidal nature of these nuclear arms that had encouraged the belief that nuclear deterrence would prevent an all-out Soviet attack on the United States and preserve peace among the superpowers. Moreover, although deterrence could fail, it *had* a historical record. The superpowers had not exchanged as much as a rifle shot in Europe where they confronted one another. Their nuclear power and their mutual fear of suicide had given them forty years of peace, Europe's longest period of peace in the twentieth century. Indeed, nuclear weapons had eliminated war among *all* the great powers, not just the superpowers. The antinuclear movement appeared to confuse the issue of using nuclear force with threatening their use to bolster deterrence.

The antinuclear movement, however, had enormous momentum by 1982. The danger of nuclear war appeared to be the nation's first concern. In New York City, three-quarters of a million people turned out for the largest political gathering in American history. For these demonstrators and the others marching, meeting, and debating the nuclear issue across the country, the ultimate goal was to eliminate nuclear weapons, but the immediate focus was to achieve a nuclear freeze. Proposals for a freeze on the testing, production, and deployment of nuclear weapons to stop the arms race were passed (or almost passed) by many town-hall meetings and voters in ten of the eleven states on whose ballots it appeared at the midterm 1982 election. Congress, especially the Democratic House, reflected this antinuclear mood, and, after coming within two votes of endorsing a nuclear freeze in 1982, it endorsed a modified version of the freeze in 1983. All 1984 Democratic presidential candidates but one came out in favor of a freeze.

Reasons for Opposition to Arms Control

This mix of concern, unease, and occasional pacifism was not appeased by the administration's professions of peaceful intent. What particularly hurt the administration as it rebuilt American military strength was its evident hostility to arms control. In part, this hostility reflected a general distrust of the Soviets, which implied that agreements with them were not desirable. Alleged Soviet violations of SALT II were constantly cited. More important was the belief of the president and many in his administration that past arms control efforts were the chief reason for America's purportedly declining strength vis-à-vis the Soviet Union. Indeed, Reagan was the first postwar president who specifically said when he came into office that U.S. military power was inferior to the Soviet Union's, an assessment with which few outside of the administration (and probably not too many in it, including the Joint Chiefs) agreed. Spokesmen for the administration asserted that arms control restrained the United States, but had not inhibited the Soviet buildup. Given this perspective, administration skepticism, if not opposition, to arms control is not surprising.

Still, this negative assessment of the value of arms control ought to be seen in perspective. Arms control was originally conceived of as supplementing the defense effort. Military strength was the basis of a peaceful superpower relationship; arms control was to ensure the stability of the deterrent balance. But during the 1970s, popular opinion and Congress resisted large increases in defense expenditures. The military, it was charged, "had plenty"; the armed services' emphasis on the growing Soviet threat was self-serving, intended only to increase their budgets. If the United States had more arms, it would only get involved in another war, for the danger was not so much the Soviet Union, but the United States itself. The impression had become widespread that arms control was not a supplement, but an *alternative* to an expensive and unilateral defense buildup whose purpose was to keep up with the Soviets and achieve strategic stability. Indeed, such efforts were often said to undermine arms control! It was charged that new arms were not needed and would endanger future agreements. This disassociation of arms control from defense policy and the pursuit of arms control in its own right, regardless of any linkages to the Soviet exploitation of foreign policy opportunities to expand its influence, ignored the fact that arms control agreements could not by themselves make peace more secure. It was often forgotten that arms competition was a symptom of the underlying superpower rivalry; arms control can neither end that conflict nor be a substitute for maintaining strength. Indeed, American strength remains the principal incentive for the Soviets to make concessions to attain stabilizing arms control agreements and not to use arms control negotiations to inhibit U.S. arms programs while theirs are growing.

The new administration therefore continued to concentrate on building up U.S. arms. But postponing new arms control talks proved difficult; public opinion equated arms control with disarmament and even more so with a sincere search for peace. The pressure on the administration grew. When negotiations finally started in 1982, the administration claimed it was shifting the emphasis from arms limitation—setting ceilings on launchers—to drastic reductions. It changed the name from SALT (Strategic Arms Limitation Talks) to START (Strategic Arms Reduction Talks). The real motives for this change were to make its approach politically appealing at home, to deflect criticism, and to weaken the freeze movement. SALT had always been concerned with restraining the arms competition and setting equal ceilings for both powers; drastic arms reductions had been the stated goal for SALT III.

In the subsequent arms negotiations, it seemed that the administration was interested primarily in gaining more support for MX. The administration argued that fruitful negotiations could be expected only if the Soviets saw the United States as willing to match the continuing Soviet arms effort; MX was critical in this respect. Why should Moscow negotiate seriously and agree to arms reductions unless it calculated that future American strength and an American counterpart to their SS-18 and SS-19 made it futile to continue its own building program? All this may have been true in the context of a negotiating strategy. But the administration's conviction that arms control in the 1970s had weakened the United States and, therefore, was a dangerous policy was by now widely perceived by the public. Its arms proposals always appeared as if they were being made reluctantly, to appease public pressures, not because the administration really had any faith in arms control.

The lesson was clear: a president can arm the United States if necessary, but only if the public also sees a genuine effort to control the arms competition and to improve the superpower relationship. The Reagan administration had not learned that lesson. MX, always a weapon of controversial merit, had been politically acceptable during the Ford and Carter administrations. The only problem seemed to be its manner of deployment. But when Reagan suggested various options for its deployment, he created enormous opposition, and for the first time since 1945 Congress initially refused to fund a major new weapon requested by the president; it finally gave him only fifty. It might fund the other fifty if the administration could find a less vulnerable mode of deployment; in late 1986, the administration suggested that these MXs might be placed on special railroad cars. The basic reason, however, for MX's continuing difficulties was the administration's inability to convince the public and Congress that modernization of the deterrent was linked to a genuine arms control strategy. To Congress, Reagan's arms control proposals appeared to be a way of gaining legislative support for MX, so Congress turned the tables on the administration: if Reagan wanted MX, he would have to negotiate seriously on arms control.

The president got the message. Public pressure and the 1984 election moved him toward expressing a desire for arms control and to talk to the Soviets. He also had a Soviet leader with whom he could talk; Gorbachev had quickly begun to consolidate his power. But the chances of success were never good. American proposals all called for massive Soviet reductions or "build down" of the SS-18s and SS-19s, while the modernization or buildup of the U.S. deterrent continued. This included the MX, which was not to be traded. (The president later confessed his ignorance of the fact that the Soviet Union, unlike the United States, relied mainly on ICBMs and that the U.S. offer had been one-sided.) The Soviets were not likely to give up the heart of their strategic force cheaply, if at all. Even had the United States been willing to give up MX, and even if it had 100 MXs already operational, this would not have sufficed for a trade against half of the more than 300 SS-18s and 300 SS-19s. As it was, MX was only a potential weapon while the Soviets had already deployed their missiles.

SALT II Provisions Renounced

The best that could be achieved in these circumstances was that the two superpowers observe SALT II. Despite his frequent criticism of it as "fatally flawed," the president committed the United States to live within its terms. He even accused the Soviets of violating this agreement, which the United States had refused to ratify. Perhaps that was as much as could be expected during a period when the U.S. emphasis was on rearmament. As it turned out, the lack of enthusiasm for arms control and preference for unilateral buildup became evident in 1986 when, the day after Thanksgiving, the Reagan administration, which had repeatedly denounced SALT II because of legitimate concerns about Soviet compliance, asserted that its limits were no longer "operational." The United States then exceeded the limits of launchers equipped with multiple independently targeted reentry vehicles (MIRVs) by deploying another bomber loaded with cruise missiles. Now there were no longer any limits on either American or Soviet acquisitions of offensive arms.

The Soviet Union made the most of a propaganda opportunity created by the U.S. renunciation of SALT by announcing that for the time being it would not follow the American example. But the Soviet Union was in a better position than the United States to increase the numbers of missiles. American production lines, except for MX, were shut down, and the huge deficit constrained Washington's capability to respond to any large Soviet buildup. These were, indeed, among the reasons the Joint Chiefs of Staff had opposed the president's renunciation of SALT II and the United States had earlier stated that it would not "undercut" it. Were possible Soviet violations, which did not alter the strategic balance, serious enough to discard an agreement that, by keeping some ceilings on the numbers of missiles and warheads, compelled the Soviets to scrap many more older weapons than the United States as they deployed new ones? The Soviets could now keep their older missiles, add new ones, and multiply the number of warheads beyond the ten allowed on each ICBM. Indeed, in the summer of 1986, they deployed a new SS-24 mobile ICBM with ten warheads.

Whether the Soviets now exceeded SALT II ceilings as well was a critical question. There was something illogical about all this, for U.S. action would legalize an increase of the same Soviet ICBMs that the Reagan administration had from the beginning labeled as destabilizing. Most illogical of all would be that the renunciation of SALT II would magnify the problems of the president's favorite program, the Strategic Defense Initiative (SDI). To destroy incoming missiles is difficult enough even with the thousands of warheads allowed under SALT II; that task will become infinitely more difficult if the Soviets can multiply missiles and warheads by several thousand beyond those permitted by mutual agreement. The only way to explain the administration's illogical action was that it was caused by the president's intense anti-Soviet feelings and hostility toward arms control.

Star Wars

Reagan first introduced SDI in the midst of the controversy about arms spending, MX, and arms control. The proposal was quickly dubbed "Star Wars" by its critics because of its reliance on sophisticated technologies such as lasers and particle beams and the fact that it would be based largely in space. The purpose of SDI was to render nuclear missiles "impotent and obsolete." This, in turn, would protect America's population. Mutual assured survival would replace mutual assured destruction. Was it not better to save lives on both sides, the president asked, than to kill the population of the aggressor in revenge for a first strike?

The best time to destroy an incoming missile is in the initial five-minute boost phase when the missile takes off. In the second or mid-phase period of flight, defense becomes more difficult because the warheads separate, vastly multiplying the number of targets to be destroyed. Those warheads that survive could be destroyed by a ground-based defense like the old ABM system in the third or terminal phase as they seek their targets on earth. According to official descriptions, SDI would be a "layered defense" using different technologies to destroy attacking missiles during each phase of the ballistic trajectory. What this amounted to was placing a protective dome over the United States.

SDI's Domestic and Security Purposes

For the president this plan served several purposes, the first of which was political. Under attack for increasing the defense budget while cutting social services, criticized for being trigger-happy and a warmonger, Reagan was able to seize the initiative with SDI. Instead of always defending himself, he could pose as a man of vision who would end the threat of missile attacks and ensure that the population of the United States, of the Soviet Union, and, indeed, of the world would survive. He had gone arms control advocates one better, not by stabilizing the balance of offensive missiles, but by banishing their life-threatening potential.

If the churches condemned nuclear deterrence as immoral, was his scheme for a strategic defense not the incarnation of morality? And if this movement condemning nuclear deterrence spread in other Western societies as well, strategic defense might be the most politically acceptable option. Reagan had with SDI, in fact, undermined the anti-nuclear movement by stealing its thunder. It did not like nuclear weapons. Neither did he, so he would get rid of them. The distinction between stabilizing and destabilizing nuclear weapons was dismissed, as was the role these weapons had played in providing for Western security since 1945. Nuclear weapons were "bad" and therefore were to be rendered harmless by U.S. technological ingenuity.

Second, SDI's utopian side was matched by a more pragmatic consideration: if it worked, it would outflank the Soviets. For years the Soviets had invested heavily in large missiles with many warheads. The fear in the United States was that these were basically first-strike weapons. The effort to respond with more accurate U.S. missiles and warheads, such as the MX, had run afoul of domestic opponents who feared further destabilization of the nuclear balance. Moreover, the Soviets were not interested in trading their actual weapons for America's potential weapons. SDI, however, not only reduced the value of the Soviet investment in missiles but also ensured there would be no nuclear war. What would be the point of attacking if the missiles could not penetrate the defensive shield around the United States?

Third, although population defense was the fundamental and long-term SDI goal, defense of the U.S. ICBM force could start more quickly. To protect population, a defense has to be virtually perfect. If only 80 percent effective—and that would be very high—and if 20 percent of, for example, 2,000 warheads get through, they would destroy urban America. But a defense against missiles can be "leaky." If it takes two warheads to destroy one missile, and an 80 percent effective SDI destroys 1,600 incoming warheads, the remaining 400 will destroy 200 U.S. missile silos. This would leave 800 of the U.S. ICBM force for retaliation. Even a less-than-perfect SDI, therefore, can be very useful: it would relieve the American fear that its ICBMs were vulnerable and increase Soviet uncertainty that they could launch a successful first strike. If the Soviets were unsure that they could destroy a sufficient number of ICBMs, there would be no point in striking at all. SDI would restore the credibility of the U.S. deterrent and the stability of mutual deterrence.

The contradiction at the heart of SDI was that it would be ten, twenty, or more years before anyone would know if population protection was really feasible; ICBM protection was possible in the near future. But SDI, Reagan emphasized, aimed to do away with missiles (if they could not penetrate a defense, they might as well be mutually abolished as both superpowers acquired such defenses); ICBM protection assumed these missiles would survive. SDI's aim was to make mutual deterrence—the reciprocal hostage relationship—safer.

Indeed, the critics questioned the long-range goal of SDI from the start. The technology would be extremely complex; the first time it was needed, it would have to work perfectly, an unlikely prospect for a system of so many interacting parts, each of which was technologically highly sophisticated. The Soviets could overcome SDI much less expensively by multiplying both missiles and warheads (as the United States had done when it added MIRVs to its missiles to overcome the ABMs being placed around Moscow, fearing that the Soviets were beginning a nationwide deployment). The Soviet Union would also seek its own SDI. The Soviets would figure out that, although SDI would be unable to protect the United States from a massive Soviet first strike because of all its technological shortcomings, SDI would be able to defend the United States against a crippled Soviet retaliatory strike *after* an American first strike against Soviet strategic forces. This Soviet fear that SDI might be a prelude to an offensive American strike rather than a defensive system was a counterpart of the same American fears in the early 1970s that the Soviet ABMs, together with their large numbers of ICBMs with their warheads, were part of a Soviet first-strike scenario; the ABMs would protect the Soviet Union against a U.S. retaliatory force greatly weakened by a Soviet first strike.

In short, according to the critics, SDI would lead to intensive defensive and offensive arms races in which the defensive technologies, even if they gained the upper hand, would do so only temporarily. Moreover, the system would be extremely expensive, threatening the budgets for other strategic and conventional forces; these expenses would rise even more because SDI, unable to defend against bombers and cruise missiles, would need to be supplemented by an additional defensive network. Therefore, it was dubious that the United States or the Soviet Union would be any more secure. Arms reductions through bilateral negotiation was the better course.

Soviet Concerns and Arms Proposals

If the critics were correct, why did the Soviets denounce Reagan's "arms race in space" and "militarization of space"? Why, after walking out of all arms control negotiations when the United States refused to suspend its deployment of medium-range missiles in Western Europe to counter the Soviet SS-20 deployment, were the Soviets so eager to resume talks? Clearly, SDI worried them. Why? Their scientists must surely have questioned SDI's ability to prevent major missile penetration. Perhaps the Soviets really were as fearful of an American first strike as the Americans had been of a Soviet first strike in the early 1970s. But surely, the main reason had to be that SDI research and development might result in American technology leaping forward a quantum jump; this fear of falling behind spurred even America's allies to cooperate with SDI, although they doubted its military value. And, of course, Soviet technology was already behind. The Soviets were well aware that the United States had the edge in technology and this advantage might grow even larger.

The Soviets, therefore, were anxious to delay, if not stop, the deployment of SDI. The United States continued to worry about the Soviet first-strike capability. A "grand compromise" seemed the obvious solution: a radical cut in Soviet ICBMs, including the SS-18s that the United States feared the most as a first-strike weapon, in exchange for SDI, or at least a delay of SDI. At a summit meeting in Iceland in 1986, Gorbachev repeated an earlier offer of a U.S.-Soviet 50 percent reduction of strategic forces in return for confining SDI to laboratory research. (This offer was a prelude to a total elimination of all nuclear weapons.) He insisted on reaffirming the 1972 ABM treaty, which, while permitting ABM research, did not allow the development or testing of space-based defensive systems. The president, insisting that this interpretation of the treaty was too "restrictive" and offering a more "permissive" interpretation that would permit the United States to do everything short of deployment, rejected Gorbachev's offer on grounds that if SDI were limited to the laboratory, that would be the end of it. Although this conclusion was questioned by scientists, it was clear that the Soviets would not cut their strategic forces until they knew whether these forces had to cope with SDI; the restriction on strategic defense research must precede radical force reductions. This was exactly the same argument Nixon had used when the Soviets proposed an ABM agreement. He could not accept that, he had said, until he knew whether the Soviets would end their continuing offensive buildup; if it continued, the United States would need more ABMs because the two were related. Reagan, however, convinced of the correctness of his long-range vision, refused to trade SDI for Soviet offensive missiles. Unless he changes his mind, no strategic arms control agreement will be concluded.

If the United States continues to hold this position, it will be the ultimate irony. When the Reagan administration came to power, its primary concern was the perceived "window of vulnerability"; it intended to make U.S. land-based missiles less vulnerable to a Soviet first strike. When Gorbachev offered Reagan a 50 percent reduction of Soviet missiles, a potentially enormous reduction of U.S. ICBM vulnerability, the president turned him down. What had been the most potent "bargaining chip" since SALT began had now apparently become a thing unto itself. When it is remembered that the president also committed the United States to the elimination of all missiles, if not all nuclear weapons, in the ten-year period following the 1986 Iceland summit meeting, this refusal to trade is even more remarkable. Why would the United States need SDI if there were no missiles left? One reason would be to ensure against cheating. But assuming that a proper verification system is in place—otherwise neither superpower could risk destroying all of its missiles—the most that would be needed would be a simpler ground-based defense, not the exotic and complex space-based defense. In the final analysis, SDI was only a research program. Only the future will tell if SDI is technically feasible and cost-effective. A future president will make the key decisions on deployment. Ronald Reagan will not. Nevertheless, he rejected Gorbachev's terms that SDI must be confined to the laboratory and not deployed for a ten-year period in return for a drastic cut of those very Soviet missiles that SDI was supposed to guard the country against in the first place. SDI had become the chief block to fruitful arms negotiations.

NATO, *Détentism*, and Disengagement

The Reagan administration's attacks on *détente*, its preoccupation with rearmament, the shift in U.S. military doctrine to nuclear war fighting, the reluctance to engage in arms control negotiations, but willingness to use force as in Grenada, upset the NATO allies in Europe. Even SDI caused considerable unease because, if the United States ever could defend itself against Soviet missiles and achieve the almost complete military security Reagan stated as its basic goal, then America's need for allies might decline and it might once more be able to withdraw in safety into isolationism.

Having complained during the Nixon-Ford administration of American-Soviet collusion and during the Carter administration of American vacillation, Western Europe now charged that American policy was too hard-line. Western Europe was determined, therefore, to preserve its own separate *détente* with the Soviet Union. Two events demonstrated how great were the differences of attitude and policy between Europe and Reagan's United States.

Martial Law in Poland

The first event took place in Poland, where domestic changes had occurred that threatened the Polish Communist party's monopoly of power and control. It was ironic that it was in Poland, a so-called people's democracy and a Communist state, which allegedly represented and protected the interests of the working class, that a truly spontaneous Marxist workers' revolution against their exploiters (the Communist party!) occurred in 1980. Stimulated by a failing economy as a result of poor political leadership, bureaucratic planning, and mismanagement, the workers demanded the right to form their own independent trade union, which would have the right to strike. Such a demand was unheard of in a Communist country where the party claimed to embody the workers' aspirations. In wanting their own union, the Polish workers were rejecting this claim and challenging the basis of the party's legitimacy.

Strikes, which resulted in a standstill of an economy already $27 billion in debt to Western banks and governments by the early 1980s, brought the government down, just as strikes had in 1970 when the ship workers had managed to replace another set of leaders who had mismanaged the economy. This time, however, the economic conditions were far more severe. The political leadership again changed, and Poland recognized the right of the workers to form their own union, which was called Solidarity. In effect, this meant a loss of the party's monopoly of power and a sharing of power with Solidarity whose demands from the beginning were not only economic but also political. The union wanted mass to be televised on Sundays, Solidarity meetings to be broadcast, censorship to be restricted, corrupt officials to be removed from office, and a farmers' union to be recognized. As the party-controlled government retreated before each demand, the demands increased and the party withdrew further in the face of strikes and threats of strikes. It was a heady experience for a still very Catholic and nationalistic people who hated the Soviets and who had been denied freedom so long. The little taste of freedom only stimulated their appetite for more reforms.

With its successes, Solidarity grew more militant. At its first national conference, it publicly asserted that it was "the authentic voice of the working class" and announced support for other East European workers who might wish to form independent unions. Domestically, it favored free parliamentary elections, free speech, and a voice in government policy, including the running of the economy. Although the Soviets accused Solidarity of provocative behavior—seeking "political power"—they refrained from invading Poland.

This restraint contrasted sharply with Soviet behavior in Hungary and Czechoslovakia, where the Soviet army had intervened when the Communist party's monopoly of power was threatened. And Poland, the nation through which every Western invader of Russia had marched and through which the Soviet Union had projected its power into the center of Europe since 1945, was geographically far more critical than those two countries had been. The situation grew more and more intolerable in Moscow's eyes. The danger of the Polish "disease" spreading to other East European states, and perhaps even to the Soviet Union if its economy suffered a further decline, made it difficult for the Soviets to stand by and do little but launch verbal criticism and hold very visible Soviet-Warsaw Pact military maneuvers in hopes of frightening the Poles. The Soviet Union could afford neither a weakening nor a collapse of its hold on Eastern and Central Europe, nor a dilution of controls at home.

But the risks and costs of intervention were also great. The Soviets recognized that Solidarity was not just a trade union seeking better working conditions, but that it represented a well-organized mass movement. The Soviets faced the possibility of a clash with units of the Polish army, the costs of occupation, and the difficulties of pacifying the population and getting it to work. In addition, the cost of paying off Poland's debt to the West would be a drain at a time when the Soviet economy was in trouble; maintaining the separate *détente* with America's European allies would become more difficult; and the possible establishment of a better relationship with the new U.S. administration would be jeopardized. Reagan could exploit a Soviet invasion of Poland to rally the North Atlantic Treaty Organization (NATO) allies. Therefore, for more than a year Moscow demonstrated remarkable restraint. When the move against Solidarity finally came, it was the Polish military and police who arrested the union leaders and imposed martial law on Poland.

Whether Moscow ordered the intervention or the Polish government acted on its own to forestall Soviet action, there can be little doubt of increasing Soviet pressure on the Polish authorities to crack down on what the Soviets called "antisocialist" and "counterrevolutionary" elements. Solidarity, by winning the sympathies of almost 10 million members, about one-third of the population, was a living refutation of the party's claim of representation; it symbolized the bankruptcy of communism. Unable either to produce a decent standard of living or to tolerate a minimal degree of freedom, communism in Poland had lost legitimacy. Force was therefore necessary to maintain the party in power; in reality, it was the army that was in power and had replaced the party. Poland was occupied by its own army! In response, the United States imposed some economic sanctions on both Poland and the Soviet Union; they were less punitive than symbolic of American displeasure. But in Western Europe, one almost heard a collective sigh of relief that the Red Army had not invaded Poland. The Polish army's crackdown was considered a domestic affair, not a matter over which *détente* was to be sacrificed.

Europe's attempt to preserve its separate *détente* with Moscow, including its profitable trade relationship, also ran headlong into Washington's determination to squeeze the Soviet Union economically. In contrast to the *détente* policy of the 1970s, which had attempted to balance the military stick with the economic carrot, to provide the Soviet Union with incentives for greater self-restraint in foreign policy, the Reagan policy concluded that offers of trade, technology, and credits had not worked. The Soviet civilian industrial and agricultural economies continued to be weak, except in the military sector. Why should the West help strengthen the economy of a hostile state? Lenin had once said the capitalists in order to make money would even sell the Communists the rope with which they would hang the capitalists. Was the West, in its eagerness to trade and sell its latest technology, not selling the Soviets that rope and even providing the money for its purchase at low-interest credit? And would the chief beneficiary of this Western "subsidization" of the Soviet economy not be the Soviet armed forces? By putting up trade barriers instead, the West could increase Soviet economic difficulties and compel the Soviet leaders to move resources to the civilian sector from the military to prevent their people's standard of living from declining even further, which might create a Soviet version of the Polish disease. Only an increase in the Soviet quota of "pain" might compel the Soviet Union to relax international tensions and moderate its behavior.

Disagreement over the Soviet Pipeline

Given the different European and American perspectives on relations with the Soviet Union and the role of trade, it was not surprising that soon after the Reagan administration took office, conflict erupted over the construction of a Soviet pipeline that would carry Soviet natural gas to Western Europe. Overwhelmingly dependent upon imported energy, Europe was eager to diversify its energy sources and become less dependent upon the Arab members of OPEC. The Reagan administration fiercely opposed the pipeline, which was to be built by the Soviets but financed by the Europeans. The principal reason was the fear that Western Europe over the years would become more and more dependent upon the Soviet Union for its energy, giving the Soviets the political leverage that might gradually undermine NATO. Another reason was that the pipeline would allow the Soviets to earn hard currencies with which they could buy Western technology. The Europeans denied that their energy purchases would make them dependent upon the Soviet Union or politically amenable to Soviet pressure. Moreover, they argued, the Soviet leadership had never hesitated to starve the consumer sector of the economy to afford the military hardware it felt necessary. Indeed, economic sanctions, argued America's allies, generally had failed as instruments of punishment. The Reagan administration's idea of cutting Western economic links to the Soviet Union to compel its leaders to behave with greater restraint would have just the opposite effect. It would produce resentment and anger and reinforce Soviet hostility toward the West. Indeed, greater Soviet moderation was more likely to be produced by an extensive network of economic relationships.

To force the Europeans to comply with American policy, Reagan ordered American companies, their branches in Europe, and European firms licensed by American corporations to produce American technology not to sell to Moscow the items needed for the building of the pipeline. These items were for the most part large turbines. The emotional and political fallout that resulted led the European governments to order their firms to comply with national policies and go ahead with the Soviet deal. Washington responded by imposing sanctions against these firms! Reagan became the first president to impose sanctions against U.S. allies (the companies, rather than nations, were penalized to minimize the level of resentment in Europe, but there was no doubt at whom American anger was aimed).

Secretary of State Alexander Haig opposed the president's course on this issue. He predicted that the Europeans were determined to go ahead; to oppose them was to risk dividing members of the alliance even further at a time when they should be closing ranks. The pipeline was one of the issues over which Haig resigned, and his successor, George Shultz, spent many of his early days in office trying to defuse it. The pipeline controversy was a symptom of the increasing divisiveness among NATO members which, in this instance, hurt the alliance more than the Soviet Union, the intended target.

The Missile Debate in Europe

By the early 1980s, indeed, it had become commonplace to say that the West Europeans wanted to pursue an independent political policy while still counting on the United States for its defense; they wanted, it was said, to "uncouple" themselves politically from Washington but to remain "coupled" to it militarily. Even the military relationship was called into question when West European opinion appeared to go back on a decision, collectively agreed to by the United States and Western Europe, on how to meet the threat of the new, mobile, and powerful Soviet SS-20 intermediate range missiles (IRBMs) that have three warheads each. The West German government had first raised the issue of the SS-20 deployment and requested the United States to counter these missiles aimed at Western Europe. The proposed American force of 572 missiles to deter the 270 SS-20s deployed in the western Soviet Union (plus 171 in its Asian part, but movable to the west) was to consist of 108 Pershing IIs (with one warhead each), whose range was sufficient to hit western Russia, plus 464 subsonic ground-launched cruise missiles (GLCMs).

Since the beginning of NATO, the Europeans had wanted the alliance strategy to emphasize deterrence. Europe had had its bellyful of wars in the twentieth century. The NATO army, therefore, was to serve as a "plate glass," which, once the Soviet invasion occurred, would sound the alarm and call in the United States strategic forces. The army's purpose was not to fight a long war like World War II, even when it was reinforced by 300,000 American soldiers. The presence of the troops emphasized America's stake in Europe and clarified to Moscow that any attack would result in war with the United States. The army's role was to "couple" Europe's defense to American strategic forces. The fear of nuclear retaliation by the United States would deter the Soviet Union from invading Western Europe.

The Soviet SS-20s threatened to uncouple Europe's defense from the American deterrent. NATO ground forces, it was claimed, were no match for the Warsaw Pact forces. Nor could NATO's tactical nuclear forces any longer compensate for the lack of manpower, including reserves. The SS-20s would deter a NATO escalation from conventional to tactical nuclear weapons. But were the American strategic forces not still the instrument of last resort? Perhaps they were, but perhaps not. Ever since the first Soviet missile test in 1957, the key question had been: Would the United States risk its own survival for the defense of Europe? Some had answered this question with a no; most had been uncertain, although United States strategic forces at the time were superior to those of the Soviet Union. Even if it were uncertain that these forces would be used, could Moscow take the chance and risk an attack on Western Europe? Probably not. Since the 1970s and the emergence of strategic parity, however, the answer to this question had grown even more doubtful. It was one thing for the United States to attack the Soviet Union when the Soviets could not attack the United States, or when America had a vast strategic superiority; it was quite another to do so when the Soviet Union could retaliate fully. Was America's strategic deterrence still credible? Washington's standard reply was yes, but in Western Europe there was more doubt than ever that this was so.

The Pershing IIs and GLCMs were supposed to reassure the allies. Because the Pershings could strike targets in the Soviet Union itself, the Soviets presumably would consider such a strike an act of American aggression and would retaliate against American missiles in Europe *as well as* the United States to forestall an all-out attack by U.S. ICBMs. The Pershings were to let the Soviets know that any attack on Western Europe could not be limited to that area and to reassure the allies that their defense was still "coupled" to the American deterrent.

Instead of being strengthened, however, the NATO "marriage," in the words of the French foreign minister, came close to a divorce. Huge crowds throughout Western Europe (except in France) demonstrated for months against the proposed deployment of the American missiles, with the greatest opposition in West Germany. The Protestant churches; the universities; the Social Democratic opposition party; and a new party, which called itself the Greens and was a mixture of environmentalists (against all things nuclear), pacifists, neutralists, and antiestablishment figures, were all opposed to the deployment, the Greens militantly so. The street demonstrators' accusations were many: America was stoking the arms race; America intended to fight a war limited to Europe; America was the aggressive party in the cold war. Moscow was not considered the chief threat. It was Washington, which had defended Western Europe since 1949 and had not yet deployed a single Pershing II, that was charged with being the bigger menace to peace. Indeed, the more SS-20s the Soviets deployed, the greater their threat to Western Europe, the shriller became the protests against the United States counterdeployment.

Certainly, the demonstrators did not represent majority opinion in their respective countries. In all NATO countries, support for the alliance remained high; so did faith in deterrence. Nevertheless, the peace movement reflected widespread concern about Reagan's *antidétente* foreign policy and an increased fear of war. (The U.S. invasion of Grenada was widely viewed in Europe as equivalent to the Soviet invasion of Afghanistan.) These concerns came together in the decision to deploy more U.S. nuclear weapons in Europe.

Ironically, the antinuclear demonstrations that took place in Western Europe stymied the American-Soviet negotiations on IRBMs. The Soviets shrewdly exploited the protests. If they might prevent the American deployment, why should Moscow make any concessions to stop the Pershings and GLCMs emplacement? Further, by repeatedly saying that they were eager to negotiate the issue, the Soviets appeared reasonable and put the United States on the defensive. The president felt compelled to respond to the demonstrations in Europe and to the Soviet initiative. He proposed a "zero option" whereby the United States would not deploy any of its Pershings and cruise missiles if the Soviets dismantled all of their IRBMs, including the SS-20s. It sounded good; all intermediate range missiles were to be eliminated. What could be more beneficial for peace and more moral than doing away with a whole class of dangerous weapons? The United States, however, did not expect Moscow to accept this offer. The zero-zero option was a public relations move; by turning it down, the Soviets would make it possible for the U.S. deployment to go ahead as a clearly necessary and defensive move, the street demonstrations would decline, and the blame for the American missiles buildup in Europe would be placed at the Kremlin's door.

Western Europe's Reluctance to Defend Itself

The intra-NATO "missile crisis" suggested something more than a concern about the direction of Reagan's foreign policy or the understandable desire to reduce the risks of war. Western Europe's clinging to *détente* and calls for arms control had a sense of desperation about them. This was not altogether surprising because the U.S. missile deployment was in fact a reminder of their dependence for protection on the United States and that this protection was not free of risk or cost. In the words of a West German journalist:

> The impending arrival of a new generation of land-based missiles thrust to the forefront of the collective psyche the irreducible dilemma of contemporary defense. Nuclear weapons not only buttress deterrence; they also drive home the fatal consequences of its failure. "Old nuclear weapons," half-forgotten, suggest a sturdy shelter; "new" nuclear weapons remind their beneficiaries that they are also the potential victims. . . .
>
> Nations that depend for their security on others want the best of all possible worlds. The Europeans want full protection but minimal risks; they will the end, which is the credibility of American power, but not necessarily the means, which entails the reassertion of American power—be it in the form of Euromissiles or confrontationist policies towards the Soviet Union.[7]

Nor were the Europeans ready to take the measures necessary for their own defense. Although their combined population and industrial output exceeded that of the Soviet Union, America's European allies were still unwilling to raise the size of their conventional forces. They wanted to continue relying on the American strategic deterrent at a time when the superpowers strategically neutralized one another, when the threat of using the American strategic forces was no longer as credible as it had once been as a deterrent to a Soviet invasion of Western Europe, and when NATO armies could not without great risk resort to tactical nuclear weapons to even the odds. One obvious response by NATO in these circumstances would be to field adequate conventionally armed military forces, including sufficient ground forces, to hold a Soviet armored thrust and blunt it without resorting to nuclear weapons unless the enemy used them first. But the European allies were opposed to significantly upgrading their defense efforts, paying more for defense, especially at a time of unemployment, or conscripting greater numbers for military service. It was less costly to try to preserve a *détente* separate from their major protector, to talk with Moscow regardless of its behavior, not to take any actions that might provoke the Soviets, to emphasize arms control instead of strengthening their own defenses and shifting public

---

7. Josef Joffe, "Peace and Populism: Why the European Anti-Nuclear Movement Failed," *International Security* (Spring 1987): 16, 17-18.

expenditures from the social to the military sector, and to blame the United States for unwise policies and leadership.

These nonmilitary policies were intended to compensate for European reluctance to increase its military muscle. One result was to stimulate demands in the United States for the withdrawal of some or all American forces from Europe over a period of years. Most of the American defense budget allocated for hardware and maintenance was not spent on strategic forces; half went for the upkeep of the more expensive conventional forces whose primary mission was the defense of Europe. When the alliance had been formed, the European nations vividly remembered the failure of appeasing a totalitarian regime, the defeats and suffering of World War II, their postwar collapse, and the need for American protection against the new threat from the East. By the 1970s and 1980s the memory of having appeased Nazi Germany was fading; the story of this appeasement was not even a part of the history or consciousness of the new generation that had grown up in a peaceful Europe. Protected by the United States, Europe seemed to forget the realities of international politics.

In France, which had fielded forces that had been withdrawn from the integrated NATO structure and was deploying a growing independent French deterrent force, the popular historical association of national independence and pride in the nation's armed forces was still alive. Moreover, there were no massive antinuclear and anti-American demonstrations. French Socialist president François Mitterrand told the West German parliament in 1983, "I'm against the Euromissiles. But I notice two terrible simple things about the current debate: Pacifism is in the West and the Euromissiles are in the East. I consider this an unequal relationship." [8] Such an imbalance, he predicted, would ensure war, not avoid it.

Elsewhere in Western Europe, defense had become, it seemed, an American responsibility. It appeared to many Europeans that the American plans for deployment jeopardized the peace; and parties that were formerly stalwart defenders of NATO, such as the British Labour party and the German Social Democrats, now literally deserted the alliance. Given that circumstances vastly differed from when NATO was founded, one had to wonder whether, if NATO had been proposed in the 1980s, there would be an alliance at all, and if so, which countries would join it? European public opinion might still be in favor of NATO, but a low-cost policy was not possible now that U.S. strategic forces could no longer deter both Soviet strategic forces and Warsaw Pact conventional armies.

NATO Threatened from Within

By the mid-1980s one thing was very clear: the intermediate-range nuclear weapons issue had become a critical political issue. The decision to

---

8. Quoted by Flora Lewis, "Missiles and Pacifists," *New York Times*, November 18, 1983.

deploy the Pershing IIs and the GLCMs had been an alliance decision. Attempts to negotiate with the Soviets a reduction of their constantly growing SS-20 force against a smaller U.S. deployment had been fruitless. Moscow refused to accept *any* American deployment and rejected the principle of superpower equality. The Soviet purpose was clearly to manipulate Europe's fear of war to drive a wedge between the NATO allies, especially between Europe and the United States. The question was whether the alliance would survive. The Soviets had no reason to compromise in separate arms control negotiations on this issue; they had every reason to test the strength of the European peace movement in the hope of aborting the American deployment. The Soviets could deploy their missiles and target every European capital, but the United States could not deploy missiles that could hit the Soviet Union. What Moscow has is not negotiable, what NATO has is, was the message.

Could NATO, having made a key decision, stay with that decision? Or would NATO be unable to stick with its defense and diplomatic strategy or to resist pressures from within that were abetted by shrewd Soviet political propaganda? The alliance itself was at stake. And the gravity of the situation was magnified by the fact that in Britain and West Germany, governments had recently been elected that had campaigned in favor of the American deployment. The democratic process was therefore also at stake. Would governments elected by clear majorities give in to the peace marches? Was the alliance and the viability of democratic elections to be negated by the politics of the street?

For Moscow the missile debate was a means of undermining the alliance. NATO had not confronted such a serious issue since German rearmament in the early 1950s and the Berlin crisis after 1957. These two issues had involved the future of the alliance, its ability to face down intimidation and remain united. Above all, they had involved a struggle for West Germany, NATO's strongest member, without whose territory the alliance could not defend itself. Moscow obviously wanted to detach it from NATO, and Washington wanted to keep West Germany within the alliance. Given the political stakes for each superpower, should it have been a surprise that American-Soviet relations reached a low point in the early 1980s, regardless of who the leaders were? Neither side was willing to compromise in what it regarded as a fundamental test of wills. When the United States began its deployment during the winter months of 1983-1984, was it really a surprise that Moscow walked out of all arms control negotiations in order to raise the fear of war in Western Europe and to push it into a greater neutralism and pacifism?

For the short term, the missile crisis faded as the deployment occurred and as Gorbachev, in a surprise move, accepted an earlier Reagan proposal for zero intermediate-range missiles for both powers. The administration's determination paid off. It had not abandoned the deployment, nor, when the Soviets walked out of all arms control negotiations in response to it, had it delayed deployment, despite widespread calls to do so. Unable to achieve Soviet goals with threats, Moscow switched to seduction. In terms of IRBMs, the zero-zero solution was a significant achievement, trading about 1,400 Soviet warheads for just over 300 U.S. warheads. This move would eliminate an entire class of weapons rather than—as in SALT I and II—place limits on their deployment.

In terms of alliance cohesion, the result was more debatable. The German Social Democrats and British Labour party were no longer strong NATO supporters; the underlying attitudes that had led to the strong reaction against U.S. deployment were still there. The question of whether Europe would assume more of the burden of its own defense remained. Symptomatic of the problem was the European governments' unenthusiastic reception of Gorbachev's acceptance of Reagan's propaganda proposal. They could hardly oppose this plan now, even though it would eliminate the weapons whose purpose allegedly was to reassure Europe about America's continued protection. In addition, it would leave the Soviets with short-range nuclear missiles while NATO had none. But when the Soviet leader offered to eliminate this category of missiles as well, they were worried about the future "denuclearization" of Europe, which would leave them in a position of conventional inferiority. In short, they were still reluctant to do what they sould have done years earlier—increase their conventional strength. It was easier and cheaper to remain dependent on the U.S. nuclear deterrent. It took U.S. pressure on the allies to gain their acceptance of NATO's own proposal.

Two things became very clear during the 1980s: one was that the Europeans' confidence in the United States had diminished since Vietnam. During the Nixon-Ford *détente* years they had complained about possible U.S.-Soviet deals at Europe's expense; during the Carter years, of vacillation and weakness; and during the Reagan years, of too much *machismo* or "Ramboism" and too hard a line on the Soviets and arms control. Europe's fear of war had also risen. Not Soviet behavior but the "arms race" was seen as the critical danger, as was "provocative" American behavior. These attitudes translated into growing public doubts about the value of NATO despite general support for the alliance. While the first cold war was characterized by U.S.-Soviet conflict and U.S.-European cohesion, cold war II was characterized by U.S.-Soviet conflict *and* U.S.-European conflict.

The other was that the European members of the alliance were still unwilling to reexamine the assumption they had accepted for more than forty years—that the Soviet Union is the naturally dominant Eurasian power against which Western Europe cannot mobilize sufficient conterbalancing power without outside help. Such an assumption is demeaning for states that have for centuries been the leading international actors and who, by the 1980s, had become the prosperous dependents of a protector whose foreign and defense policies they increasingly distrusted and who, in turn, had become increasingly restive in that role.

The Declining American Economy
and Global Commitments

In a fundamental sense, the critical problem facing the Reagan administration from the day it took office was not the Soviet Union or NATO, but the state of the American economy, which had been in the doldrums since 1973. No president in the 1980s could afford to neglect this problem because without a growing economy the United States could not support a global foreign policy. America had long been the world's leading industrial power, and its huge productive capacity was the basis of victory in the two world wars. Most especially, the enormous wealth created by American industry and agriculture had made it possible for the United States to accept commitments in many areas of the world and simultaneously to afford sizable deterrent forces and a conventional military capability.

The key question that American policy makers after World War II repeatedly asked themselves was whether a particular area or country was of vital interest to the security and/or prosperity of the United States. If they decided it was, the appropriate policy followed. The question of affordability was only rarely asked; rather, it was assumed. Only conservatives on occasion asked whether the United States could afford a Marshall Plan or large deterrent and conventional forces. The Eisenhower administration was particularly concerned with the question of costs, federal deficits, and balanced budgets. But in the words of presidential candidate John Kennedy, the country could afford anything it needed for its security. Although funds obviously were not unlimited, the assumption was that the nation was wealthy enough to support a high standard of living at home and a global policy abroad.

The 1950s and 1960s were decades of very rapid economic growth. It became commonplace to refer to the United States as an "affluent society," to Americans as the "people of plenty." Wages for workers rose rapidly during this period as trade unions grew powerful and negotiated sizable annual pay raises. American industry apparently could afford such raises in an increasingly consumer-oriented society while still earning handsome profits. The Kennedy administration vastly expanded the welfare state, as did Lyndon Johnson's. The payments made by older programs such as Social Security were frequently raised, and new programs were initiated. Some, like Medicare, started small but grew rapidly in cost as more people became eligible for them and the benefits were adjusted to meet inflation. These "entitlement" programs were made possible because the economy was growing rapidly and producing sufficient wealth to support both a high standard of living and welfare payments, as well as an extensive foreign policy. President Johnson went to war in Vietnam thinking he could finance both the Great Society programs and the war (which originally was expected to last two years and involve 200,000 troops) without increasing taxes.

The enormous expense of the Vietnam War, plus the dramatic rise of oil prices, which simultaneously produced high inflation and large-scale unemployment, put a brake on the economy. Instead of growing rapidly, it stagnated. The United States could no longer afford both guns and butter. It had to make choices: an economy that was growing only slowly could not afford constantly rising wages, rapidly rising annual welfare costs, and expensive foreign policy commitments. When the ecomony slows down, growth in one program comes at the cost of others. In a democracy these choices are painful: workers do not gladly accept pay cuts; voters are unhappy with a slowdown in the increase in welfare programs, let alone cuts; and, although defense cuts are often advocated and followed in these circumstances, the nation also needs to guard itself against foreign threats.

Reaganomics and U.S. Competitiveness in the International Economy

Reagan, asserting that defense spending had been held back during the 1970s, stepped up military spending and cut back the growth of social programs. Politically, of course, this can be done only for so long. The longer-term solution, according to the Reagan administration, was to stimulate the economy so that it would once more grow as rapidly as it had during the 1950s and 1960s. The policy advocated was supply-side economics. Whatever the validity of this approach, the fact was that the American economy had changed greatly since the 1960s. Although American agriculture was the most bountiful in the world, and the export of food was a major source of earnings in foreign trade, by the middle 1980s overseas markets were declining. Other developed countries like Britain and France had become food exporters, as had less-developed countries such as India, China, Thailand, and Indonesia. The future of American agricultural exports looked dim as conflict over markets became an increasingly tense and divisive issue among the United States, it allies, and other friendly nations. The traditional smokestack industries like steel were especially hard hit because they had become increasingly uncompetitive internationally and had declined. There were many reasons for this decline: underinvestment in the American economy because of high U.S. wages, a desire to be nearer overseas markets, and the Common Market's tariff barriers against imports. American industry was going overseas where it could save transportation costs and where wages were lower, especially in Third World countries. American manufacturers could avoid the Common Market's tariff wall by building factories in Western Europe. Industry considered its actions rational: goods could be produced more cheaply outside of the United States, where large-scale markets and opportunities were also opening up. Goods, for consumers both abroad and at home, it argued, would be less expensive and more competitive with foreign goods while also increasing corporate earnings.

Another reason was that America's allies and friends, whom it had helped to rebuild following World War II, became by the 1970s major industrial competitors. Older industries such as textiles, steel, shipbuilding, and automobiles (in Europe) were rebuilt, and new industries such as automobiles (Japan) and electronics (Japan, Taiwan, and South Korea) were started. Because U.S. industries were accustomed to having an enormous domestic market virtually to themselves, they had not made the necessary investments in research and development. U.S. textiles, steel, shipbuilding, automobiles, even electronics, became successively unable to compete with goods produced by newer technology, but at lower wages. Europe and the Far East found new markets in the United States, as American consumers were eager to buy less expensive, and better-made products from abroad.

Industries like steel foundered. In 1986 U.S. Steel, once the symbol of American industrial might, changed its name to USX as it cut back further on steel production, which was no longer the main part of its business. Japanese steel, produced by more modern methods, could be shipped to the United States and sold more cheaply than steel made in Ohio. Although the automobile industry invested money, it kept mass-producing the same large, gas-guzzling, showy cars year in and year out, expecting customers to trade them in every few years for another large car. When the oil crisis hit, the industry was caught without small, fuel-efficient, well-made automobiles. Japan had them and captured a sizable sector of the market. Despite Detroit's recovery, which resulted not only from its increasing efficiency but also from a ceiling on Japanese imports, many of the workers laid off during the 1970s recession were not reemployed; robots worked better and were cheaper.

Even the high-technology sector of the economy (computers, machine tools, robotics, and aerospace technology), often acclaimed as the basis for future economic growth and prosperity, experienced difficulties. American capital investments and funds for research and development were among the lowest in the Western industrial world (Canada, Western Europe, and Japan), and the American labor force was declining qualitatively, a reflection of lower U.S. educational standards. Japanese and West German school children attended school longer each day and up to two months longer per year. These children learned more science and mathematics, the cutting edge of all contemporary innovations. Even when the United States achieved technological breakthroughs, as in video recorders, microwave ovens, and robots, American manufacturers chose not to produce them.

The Imbalance Between Economic Power and Political Commitments

The economic base of the U.S. international role was eroding. America's superior productive capability had been the basis for its victory in World War

II; after the war, the economy had underwritten America's role abroad. The decline raised the critical question whether the economy can still support a foreign policy that keeps 300,000 men in Western Europe, defends Japan, is committed to the Persian Gulf, and is increasing its commitments in Central America. Can it do all these *as well as* support higher wages and extensive welfare programs and still find the investment capital necessary to restimulate the growth of the private sector? Given the expenditures needed to make the American economy internationally competitive, including investment in education, transportation, and basic urban services, all of which contribute to U.S. competitiveness, how much can the nation afford to spend on commitments abroad and on defense? Will these commitments divert funds from social programs, thereby risking domestic dissatisfaction, hardship, and conflict? Should ailing industries be protected with tariffs and subsidies or compelled to become more efficient (assuming they can survive), even if that means forcing wages downward? How much should the government become involved through tax policies in the reindustrialization of America?

Starting in the 1970s, it became apparent that the nation was no longer capable of supporting a global foreign policy role, maintaining a high living standard, funding an extensive welfare state, and, at the same time, finding the funds necessary for the regeneration of the economy through a new industrial revolution, which was necessary if the other aims were to be achieved. How the United States responded to this dilemma was obviously critical for its security.

The Reagan administration placed great emphasis on the recovery of the economy. But it sought to do so by simultaneously increasing the defense budget while lowering taxes and, therefore, revenues. The result was a huge budget deficit of more than $200 billion. As the government competed with industry for capital to cover the deficit, interest rates rose. This in turn attracted huge foreign investments, boosting the value of the dollar. The result was that American export prices shot upward, hurting exporting industries. At the same time, import prices dropped, undercutting American firms at home. While American consumers and tourists benefited from this state of affairs, American farmers, overproducing and very dependent upon exports, were badly hurt; many smaller family-owned farms went bankrupt. Industry also suffered as lower earnings meant less investment capital. In 1986 the United States became the world's largest debtor nation, with a bigger debt than all the less-developed countries put together. More than 2 million jobs were lost in industries that export, which resulted in a demand for protectionism. If other countries followed America's protectionist lead, however, that would cut U.S. exports even more as other countries' earnings with which to buy American goods declined. Simultaneously, the U.S. inflation would increase because the American manufacturers would not have to compete against foreign products. But protectionism would not arrest the decline of the economy or boost its ability to compete against the world economy. It would only disrupt the flow of trade, hurt friendly nations and allies, and perhaps endanger important political and military ties. Despite reductions in inflation, interest rates, the value of the dollar, and oil prices, the U.S. economy remained sluggish, and the 1986 trade deficit was $170 billion, up from $148 billion in 1985.

In the final analysis, the United States must give priority to rebuilding its economy by following its own earlier history. The United States, like Germany, at the turn of the century did not just compete with Britain, then the world's leading industrial power, in areas in which it had attained industrial primacy, such as steel and shipbuilding; both developed new products such as chemicals, electrical devices, and automobiles. The United States has had a history of successful transformations from older to newer industries. The question is whether it can do so again. One thing is certain: if the United States cannot revitalize its industry, the decline of the U.S. industrial base will continue, and America will no longer be able to serve as the "arsenal of democracy." A productive and competitive economy is a basic prerequisite for playing an active global role in the world. The United States cannot indefinitely continue to expand its imperial role or political and military commitments while the foundations of its power are eroding.

chapter twelve

Cold War II in Central America and the Middle East

DESPITE Americans' growing concerns about "imperial overstretch," President Ronald Reagan's administration expanded U.S. commitments in the Central American-Caribbean area, just as the Carter administration had in the Persian Gulf.[1] Neither felt it had much choice; both were concerned about stopping the growth of Soviet influence. But the Third World was no longer "a homogeneous area of underdeveloped nationalists, full of 'vacuums' waiting to be filled by one superpower or the other."[2] The containment policy, therefore, had to take into account the Third World's more complex realities: the instability of many governments; the proliferation of regional conflicts, including ethnic and religious differences; the increasing use of terrorism; the bursts of intense nationalism, often directed against the United States; and the economic stagnation of many countries, some of which were deeply mired in debt.

Despite his conviction that Third World problems had to be viewed through the prism of the East-West struggle, Reagan found containment in the less-developed areas a frustrating experience. Memories of Vietnam and congressional restraints on the use of the armed forces made it impossible to deal with the Marxist regimes in Nicaragua as other presidents had dealt with them: by covert or overt intervention. And the Middle East-Persian Gulf area remained as volatile as ever, if not more so because of the Iran-Iraq war and Iran's determination to spread Islamic fundamentalism. The president found himself completely stymied in advancing the Arab-Israeli peace process.

1. Paul Kennedy, "The (Relative) Decline of America," *The Atlantic Monthly,* August 1987, 29-38.
2. Robert Osgood, "Reagan's Foreign Policy" in *Reagan's Leadership and the Atlantic Alliance,* ed. Walter Goldstein (New York: Pergamon-Brassey's, 1987), 27.

Moreover, his administration was weakened and his reputation damaged when it was revealed that the United States had sold arms to Iran to gain the release of U.S. hostages in Lebanon and then used the excess profits from the deal to finance a covert war against the Nicaraguan government over the opposition of Congress.

The Reagan Intervention in Central America

Virtually from the day Reagan took office, his administration placed El Salvador, a country the size of New Jersey with a population of 5 million, within the context of superpower conflict. The roots of El Salvador's problems were—as in Nicaragua, Guatemala, Honduras, and even in democratic Costa Rica—largely domestic. All except Honduras had been rapidly modernizing since 1960, but their economic growth had benefited mainly a small elite of landowners, businessmen, and generals while leaving the mass of the urban population and peasantry poor. In addition, a high birth rate weakened the semifeudal structure in the countryside and forced many peasants, many of whom did not own land, to move to cities. Here they were exposed to new ideas and saw a better way of life to which they aspired. With governments unable to meet their peoples' new expectations, these countries suffered rising social discontent and tensions. Their attempts to modernize undermined the traditional, conservative political systems, and the high price of imported oil caused high inflation. Military regimes or militarily supported regimes prevented social reform and political change. Peaceful change being impossible, the authoritarian governments in Nicaragua, El Salvador, and Guatemala increasingly faced the opposition of leftist guerrillas.

The first result of guerrilla action, the collapse of the regime of Anastasio Somoza in Nicaragua in 1979 and the victory by the Sandinistas, led to increased disturbance throughout the region, as the extreme left and right sought to achieve or preserve power through violence. America's major setback to its primacy in the area had begun in the 1960s when Washington tolerated Soviet presence in Cuba. Now U.S. influence eroded further. Somoza's fall, coming after forty years of rule by his family, who were friends of the United States, encouraged armed, left-wing forces to make a military bid for power. The traditional right-wing authoritarian governments (except in Costa Rica) responded fearfully with force. Each side attacked elements of the other side, the right even assassinating nuns and priests, including an archbishop in El Salvador. Moderate political leaders who advocated peaceful reform and change, such as some of the Christian Democrats who came to power in El Salvador, were targets for assassination. The moderates had difficulty controlling right-wing death squads and factions of the military who, while fighting against leftist guerrillas, also tried to eliminate the center. In Guatemala, government-controlled murder squads carried out thousands of political killings; victims included Christian Democratic leaders, trade union leaders, and priests. Such action further polarized society in these countries.

The Reagan administration made El Salvador an international issue because, after years of Soviet-Vietnamese-Cuban successes in the Third World, the administration was determined to send Moscow a message to stop expanding Soviet influence by means of proxies. Asserting that the government of Napoleón Duarte was moderate, the administration decided that Duarte had the best chance of carrying out domestic social reforms while preventing a radical left-wing assumption of power. Therefore, the Reagan administration backed him with shipments of military equipment and fifty U.S. advisers to the Salvadoran government forces. This assistance, it was claimed, was necessary to counter the arms sent to the Salvadoran guerrillas by Cuba, Ethiopia, Libya, and Vietnam at Soviet direction. Further, it was alleged that most of these arms had been shipped via Nicaragua, which was punished for its complicity by a cut-off of American economic aid.

In addition to arms, the Communist states were said to be giving the Salvadoran guerrillas money, training, and advice. The war in El Salvador, the State Department claimed, was a "textbook case of indirect armed aggression by Communist powers." Because of Washington's determination to publicize and stop Soviet-Cuban expansion in the Third World, especially so close to the United States, the war received widespread international attention. Washington was concerned that if, after Nicaragua, El Salvador also fell to left-wing guerrillas and established a second Marxist mainland regime, the rest of Central America would follow. But the threat was not only to Panama or Mexico, but to the wider U.S. position throughout the world. "If Central America were to fall," the president asked, "what would the consequences be for our position in Asia, Europe, and for alliances such as NATO? If the United States cannot respond to a threat near our own border, why should Europeans or Asians believe that we are seriously concerned about threats to them?" [3] In brief, U.S. stakes were very high in Central America, and the nation could not ignore or be indifferent to the danger of governments with close ideological and military ties to the Soviet Union.

Whether El Salvador was the right place to take a stand against Soviet communism and its proxies or whether the revolution should have been allowed to follow its natural course was energetically debated in the United States. Critics of the administration's plans argued that the arms were not the principal cause for the civil war; rather, the appalling social and economic conditions and political repression were the true causes. The United States should not support the privileged few who had long exploited the poor. Social justice demanded nonintervention; so perhaps did expediency, if the United States wished to avoid being identified with the losers, as it had been so many

---

3. Ronald Reagan, "Central America: Defending Our Vital Interests," U.S. Department of State, *Current Policy,* No. 482, April 27, 1983.

times before. The Vietnam War frequently was cited as a reminder of the dangers of supporting the wrong side—an unpopular political elite whose vested interest lay in the preservation of the *status quo*. In any event, no purely military solution was possible. Much was made of human rights violations in El Salvador. The United States, which stands for human rights, it was said, should not be backing a regime whose security forces were so brutal. Moscow would be the only winner. Indeed, in Western Europe, as well as in many Latin American countries, especially Mexico, El Salvador's northern neighbor, the Salvadoran guerrillas were thought to deserve more support than the government because they would create a more equitable society.

The Administration's Distinction Between Authoritarian and Totalitarian Regimes

Rejecting these arguments, the Reagan administration insisted that the United States was in El Salvador not to help a right-wing government but Duarte's Christian Democratic government. The Duarte administration was committed to peaceful reforms, but it was under attack by militant left-wing forces who were seeking to bring it down by destroying the nation's economy. In any event, even if El Salvador was not a democracy, the Reagan administration declared that in its view it was preferable to support a right-wing authoritarian regime to a left-wing totalitarian one. Admitting that violations of human rights occur in the midst of a civil war and that authoritarian regimes do repress criticism of and opposition to their political rule in order to preserve the *status quo,* the administration claimed that such governments at least do not stifle all criticism, jail all opponents, or squash all personal freedoms. Such regimes can be reformed, even democratized, as happened in Greece and Spain. When they were pro-American, such regimes deserved U.S. help if there are no alternative political groups to support at a time when the Soviet Union and its friends back the opposition. Otherwise, victory for the radical left meant both an extension of Soviet influence and increasingly totalitarian rule.

Reagan officials pointed to Nicaragua, where Jimmy Carter, not wishing to block a "progressive Third World revolution" and preferring to be on the "right side" of history, withdrew support from Somoza and supported the Sandinistas. The Carter administration believed the Sandinistas would bring Nicaragua a more democratic regime and social justice. But, once in power, the Sandinistas began to consolidate their hold on government, gradually suppressing the voices of criticism as counterrevolutionary. They postponed general elections while building an army larger than Somoza's and establishing relations with Cuba and the Soviet Union. The question was not how Marxist the regime would become, as it turned against the Catholic church, the business community, professional organizations, trade unions, and student groups that had helped it depose Somoza, but how dictatorial it would become and how closely it would align with Havana and Moscow. The Sandinistas imposed censorship on opposition newspapers, restrained activities by other political parties, established neighborhood surveillance committees to watch citizens, and extended control over worker and peasant organizations. With the help of Eastern bloc and Cuban personnel, Nicaragua strengthened its police and security apparatus. The original Sandinista commitment to political pluralism was very much in doubt, but there was no doubt as to its international sympathies. Despite the Carter administration's initially favorable attitude, its withdrawal of support from Somoza, and extension of foreign aid, Nicaragua soon turned toward Cuba and the Soviet Union. The United States was forced to reassess its policy even *before* the arrival of the Reagan administration and its organization of the "contras," the fighters trying to overthrow the Sandinista government.

Reagan did not intend to repeat in El Salvador what he regarded as Carter's error in Nicaragua. But American public opinion was not enthusiastic about becoming involved in that tiny country. Economic and military aid, but no military intervention, was what it was willing to tolerate. Congress even made that aid contingent upon an improvement of the Salvadoran regime's human rights record. This left the administration little choice but to support the Salvadoran government while encouraging it to continue its social reforms and to discipline any soldiers and security forces accused of killing civilians. A key aspect of American policy was to legitimate the regime by holding general elections.

The left, however, opposed participation, and the guerrillas threatened those who tried to vote. Nevertheless, to the surprise of American observers and others watching the election for fraud and intimidation, more than 80 percent of the electorate turned out. The results of the 1982 election were ironic. The Christian Democrats, who were in power, received the largest vote of any single party, but the several right-wing parties together polled a larger vote and organized a coalition government. Those who had opposed the Christian Democrats and the reform-minded military officers, both supported by the United States, were therefore the beneficiaries of the American-sponsored free election. Duarte was out. The election, however, demonstrated that the formerly strong support for the guerrillas among peasants, students, and workers had eroded.

Nevertheless, the war went on. The army was poorly led and trained. As death-squad killings of civilians continued and no government official or soldier was convicted of any of the thousands of murders, Salvadoran politics became further polarized between right and left. Reagan wanted to send in more military advisers and greater military assistance. But Congress, still haunted by memories of Vietnam and questioning whether the Salvadoran army could win the war, no matter how much aid it received, opposed the president on sending in more advisers and only reluctantly supported him with funds for military and economic assistance. For the administration to succeed, the United States would have to exert greater control over the Salvadoran right, strengthen the moderates and build public support for the center, rebuild an economy deliberately ravaged by the guerrillas to force the government to its knees, and transform the military into an effective army. That was a formidable task. The president was determined to stay the course because, given the stakes he saw at issue in central America and the world, he was unwilling to lose.

The Shift to Centrist Politics

The key to mobilizing support domestically and perhaps achieving success in El Salvador was to find a moderate center. The United States often appeared trapped between reactionary forces whose rigid commitment to the *status quo* only intensified revolutionary sentiment and endangered American interests, and radical forces that tended to be Marxist and to look to Havana and Moscow. But it was rescued from this trap by the 1984 Salvadoran presidential and 1985 legislative and municipal elections, which brought Duarte back to power. Duarte's election strengthened the Reagan case for assistance to El Salvador because Reagan could rightfully claim that the United States was not supporting the right wing as an alternative to the radical left. Washington sent Duarte military aid, including helicopters to fight the guerrillas and Americans to train the Salvadoran army; it also encouraged domestic reforms without which all the military assistance in the world could not win the war. It hoped in these ways to avoid both another Cuba in Central America and another Vietnam.

This course promised success. The Salvadoran army, as a result of U.S. training, aid, and advice, greatly reduced army misconduct and improved its treatment of civilians. It also became more of a professional force, driving the guerrillas to resort to urban assassinations as they suffered defeats in the field. The guerrillas stepped up their campaign of economic ruin, knocking out bridges and electrical pylons and destroying crops. This destruction, in turn, required continuing large-scale U.S. economic assistance to ensure Duarte's political survival. Although the rebels were unlikely to win the civil war, they could continue a war of attrition. In the meantime, the fundamental problems of Salvadoran society—its vast social inequality, class divisions, and authoritarianism—persisted. American policy had denied the guerrillas victory; it now found itself committed to the more difficult and elusive task of building a nation from a deeply fragmented society. At the same time it remained committed to assisting Duarte, who was still beset by the radical left and the extreme right wing. But rising unemployment and inflation and the failure to implement any fundamental social and economic reforms resulted in the narrowing of Duarte's base among the workers and peasants, and therefore the possibility of failure remained.

The Reagan Doctrine:
El Salvador and Nicaragua

In the broader context the Reagan administration's policy in Central America was not merely to hold the line in El Salvador, but to reverse what it saw as Soviet gains in Third World contests that had taken place in Angola, Ethiopia, Yemen, Afghanistan, and Cambodia after the Vietnam War. The Soviets and their allies had been using force as an instrument of statecraft. They had been allowed this monopoly because of the widespread feeling in the United States that the use of force had become counterproductive, that it was so clearly immoral that short of an attack on the United States or its allies in Western Europe, force was not a legitimate means for protecting or advancing American interests. "Force will not solve political problems" became the commonplace phrase. In this atmosphere of American nonintervention, neither Moscow nor Havana were penalized for intervening; the absence of sanctions, indeed, provided them with an incentive for exploiting favorable political opportunities. The Reagan administration had been skeptical from the beginning about the notion of the disutility of force. The U.S. invasion of Grenada in 1983 was intended to raise the risks and the costs for the Soviets and Cubans should they continue to try and extend their political and military control in this hemisphere, as well as elsewhere. Asserting that it had intervened just in the nick of time to prevent Grenada from becoming a "Soviet-Cuban colony," the administration called Grenada a "warning shot."

Cuban-Soviet presence on Grenada had been of concern to the administration earlier. Grenadians, it ought to be added, overwhelmingly welcomed the intervention, which rescued them from Cuban control and domestic repression. As it turned out, many of the 700 Cuban "construction workers" resisted the American landing, which the president called a "rescue mission," not an invasion. Soviet military personnel, North Koreans, and East Germans were also present on the island. Caches of arms were found, as well as documents showing that larger shipments of arms were to be transported in the future, presumably to be sent to leftist rebels in Latin America or used for training guerrillas. For Cuba, the invasion of Grenada was certainly a blow. Fidel Castro lost a bridgehead and influence in the Caribbean—the leftist government in Surinam, a former Dutch colony, immediately expelled the Cuban ambassador—and in Central America, because Castro announced that he would not be able to help Nicaragua if it were invaded. The U.S. action was obviously aimed at Nicaragua. American pressure against the Sandinistas had been increasing for some time with the support of the contras and the stationing of sizable American naval forces off both the Atlantic and Pacific coasts of Nicaragua. Grenada was intended to escalate this pressure and demonstrate to the Sandinistas, Cubans, and Soviets that the United States

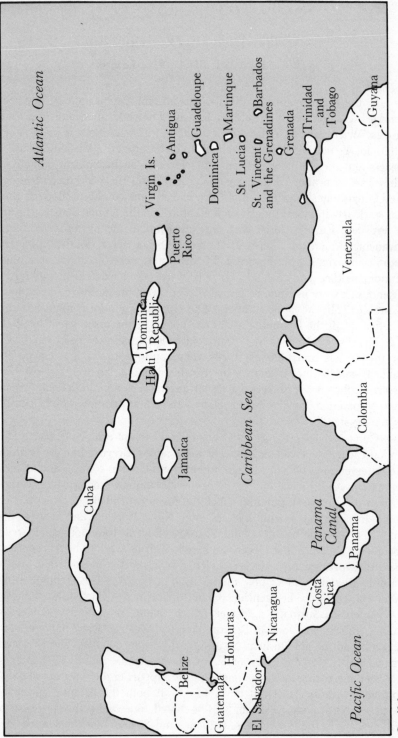

Caribbean

would once more use force if the administration thought it necessary. The Soviet Union and its proxies might mock the United States for attacking a minuscule state, but presumably they would exercise more restraint in the future—at least in Central America and the Caribbean.

But Grenada did not resolve a key problem. American foreign policy had always assumed the security of U.S. borders. The nation's ability to project power to Europe, Asia, or the Middle East, all far away from the United States, was predicated on peace in the Western Hemisphere. By contrast, this strategic luxury had been denied to the Soviet Union, which has always had to be concerned with the security of its long frontiers. It was to enhance his country's sense of security that Joseph Stalin transformed Eastern Europe into a Soviet buffer zone and that Leonid Brezhnev later formalized the Soviet right to intervene in that area to prevent "counterrevolutions," which might jeopardize socialism. The Brezhnev Doctrine, announced at the time of the Soviet intervention in Czechoslovakia in 1968, had already been practiced in East Germany in 1953 and Hungary in 1956. The Monroe Doctrine historically had reserved the Western Hemisphere as America's sphere of influence. But, if it was anything, the Monroe Doctrine was really a Caribbean Doctrine, making that area America's buffer zone. (The southern tip of Argentina was, after all, farther away than Western Europe.) Castro's survival in Cuba had altered this situation.

The Reagan administration now viewed the Caribbean-Central American area as America's "soft underbelly," a potential "Eastern Europe." The reason was the combination of unstable political conditions throughout the area and the rise of Soviet-Cuban-Nicaraguan influence. Washington, therefore, was confronted with three undesirable options: much larger defense spending to guard against future efforts to expand Communist influence and the stationing of larger military forces, including carrier battle groups, in the area; a reduced role and capability to defend more distant areas, including Western Europe; or eliminating the regime in Nicaragua that had transformed the nation into the first "Cuba" on the mainland. It was the third option that the administration actively pursued.

The administration was absolutely convinced that the Sandinistas harbored ideologically motivated ambitions beyond their own frontiers. Because they also accepted support from Havana and Moscow, Washington saw them as a continuing source of instability and tension in an area of vulnerable states. The Sandinistas' pledge to confine themselves to Nicaragua was regarded as unlikely to be honored as their pledge in 1979 to political pluralism, a mixed economy, and a nonaligned foreign policy. By the dynamics of their own revolution, the Sandinistas were expected to support "fraternal" revolutionary movements among their neighbors; theirs was a "revolution without frontiers."

What the Reagan administration sought in Nicaragua was to undo the Sandinistas' increasing monopolization of power and turn Nicaragua back to the post-1979 period when the popular anti-Somoza revolution had produced a new government composed of the major groups that had helped overthrow Somoza. Past administrations had been committed to containment and had not hesitated to intervene to save a friendly regime from being attacked externally or from within by the Soviet Union and/or its friends. However, except for episodic efforts such as Harry Truman's effort to "liberate" North Korea, or John Kennedy's Bay of Pigs operation in Cuba, it had never been the official policy of the U.S. government to unseat Soviet-supported regimes. Dwight Eisenhower's administration had spoken of the liberation of Eastern Europe, but had never acted upon that wish. Containment was a defensive doctrine. The new Reagan policy went "beyond containment" and was inclined to take the offensive.

Dubbed the Reagan Doctrine, its aim was to undo the results of Soviet expansion, not only in Nicaragua but also in Angola and Afghanistan, the Soviet Union's neighbor. Afghanistan was included, although the Afghan resistance had been receiving assistance even before Reagan took office. (Henry Kissinger had tried to help the opposition in Angola until Congress cut off the funds.) All three countries had become Marxist states, but the new governments had not yet fully consolidated their power, and all faced resistance movements. In a sense, Reagan's strategy of "national liberation" set out to disprove the Brezhnev Doctrine—once a nation became part of the Soviet bloc, it could never leave—at least in the Western Hemisphere. The Reagan Doctrine was based upon certain assumptions: that the Soviet Union had become overextended in the 1970s; that the "correlation of forces," as Moscow called it, after favoring Moscow in the 1970s, was shifting back to the United States as a result of its military buildup; that the Soviet Union's most critical problems were domestic; that, except for Afghanistan, only peripheral Soviet interests were involved; and that the Soviet Union would not want to risk a confrontation with the United States.

The Gap Between Ends and Means

In practice, however, the Reagan Doctrine amounted to little more than bleeding the targeted governments; if these governments wanted to stop the hemorrhaging, they would have to negotiate a political solution with the insurgents. Because the insurgencies were not strong enough to overthrow the Marxist regimes, the aim was to transform them diplomatically. In Nicaragua, for example, this meant that the Sandinistas and the contras would have to negotiate about genuinely free elections in which all parties participate unhindered and have equal access to the mass media. The result, it was expected, would be the political pluralism, mixed economy, and nonaligned foreign policy to which the Sandinistas had committed themselves in 1979. In this way, the Sandinistas would help dismantle their post-1979 revolution and become good democrats! The proposition is, of course, ludicrous and demonstrates only that in a civil war there is nothing to negotiate. As Vietnam should have illustrated, civil wars cannot be resolved peacefully. The Sandinistas refused to negotiate with the contras, whom they called American puppets; and the United States would not negotiate any settlement that did not include the contras, whom the president called freedom fighters. The United States was unwilling to accept any solution that left the pro-Soviet regime in power in Nicaragua, and the same was true for Angola and for Afghanistan, which was not just a peripheral interest to Moscow.

This meant that the Reagan Doctrine was flawed by a contradiction. Its aims were very ambitious, but its means were very modest—just a few million dollars of material aid. Either the means would have to be greatly increased or the ends reduced. Increasing the means was precisely what many in Congress feared. Sooner or later, if the insurgents failed, the end could be achieved only by American forces, at least in Nicaragua, which the administration considered a vital interest. Given the involvement of American prestige, could the United States allow the insurgents to lose? Would it not be claimed that American resolve was at stake? In short, was not escalation (and the possible loss of public support) built into the Reagan Doctrine and its ambitious goals? That the United States might at some time have to escalate its efforts or cut its losses was demonstrated by the Soviets in 1985 and 1986. They showed that they were both capable and willing to support their friends by raising their military assistance to the Nicaraguan and Angolan armies. In Afghanistan, the Soviet army did virtually all the fighting. Clearly, Soviet leader Mikhail Gorbachev was determined to maintain his country's imperial outposts.

In Nicaragua the result was that the contras suffered severe losses. Basically defenseless against Soviet-supplied helicopter gunships, reportedly flown by Cuban pilots, and heavy artillery used by the Soviet-Cuban trained Nicaraguan troops, the contras were driven out of Nicaragua into neighboring countries. In Angola Jonas Savimbi, the leader of the insurgents, came to the United States to appeal for more military aid after his troops suffered severe setbacks at the hands of government and Cuban forces. And in Afghanistan, where the fierce resistance had already involved the Soviet Union in a war longer than that against Nazi Germany, the question of Soviet determination to control the country could not be doubted. The Soviets taught the Russian language and Marxism-Leninism in the schools in the towns they controlled, sent thousands of young Afghans to Soviet and Eastern bloc universities, and integrated the economy into that of the Soviet Union. At best, the United States could raise Soviet costs in an area where its vital interests suggest that a complete Soviet disengagement was unlikely, even though the establishment of a genuinely neutral government sensitive to Soviet security concerns would allow the Soviets to withdraw.

Under the circumstances, the dilemma of raising the means or cutting the ends—accepting the "loss" of the countries to the Soviet Union—could be avoided only if historical trends were judged favorable. That is precisely what the Reagan administration claimed. A democratic revolution was sweeping the Third World; modest means could achieve immodest ends. For evidence the administration pointed to Latin America. During the Reagan years— besides El Salvador, Grenada, and Haiti (in whose transformation it had been involved)—the administration cited Argentina, Bolivia, Brazil, Guatemala, Honduras, Peru, and Uruguay as having become democratic. Whatever the reason for this phenomenon—administration policy, the sudden political blossoming of Iberian culture in Latin-America and the Philippines after Spain and Portugal became democratic in the 1970s, or sheer coincidence— the administration expressed its optimism that this was part of a global trend. The Soviet bloc, by denying human freedom and dignity to its citizens, was running against the tide of history. This was the reason why at the periphery of the bloc there were revolts against governments that had come into power with Soviet bloc help and were kept in power by it. The United States, as a free society, Washington asserted, was duty-bound to support such struggles for national independence and self-government.

The Salvadoran Precedent

Admittedly, early administration pronouncements on the superpower struggle in the Third World had not sounded as if the United States would be a contributor to this democratic tide. The clear-cut preference for pro-American authoritarian regimes over pro-Soviet totalitarian regimes had not seemed particularly compatible with American values, even if it could be justified in strategic terms and the memories of what happened in Iran and Nicaragua. But in fact the Reagan Doctrine of support for anti-Communist insurgencies always had involved the Salvadoran example of support for the moderate center. The initial distinction between authoritarianism and totalitarianism was based on the assumption all too true in the past in the Third World: that one or the other was the only choice, that there was no third force between these two extremes, as in China or Vietnam. The rise of Duarte in El Salvador provided the Reagan administration, despite its rhetoric, with a democratic politician and party to back. (Congress, of course, also deserves credit for this development for compelling the administration to switch from total anticommunism to support for democracy by insisting that, in return for military aid, El Salvador would have to demonstrate greater respect for human rights. This helped win the military's support for Duarte because of its desire to continue receiving U.S. weapons.) In brief, even in the midst of a civil war, there were elements upon which to build democracy; social justice and strategic concerns did not always have to be incompatible. The Salvadoran center was admittedly fragile, beset as it was by guerrillas on the left and resistance to reforms on the right, but it curbed the death squads and created a more hospitable climate for democratic politics.

The Salvadoran precedent was not widely recognized until after the events in the Philippines in 1986. The United States had long supported

President Ferdinand Marcos. In August 1983 opposition leader Benigno Aquino returned home from exile in the United States and was assassinated by Marcos's supporters. As public opposition to the Marcos regime grew, the United States urged him to restore democracy, economic growth, and military reforms. His despotism, economic mismanagement, widespread corruption, and the military's abuses also were fueling a rebirth of the Communist guerrilla army. In the absence of basic reforms, the guerrillas might defeat the poorly trained and badly led Philippine army. Marcos, however, refused to heed these suggestions and, to prove his legitimacy to the Americans, called for an election, confident that he could control the outcome, as he had done before. But this proved to be his undoing. The opposition ran Aquino's widow for the presidency; she had become both a symbol of democracy and a rallying point. Marcos tried to alter the election results with widespread fraud, but, as the election was closely covered by the U.S. media, the fraud was not difficult to discover. Marcos lost his legitimacy even while "winning" another term. When top army commanders defected, Marcos fled to Hawaii and Corazon Aquino became president.

Almost simultaneously, the Reagan administration helped Haiti get rid of Jean-Claude "Baby Doc" Duvalier, who had succeeded his father as dictator. The United States first advised Duvalier not to use force against protesting crowds and then furnished him with an airplane to flee to France. The Reagan administration now declared its new policy: "The American people believe in human rights and opposing tyranny in whatever form, whether of the left or the right." [4] The United States would support those struggling for democracy and oppose not just radical left-wing regimes but also pro-American right-wing authoritarian regimes. And it did so. In 1987, after considerable turmoil in South Korea, which had flared on and off for years, the military-supported regime promised free elections for the presidency. Administration pressure upon South Korea's rulers had helped smooth the long-awaited transition.

Had the Reagan administration gone Carteresque? Was it now doing what it had accused Carter of doing in Iran and Nicaragua, that is, "destabilizing" conservative pro-American regimes? The administration rejected this comparison. The impetus for change in the Philippines and Haiti had been local. American help had come only as the despots' power was already crumbling because of popular revolts. Most important, in the Philippines, the opposition appeared genuinely democratic, reform-minded, and pro-American. By implication, however, this also meant that in countries where there was no democratic center as a political alternative, American pressure might make things worse, not better. In Chile American pressure might work although the administration seemed not to be actively influencing its regime; in Indonesia, it was less likely to work, as American pressure on

---

4. President Reagan's March 14 Message to Congress, *New York Times*, March 15, 1986.

the shah of Iran for political and social liberalization had demonstrated. In Iran, like Nicaragua, the center had been a mirage seen by U.S. policy makers. They had expected democratic forces to take over from the shah and were not especially concerned with his overthrow. In Nicaragua they had expected the centrists to share power with and preserve control over the Sandinistas. Ayatollah Ruhollah Khomeini and the Sandinistas, however, quickly and easily destroyed the fragile center and consolidated their respective power. In the absence of a democratic center that had a genuine chance of blossoming, right-wing authoritarianism would presumably still be preferable to left-wing totalitarianism. The administration had shrewdly remarried democracy or human rights concerns to anti-Sovietism. Where democracy had a chance to grow, it was the best antidote to communism.

The Criteria for Success or Failure

For the most part, however, the Reagan administration invoked its claim of a global prodemocratic tide as a rationale to support the resistance movements in Afghanistan, Angola, and Nicaragua. It took a strong verbal stand against apartheid in South Africa, but had to be pushed into imposing economic sanctions by Congress. In any event, whether the insurgencies it supported in the name of spreading freedom represented democratic tendencies was questionable. In Afghanistan, the opponents to Soviet rule were Islamic fundamentalists who, if they won, were more likely to establish an Iranian-style theocracy than a democracy. Still, that they were a genuine resistance movement cannot be doubted. In Angola, Savimbi, the rebel leader representing Angola's largest tribal group, was trained in Communist China and was quite willing to rely on South Africa for help. And in Nicaragua, some of the principal contra commanders were former members of Somoza's National Guard who remained very conservative. They held more power in the opposition movement than the Social Democrats and liberals who, having initially cooperated with the Sandinistas, joined the contras' civilian directorate in protest against the Sandinistas' increasing regimentation of Nicaragua. But this civilian directorate was basically powerless. The suspicion of the Somocistas was a major cause for the contras' inability to exploit the growing alienation of Nicaraguans from the Sandinistas.

Admittedly, the 20,000 contras could not be effective, let alone win, when Congress, fearful of another Vietnam, cut military aid and/or substituted "nonlethal" or "humanitarian aid" of food, medicine, and such items— although the administration funded the contras secretly so that they could survive until Congress changed its mind again—while the Soviets supplied $500 million in arms over a period of five years. Nevertheless, an effective guerrilla movement should have been better able to exploit the worsening social and economic conditions in Nicaragua. The contras have yet to capture a single village and they keep killing the civilians whose support they need to enhance their following. In short, the contras have never been able to spark the kind of devotion and following the Sandinistas did in an earlier era or that even the Salvadoran opposition had to some extent.

Partly because of this, the contra war never gained much popular support in the United States. Quite the opposite: Congress, especially the Democratic-controlled House during the first six years of the Reagan presidency, generally opposed the war. Moreover, the president has never been able to convince the public that U.S. security interests were endangered by the Sandinistas. Indeed, there has been a good deal of speculation that the administration, determined to overthrow the Nicaraguan regime, had not seriously pursued a diplomatic solution. The lack of support drove the administration to fund the war illegally during the years Congress cut off military assistance to the contras, as well as after Congress resumed funding.

The contrast to Afghanistan is instructive. The Soviet invasion meant that the resistance to the Soviet-imposed government had genuine popular support. The resistance fighters fought courageously and successfully against the Soviet army despite their general lack of modern weapons. Many states throughout the world were sympathetic to the rebels; the Moslem states were largely united in their condemnation of Moscow. Unlike the U.S.-supported contra war, which most states in the region and elsewhere opposed, America's covert assistance to the Afghan resistance was not condemned by neighboring states; and it had congressional and popular support in the United States.

The issue in these instances, as well as Angola, was not so much the advancement of the democratic cause as the likelihood of success in the field and the identification of the United States with a widely approved course of action. Where could the United States legitimately support anti-Soviet insurgencies? The Reagan Doctrine evaded asking the key questions before committing the United States. How close to Moscow are the governments in these nations? How likely are the insurgents to achieve their aims without U.S. assistance? If they gained power, would that improve the lives of their people and advance U.S. regional interests? Do U.S. allies and friends, especially those in the area, approve American support of the insurgency? When U.S. security is clearly at stake, when the rebels are worthy of support and have some hope of success, where other states approve and support the insurgency, and diplomacy is likely to fail, a president can expect the country to support him. Otherwise, if the president persists, like Reagan, he may find that the attempt to justify covert anti-Soviet interventions ends up in scandal, weakening the presidency and undermining the cause itself.

Perhaps because of that risk and because the presidents of Costa Rica, Nicaragua, El Salvador, Honduras, and Guatemala agreed to a regional peace plan in 1987, Reagan supported it. If the plan failed and if the failure could be clearly attributed to the Sandinistas' unwillingness to open up Nicaragua to genuine democratization, as stipulated by the peace plan, Reagan might regain support for further financial assistance of the contras. If the plan were successfully implemented, the Sandinistas would be diluting their control of Nicaragua and sharing power with opposition groups in the type of political pluralism they had committed themselves to in 1979. They would certainly set a precedent: a Marxist-Leninist regime voluntarily surrendering its virtually complete control of society. A more likely end to the fighting would come from an agreement that left the Sandinistas' power essentially intact while reducing Cuban and Soviet advisers, military supplies, and the size of the Sandinistas' army—the kind of formula Reagan had been unwilling to accept. Whether the United States would enforce such an arrangement, which would also have to include a Sandinista pledge not to export their revolution to their neighbors, was questionable. The Reagan administration had expressed a belief in the necessity for the use of force in advancing U.S. purposes. It ended up, as its predecessors, unable to resort to force even in a situation where it believed vital interests were involved. The post-Vietnam administrations' ability to use force for any prolonged involvements remained restrained by public opinion.

The Middle East and the
Anti-Soviet Strategic Consensus

The oil in the Arabian peninsula and in some of the nearby countries had made security in this area critical for the United States and the West since the early 1970s. But the region was both threatened and unstable. With a sizable army in Afghanistan on the border of Pakistan (a nation caught between the Soviet sphere and unfriendly India), and with the use of air and port facilities in Ethiopia and South Yemen, the Soviet presence in the area and its threat to the oil and shipping lines were real. The increasing nearness of Soviet power and influence frightened Saudi Arabia and the other oil kingdoms, which were already confronting the possibility of domestic instability as a result of the presence of foreign workers, such as Palestinians and fundamentalist Islamic groups opposed to Western-style modernization.

The Carter Doctrine was a symbol of America's vital interest in the area. The establishment of the Rapid Deployment Force (which in 1984 was still not rapid, deployed, or a force); the search for bases in Kenya, Somalia, and Oman; the modernization of the base on the island of Diego Garcia in the Indian Ocean; the sizable U.S. fleet in the Indian Ocean-Persian Gulf area; and the discussions of possible military cooperation with Egypt, with whose forces the United States held annual exercises—all these were part of an effort to establish an American presence and to balance Soviet power in the area. The superpower rivalry was imposed on top of the instability of key countries, as well as on regional rivalries, such as those between India and Pakistan, and Iran and Iraq. Arab unity was shattered by the Iran-Iraq war. Libya and Syria supported non-Arab Iran, while former adversaries of Iraq such as Jordan helped it; even Egypt, the target of Iraq's Rejectionist Front, sent arms. And, of course, the politics of the area could not be separated from the Arab- (minus Egypt) Israeli quarrel. The area was a veritable tinderbox.

The Reagan administration pursued a twofold foreign policy strategy toward the Middle East-Persian Gulf area to reduce this insecurity. First, based upon the assumption that Saudi Arabia, the key oil country, kept its distance from the United States because of its lack of confidence in American leadership and power, the new administration decided to upgrade the U.S.-Saudi relationship by agreeing to sell the Saudis the fuel tanks and air-to-air missiles they requested for their F-15 fighters, as well as five Airborne Warning and Control System (AWACS) aircraft—Boeing 707s with large disklike antennas mounted on them. The sale took place even though Israel worried about the threat these aircraft posed because of their ability to collect information on Israeli air force movements. Reagan vowed the United States would not permit Saudi Arabia "to be an Iran," thereby upgrading Carter's commitment to protect Persian Gulf states against external forces. This statement implied that the United States would protect the Saudi government even against internal insurrection.

If reassuring Saudi Arabia of its special relationship with the United States and America's ability and willingness to protect the kingdom's security was fundamental U.S. political strategy, what about the Arab-Israeli conflict? Reagan administration officials were fond of stating that the region's various rivalries and domestic instabilities were only marginally related to the Arab-Israeli struggle, thereby suggesting that, if the United States could establish its power in the area and the pro-Western Arab regimes then felt more secure, the oil supplies for the West would also be more secure. The key issue was American leadership and the credibility of American power, not the self-determination of the Palestinians, the critical issue blocking a more comprehensive Arab-Israeli peace.

The second part of the Reagan strategy, therefore, was to stress the anti-Soviet nature of its policy. Fundamentally, this attempt to forge an anti-Soviet "strategic consensus" was intended to overcome the Arabs' resistance to joining forces with the United States because of their resentment of Israeli policy. Specifically, Reagan's purpose was to gain the cooperation of countries such as Egypt, Jordan, Saudi Arabia, and Pakistan, as well as Israel. They should all give priority to containing Soviet influence, subordinating their local quarrels to this more important task. This approach amounted to downplaying the central Arab-Israeli conflict and postponing a settlement of the most critical problem preventing a settlement, the Palestinian problem.

It was not a successful strategy. The Israelis were very anxious about any weapons sold to any Arab state, and Saudi Arabia, as an Arab state, could not ignore the Palestinians and other issues of concern. In fact, the Saudis argued strongly that the increasing frustration and anger about the lack of progress on the Palestinian issue was the *main* danger to the U.S. interest in keeping the oil flowing and that *all* Arabs, not just Israel's neighbors, felt the same way. Only the establishment of a Palestinian state would alleviate the regional anti-U.S. feeling, which had made it impossible for any Arab state to be closely linked to the United States or to cooperate with it fully on oil or military issues. In short, the countries in the area gave priority to their quarrels while the United States searched for ways of resolving both the oil and the Arab-Israeli problems, problems that refused to be divorced from each other.

Events Undermining Reagan's Policy

Four events took place that frustrated the administration's policy for the region. The first was in Lebanon, Israel's small northern neighbor, which several years earlier had disintegrated into civil war between Christians and Muslims. The Christians, long the wealthier and more politically influential, sought to retain their position by suppressing the Palestinians, whose presence had become sizable after Jordan's King Hussein had driven them out of his country during the early 1970s. Sympathetic to their fellow Arabs and their aspirations for a greater say in Lebanese affairs, which would reflect their rapidly growing numbers, the Palestinians, heavily armed, constituted a threat to the integrity of Lebanon. They upset the agreement of the Christians and Lebanese Muslims for a domestic redistribution of power because the more militant left-wing forces felt that they could militarily defeat the Christians with the help of the Palestine Liberation Organization (PLO) and win most of the political power. Syria opposed a solution that would probably have led to a Christian secession from Lebanon and the establishment of two states, one Christian and one Muslim. It sought Lebanon's survival and political integrity, first through political mediation and, when that proved unsuccessful, through military intervention. Syria did so for several reasons: to boost its prestige; to prevent creation of a Muslim neighbor with a more radical and militant leadership than Syria's own; to avoid being dragged into a war with Israel by such a leadership; and most important, to establish its dominance in Lebanon, essentially incorporating it into Syria's sphere of influence.

An uneasy peace, frequently violated, prevailed as the Syrians tried to prevent outbursts. But this Christian-Syrian alliance was an unnatural one. The Christian-Israeli alliance was a better partnership because the two groups shared an interest in containing, indeed in weakening, PLO influence. The Israelis and the Lebanese Christians cooperated after an Israeli invasion of southern Lebanon to destroy PLO bases. The Israelis let the Christians take over the area and supplied them with arms to provide a buffer zone between Israel and the PLO; they also secretly committed the Israeli air force to defend the Christians against Syrian air strikes. The Syrians, in their turn, were sympathetic to the Muslim majority fighting the Christians. The character of Lebanon's civil war was changing as each side was supported by an external power. As a result, Israel and Syria almost came to blows in 1981.

Because such a military clash would inflame regional tensions and place the Soviet Union, with whom Syria had a treaty of friendship, on the Arab side, the Reagan administration mediated the issue. Thereafter the situation quieted for a while; nevertheless, it demonstrated dramatically once more that the Arab-Israeli conflict provided the powerful political and emotional context through which most other problems were filtered.

In the midst of these negotiations, the second event occurred, an even more dramatic reminder for the Reagan administration that the Arab-Israeli conflict could not be subordinated to an anti-Soviet strategic consensus. Asserting that Iraq, an oil-rich nation, would use its new nuclear reactor to produce nuclear bombs, which it would then drop on Israel, the Israeli air force attacked and destroyed the reactor just before it became operational. Whether Iraq, which had signed the nuclear nonproliferation treaty, would have produced such bombs or used them to destroy Israel, which had not signed this treaty, is unknown. Israel's claim was based upon Iraq's possession of a reactor, Iraqi leadership of the Arab states that rejected the Camp David peace process, and an Iraqi leader whom Israeli prime minister Menachem Begin claimed was a "tyrant" and "crazy." Clearly, the Israeli idea of self-defense was very broad and included the right to attack a potentially hostile neighbor who might develop nuclear arms and attack Israel with them.

Washington viewed this air strike as politically damaging. It revived the Arab perception of Israel as the prime Arab foe, set back U.S. efforts to portray the Soviet Union as the chief threat to the area and to forge an anti-Soviet alliance with moderate Arab states, and endangered further efforts toward achieving a broader Arab-Israeli peace. The air strike also confronted the president with an unpleasant dilemma: if the United States acquiesced in the Israeli action it would risk alienating the moderate Arab states, including Saudi Arabia; if it punished Israel, it would stir domestic opposition. As a way out, the United States joined Iraq in the United Nations in condemning Israel, but the condemnation had no teeth in it. The United States insisted that no sanctions be applied, although it temporarily withheld several jet fighters from delivery. This mild slap on the wrist was viewed by the Arabs as confirmation of America's one-sided attitude, regardless of how extreme or provocative Israel's actions were.

The third jolt to the Reagan strategy of subordinating the Arab-Israeli conflict to an anti-Soviet strategy was the reelection of Begin as prime minister of Israel. Begin, having made peace with the only Arab state that had potential power to be a threat to Israel, saw no reason to be accommodating on other issues. Washington had hoped that the Labor party would win the election and take a more flexible approach when the peace process was resumed. Instead the most right-wing government in Israel's existence came to power. Begin appointed a foreign minister who had opposed the peace with Egypt and a defense minister who as agriculture minister had been in charge of an aggressive policy of settling the West Bank. Symbolic of Begin's conviction that the West Bank was part of Israel, he put his *interior* minister in charge of the Palestinian autonomy talks. Begin had always pursued Israeli interests, as he defined them, regardless of American preferences, offering occasional demonstrations of the natural order of things turned upside down—of a small country manipulating its far stronger protector. He was able to do so because most U.S. presidents were genuinely concerned about Israeli security as well as fearful of domestic repercussions if they pressured Israel.

The fourth blow was the biggest of all to the administration: the assassination of President Anwar Sadat of Egypt in October 1981. Both Israel and Egypt immediately announced that they remained committed to carrying out the remaining provision of their peace treaty. Still, uncertainty over the future increased. Israel remained bent on annexing the West Bank. Sadat's whole policy had been based from the beginning upon the expectation that the United States would pressure Israel; in that respect, the United States had clearly failed him. No American administration had been willing to take that risky political course. None had been willing even to speak out publicly about the U.S. interpretation of Camp David and how the peace process was supposed to evolve, or to say that Begin's policy was a reason for Egypt's isolation in the Arab world, for the criticism of—and opposition to—Sadat at home, and for the increasing perception in the region of the United States as either one-sided or an ineffective mediator.

The Palestinian issue was not the only question on which Washington and Israel differed, as Begin quickly demonstrated when, unexpectedly and without consulting the United States, he formally annexed Syria's Golan Heights, an area important to Israeli security. Begin again showed his willingness to act unilaterally, motivated by his concern only for Israeli interests as he interpreted them, and his lack of sensitivity to the interests and concerns of the United States, Israel's principal source of protection and military and economic assistance. When the United States, feeling that cooperation between the two countries was a two-way street, voiced its displeasure, Begin lashed out, accusing the administration of practicing anti-Semitism, breaking its word, and treating Israel like a "banana republic." Begin clearly thought that Israel should be able to do whatever it wanted and that America should support Israel, regardless of the consequences its action had on American interests. Even if the United States thought Begin's moves jeopardized the peace process, increased Egypt's isolation, and weakened America's position in the area, it should support Israel.

What the Israeli action did, however, was to raise the key question of whether Israel and the United States could work together for peace. The American assumption had always been that a Middle East peace could be built upon an exchange of the 1967 Israeli-conquered Arab territories for Arab acceptance of Israel; the Israeli withdrawal from the Sinai suggested that Israel shared that belief. But increasingly since the peace treaty with Egypt, it had become clearer that Begin's Israel preferred the expansion of territory to peace with its neighbors based fundamentally on the 1967 borders. Negotiations were replaced by annexation—of East Jerusalem, the Golan Heights, and, for all practical purposes, the West Bank and Gaza. Could the United States in these circumstances still assume that Israel would withdraw from these areas in return for Arab acceptance of Israel, and more fundamentally, that American and Israeli interests coincided?

Israeli Invasion of Lebanon

The 1982 Israeli invasion of Lebanon to crush the PLO and solve the political problem of the Palestinians by purely military means dramatically underlined the question of U.S.-Israeli common interests. Israel gave as its reason for the invasion the danger to its citizens in its northern settlements from PLO artillery and rocket fire. The stated purpose was to drive the PLO back from the border and establish a rocket-free zone. The immediate cause for the invasion was the assassination of the Israeli ambassador to England by, the Israelis claimed, the PLO. The PLO denied the charge. Clearly, the Begin government was looking for a pretext to set in motion detailed plans for an invasion long planned.

Once the invasion began, it also became very clear that the Israeli goal was more than the security of its citizens living along the border with Lebanon. No immediate danger to their lives existed; the American-negotiated truce had held over nine months. The very fact that the Israeli forces hardly stopped for refueling once they were twenty-five miles deep into Lebanon but continued their rapid advance toward Beirut suggested that West Beirut, the Moslem half of the city where the PLO had its headquarters, had been the principal goal all along. If the Israeli forces could militarily defeat the PLO and politically humiliate it, they would be doing more than ensuring the safety of Israeli citizens by destroying the PLO as a "state within a state" in Lebanon and eliminating terrorist attacks in Israel. Crushing the PLO would also, it was hoped, destroy Palestinian nationalism on the West Bank and either force the Palestinians to move to Jordan or submit to permanent Israeli domination. A third aim was to place Lebanon more firmly in control of the Christians, who were friendly to Israel, and thus enhance Israeli security on its northern border.

But the siege of Beirut backfired and once more demonstrated that a military victory cannot always be transformed into a desirable political settlement. Every night for several weeks, television showed Israeli warplanes, tanks, and artillery pounding West Beirut, bringing destruction and human misery, and world criticism of Israel grew. Even though it was the PLO that decided to fight in the city among the civilian population, the heavy Israeli fire greatly damaged Israel's reputation in the West. In its previous three wars, Israel had attacked only after it had been struck or was certain an attack would occur. No such danger to Israeli security existed before the invasion of Lebanon. The invasion was widely viewed as an unprovoked offensive action, and none of the ever-changing, publicly stated reasons given for it had much to do with the real reasons why it was launched. Israel not only shocked many of its admirers by the transparency of the rationales it offered but also by the disproportion between the means it used and the limited ends it claimed to be seeking. The massive use of force, however, achieved the central Israeli aim: the expulsion of the PLO from Beirut. Abandoned by their fellow Arabs, as well as their Soviet friends, the PLO finally gave in and accepted an American-negotiated truce that kept Israeli forces out of West Beirut and provided for a multinational peace-keeping force composed of Italian, British, French, and American troops to supervise their exit to the twenty-odd Arab countries.

Yet, ironically, in victory the Israelis defeated themselves. Seeking to crush the PLO and thereby Palestinian nationalism, they made the Palestinians a central political issue. Initially, the Israelis shamed everyone: the Arab states that did not lift a finger to help the PLO (and only reluctantly accepted their "freedom fighters" after their defeat); the front-line Arab states, including Syria, whose Soviet-equipped and -trained army in Lebanon was badly mauled by the Israelis; Egypt, whose peace with Israel seemed even more of a betrayal of the Arab cause (and whose only action, short of violating that peace, was to recall its ambassador from Israel); the Soviets, who said that they were not going to bail out the PLO when the Arabs themselves stood by; and the United States, which in Arab eyes had tacitly approved the Israeli invasion because it had failed to stop it. However, the pounding of West Beirut angered President Reagan and tested his strong pro-Israel feeling, which had already been eroding as a result of Begin's earlier actions.

It now appeared to the president that the Palestinian problem could not be subordinated to regional anti-Soviet policy; that the Arab-Israeli problem was a separate issue; and that the key to resolving that conflict, as well as establishing closer and more cordial relationships with the Arab countries, including the oil producers, was resolving the future of the Palestinians. The Israel government now found itself alienated from the United States and faced by an American initiative it had neither expected nor welcomed. Clearly separating himself from Begin's policy, Reagan proposed a new peace plan whose basic features were genuine autonomy for the Palestinians living on the West Bank and Gaza and the association of the West Bank with Jordan. In short, there would be no Palestinian state, which Israel constantly declared was unacceptable because it would pose a security risk. But there would also be no Israeli annexation of the West Bank; instead, Israel was expected to withdraw from most of it. The initial Arab and PLO reaction was to show interest, but Begin's immediate reaction was a swift and total rejection.

The Massacre in the Palestinian Camps

Israel appeared to be isolating itself in the world, even among Jews. The always loyal Jewish community in the United States largely supported the president in his peace efforts. The World Zionist Congress, meeting in Israel at the time, denounced Begin's effort to annex the West Bank. And then came the real shock, a human tragedy that placed the Israeli invasion, Begin, and his defense minister, Ariel Sharon—the man largely responsible for Israel's policy on the West Bank and the invasion of Lebanon—in the global limelight. In Lebanon Bashir Gemayel, the newly elected pro-Israeli leader of the Christian, or Phalangist, militia was assassinated on the eve of becoming president. Begin and Sharon immediately sent Israeli forces into West Beirut in violation of the truce (the multinational peace-keeping forces had already been pulled out). Ostensibly they did so to protect the Muslim population from Christian revenge, but the real aims appear to have been to gain control over West Beirut and to make the United States (which had arranged the truce that was supposed to keep the Israelis out of West Beirut) look helpless. This, in turn, would undermine the support the president needed from the moderate Arab states for his peace plan. Once in West Beirut, the Israelis called on the Christian militia, the Phalangists, to go into the Palestinian refugee camps to rout out any remaining PLO terrorists. The stated purpose was to save the lives of Israeli soldiers. But the Christian forces proceeded to slaughter several hundred Palestinians, mainly women, children, and old men.

The Israelis, along with the rest of the world, were shocked. To what extent were Israel's leaders and army implicated? At best, knowing of the hatred and past killings between Christians and Moslems, the Israeli authorities should have known better than to send the Phalangists into the Palestinian camps in the wake of their leader's death, presumably at the hands of Muslims. Begin denied any Israeli responsibility and harshly denounced the critics. But the strength and decency of Israeli democracy insisted otherwise. Begin refused to establish an impartial judicial commission of inquiry. The president of Israel, normally a symbolic figure, intervened and publicly called for such an inquiry as a moral necessity. Street demonstrations occurred, and Jewish leaders in Europe and America also protested Begin's decision. The prime minister was compelled to change his mind. How could a Jewish state, composed of people so long persecuted themselves, do otherwise than investigate the tragedy, even if direct responsibility for the massacre lay with Lebanese Christians? How could a country that arose out of the slaughter of 6 million Jews by the Nazis not feel that Israel's moral reputation had been stained? How could Israeli officials be held blameless, especially after they had sent Israeli troops into West Beirut allegedly to protect the Muslim population?

For many Jews in Israel and outside, Begin and Sharon had squandered

Israel's most precious asset, its self-respect and the respect of the world. The findings of the judicial commission did, indeed, hold Israel "indirectly responsible." It issued separate reports on Begin, Sharon, Israel's foreign minister, the chief of staff, and the commanding general in Beirut, among others, assessing their responsibility. Specifically, it recommended Sharon's dismissal as defense minister and, by implication, from the government. Characteristic of Begin's general insensitivity and refusal to accept any blame for Israel, he asked Sharon to give up the Defense Ministry but kept him in the cabinet, thereby accepting the commission's recommendation but violating its spirit.

If Begin and Sharon appeared morally callous and Israeli policy too eager to use force to resolve problems, the events in Lebanon also showed the Arabs to be lacking in foresight and courage. Although neither the Arab states nor the PLO completely rejected Reagan's peace plan, they soon reaffirmed their commitments to an Israeli withdrawal to the 1967 borders, to a Palestinian state, and to the PLO as the representative of Palestinian nationalism. Nothing changed, despite past statements that they were willing to accept coexistence with Israel, and despite several meetings between King Hussein and PLO leader Yasir Arafat during which the two men explored the possibility of Hussein's negotiating on behalf of the PLO. Little attention was given to Hussein's reported warning that if the Reagan initiative were allowed to die, Israel would determine the West Bank issue once and for all with its settlements. There was little time left for the Arabs to negotiate, reverse the Israeli policy of annexation, and gain American backing. The time may have passed for a Palestinian state, and the Reagan plan might be the most that could still be achieved to advance Palestinian goals.

But the PLO remained divided between moderates and rejectionists who sought the destruction of Israel. As in earlier years, Arafat was unwilling either to crush the extremists or to split the organization to get the best deal possible before time ran out. The Arab leaders were also unwilling to take the initiative. This included Hussein, who would not proceed without PLO consent. Despite its military defeat, the politically weakened PLO was allowed to exercise a veto to prevent the moderate Arab states from exploring the Reagan plan. This time there was no leader of Sadat's stature who was willing to seize the opportunity and announce a willingness to accept Israel and negotiate with it on the basis of the American formula. The postponement of negotiations and a settlement also risked transforming the character of Israel, a state composed of 3.5 million Jews ruling over 2 million Arabs (1.3 million in the West Bank), whose high birth rate threatened Israel's Jewish character, its democratic character if it denied them the vote, and its humane character if it kept them as second-class citizens, treated them as noncitizens without basic rights as on the West Bank, or uprooted most of them and drove them out.

With the PLO defeated, its soldiers scattered over many Arab countries, all of whom exercised tight control over them, its armed struggle against Israel no longer feasible, and Arafat's control contested by Syria—and with a global oil glut rendering the Arab oil weapon impotent—was there an alternative to a diplomatic solution? With the United States having distanced itself from Begin (who resigned in 1983) and having advanced a peace plan more sympathetic to Palestinian aims than any previous American plan, the enormity of the Arabs' lack of political courage to seize this fleeting opportunity was startling. American officials were especially disappointed that the Saudis, the recipients of so much political and military assistance from the United States, were unwilling to use their influence to urge the PLO and/or Jordan to negotiate within the Reagan framework.

Naturally Hussein felt vulnerable. Sadat had been confident because Egypt was the strongest Arab state. Jordan was a small state. But the failure to take risks meant that the situation on the West Bank was bound to deteriorate: Jewish settlers would increase in numbers and determination to make it part of Israel; and the 60 percent of the West Bank population that was under the age of twenty—a youth that had never known anything but Israeli occupation—would become politically radicalized and intensely nationalistic. The young people were drawn to Arafat as a symbol of their desire for a Palestinian state, even as he was relegated to the political sidelines because he had allowed the PLO rejectionists to block negotiations.

Who Gained? Who Lost?

Nor did the United States escape from Lebanon unscathed; it too blundered there as a result of Lebanese politics and regional rivalries. Lebanon, as noted, had long been divided between the wealthier and politically powerful Christians and the poorer and politically less influential Arabs (Druse, Sunni, and Shi'ite Muslims). As the Muslim sects grew in numbers and the demographic balance between Christians and Arabs changed, the Arabs demanded a redistribution of power. The PLO, settling in Lebanon after being ejected from Jordan, in the 1970s had backed this demand with support and arms. The Israeli defeat of the PLO in 1982 had shifted power back to the Christians and had led to the formation of an Israeli-supported, Christian-dominated government. But this did not settle the fundamental constitutional problem of how Lebanon could end its civil war and govern itself peacefully; quite the contrary, it fired up the domestic war among the various political and religious factions, all of whom had their own armies.

The Israelis also demanded a normalization of Lebanese-Israeli relations; in short, they demanded a peace treaty as the price of withdrawing their troops. This, it was widely assumed, would then lead to a simultaneous Syrian troop withdrawal, allowing Lebanon once more to govern itself. Israel demanded more than security arrangements for its northern border with Lebanon—the original pretext for the invasion—because the Israelis had suffered high casualties and the war had for the first time led to domestic protests. The government needed to justify these losses and pacify the opposition. Peace with another Arab state appeared to be a prize worth Israeli sacrifices. Lebanon's fragile Christian-dominated government was reluctant to accede to Israeli terms, however, because most of its Arab population would refuse to go along. But Lebanon finally accepted an American-mediated agreement because that appeared to be the only way to get the Israelis and Syrians out.

Not only were Lebanon's Arabs opposed to the government because it was Christian-dominated, but now they faced the added factor of peace with Israel. Most important, Syria, which had opposed the Israeli-Egyptian accords, opposed the terms of this peace as well and refused to withdraw its 50,000 troops. As Israeli forces, tired of the casualties, pulled back to southern Lebanon, Syrian influence grew. During the months that the Israelis had refused to pull back and had pressured the Lebanese government to accept the normalization agreement, the Soviets had reequipped the Syrian armed forces, badly defeated by the Israelis in 1982, and had sent 7,000 military advisers to Syria. This strengthened Syria's resolve and its hand in settling Lebanon's future. Besides helping the PLO dissidents to destroy Arafat, the Syrians now supplied the military hardware the various Arab militias needed to attack the Lebanese government and its small, new, and poorly trained army.

In the midst of this escalating and fiercely fought civil war, the multinational peace-keeping force, which had returned to Beirut after the slaughter in the Palestinian camps, no longer had a peace to keep. The approximately 1,500 U.S. marines, even with the fleet offshore, were in no position to impose domestic peace. There were only two possible ways of doing so: an Israeli attack on the Syrian army in Lebanon, if Israel wished to preserve the pro-Israeli Christian government and the peace agreement; or an American attack on Syrian forces or Druse and Shi'ite forces around Beirut. Only if Syria or its Lebanese friends were bloodied and weakened would they have reason to be more accommodating in negotiations with the Christians about Lebanon's domestic political power distribution and Lebanon's withdrawal from the Arab confrontation with Israel. But Israel had wearied of the war it had started, and Washington could not politically send sizable U.S. forces to Lebanon to battle Syria. Much of American public opinion was not persuaded that preventing Lebanon's partition between Syria and Israel was a vital interest of America.

Nevertheless, without ever announcing it, Reagan changed the marines' mission. He judged it important to preserve the Lebanese government from its domestic opponents and their Syrian supporters. Their victory over the government, whose jurisdiction at the time did not extend beyond Beirut's city limits (if that far), was likely to result in a basically anti-American, anti-Israeli government controlled by Syria, which had close relations with the Soviet Union, Libya, and Iran. The role of the marines and the fleet was shifted from keeping the peace to enforcing it on behalf of a pro-American and pro-Israeli government. This meant that the United States was now supporting one side in a civil war, and the Arab factions saw the marines and the navy offshore as enemies. They began to fire on the Beirut airport, where the marines had dug in to protect themselves. The marine position proved indefensible as pro-Iranian Shi'ites filled a truck with gas-enhanced explosives equal in tonnage to an atomic bomb and, in a suicide mission, destroyed a barracks where the marines were sleeping. The marines lost 241 men as a result of this terrorist attack, which could not possibly have been organized without Syrian knowledge, if not help. An earlier suicide mission on the U.S. Embassy in Beirut had also caused a large number of deaths. Demands to bring the marines back to the United States grew stronger.

The president resisted these demands, although 1984 was an election year and Lebanon was a political liability for him. Events, however, compelled him to change his mind. He pulled the marines out, as the Syrian-backed Muslim factions defeated the Lebanese army, many of whose Muslim soldiers deserted. The Lebanese cabinet resigned. The Christian president, who had been unwilling to make sufficient concessions to achieve "national reconciliation" because of American support, was forced to make the government more representative and to renounce the agreement with Israel. But the victorious Muslims and Syria said these concessions were too little and too late. They were clearly bent on destroying the American-supported government. The Syrians appeared determined to humiliate Washington and show the world who was the victor. Lebanon was in effect partitioned between Syria in the east and Israel in the south, with Syria the dominant influence in Beirut as well. Most of Lebanon fell under Syria's sphere of influence. Meanwhile, everyone else looked back at the Lebanese quagmire, recalled their original expectations and aims, and then assessed the rather meager results.

For the United States the withdrawal of the marines and the collapse of the Christian-dominated government and the Lebanese-Israeli treaty was a bitter experience—a defeat, to put it frankly. The Reagan administration had tried to demonstrate to Arab moderates that, unlike its predecessor, it would be a staunch friend they could rely on in a crisis. The result in Lebanon suggested the contrary. Apparently, the better part of wisdom might be to keep one's distance from the United States, an unreliable and weak friend with little stomach for a fight with Syria, a small but tough adversary. American prestige, on the line once the marines became civil war participants, suffered a serious blow when they were pulled out and the Beirut government and its army collapsed. For many observers in the area, the friends of America—as in Vietnam and Iran—had lost again.

This was surely the lesson that America's enemies wanted the states in the region to learn. Syria, a poor country with fewer than 10 million people had finished what Israel had started and did so while the whole Arab world stood by meekly. It had humiliated Arafat and asserted Syrian control over what was left of the PLO by militarily supporting the rejectionists in the organization, who destroyed the remainder of Arafat's forces, once more hiding among civilians (this time in Tripoli). It had outlasted Israel, which had withdrawn its forces to its northern border. It had forced Reagan to pull out the marines while it established its influence in Lebanon and simultaneously tried to make itself the powerbroker for any future Middle East negotiations.

Iran, whose aim was to destabilize the pro-American oil regimes in the Persian Gulf, could also feel great satisfaction. As an Iranian official reportedly was heard to remark crudely: "All it took was two martyrs to push the Americans out of Lebanon; one to blow up the embassy, another for the marines." When vital interests seem ambiguous, or even when they are starkly clear, if the United States was unwilling to use force on a scale larger than 1,500 marines—and use it effectively—less prestige is lost by avoiding involvement altogether than by intervening and failing.

Indeed, as Hussein and Arafat met again to form a united political position for negotiations with Israel, the United States remained on the sidelines. Hussein still would not act alone, although he threatened to do so if Arafat continued to block negotiations. In the meantime, PLO fighters reinfiltrated into Lebanon (where the Syrian-supported Shi'ites tried to destroy them). Negotiations predictably broke down. The peace process was stalled again, and in 1987 Arafat reunified the PLO by committing himself once more to the military struggle against Israel. The "inalienable right" of Palestinians to self-determination, which the Arab states ignored while they controlled the West Bank and Gaza, remained a critical stumbling block. Meanwhile, Israel was still unwilling to surrender its 1967 conquests.

Indeed, the military victory in the Six-Day War was becoming a burden. As the occupier of the West Bank, Israel found itself cracking down on Arab resistance as the local youth became more and more radicalized and devoted to Arafat's cause. The legacy of that war was the question whether Israel could preserve both its Jewish heritage and democratic values. The more recent Lebanese war had not turned out as expected. It had not resulted in an Israeli-Lebanese peace, but in Syrian influence over the Lebanese government. The Israeli occupation had transformed the once friendly Shi'ites on the Israeli border into bitter enemies, and the pro-Iranian and militantly anti-American and anti-Israeli radical terrorists had gained a secure foothold in the ruins of Lebanon. The Reagan administration, dispirited after its bumbling in Lebanon and the loss of the marines and weakened by the Iran-contra scandal, had neither the imagination nor the will to risk taking the initiative in the peace process before the situation grew even more unstable and violent. So it continued to stand passively by.

Terrorism, the Iran-Contra Affair, and the Reagan Downfall

With the Middle East in a turmoil and Arab radicalism on the rise, the United States became more and more concerned with terrorism. The kidnappings continued in Lebanon. The Americans and French were particularly targeted by pro-Iranian Shi'ite groups like Islamic Jihad and the Party of God, who had bombed the U.S. Embassy and the marine barracks. These groups were also involved in the seizure of a TWA airliner in which a marine in civilian clothing was murdered. Other Palestinian groups were also active, including the PLO and groups opposed to Arafat and to any moderate Arab leaders who might favor peace negotiations with Israel. Especially ruthless was a faction led by Abu Nidal. Members of this group seized an Italian cruise ship in the Mediterranean, killing an elderly American in a wheelchair. In other terrorist incidents, a bomb exploded on a TWA airliner during landing, and several people were killed; an Egyptian airliner was hijacked; a simultaneous attack was carried out on the Rome and Vienna airports, injuring and killing many, including an eleven-year-old American girl. Several other plans, like the bombing of the U.S. Embassy in Rome, were aborted.

The common link in all these attacks was that the terrorists were state-sponsored: Iran and Syria backed the groups in Lebanon, and Libya and Syria the extremist Palestinian groups. Such state-supported terrorism (providing camps and training, furnishing weapons and money) was a "poor-man's war." It was a way of striking at an enemy whose military strength was too great to face in a state-to-state confrontation. The enemy was the United States, and all Americans were targets—soldiers, officials, and tourists. There were no "innocent" Americans; even those who worked and taught for years in Arab countries were not exempt.

The motives for terrorism varied. To the ayatollah, America was the representative of a secular (and, therefore, atheistic), dynamic, successful Western civilization that was undermining Iranian traditions and customs, including the influence of the clergy. Opposed to modernization, seeking to revive the glories of Islam, and to expand its influence, Khomeini wanted to eliminate completely American influence from Southwest Asia and the Middle East. For Syria, the goal was a greater Syria, including Lebanon; Syria's preeminence in the Arab world; and the proof that "all roads went through Damascus" in any Middle East negotiations. Having helped destroy the PLO in Lebanon, Syria was not much concerned with the fate of the Palestinians, except to use them for its own purposes. And Libya's Muammar Qaddafi believed himself to be a revolutionary leader and global figure. But how could he play a prominent role on the world stage as leader of a country with fewer than 4 million people? He sought to do so by making himself a champion of the Arab world and seeking the elimination of the state of Israel, as well as supporting other terrorist groups whose stated goals were radical. Obviously, Palestinian grievances were a genuine cause for some, but, even if the Palestinian problem were solved, the settlement would be unacceptable to many. Terrorism would continue against those who had accepted the settlement, as well as against Israel. Whatever the motives, the terrorists considered themselves "at war" with the United States, if not the West.

Personal ambitions, dedication to a higher cause, and hatred of the United States by certain leaders of specific countries are, then, key ingredients. But because Americans think of their fellow citizens who are kidnapped or killed as innocent bystanders, the other side of the coin—the role the United States plays in the world—needs to be examined. As a global power whose decisions and policies affect other governments, often unfavorably, the United States is deeply involved in the affairs of many nations. Given its enormous power and the fact that isolationism is not a genuine alternative, the United States has no other choice but to play this role. As Israel's close supporter, the United States is not seen as an innocent bystander when Israel invades Lebanon and destroys Beirut, or when the United States intervenes militarily in Lebanon's civil war. There are states and factions within states that strongly oppose U.S. policies and blame the United States—and, therefore, all Americans—for what happens to them. There are no "innocent" Americans in their eyes. As the weaker parties, they fight by any means they can, not by the "rules" of warfare. The terrorists do not see themselves as madmen, but as fighting back against an omnipresent and interventionist United States. This does not mean that the United States, or any other nation beset by terrorists, should not react, as it would with any other adversary state.

Reagan, who had been inaugurated as the first Iranian hostage crisis was ending, had long promised retaliation against terrorism waged on Americans. But as one attack after another occurred on American installations in Lebanon, no retaliation occurred. The United States managed to intercept the cruise ship hijackers in a flight over the Mediterranean. But the United States did not react militarily until the attacks on the airports in Vienna and Rome and a bomb blast in a West Berlin discotheque full of U.S. servicemen. According to U.S. intelligence, the Libyans were deeply involved in these terrorist incidents. It turned out later that the Syrians may have been responsible for the attacks, but the the United States struck Libya, not Syria, with its thousands of Soviet military advisers and ground-to-air missiles. Qaddafi, who had been a troublemaker for all his neighbors, was generally disliked by other Arab governments, and they probably would have quietly cheered his demise. After the United States sent aircraft carriers into international waters claimed by Libya, to which the Libyans responded by firing a few missiles, the United States launched a quick strike at Libya, which was followed by a larger attack, partly from carrier aircraft and partly from bombers based in England. The main target for some of these bombers was reportedly Qaddafi himself.

Apart from the British, no European government supported the attack. Even British public opinion was strongly against it, and there were demonstrations in many European cities against the United States. The main U.S. attack had occurred only after Washington had repeatedly sought to get its allies to act with it and impose economic sanctions on Libya, a country highly dependent on foreigners, mainly Europeans and Americans, for the operation of its oil fields and other industries. But the Europeans, fearful of negative economic consequences, had refused to go along. After the United States had acted unilaterally, and probably only to prevent another U.S. military act, the Europeans reduced the number of personnel in Libyan "people's bureaus" (embassies) and restricted their freedom to travel. Some months later, after an attempt to place a bomb aboard an Israeli airliner in London, the British government, convinced of Syrian involvement, broke relations with Syria. At that point the European governments agreed to an arms embargo and restrictions on Syrian diplomats. Ironically, at the very moment that a European consensus on terrorism was emerging, the Reagan administration was undermining its own position on terrorism and eroding its credibility in the conduct of foreign policy.

Iran Scores Again

Iran came to haunt the Reagan presidency as it had the Carter presidency. Carter had come to grief over fifty-two U.S. hostages held for more than a year in the embassy at Tehran; Reagan now came to grief over six U.S. hostages seized by Iranian-supported terrorists in Beirut. Claiming that the United States had wanted to deal with Iran because it was strategically important and that it would be beneficial to make contacts with "moderate" elements in the leadership before the question of Khomeini's successor was settled, the president—after a leak in a Middle East newspaper—admitted that he had sent arms shipments to Iran. He also stated that he wanted to try to end the six-year Iran-Iraq war, which, if won by Iran, the larger state, threatened to spread Islamic fundamentalism to the oil sheikdoms in the Persian Gulf and the Middle East.

It was a bizarre explanation that raised more questions than it answered. However persuasive the geopolitical rationale for approaching Iran might be, did it have to be accompanied by arms? How could giving arms to Tehran possibly help end the war? Why were negotiations not quietly conducted in some neutral country? Among the Khomeini loyalists, were there in fact moderates? Would not their contact with Robert McFarlane, Reagan's former national security assistant, expose these moderates, if they existed, and end their influence? Above all, how could the president square the shipment of arms with the U.S. arms embargo against Iran, his own consistently strong stand against terrorism, his efforts to mobilize allied support, Iran's earlier humiliation of the United States, and Iran's involvement in the attacks on the U.S. Embassy and annex in Beirut and the marine barracks?

It soon became clear that geopolitics was not the real reason for approaching Iran, but a convenient justification to cover the administration's embarrassment once it had been caught doing what it publicly and repeatedly had condemned other countries for doing. The U.S.-Iran opening was a straight arms-for-hostages deal. Ransom money even had been raised from a private source. Apparently, the deal was that all six hostages were to be released with the arrival of the first arms shipment. When none were freed, instead of calling the trade off, the administration made three further shipments. Each time, one hostage was released, making it obvious that, for all the president's denials, his motive had been to gain the release of the hostages. Moreover, by trading on a one-to-one basis, the administration was giving the terrorists an incentive to replace the freed captives, which is exactly what they did by kidnapping three others. All of this went on despite the opposition of the secretaries of state and defense, who were cut out of the decision-making process as a result. John Poindexter, the president's national security adviser, and his staff, usually a coordinating and advisory body, now played the key operational role, which it was not well equipped to handle.

Worse, however, was the fact that little consideration was given to how this would look if it became public and the damage it would inflict on the administration and on U.S. relations with its allies and moderate Arab governments. First, the United States would be exposed as hypocritical, as saying one thing but doing another and, in the process, ignoring its own arms embargo against Iran and the president's condemnation of Iran as an "outlaw state" run by "misfits, Looney Tunes, and squalid criminals." Second, the United States, having slowly mobilized allied support for some actions and sanctions against state-sponsored terrorism, undermined its credibility, and probably weakened the new allied resolve. Third, the United States shocked and dismayed its Arab friends, all deadly fearful of an Iranian victory over Iraq, which would endanger Egypt, Jordan, perhaps even Syria, and certainly the oil sheikdoms, including Saudi Arabia. This threat was real even though the Saudis, fearful of an Iranian victory, had made a number of accommodating moves toward Iran. But in 1987, after provoking a bloody riot in Mecca, Iran called for the overthrow of the Saudi regime.

While weakening the U.S. position in the Arab world, the United States had simultaneously helped raise Iran's prestige and influence. Worse, if Iran should win the war, it would virtually control the Persian Gulf with two-thirds of the world's known oil reserves, which would enhance its ability to eliminate U.S. influence from the Middle East. It was for these reasons that in 1987 the United States tried to recoup its influence by making a dangerous move in the Iran-Iraq war. Iraq had failed to achieve a victory after its 1979 attack on Iran, and the war had become a grim war of attrition. Given Iran's three-to-one superiority in men, it would ultimately wear down Iraq, which had superiority in arms. Iraq in 1984, therefore, attempted to bring the war to an end by attacking oil tankers doing business with Iran, as well as Iranian loading facilities, in an effort to shut off its oil exports and strangle Iran financially. In late 1986 Iran retaliated by attacking the tankers of Iraq's virtual ally, Kuwait, which contributed financially from its oil exports—together with Saudi Arabia and other sheikdoms—to Iraq. Moreover, Kuwait allowed its harbor to be used for transshipment of Soviet arms for Iraq. In the wake of Reagan's dealings with Iran, Kuwait appealed to the Soviet Union for protection of its tankers. Moscow agreed, whereupon the United States, which had also been asked but had not responded, said it would reflag eleven Kuwaiti tankers as U.S. ships and protect them. That an Arab state would ask Moscow to play a role in the Gulf, *the* geopolitical prize of the late twentieth century, may have been the most damaging result of the Reagan approach to Iran.

In fact, the United States, by trying to rebuild its influence with the oil kingdoms and moderate Arabs, and limit Soviet encroachment in the area, had involved itself in the war and had tilted toward Iraq. The danger to U.S. ships in the Gulf was real; an Iraqi pilot mistakenly launched two missiles at a U.S. frigate and killed thirty-seven men. Congress reacted strongly, recommending that the reflagging be postponed, if not canceled. What would the United States do if the Iranians attacked the tankers or U.S. naval escorts? And if the Iranians used their land-based short-range missiles to cut off the oil flow from the Gulf, would the United States retaliate by attacking the air bases or missile launchers? Would it strike preemptively rather than retaliate? How could U.S. ships be protected without air cover? Should the United States protect tankers without the help of the allies to whom most of this oil was being shipped?

As the Reagan administration hastily organized its escort services, the main question was whether it had thought through its intervention on behalf of Iraq better than its earlier intervention in Lebanon. This seemed particularly pertinent after the first escorted ship struck a mine. The U.S. Navy, in its concern with carriers and nuclear submarines, had neglected to build minesweepers, although it had helicopters that could deal with mines floating near or on the surface. Iran, with World War I technology, posed a threat to the safety of all the tankers and the high-technology U.S. warships. Britain and France, worried about their tankers and their deteriorating relationships with Iran, sent minesweepers. The U.S. action also had two other immediate and ironic results. A simultaneous, although perhaps only temporary, suspension of Iraqi air attacks on tankers doing business with Iran increased Iranian oil exports, thereby enabling Iran to buy more arms on the world arms market. The Soviets also benefited geopolitically as their relationship with Tehran became friendlier as the result of a number of economic agreements signed after the start of the U.S. naval escorting service, even though they had also assisted Kuwait.

The Contra Connection

The issue of the administration's competence, sense of judgment, and policy-making procedures had already become the central issue in the arms-for-hostages deal. Then it was revealed that profits from the arms sales to Iran had been placed in a secret Swiss bank account to fund the Nicaraguan contras during the period from late 1984 to 1986 when the Congress had expressly forbidden the use of U.S. funds for this purpose. In fact, in an end-run around Congress, the administration had shifted the conduct of the contra war from the Central Intelligence Agency (CIA) to the National Security Council (NSC) staff. But on the hostages and contras, McFarlane, a former marine colonel, and Vice Admiral Poindexter, both staff officers with neither a great deal of foreign policy experience nor competence, were not in charge. Both operations were really run by the CIA director William Casey and his point man on the NSC, Oliver North, a marine lieutenant colonel.

Referred to in the later congressional investigation as the only "five-star" lieutenant colonel in the U.S. military, North supervised the arms-for-hostages deal, during which he reportedly assumed presidential powers by telling the Iranians, among other things, that the United States would defend it against a Soviet invasion and committing the United States to depose Iraq's president! He also directed the raising of private funds for the contras through individuals, mainly people formerly involved with military intelligence, from tax-exempt organizations, and from wealthy U.S. citizens and foreign governments. Moreover, North commanded a vast network of arms dealers, ships, and airplanes to supply the contras, for whom he also provided tactical intelligence and advice on how to conduct the war. Although CIA agents, an ambassador, and other public officials were also enlisted to help in the various tasks, from fund raising to pressuring Central American governments to allow this network of what were in fact U.S. agents to operate in their countries, the total effort amounted to an attempt to "privatize" foreign policy.

The NSC became a "shadow government," which, in turn, organized a "private CIA" and a "private Treasury" to direct and fund the contra war effort. The U.S. Constitution, however, requires that foreign policy be made by the president and Congress in a publicly visible manner; nowhere does the Constitution sanction private groups to conduct the nation's policy. The State Department would not be needed any more or, for that matter, Congress, which in the American political system has the right to decide whether to support policy by appropriating the necessary funds to carry it out.

Although Reagan remained personally popular and the nation was not ready for another Watergate—the scandal over which Richard Nixon had been forced to resign—the violation of the presidential oath to "take care that the laws be faithfully executed" was raised again. The abuses of power this time were the selling of arms in violation of a law banning such sales to states that sponsor terrorism; the failure to notify Congress's intelligence committees of this covert operation; the diversion of funds from the sale to buy arms for the contras; and the private solicitation of money for the contras in the United States and abroad. Even the president had solicited funds from Saudi Arabia, which increased its monthly contribution from $1 million to $2 million right after its king had met with Reagan. The president also met with individual Americans who had contributed generously. When discovered, the NSC attempted a cover-up by constructing a false chronology of events to minimize the president's role in these events. Relevant documents were shredded. Throughout the operation, the administration kept any knowledge of what it was doing from Congress. Furthermore, as the story broke, the president first denied knowledge of many of the details of these events, making it appear as if McFarlane, Poindexter, and North who had spent most of their adult lives acting as links in chains of command, would suddenly and blatantly flout the law and take the foreign policy of the United States into their own hands.

Public opinion polls showed that most Americans thought Reagan was lying, and the congressional hearings made it plain that he was actively involved and informed, especially on the contras. He suddenly reversed gears and claimed that he knew everything except for the diversion of funds and that the congressional restrictions did not apply to him or his staff. When Congress had first forbidden military assistance, the administration had claimed repeatedly that it was obeying the law. Obviously, the secrecy with which the Iran and contra operations were carried out suggested that the administration knew very well that it was breaking the law. All the participants, once they were caught, claimed only to be acting for patriotic motives, but in several cases, the patriotism seemed well greased by private gain.

Poindexter testified that he had never informed Reagan of the diversion of funds, but he added that he had made that decision so that the president would—as often occurs in secret operations—be able to deny knowledge of what would be an explosive political event and embarrassment if revealed. North stated that he had offered himself as the fall guy if news of the operations ever leaked to the press and the public, but he was told by the CIA director that he might not be big enough and that Poindexter might have to play that role. Poindexter's apparent willingness to take the blame made the case that the president was lying all the more convincing.

Clearly, Reagan had damaged himself badly by this affair. He was, after all, the presidential candidate who had accused his predecessor of weakness in dealing with the Iranian hostage situation. He had consistently projected a image of toughness and confidence, and he had claimed that the nation could "stand tall" again. Many Americans shared this new sense of patriotism and regarded the president as the man who made them proud again and who could—and did—stand up to the Soviets. But Reagan had almost done the impossible by making Carter's hostage policy look good; Carter had not sent arms to Khomeini. Even the president's admirers and supporters were puzzled. The president's judgment and competence were particularly questioned after his Iceland meeting with Soviet leader Mikhail Gorbachev.

Presidential Incompetence

At the 1985 Geneva summit conference Reagan and Gorbachev had agreed that the 1986 and 1987 summits were to be held in Washington and Moscow, respectively. In 1986, however, Gorbachev refused to set a date; he said he would not come to a meeting unless there was progress on arms control. Reagan informed him that if no meeting were held by September, the mid-term election would postpone a conference until late November at the earliest. Gorbachev suddenly pressed for an October "pre-summit" to which Reagan agreed—only ten days before it was to take place in Iceland. This left little time for detailed preparation. The president assumed that the purpose of this meeting was to set a date for the Washington summit, to put the finishing touches on a European intermediate-range missile agreement, which had been arrived at after lengthy negotiations in Geneva, and perhaps to move toward the gradual cessation of all nuclear testing, which Moscow had repeatedly demanded. Because he had not checked what the agenda would be, Reagan was unprepared for the radical arms plans Gorbachev sprang on him. Gorbachev offered to accept Reagan's old plan to eliminate completely the Soviet SS-20s and the U.S. Pershing IIs and cruise missiles—the so-called zero-zero option; the previously mentioned 50 percent cut in Soviet and U.S. intercontinental missiles within five years; and the total elimination of all nuclear weapons in the next five years. Reagan initially agreed only to the elimination of missiles, but, when Gorbachev insisted on all nuclear weapons, the president quickly assented.

After Iceland, there was considerable confusion over what the president had undertaken because, although he did not deny that he had agreed to the abolition of all nuclear arms, the president now said that his position was that he went along with Gorbachev's proposal solely as a long-range aim. Nevertheless, it is astounding that in a weekend meeting the president could agree to such a radical proposal without consulting his own Joint Chiefs of Staff, the State Department, and U.S. allies. Had he simply said that he would consider the Soviet proposal and discuss it with the Soviet leader at their scheduled Washington summit, he would have had the time to consult and consider the consequences of his acceptance. For example, how could such an elimination of all nuclear weapons be verified? Would it not place a premium on cheating? The side that could hide a few missiles would be able to dictate terms to the side without any nuclear arms. And would the side most able to cheat not be the totalitarian rather than the open society? Because NATO for four decades had depended for its defense on the U.S. nuclear deterrent, would its abolition not destroy the alliance, given the Soviet Union's conventional superiority? How would NATO match the Soviet

Union and its allies' peacetime conventional superiority after all nuclear weapons had been destroyed? Would it not be extremely difficult to mobilize support in the Western democracies for a large-scale conventional rearmament in the midst of the euphoria accompanying nuclear disarmament, when they had not rearmed during more threatening times? Even if NATO were capable of raising such conventional forces to match those of the Warsaw Treaty Organization, how long could a conventional deterrent, not backed up by the dreaded and destructive nuclear weapons, ensure the peace? Without a nuclear backup, conventional deterrence could not threaten the total destruction of the aggressor, the consequence which had so long deterred aggression.

Indeed, what was truly breathtaking in Reagan's quick acceptance of Gorbachev's ten-year timetable—despite the denials after the summit and the hasty retreat even from his own position of abolishing only offensive nuclear missiles—was the almost casual rejection of the fundamental assumption shared by other postwar presidents. That assumption was that nuclear deterrence was the best way to eliminate any Soviet temptation to risk war. Indeed, from the beginning of his administration, the president had energetically strengthened deterrence because of his fear that Moscow might otherwise be tempted to strike first. The fact that all of the Soviet proposals came to naught because Gorbachev tied them to a postponement of SDI deployment, the reaffirmation of the 1972 ABM treaty which forbade the testing of space-based exotic defense technologies, and the restriction for ten years of SDI research to the laboratory—which Reagan rejected with the assertion that this would "kill" SDI—did little to enhance Reagan's reputation as a negotiator and steward of the Western world's security.

As noted earlier, he had rejected the "grand compromise" of a 50 percent cut of Soviet and U.S. missiles for a delay of SDI. Now he was willing to eliminate all missiles, if not all strategic weapons, because he thought he could convince Gorbachev of the sincerity of his defensive intentions. The Soviets had publicized their fear that SDI would provide the back-up for a U.S. first strike; by endorsing the elimination of these weapons that could deliver such a strike, Reagan was trying to reassure the Soviet leader that SDI would not constitute a threat to Soviet security. Why deploy SDI at all in a missile-free world? asked Gorbachev. Reagan could only speak of the need for insurance against possible cheaters, even though that would hardly require the same exotic space-based defense system needed to protect the United States from thousands of incoming Soviet warheads. But the president was stubborn: he wanted the full-scale SDI he had proposed and he was willing to give up all U.S. offensive missiles in return.

At a minimum, the Iceland summit left Gorbachev with a major propaganda victory in which he appeared to be the spokesman for disarmament and a less dangerous world, and the president, stubbornly clinging to SDI to defend the United States against missiles that would be abolished, seemed to be the obstacle to the relaxation of international tensions and the elimination of weapons that might otherwise destroy humanity. No doubt Gorbachev had calculated that Reagan would be inflexible on his Star Wars vision because the president and the civilians in the Defense Department had been against arms control from the beginning. Therefore, Gorbachev felt safe offering his proposals, and the Iceland meeting may well have been a propaganda trap for the president.

In any event, the accumulation of all of these events in a matter of a few weeks kept in the public eye questions about the president and his administration's sense of judgment, competence, and policy-making procedures. The overall impression remained that the president did not understand that the key to Western security was the U.S. nuclear deterrent. The United States had deployed the triad of bombers, ICBMs, and SLBMs to defend against a Soviet first strike and to frustrate Soviet defense against U.S. retaliation. A triad also guarded against the possibility that if one or even two "legs" of the triad became vulnerable, the third would then still be able to retaliate fully and thus deter a Soviet strike. The nuclear submarines with their missiles were the most invulnerable part of the triad in the 1980s; they contributed the most to preserving the stability of the nuclear balance. But, in a weekend the president proposed to get rid of all U.S. missiles, including those that stabilized the balance, to protect what was still only an ongoing research program.

It would probably not be known until well into the twenty-first century whether such exotic technologies as lasers and particle beams were feasible for the type of space-based defense the president had in mind. Reagan was not a pacifist, but, in adopting the antinuclear stance of the Catholic and Methodist bishops in the United States and the Labour party in England, he was not only fortifying those who condemned nuclear deterrence as immoral and sought to delegitimate U.S. deterrent policy, but, in the view of many experts in both the United States and Europe, heedlessly endangering U.S. and NATO security.

The Iran-contra issue may have embarrassed the administration and hurt its credibility, but it did not affect the strategic balance. The Iceland summit could have been far more damaging to U.S. security interests. Reagan's rebuff of Gorbachev may have given the Soviets a propoganda advantage, but the president's effort to protect SDI not only blocked fruitful arms negotiations but luckily saved the United States from either dismantling its deterrent forces or signing agreements from which it would have had no choice but to withdraw later. In short, SDI's main service may have been to save the United States and its allies from Reagan's folly, as well as to expose the president's shallow knowledge of foreign policy and defense issues and his failure to think through the consequences of his proposals. In these respects, Iran and Iceland were alike.

The Third World: Democratic Capitalism, the 'Debt Bomb,' and OPEC's Decline

Despite the domestic troubles the administration got into in pursuing the Reagan Doctrine in Nicaragua and by trading arms for hostages with Iran, its general attitude toward the Third World was one of "benign neglect." It was involved in the Third World mainly because it saw the less-developed areas in terms of Soviet activities and the continuing superpower competition for influence. Revolutionary changes, seen as either Soviet-inspired or exploited, were opposed. The "globalist" viewpoint prevailed once more. But the administration's attitude was unsympathetic toward Third World demands for a new international economic order and complaints about Western capitalist exploitation, or "imperialism." It held a rather similar point of view of the world's poor as it did of the domestic poor; namely, that they were poor because they did not work hard enough. The less-developed countries (LDCs) should not look for Western "charity" to do for them what they would not do for themselves. From the beginning, the administration emphasized that the LDCs were responsible for their own welfare, just as it held individuals responsible for their personal welfare.

Instead of aid—of which the United States in 1979, the last Carter year, gave only 0.20 percent of its gross national product, which ranked it ahead of only Austria and Italy among all Western nations—the stress was on "the magic of the marketplace," private enterprise, investments, and international trade. Selling their goods in the huge American market was, Reagan emphasized, the best contribution the United States could make to the LDCs' economic progress. In 1980 non-OPEC countries earned $63 billion with their exports to the U.S. market, more than half of these nations' manufactured goods. An improvement of the American economy would presumably help them sell even more of their exports as the U.S. demand for their goods would rise. The administration could claim that the priority it had given to the U.S. economy was not only the best domestic course it could pursue, but also the best foreign policy for the Third World.

As it did with regard to the Soviet Union, the administration was quick to react to Third World complaints that their problems were not their own fault and assertions that the West owed them aid and technical assistance because of past and present exploitation. The administration considered these charges unfair and rejected them. It also attacked the Third World's preference for socialism as a system allegedly superior to capitalism for encouraging development. The administration not only argued that those less-developed nations most deeply involved in the present international economy were the best off, but also that it was the policies of the national governments of these self-styled Socialist states that were to blame for the lack of development. There was considerable evidence to support this contention, such as the conspicuous consumption and corruption among the governing elites, the long neglect of agriculture so that many of these nations could no longer feed themselves but had to import food, and the vast spending on military hardware. The administration therefore recommended a course of self-help by means of greater domestic austerity, high savings, and productive investments.

At Cancun, Mexico, in 1981 at a meeting of twenty-two developed and less-developed countries, including China and India, the LDCs tried to impress upon the U.S. president their situation and their needs. They urged that "global negotiations" between the rich and poor countries deal with problems such as the distribution of wealth, food, and energy. The president, however, continued to stress the virtues of democratic capitalism and the creation of new wealth rather than the redistribution of existing wealth. He also pointedly noted that the Soviet Union's absence from the conference was a tacit admission that it had nothing to contribute, despite its claim that the world's economic problems were the result of capitalism and all solutions lay with socialism. "Who's feeding whom?" Reagan asked. (The Soviets' response was that they had not cared to attend a meeting of the "civilized plunderers" and "the plundered.") The United States was taking a critical and adversary position and reminding the LDCs that the American experience had combined economic development, political freedom, and respect for human dignity.[5] This emphasis on private investment and trade, rather than government assistance, was the focus of the president's Caribbean Basin plan. The plan would help the non-Communist Caribbean and Central American nations combat further domestic radicalization by dealing with their social and economic problems.

The American decision not to accept Third World charges that their poverty was due to an exploitive Western-dominated international economy, or that the West was morally obligated to assist the LDCs by creating a new international economic order, spilled over into a general critique of their self-professed nonalignment. In October 1981 a delegation from ninety-three Third World nations issued a communiqué harshly criticizing the United States for stimulating the arms race (without mentioning the long Soviet buildup), not granting independence to Puerto Rico (even though in several elections its population had rejected this option), attempting to "destabilize" a number of Latin American countries, committing "aggression" against Libya by downing two of its planes when they attacked U.S. planes, and having a friendly attitude toward South Africa. By contrast, in mentioning Afghanistan and Cambodia, the communiqué referred only to the withdrawal of "foreign forces," not Soviet and Vietnamese forces. Jeane Kirkpatrick, the American delegate to the United Nations, thereupon asked the delegates of forty nations

---

5. The Reagan administration's attitudes toward the Third World are well expressed in Peter Berger's "Speaking to the Third World," *Commentary*, October 1981, 29-36.

to explain why, professing nonalignment, they had supported such a one-sided communiqué with its "base lies and malicious attacks" upon the United States. Asserting that she could not believe that these statements accurately reflected their governments' views, she asked what the United States was to think when they joined in such charges instead of dissociating themselves from them?

In 1983, at the conference of 101 nonaligned states, things were not very different. Although the conference mood was described as more moderate, the United States was denounced for "aggression" against Nicaragua. But the conference again refused to denounce the Soviet Union for its invasion of Afghanistan, a Third World country. Once again, the nonaligned states called for the withdrawal of "foreign forces," with no reference to the Vietnamese in Cambodia. Israel and South Africa were subjected to their by now routine denunciations. Nonalignment was certainly losing credibility—the 1979 conference had been held in Havana—as the movement embraced Communist states like Cuba and Vietnam, which, like the Soviet Union, boycotted the Olympic Games in 1984, and accused the United States of gross injustices but refused to accuse the Soviet Union. How seriously could these denunciations be taken when most of the Third World's non-Communist leaders do not represent democratic opinion and when many preserve their power with brutality and repression and are guilty of aggression? How seriously should their accusations be taken of white South African treatment of blacks or Israeli treatment of Palestinians, when not a word was said about human rights abuses by Third World states of their own or other citizens—for example, the cruel expulsion of more than 1 million aliens by Nigeria in 1983? In any event, as evidence of America's mood, the United States withdrew from the United Nations Educational, Scientific, and Cultural Organization (UNESCO) because it had become thoroughly politicized, and constantly attacked Western values, institutions, and interests.

The Reagan administration's vigorous defense of American policies and its unwillingness to acquiesce in what it regarded as unjustified and one-sided attacks were symptomatic of a new mood in America not to put up with such hypocrisy. Yet at the same time there could also be no doubt that the Third World was of increasing importance and concern to the United States. The developing countries had become a larger export market for the United States than Western Europe and Japan combined. The United States also depended on the LDCs for tin, natural rubber, bauxite, and other strategic materials besides oil. And, of course, prosperous developing nations were less likely to suffer domestic instability, which might threaten American security interests. Negatively, the enormous $600 billion debt of the LDCs at that time to Western banks also demonstrated the growing economic closeness of the First and Third Worlds. Of this amount, almost $400 billion was owed by Latin American states, most prominently by Brazil ($104 billion), Mexico ($98 billion), Argentina ($45 billion), and Venezuela ($38 billion). The fear was that one or more of these countries might refuse to pay its debt and bring down major Western, including American, banks.

The needs of the Third World could not be ignored. In the early 1980s, these countries suffered from the lowest nonoil commodity prices in thirty years. Their earnings were down because of the West's recession; so was Western aid. Their alternative was either to tighten their belts or continue their economic development. Western banks, holding huge amounts of "petrodollars" the oil-producers had deposited, were only too eager to lend that money and earn handsome profits. They did not worry too much about collateral, especially from oil-producing states like Mexico. The LDCs did not worry either; the high American inflation rate meant that they expected to repay the dollars borrowed with cheaper dollars in the future.

But the dollar rose sharply in value as not only commodity prices but also oil prices fell. This combination of existing debt and falling prices created a huge "debt bomb" whose explosion could hurt borrowers and lenders alike. Even to repay their annual interest on loans, the LDCs had to borrow more money, and Western banks had little choice but to extend further loans if they wished to avoid defaults. To receive new loans, however, the LDCs were required to balance their budgets and cut government spending, including the subsidies for all sorts of social programs. In countries with many poor, that led to rioting, strikes, and general social upheaval because many of the hard-earned benefits gained over the last four decades were wiped out. Increasingly, the idea of debt repudiation grew more attractive to the debtors as their standards of living fell and unemployment grew. Fear of losing their credit rating prevented this radical solution. Clearly it was in America's interest to do something, if only to save some banks from collapse and to stabilize the growing number of new and fragile Latin democracies, such as Argentina and Brazil, which were among the leading debtors. Moreover, assistance to the debtors ultimately would benefit the United States because it would enable these countries to buy U.S. goods and help the economy. The United States, therefore, shifted toward the position that economic growth was more likely to enable the Latin American countries to pay off their debts. More money was to be made available to them from not only commercial banks but the World Bank, and private enterprise and market-oriented policies were to be encouraged.

Whether this policy succeeds remains to be seen. What is clear, however, is that the debt crisis was part of the greater issue of the division of wealth between the rich and poor states and was not just a financial problem. It was also clear that the LDCs would have to rethink their ways of development. By the 1980s many of them were increasingly attracted to private enterprise as state-owned enterprises foundered. More basically, the LDCs increasingly questioned their earlier attitudes that profits and private markets, identified with capitalism, were selfish and exploitative while the public sector was selfless and oriented to improving everyone's lot. Socialism, as they had usually called their economic system, had proven disappointing, especially in comparison to the economic successes of Asian societies. Not just Japan, but other newly industrialized countries, such as Hong Kong, Singapore, South Korea, and Malaysia, had adopted free-market policies and were very export-oriented; that is, they were integrated into the international economy that so many LDCs held responsible for their continued lack of economic progress. By the latter part of the decade, therefore, the LDCs were less confrontational on aid, trade, and Third World development.

One other reason for the LDCs' chastened mood was the collapse of OPEC. OPEC's huge price escalation after the fall of the shah in 1979 proved its own undoing, for it led to genuine Western conservation of energy (in 1983, U.S. oil imports from the Gulf were down to less than 5 percent of total U.S. oil imports, Europe's to 25 percent, and Japan's to 50 percent). High oil prices also created a deep recession that idled many factories and workers, which lowered the market for OPEC oil even further. OPEC's policies encouraged an increase in the supply of non-OPEC oil (for example, from Mexico, Alaska, and the North Sea) and the use of alternate energy sources like coal. The result was an oil glut, and the real price paid for oil fell below the official price of $34 per barrel.

The only way OPEC could ensure its future as a cartel and regain control over oil prices was to cut production. But in general, the countries with larger populations, such as Nigeria, Iran, and Algeria, expected the less-populated Arab Persian Gulf countries to absorb most of the cuts. Presumably, these countries needed less money; Saudi Arabia was expected to accept the biggest cuts. But the cartel members had many conflicts with one another. Libya accused Saudi Arabia of betraying the Arab cause by being pro-American; Iraq was at war with Iran; and Iran, needing to finance the war, refused to accept its OPEC-set production levels. Given the members' conflicting national interests, OPEC found it impossible to control production. Even when OPEC finally agreed on new production levels and lowered the official price to $28 per barrel, its influence to keep that price up was in doubt. Its success depended on non-OPEC producers like Britain, Mexico, and the Soviet Union (the world's largest oil producer) not underselling OPEC and on OPEC members not seeking advantage at one another's expense. However, Britain refused to go along with an OPEC request for the non-OPEC oil producers to cut their production. Saudi Arabia, tired of losing revenues while its market share declined, decided to increase its production and regain its share of the world oil market. Oil prices plunged to below the 1973 level of $9 to $10 a barrel.

While this decline in oil prices was undoubtedly beneficial to economic growth, lower inflation, and interest rates in the oil-importing countries, it worsened the lot of oil-producers and debtors like Mexico and Nigeria. Many Westerners now enjoyed watching the OPEC members' misery as their revenues plunged. However, the drop in oil prices also halted oil exploration in the United States, hurting the economies of Texas, Louisiana, and Oklahoma, while increasing consumption. The danger was that in the not-too-distant future, this increased consumption would lead to another oil crisis as demand rose, a demand that only OPEC, still possessing the world's largest oil deposits, could satisfy—at higher prices. OPEC, seemingly on the ropes as an oil cartel, was not yet dead. By early 1987 oil prices had already recovered to $18, twice the mid-1986 level, and experts were predicting an energy crisis in the 1990s far worse than that of the 1970s. Whether U.S. policy in the Gulf might send oil prices sharply up before then remained to be seen.

But clearly, as the administration was coming to the close of its second term, the health of the American economy remained *the* critical issue confronting the nation. The United States, once the world's wealthiest nation, was the world's largest debtor. The nation it had defeated in 1945 had become the largest creditor. Despite the dollar's sharp fall since 1985, the trade gap between the United States and Japan showed no sign of closing, even with the boost of lower oil prices. An oil price increase could widen the gap even further. The United States had to become more competitive and export-minded. Yet cries for protectionism—a sure sign that other countries are now economically more proficient—were heard more frequently, and trade wars between allies and friends threatened to break out.

The failure to resolve the LDCs' debt problem was an additional reason for the sluggish American economy. In a way, the United States was becoming a less-developed country itself. Manufacturing of industrial products was being transferred to the low-wage workers of the Third World, who had also mastered the techniques of mass production. The U.S. economy was becoming a service economy; its main export, until that too suffered from competition, was agricultural staples. It depended increasingly on attracting foreign funds, especially Japanese and European, to cover its deficits. The United States is actively selling itself; Japanese investors, for example, bought $3 billion worth of real estate in 1986, twice the amount of 1985. Direct investment in American industry by all foreigners grew from $109 billion to $209 billion since 1982.[6] As the LDCs have long argued, the greater the share of a nation's production that is controlled by foreigners, the more dependent that nation becomes on foreign governments' decisions. The fundamental issue of economic health, its general competitiveness, especially in high technology, looms over the central issue of whether the United States can continue to meet ever-widening global obligations while its economic capability declines.

---

6. "What Can America Sell?" editorial in *New Republic,* May 25, 1987, 5.

Containment:
A Reappraisal

DURING the twentieth century the United States has been repeatedly compelled by the changing Eurasian distribution of power to emerge from its historically isolationist course. In both world wars Germany appeared likely to achieve dominance over continental Europe and threaten Britain, whose navy during the nineteenth century had guarded the Atlantic approaches to the Western Hemisphere. In 1917 Germany's submarine campaign against all shipping, including American vessels sailing to England, propelled the United States into the war. After Germany's defeat of France in 1940, the United States became engaged in a limited naval war with Germany in the Atlantic as the United States sent supplies to Britain to keep up its war effort. Had the Japanese not attacked Pearl Harbor in 1941, Germany sooner or later would have attacked American shipping again to bring Britain to its knees. War with Germany had become unavoidable, just as it had earlier in the century.

In short, the nature of the state system and the shifting balance between Germany and Britain left the United States little choice but to become involved in both wars. American leaders have long considered the dominance of Europe by any power that could mobilize Europe's population and resources to be a potential threat to American security. In neither 1917 nor 1941 did American leaders or the public *want* to go to war; the preference was to remain at peace. But as Germany appeared about to achieve a superiority of power and continental control, peace was no longer possible. This pattern was repeated after World War II as the Soviet Union, the heartland power, expanded into Eastern and Central Europe; exerted pressure southward toward Iran, Turkey, and Greece; and constituted a threat to postwar Europe. The repetitive nature of U.S. interventionism to protect the western rimlands of Eurasia in this century is very striking.

The Continuity of Containment

The need to balance Soviet power was first recognized by Britain. American recognition came more slowly and occurred only after Britain said it was no longer able to contain the Soviet Union; until then, the United States thought its primary function was to mediate what appeared to be only a Soviet-British conflict! Again, the American preference was to withdraw from international politics and to limit its role mainly to the Western Hemisphere and to participation in the United Nations. But the emergence of a bipolar world made that impossible as the Soviet Union, with a very large army and straddling Europe *and* Asia, was seen, like Germany before it, as a threat to American security.

The containment of Soviet power, therefore, became the centerpiece of postwar U.S. foreign policy. Note the expansion of America's territorial commitments. The initial commitment in Iran, Turkey, and Greece came as British power in the region declined. The major commitment to Western Europe followed the defeat of Germany and the exhaustion and collapse of all of the former European great powers, including Germany. The incorporation of South Korea in the U.S. defense perimeter in Asia occurred after North Korea invaded the South. Japan became an ally after Nationalist China's demise, and South Vietnam after France's defeat in 1954. Britain's withdrawal from Palestine in the late 1940s and the later collapse of the Iraqi monarchy led to U.S. involvement in the Middle East, which was extended to the Persian Gulf after Britain's withdrawal from territory east of Suez. Since 1979 domestic changes within El Salvador and Nicaragua have once more led the United States to pay attention to Central America and the Caribbean.

From the Truman Doctrine until the war in Vietnam, American foreign policy was based on certain widely accepted assumptions. One is that the central conflict in the world was between the Soviet-led Communist world (which after 1950 was seen as including Communist China) and the American-led "free world." Another assumption was that any Communist gain of influence was a loss of influence for America and its allies and friends. It was the task of the West to oppose such expansion, and, because the United States was the only Western country that had the requisite strength, it had to assume the role of containing the Soviet Union and its allies. When the cold war was replaced by *détente,* the new policy was essentially containment adapted to superpower strategic parity, the Sino-Soviet schism, and neo-isolationism in the United States. Given the conflict between the two leading Communist powers, American policy refocused on the stronger Soviet threat and moved closer to China, which was also interested in containing its large northern neighbor.

Détente as the continuation of containment by other means was based upon the recognition that, with its growth in military power, the Soviet Union constituted an even greater threat than before. Deterrence was not based on any illusions that the Soviet Union had been transformed into a *status quo* state. The aim was to persuade Moscow to act with greater restraint by providing an ever-changing mixture of carrots and sticks. *Détente* was intended to be a political strategy, a holding operation until the American people "recovered their nerve." While President Jimmy Carter sometimes appeared to believe that American-Soviet rivalry was a thing of the past, Zbigniew Brzezinski often tried to remind him that it still existed. The Soviets reminded Carter in no uncertain terms when they invaded Afghanistan. Thus, from Harry Truman to Ronald Reagan, American foreign policy has displayed a remarkable continuity, despite frequent changes of administration (Dwight Eisenhower was the last president until Reagan to serve two terms), changes of parties in power, and the erosion of the original cold war consensus. The U.S.-Soviet rivalry has become a fixture on the international scene, and there is no reason to believe it will disappear soon.

Since the Vietnam War, however, many former supporters of containment have become its strongest critics. Although American power was very great, they asserted, the United States was not omnipotent and therefore could not pursue global commitments. Policy makers had to rank carefully the external priorities and concentrate on these; this meant giving priority to Europe and Japan besides the Western Hemisphere. By being more selective in commitments, the United States could bring into balance the ends of policy and the means of its implementation. The Vietnam War was seen as a tragic product of an indiscriminate anticommunism that had led the nation to overextend itself. It also was seen as a chastening experience that should result in the reduction of American commitments, a greater concentration on urgent domestic problems, and a generally more sober and restrained international behavior. America was no longer to be "the world's policeman"; its future conduct should reflect its "limited power." A more discriminating policy would commit American strength only to the defense of its truly vital interests, not lesser concerns.

The Impact of the State System on Containment

These broad recommendations were useful reminders to policy makers, but had they in fact been ignored in the earlier conduct of foreign affairs? After four decades of containment, some observations about the policy can be made. The first is that American policy makers in the immediate postwar years were certainly aware of the nation's limited power and of the need to rank commitments in terms of priorities. This awareness was the basis for the Truman administration's decision to give priority to Europe, the cradle of the American heritage, the area where an imbalance of power had twice dragged the United States into total wars. This focus on Europe was the chief reason the United States did not intervene in any major way in the Chinese civil war between the Nationalists and the Communists. Although the United States furnished the Nationalists with some economic and military assistance, limits to its intervention were dictated by the resolve not to become militarily engaged. Similarly, in husbanding the nation's resources and trying to keep a balance between America's commitments and its "limited power," troops were withdrawn from South Korea. Continental Asia was strictly of secondary interest, and the American defense perimeter in the Pacific was publicly defined in terms of the island chain, including Japan, off the Asian coast. The Soviets and North Koreans apparently drew the logical conclusion that the United States had written off the Republic of Korea. Consequently, in June 1950 the North Korean army marched southward across the thirty-eighth parallel, and America was suddenly and unexpectedly engaged in its first "frontier war."

A second observation about the containment policy, however, is that, despite efforts to arrange American interests on a scale of priorities, the United States repeatedly became involved in places where it would have preferred not to become involved. Despite a nation's best intentions, commitments were not always determined by *a priori* selection but by contingencies and events over which even a great power had little or no control. Twice in the twentieth century the United States had become involved in world wars, although no commitment to defend France and Britain had existed. It had little choice on both occasions if it wished to guard its security.

A rather quick and painful postwar reminder of this lesson came in Korea when the United States decided to fight a "limited war" in defense of South Korea. American forces were committed not because the United States had a legal obligation to defend South Korea or because the southern half of the Korean peninsula was a strategic American interest, but because the political and psychological consequences of inaction were believed to affect the global balance. Specifically, the impact of not defending South Korea in a bipolar world would result in the neutralization of Japan and Europe. Suddenly, American security was recognized as very much involved in this area of secondary interest. Overnight, an area deliberately excluded from the defense perimeter because it did not seem vital, became a primary commitment. Had the United States made a prior commitment to help in case of attack and backed it with a few thousand troops, America might have deterred the Communist invasion and been spared a costly war. One need only compare Korea with the situation in Europe, including the divided city of Berlin, where the American presence and a defense commitment have kept the peace for more than forty years.

The post-Vietnam period reinforced this lesson about commitments. Despite the longing for relief from the active role it had played during the cold war and the desire to assume a lower profile on the international scene, America was affected, often deeply, by virtually all problems, whatever the origin, wherever they occurred, and whether the Soviets sought to exploit these issues. The United States stayed extensively involved in the state system. Indeed, by the 1980s it was even *more* extensively involved than during the days of the cold war and its most active days as global policeman. Many of these problems, as in southern Africa, the Horn of Africa, and especially the Persian Gulf area and Central America, not only held important consequences for the United States that might lead to commitments far beyond those of the Truman and Eisenhower doctrines of the 1940s and 1950s, but also they could not be easily isolated from the American-Soviet rivalry. Even before the shah's collapse in Iran and the Soviet invasion of Afghanistan, it had become clear that American and Western interests in oil required a commitment of American power in an area in which the United States had not previously been engaged. Again, it was not so much a question of what the United States wanted to do but of what it had to do. Ironically, Carter, who spoke constantly of America's "limited power," placed his name on the doctrine that formalized this new commitment and thereby extended America's policeman role to a new and dangerous area.

The 1980s have led the United States to a growing preoccupation with its own backyard because of Nicaragua, the Sandinistas' revolutionary character, and their ties to Cuba and the Soviet Union. American foreign policy has always assumed security in the Western Hemisphere; this was the precondition for the projection of American power across the Atlantic and Pacific oceans. The potential of an "Eastern Europe" on its doorstep expanded U.S. commitments even further. Indeed, it was not until the 1980s that the United States became a truly *global* power.

A third point about the containment policy is that this extensive American involvement was not due to any "arrogance of power" or desire to dominate the world or a quest for capitalist profits; rather, it was due to the postwar bipolar distribution of power. In a reevaluation of containment, it is worth stressing once more that a bipolar distribution of power is the most sensitive of all balances. In a bipolar balance, each power sees its adversary as its foe; for the opposing power is the only one who can hurt it and threaten its security. The balance is therefore continuously at stake, because each power fears that once the adversary has shifted the balance in its favor, the shift may be irreversible. For reasons of security, therefore, when one side sees the other push, it feels compelled to push back. A bipolar balance is consequently one of continuous confrontation, frequent crises, and occasional limited wars. Moves in areas of even secondary interest will be opposed because each power fears a domino effect; that is, if one of its allies, protégés, or satellites is allowed to fall, others will follow, and an accumulation of small losses of power—each one of which would by itself be tolerable—would add up to a major loss of power that would be intolerable.

The Korean War, the rise of Communist China, and the subsequent Chinese intervention in Korea as American armies advanced toward China's frontier, plus the Sino-Soviet alliance, reinforced this bipolar pattern: the Soviet Union and China, extending across most of Eurasia, versus the United States and the North Atlantic Treaty Organization (NATO) on the western rim of Eurasia and South Korea-Japan on the eastern rim. After the United States, the Soviet Union, and China accepted the division of Vietnam in 1954, the seventeenth parallel became part of the frontier drawn between the Communist bloc and the free world. When North Vietnam refused to accept this division of Vietnam and initiated the Second Indochina War, the United States felt obliged to defend it. The containment policy was applied in South Vietnam without any reassessment of whether it was a vital interest in the context of a Communist world that showed increasing signs of division. Nationalism was eroding the cohesion even among Communist countries that had claimed that their unity resulted from sharing a common ideology.

After Vietnam, the superpower rivalry continued, although for a while the United States was in no mood to respond to Soviet moves as frequently or vigorously as before. The Soviets quickly exploited this postwar weariness and mood of withdrawal by taking advantage of opportunities for expanding their influence. This, in turn, caused increasing American disillusionment with *détente,* which came to be widely viewed as a one-way street. Reagan was elected in part because of this disillusionment. His administration refocused American policy on opposition to the Soviet Union. Even in a world that is no longer strictly bipolar, American-Soviet competition remains the central preoccupation of U.S. foreign policy.

A fourth point about containment is that the bipolar distribution of power resulted in the militarization of containment. During its first few years, the policy was implemented mainly by economics. But the attack upon South Korea and the resulting fear that the Soviets might try something similar in Europe led to a vast American and Western rearmament. After Korea, the concept of deterrence as a drawing of frontier lines and a threat of major retaliation if these were crossed was extended from Europe to the Middle East and Asia. Because the rise of nationalism in these areas was frequently accompanied by anti-Western overtones, the alliances formed to support such lines proved relatively useless as containers. They caused a great deal of turmoil among the nations of these regions, frequently drew the United States into their quarrels, and led the United States to support some rather despotic regimes in the name of defending freedom.

The emphasis on drawing lines of containment by establishing military alliances—multilateral partnerships such as the Southeast Asia Treaty Organization (SEATO), the Central Treaty Organization (CENTO), and NATO, as well as bilateral agreements between the United States and Japan or the United States and Taiwan—largely reflected the bipolar division of power. Given the great sensitivity of the superpowers to any changes in the balance, especially by the United States, which saw itself as essentially on the defense against Soviet (and for a while, Chinese) expansionism, the essence of the cold war was the delineation of "frontiers" to mark off the respective American and Soviet spheres of influence, and then the defense of the resulting territorial *status quo.*

In short, each superpower formed alliances primarily as a means of defining the areas of vital interest to it and communicating this information to its adversary in order to deter an attack. Each superpower was determined to maintain the cohesiveness of its alliances and to prevent defections, even if that required military or covert intervention. Perhaps most symptomatic of the bipolar rivalry was an intense arms competition spurred by the fear that, with rapid changes in the technology of modern weapons, the opponent might achieve a technological breakthrough that it would then exploit to gain a perhaps irreversible superiority of power. A bipolar balance is particularly sensitive to any changes of military power.

A fifth point about containment is that a gap exists between operational or actual policy and declared policy with its rhetoric of universal anti-communism. By and large—certainly in the early cold war years—anticommunism was less a motive for American foreign policy than a tool used by American leaders for mobilizing public support. The United States traditionally has been an inwardly oriented society. This is not accidental; quite apart from the self-absorbing tasks of westward expansion and modernization, the United States is based on a political system in which the people vote and those elected must be responsive to mass preference. The system concentrates upon domestic affairs and welfare issues rather than on a burdensome, costly, and distracting foreign policy. To arouse the public to support external ventures, the struggle for power and security inherent in the state system had to be disguised to appear as a struggle for the realization of the highest values. From the beginning of its existence, the United States has felt itself to be a post-European society—a New World standing as a shining example of democracy, freedom, and social justice for the Old World.

Anticommunism fitted beautifully into this traditional dichotomy. America could practice *Realpolitik* as long as it could be disguised as *Idealpolitik,* which suited its national style of conducting foreign policy. Power politics needed ideological justification in a nation that had always felt that the use of power internationally was evil. Domestically, power was legitimated by the democratic purposes for which it was used; externally, its employment had to be justified in the same terms. The conflict between the United States as a democracy and the Soviet Union, a totalitarian threat, fitted perfectly the American penchant for explaining international politics as a moral struggle between good and evil. Unfortunately, while anticommunism provided an easily understandable public explanation for the U.S. postwar international role, it also had profoundly negative effects on the conduct of that role.

The Persistent Influence of National Style

A final point can be made about containment: although the United States was basically concerned with maintaining the balance of power and behaved as other great powers had done in the past, its role was shaped not only by the state system but also by the American national style. An anti-Communist crusade may have been intended primarily to arouse the public and to mobilize popular support for cold war policies while the nation in fact pursued more limited aims. However, once an administration had justified its policy in terms of an anti-Communist crusade and aroused the public by promising to stop communism, it opened itself to attacks by the opposition party in case of setbacks, even if they occurred for reasons beyond America's ability to prevent them. The out-party could then exploit such foreign policy issues by accusing the in-party of "appeasement," of having "lost" this or that country, and of being "soft on communism." This sort of accusation made it difficult to recognize Communist China, to build bridges to Eastern Europe, to negotiate with the Soviet Union, and especially to discriminate between areas of vital and secondary interest to U.S. security.

Democratic administrations were more deeply affected by this political rhetoric than Republican administrations. The Democrats were in power when Nationalist China collapsed; the Democrats were accused of "treason," of "selling out" China, and they lost the 1952 presidential election as a result. The desire to avoid accusations of being soft on communism had pushed Truman to advance northward across the thirty-eighth parallel before the 1950 midterm elections and made it impossible for him to negotiate any settlement of the war that would leave Korea divided. The wish to avoid similar accusations made it impossible for John Kennedy, who had campaigned on a tough anti-Castro platform, to reject the Eisenhower-initiated plan to invade Cuba, even though the new president had serious qualms about it. It led the Kennedy and Johnson administrations to make their piecemeal commitments in Vietnam, lest the Democrats be charged with the "loss of Indochina" as well as China, and it influenced Lyndon Johnson to bomb North Vietnam and to escalate the war by sending in the army. Finally, it persuaded Johnson to land troops in the Dominican Republic to prevent "another Cuba" from being established.

These examples illustrate the high price the United States consistently paid for the need to moralize power politics: overreaction, diplomatic rigidity, and overt or covert interventions that it might otherwise never have launched. National style was a principal cause for the long delay in recognizing Communist China and the failure to exploit Sino-Soviet differences. Worse, it was the main reason for misunderstanding the nature of Asian communism, including the character of the war in Vietnam. It was certainly a key reason, if not *the* reason, for the subsequent intervention. Because the domestic costs of losing a country to communism were so high, those in power felt compelled to intervene with the Central Intelligence Agency (CIA), marines, or army to avoid such losses. The desire to avoid accusations of appeasement, of betraying the nation's honor, of weakening its security was keenly felt. The domestic costs of intervention appeared far smaller than the domestic costs of nonintervention. This was especially true just before elections, and there was always an election coming up.

These costs should not be underestimated. The president would lose prestige; in turn, this loss would affect his ability to gain support for the rest of his foreign, as well as domestic, policies. He would be vulnerable to congressional attacks, and his entire program for the nation, abroad and at home, would be jeopardized. Far more than the president's personal reputation, his ability to be reelected, and his party's electoral future were at stake, although these were not minor concerns. The basic rule of domestic politics during the cold war years, therefore, was to avoid what appeared as major losses to communism overseas.

Conservative Republican administrations were less vulnerable to such attacks. Eisenhower was the first president during the cold war to meet the Soviet leaders. He signed the same peace agreement in Korea that Truman could not. Eisenhower did not feel compelled to intervene in Indochina in 1954 and, although he supported the regime of Ngo Dinh Diem in Saigon, he carefully limited U.S. support. Richard Nixon could do what a rational foreign policy would have done years earlier—seek a reconciliation with China and try to exploit the Sino-Soviet schism. Neither Republican president could be accused of being soft on communism; their credentials as strong anti-Communists were above reproach. They were "hawks," not "fuzzy-minded liberals." Reagan did not follow in the footsteps of his Republican predecessors because he perceived the necessity of rebuilding American military strength before negotiating seriously with the Soviet Union. He also was more skeptical about arms control, and his commitment to SDI blocked fruitful results. But as he moved closer to a major agreement with the Soviet Union on medium- and shorter-range missiles, he could hardly be charged with betraying U.S. security, even if some critics expressed concern over verification procedures.

The main point is that liberal Democratic administrations before the war in Vietnam tended to be more interventionist and to take a harder line in policy toward the Communist bloc (with the exception of Yugoslavia) than Republican administrations. But many liberal Democrats were so badly burned by the war in Vietnam that they turned away from intervention, finding few vital American interests outside of Western Europe that might require the threat or use of American military forces or covert intervention. Their ideal president, ironically, was Eisenhower. In the 1950s liberal Democrats had denounced him as a lazy and mediocre president who had not been vigorous enough in the world; now they praised him for his moderation, his reluctance to intervene, and his careful calculation of the national interest.

Eisenhower's forbearance in Indochina and in Quemoy and Matsu on two occasions, his refusal to escalate the Berlin crisis after 1958 or to be panicked into a new arms race after Sputnik and the first Soviet ICBM test, became the very incarnation of wise American policy for liberals.

National style was also evident in the continuity of American moralism in foreign policy and the reappearance of the pendulum-like swings from pre-cold war isolationism to crusading and back again. After years of cold war interventionism, these swings showed up as a desire for a lower American profile in the world. Indeed, it was widely asserted during the 1970s that "the cold war was over"; *détente* was often understood publicly as its opposite state. The cold war was a condition of conflict and confrontation, *détente* one of peace and negotiation. This was typical of America's national style with its view of the world in either-or terms: war or peace, force or diplomacy, harmony or conflict. All of this was attended by the guilt and shame America has felt when it thought its power was being abused and misused. Historically it was thought that, because power politics is morally bad, the best course is to abstain from using it; but once used, it can be justified only by the nobility of the purposes pursued. The total destruction of the antidemocratic regimes in two world wars was seen as a worthy goal. The United States was making "the world safe for democracy." American power had to be righteous power.

But America intervened in Vietnam on the side of an undemocratic regime, and the conduct of war, particularly the massive bombing, was for many Americans morally ambiguous, if not downright immoral. Self-accusation followed. The nation was pictured as an evil country whose policies were wicked; it had not just gone astray or made a tragic mistake, which could be corrected. The idea that the United States was a force for good in the world was replaced by disillusionment and cynicism. Soon the United States was blamed for any evil anywhere in the world. It was viewed as responsible for right-wing regimes in the Third World, which were supported in the name of anticommunism, overthrowing Allende in Chile, bringing into power the Cambodian Communists. The United States was held accountable for the maintenance of apartheid in South Africa because of a lack of U.S. political and economic pressure on its white government.

The best course for the United States, therefore, was to withdraw from the international scene, renew and purify itself by concentrating on its domestic affairs, and build a fully free and socially just society whose example would radiate throughout the world. Power politics would be replaced by social politics; America's foreign policy would be its domestic policy. In the words of a former chairman of the Senate Foreign Relations Committee, America should "serve as an example of democracy to the world" and play its role in the world "not in its capacity as a *power* but in its capacity as a *society.*" [1] Virtue, not power, would be the hallmark of American foreign policy;

---

1. J. William Fulbright, *The Arrogance of Power* (New York: Vintage Books, 1967), 256.

other nations would be attracted to the United States by the merit of its principles, not by its superior strength.

Expressions of the priority of domestic policy and abstinence from international politics were symptoms of the nostalgia for the old isolationism. "Come home, America" was a slogan that expressed the longing of millions. The consequences were restraints imposed upon the presidency and the CIA, the chief arms of overt and covert U.S. intervention, and the cutbacks of military budgets as a percentage of the gross national product to pre-Korean War (1950) levels at a time of unprecedented Soviet spending on arms of all kinds. These measures were clear evidence of this anti-national security mood. They were intended to assure America's lesser role in the world, one limited basically to the defense of the democracies in Europe and Japan and security in the Western Hemisphere. Revisionist histories, in the meantime, stressed that the cold war was largely the fault of a U.S. policy to which Joseph Stalin, whose aims were only limited, defensive, and legitimate, had reacted in fear. If America, then, reduced its international role, the world would be a more peaceful place. America was the problem, not the Soviet Union. Restraint of the United States, not the containment of communism, was the chief task.

In these circumstances of neo-isolationism, self-blame, and self-flagellation, the United States was again stirred up by its enemies. Just as Stalin's seizure of Czechoslovakia and the Berlin blockade had provoked the United States in the late 1940s, so Iranian and Soviet actions in late 1979 angered and aroused public opinion once more. The retrenchment of American power, the failure of the United States to act like a superpower in defense of its vital security and economic interests, the obvious revulsion many Americans felt about the past employment of American power, and the hesitation and reluctance they betrayed in using power in the post-Vietnam period—these attitudes were visible to the entire world. Instead of praising America for its restraint, many states—allies and adversaries alike—criticized it for a loss of a will to act. Not only a superpower such as the Soviet Union but a relatively minor state such as Iran felt that in these circumstances it could act with impunity even if it hurt and insulted American interests.

National impotence was bound to lead to national humiliation. If the lesson of Vietnam was no more interventions, the lesson of Iran was no more being pushed around while we flounder helplessly. That was the mood of the country when it elected Reagan instead of reelecting Carter, a late convert who had for most of his term reflected the earlier passivity and guilt, as well as the hopes for a new post-power politics world in which the nation-state, national egotism, security and power considerations, and the use of force would play a lesser role, if not be replaced by a more beneficient world order. Still, even with Reagan at the helm, the nation continued to sway somewhere between the post-Vietnam and post-Iranian moods—between Grenada on the one hand and Lebanon and Nicaragua on the other.

In terms of using force in support of U.S. foreign policy, Grenada appeared to be the model for the future. During his years in office, Reagan had resorted to force several times, but always against minor opponents such as Grenada and Libya. The president was always careful not to take on any serious adversary. Syria was more involved in terrorist attacks against American targets than Libya, but the president refused to retaliate against Syria, even after the bomb attack on the marine compound in Lebanon. Syria was a small country but well armed with sophisticated Soviet arms; American casualties would have been greater than against Libya. A brief clash with Syrian forces in Lebanon had led to the loss of two planes. And using the U.S. military to overthrow the Sandinistas, it was felt, would run into strong domestic opposition. Clearly, the mood of the country was to use force, but only if it appeared in advance that its use would be effective, quick, and relatively free of cost.

Long-term involvement without a promise of a favorable result was out. "Let's get in, win, and get out" was the attitude. Grenada was the ideal situation because American strength was overwhelming. The United States not only could not lose, but also it won in a few days, suffered few casualties, and shortly thereafter withdrew its troops and left in place a freely elected government.

Johnson had set the precedent in 1965 in the Dominican Republic by intervening with the marines, holding elections, and then withdrawing. The facetious question was how more enemy-held small islands were there for the United States to invade. The serious question was whether the United States could use force in other circumstances if that were necessary. Were there any objectives in the Persian Gulf or elsewhere that the American public and Congress could still agree on that were of sufficient importance to resort to force, even if the opponent—such as Iran—were more formidable than Grenada?

The fact that Reagan could say that Nicaragua was a threat to U.S. security and yet promise not to send U.S. forces—and resort instead to clandestine means and a covert war against the Sandinistas—was a symptom of the U.S. reluctance to use force in situations where the fighting might be prolonged and costly. It may well be argued that in the post-Vietnam era the United States must be more selective about where to intervene and must persuade Congress and the public that vital interests are at stake. But it is also true that, despite the restraints placed by Congress on U.S. military help for the Salvadoran government in the fight against Marxist guerrillas and the contras in their war against the Sandinistas, the Reagan administration did *less* than its predecessors. This has been overlooked in the revelations of the Iran-contra affair. However scandalous and illegal that was, and whether opposing the Sandinistas was wise or not, Reagan's action pales beside Eisenhower's in Guatemala, Kennedy's at the Bay of Pigs, and Johnson's in the Dominican Republic.

The Future of the U.S.-Soviet Struggle

In the 1980s the containment policy continues, although in a much more complex world than during cold war I. For one thing, the American-Soviet relationship has become what might be called an "adversary partnership." The competitive and conflictual nature of the relationship is clear. The growth of Soviet military power has intensified this rivalry because it has been accompanied by a more assertive Soviet foreign policy. In cold war I, the United States held strategic superiority, naval supremacy, and an ability to apply U.S. power rapidly in almost every area of the world. The Soviet Union, whose superiority was long limited to conventional, land-based forces, which held America's European allies hostage while it built up its intercontinental strategic forces, therefore had to act with great caution. Essentially, until the 1970s the Soviet Union remained a Eurasian power whose challenges were low-risk operations. The Soviet Union might probe, but if it met effective counteraction, it would desist. Above all else, it wished to avoid a conflict with the United States that might escalate, endangering the Soviet Union's survival.

But after 1975 the Soviet Union began to exploit opportunities for expanding its influence. There are two reasons for this shift in Soviet policy, and they occurred almost simultaneously. One was the achievement of strategic parity and the modernization of large conventional forces, including an airlift and sealift capability that gave Moscow the ability to project its power beyond Eurasia. The Soviet leadership saw its growth in military power as part of a shift in what it calls the "correlation of forces" from West to East. Soviet military strength would now allow Moscow to exploit opportunities it saw in the Third World to weaken the West while simultaneously deterring any U.S. military countermove. Moscow in the 1970s was particularly optimistic that Third World radicalism was on the rise and that it could win new allies. Because these would be Marxist regimes, Soviet gains would be irreversible and cumulative. Convinced that the United States was a declining power, Moscow also calculated that the United States had no choice but to adjust to these new circumstances and accept the consequences.

The other was America's post-Vietnam mood of isolationism; Americans looked very hard and skeptically at any interventions beyond the nation's borders. Even in the 1980s, after U.S. activism had been revived and the U.S. military buildup was proceeding, the constraints on policy remained in place. The loss of strategic superiority; the passing of U.S. economic primacy and leverage; increasing doubts about the deterrence extended to Western Europe; the growth of antinuclear peace movements in all Western democracies; and growing domestic and international economic difficulties, ranging from inflation and unemployment to budget deficits and trade imbalances—all these problems had a profound effect on U.S. policy.

The Soviet Union too was confronted with constraints because of several problems of its own: ideological disillusionment at home and the Soviet Union's lack of appeal as a model to the rest of the world, including other Communist states; the growing minority status of the Russians who, as the majority ethnic group historically, have always controlled Russia, czarist or Soviet; and the economy. Economic growth rates, already declining, were falling even further as agricultural and nonmilitary industrial production continued to face problems resulting from too much centralization, too much bureaucratization, too little high technology, a declining incoming labor force, and a general lack of worker productivity (not helped much by high rates of absenteeism and alcoholism). One especially critical problem is that if the Soviet government continues its large-scale investment in military production, it could jeopardize the small increases in the standard of living the Soviet people had come to expect, thereby increasing social tensions. The Soviet Union is too top-heavy for its economy, with too many bureaucrats. The irony is that after seventy years of communism, the Soviet Union faces a crisis that Karl Marx predicted for capitalist states: the economic base is in conflict with its political-social "superstructure" or political order.

Unless there are major structural reforms in the Soviet economy, as in Communist China, with greater recognition of market forces and private incentives and initiative, the economy will continue to fall behind not only the West, including Japan, but also states such as South Korea and Singapore. Star Wars research may increase the technological and scientific gap. Despite Soviet leader Mikhail Gorbachev's entreaties and reform efforts, the party, military, secret police, and economic planners all have a strong vested interest in the *status quo*. They fear change because it threatens their jobs and privileges; the party is especially concerned that decentralization and more autonomy for factory managers will threaten its monopoly of political power. Moreover, these elements fear that *any* loosening of central controls would be harmful, if not fateful. The Russian portion of the population, which controls the levers of power, is particularly fearful that such a devolution of power from Moscow would result in greater political self-determination to the non-Russian nationalities. Economic decentralization might spill over into political decentralization. In other words, the fundamental structural reforms the Soviet Union needs might threaten Moscow's imperial control over its own vast country. Quite contrary to Marxist analysis, then, the political substructure determines the fate of the economy rather than the other way around; the political system is the greatest obstacle to economic modernization.

This situation confronts the Soviet leadership with a genuine dilemma. Can it risk basic reform and yet not lose control over the consequences (assuming it can get the various bureaucracies to go along)? It really has no choice, if only because without reforms the Soviet Union cannot sustain its superpower status and enhance its global role. Gorbachev's leadership is intimately tied to the success of the Soviet economy *and* success in Soviet foreign policy. The Soviet Union has achieved a superpower status and equality with the United States; it belongs to a club of two. It is proud of that achievement, and no Soviet leader who would cut back, let alone abandon, that status could survive. All these considerations suggest that the Soviet leadership will require a prolonged period of *détente* and arms control agreements to have time to carry out its domestic changes and to shift resources from the military to the civilian sector, as well as to attract Western trade, technology, and credits.

There is, however, an opposite thesis—held by Henry Kissinger, Alexander Haig, and Brzezinski—that Soviet weaknesses, domestic and foreign, will not constrain Soviet foreign policy, but impel it to further expansion. A principal reason that internal decline will lead to future foreign policy adventures is that any leadership must justify its rule, even one that holds a monopoly of power and crushes dissent. How can the Soviet Communist party, which has for decades promised to create a better life for its citizens, continue to legitimate its power as domestic problems grow? The party had long done so by claiming that foreign enemies surround the Soviet Union. A "garrison state" cannot justify itself unless it invents enemies who are laying siege to it. Nevertheless, to the extent that it fails to deliver on its domestic promises, the regime's sense of legitimacy becomes even more insecure, reinforcing the need for ideological conformity and a foreign enemy.

The danger, therefore, is not that the Soviet Union will grant priority to economic modernization over its global ambitions. The danger is that its internal decline may produce pressure for external expansion, substituting Soviet greatness for an unsuccessful domestic system and providing a cover for the painful and risky process of internal change. Given the contrast between the Soviet Union's bankruptcy of official ideology, a stagnating economy, and potentially divisive nationality problem and enormous military strength, the Soviets may not be able to resist the temptation to use the one instrument the leadership has in abundance. Soviet leadership, after all, confronts not just serious domestic problems; it also faces an unstable political situation in Eastern Europe and the continued enmity of Communist China, whose willingness to restructure its economy stands in strong contrast to that of the Soviet Union.

The Soviet leadership, therefore, might be attracted to the idea of uniting the nation and mobilizing popular support by extending Soviet influence in the world. In 1914 *czarist* Russia had, along with Austria-Hungary and Germany, attempted to "export domestic dissatisfaction" and unify their people by following highly nationalistic policies. This had helped precipitate World War I. Observers were concerned that the Soviet Union's domestic weaknesses and problems with its Eastern bloc allies might similarly aggravate the international situation and entice it to resort to its formidable military forces. Moscow no longer emphasizes, as it did in the past, the defense of the motherland and Eastern Europe; rather, it emphasizes the development of forces capable of engaging the United States anywhere in the world. The new surface navy, has become the symbol of the Soviet Union's new global reach and status; the building of three large new aircraft carriers for this navy gives the Soviet Union an extra dimension to fulfill its global ambitions.

Whatever the validity of this "internal decay, external expansion" thesis, a number of things are clear from the experiences of the 1970s and 1980s. First, as already noted, the newly acquired Soviet conventional military capabilities have allowed the Soviet Union within the context of strategic parity to project its power beyond Eurasia as a means of extending its influence and as a low-risk, low-cost policy of chipping away at U.S. power and prestige. Moscow has intervened repeatedly to protect its friends from defeat and to produce political results that benefited them as well as itself. Large-scale "proxy interventions," such as in Angola, Ethiopia, and South Yemen, had not been possible before. Second, the Soviet Union was willing to use force. The invasion of Afghanistan by the Red Army was Moscow's first direct use of force outside of Eastern Europe and the first in a Third World country. The Soviet Union more often used military advisers, arms transfers, treaties of friendship, and proxies, ranging from Cuban soldiers to East German policemen.

Third, the Soviet Union has been willing to increase its commitments to regimes like those in Angola and Nicaragua when, during the Reagan years, the United States supported anti-Marxist guerrillas. In the 1980s Moscow may not be looking for new client states, as it did in the 1970s, because of the economic drain they place on the Soviet Union, the number of Soviet advisers and Cuban troops engaged in counterinsurgency operations, and the effects of more proxy interventions on Soviet-U.S. relations. It may also have been simply a matter of not finding sufficiently attractive opportunities. Whatever the reasons, however, it was determined not to abandon its old friends when they came under attack. Fourth, in the process of enhancing its influence and exploiting opportunities to do so, the Soviet Union has acquired a number of regionally active and powerful clients: Cuba and Nicaragua in Central America, Vietnam in East Asia, and, to some degree, Syria and Libya in the Middle East. These states are less satellites than partners who have interests that often coincide with Moscow's. They are also economically and militarily dependent upon the Soviet Union.

Fifth, the Soviet Union responds less to American expressions of good will and appeals for restraint than to firmness. It respects power as much as it harbors contempt for weakness or the failure or unwillingness to exercise power effectively. It did not hesitate to exploit America's isolationist mood in the 1970s. This last point was a lesson that every U.S. administration has had to learn in its turn; namely, that expectations of unilateral Soviet restraint are bound to be disappointed. After almost half a century the United States has not yet really learned that a state, which has sought security in expansion, will not restrain itself unless confronted with determined opposition.

As American forces were shifted from Europe to the Far East after Germany's defeat and were demobilized after Japan's defeat, the Soviets consolidated their hold on Eastern Europe and began to probe for soft spots from Iran to Western Europe. Eisenhower's efforts to reduce tensions with the new post-Stalin leadership at a summit conference in 1955 were followed shortly by the Soviet arms deal with Egypt, the prelude to the 1956 Suez War. Similarly, a year after the celebration of *détente* at the 1972 summit, Moscow shipped to Egypt and Syria the arms needed to launch their 1973 war and then encouraged the other Arab states to help them. It approved the subsequent Arab oil boycott of the United States and counseled against its lifting in 1974. A few years later, with an administration in power that stated that the cold war was over and that it wished to improve American-Soviet relations, the Soviets intervened in the Third World, even though they knew that the cost might be the SALT II agreement, which they wanted. Throughout the 1970s the Soviet military buildup went on without interruption, despite American restraint. Defending its Third World friends and seeking new opportunities to expand its influence in the Third World were more important to Moscow than cooperation with the United States to prevent dangers arising from regional conflicts or to enhance *détente*.

Military strength alone was not enough to deter Soviet probes for weak spots into which to expand its influence. America's atomic monopoly did not suffice in 1945. Moscow showed restraint only when faced with determined opposition. American power, economic as well as military, had to be linked to a will to use that power. The pattern has been clear since the Soviet attempt in Iran at the end of World War II. Weakness invites challenges; strength deters them and leads to their being called off. The fact that almost every administration has had to relearn this elementary lesson testifies to America's continuing optimism that if only it could demonstrate its sincerity and desire for peace and friendship, the Soviet Union would reciprocate.

Characteristic of its approach to foreign policy, the United States continues to place its faith in change, which will be for the better. Despite repeated instances of ruthless behavior that shock Americans—the shooting down of the South Korean airliner, the treatment of dissidents within the Soviet Union, or the invasion of Afghanistan, for example—the hope remains that the Soviet Union, like a bad boy, will be redeemed. The belief is strong that a "liberalization" or transformation of Soviet society will occur with each change of political leadership, attempt at domestic reform, or faltering of the economy, which, it is hoped, will distract Soviet attention from its foreign policy goals. Indeed, this expectation is often aided by the wishful thinking of those in the United States who justify Soviet behavior by American words or deeds. It is the United States that has somehow provoked Moscow by its "cold war acts" or "tough language." If the United States changed its attitude toward the Soviet Union, tensions would subside and a more cooperative and peaceful relationship emerge. Peace is the normal condition in the American outlook; conflict is abnormal. That the Soviet leaders continue to regard the United States as the enemy is unacceptable; it is preferable to believe that given their history they misunderstand the United States and that U.S. policy reinforces rather than reduces their misperceptions.

Nevertheless, the critical task of American foreign policy since 1945 has been to communicate clearly to the Soviet leadership the limits beyond which Soviet efforts to expand would be resisted. And, ironically enough, Moscow has been more comfortable with American administrations that have drawn these lines than with those that have left their intentions uncertain. With the more forthright administrations, the Soviet Union has been willing to exercise restraint and arrive at major accommodations; with the less direct administrations it has been tempted to probe, which has often resulted in an increase of tensions. The problem is that the Soviet Union cannot resist the temptation to exploit opportunities. The chief aim of the United States, therefore, is foreclosing such opportunities. A militarily powerful Soviet Union will continue to challenge American interests, values, and policies in a protracted rivalry that can be resolved neither by one quick military blow nor by one dramatic act of reconciliation.

Yet, the two superpowers share a common interest in avoiding a nuclear holocaust. Arms control negotiations have reflected this desire in the past. More specifically, the two countries shared an interest in stabilizing the strategic balance, preventing or slowing down further nuclear proliferation, improving crisis management, and, on occasion, cooperating in certain regions to avoid a superpower clash. Every postwar American president before Reagan has been an arms control president. Each has felt the awesome responsibility of the enormous power he controlled, that he could literally destroy the world at the push of a button. And none, regardless of party affiliation, regardless of whether he was a hawk or a dove, took this responsibility lightly. As the commander-in-chief, charged with the defense of the United States, each president confronted the difficult task of protecting the nation's vital interests as he perceived them by preserving the nation's military strength and simultaneously trying to avoid a nuclear war. And each has succeeded. This is also true of Reagan, who has concentrated on rearmament rather than arms control.

Reagan abided by the terms of SALT II for six years. Probably no president, not even one less skeptical about the value of arms control, could have negotiated a new arms control agreement during the first years of disillusionment with *détente*, whose symbol was the SALT process. Unable to use MX to provide Moscow with sufficient incentive to reduce its first-strike ICBM capability, the president decided to outflank the Soviet ICBM force with SDI. That gave Moscow the necessary incentive to negotiate seriously and provided the basis for a proposal for a dramatic and deep reduction of ICBMs for constraints on SDI. But the president, committed to his vision of a missile-free, if not nuclear-free, world, was reluctant to accept any such constraints. However, he did seek a significant arms control agreement: the worldwide elimination, not just reduction, of all intermediate- and shorter-range missiles. But the president was mainly interested in unilaterally exploiting new technologies to achieve strategic stability; whether these new technologies would or would not lead to stability became a matter of intense controversy.

What is most striking about U.S.-Soviet relations over the last forty years is that these most heavily armed states have successfully avoided sparking a war from any of their political quarrels, confrontations, crises, limited wars, and interventions: Iran (1946), Greece (1947), Berlin (1948-1949), Korea (1950-1953), East Germany (1953), Hungary (1956), Berlin (1958-1961), Cuba (1962), Czechoslovakia (1968), Vietnam (1964-1973), the Arab-Israeli wars (1956, 1967, 1973), Afghanistan (1979), Poland (1981), and the Korean airliner incident (1983). The United States and the Soviet Union have acted with a restraint they might not have demonstrated if nuclear weapons had not existed. This is the impact of "the bomb"; its enormous destructive power has disciplined the conduct of the superpowers' foreign policy. The age of the "absolute weapon" that can destroy the nations that dare use it is also the age of deterrence, crisis management, limited wars, and wars by proxy. For forty years, twice the time between the two world wars, the nuclear peace has been kept. Indeed, the nuclear age has not only avoided a superpower war but has *eliminated all great power wars*. This is in no small measure due to the caution exercised by American and Soviet leaders, fearful of committing mutual suicide. Indeed, during the Reagan years, despite the strong rhetoric the superpowers hurled at each other, there were no Berlin or Cuban crises or Middle East wars that threatened to draw in the United States and the Soviet Union.

Nations were less cautious about going to war when they believed that the gains would exceed losses. That there were two global wars before 1945 demonstrates the restraining impact of nuclear weapons. To emphasize this key point is not to deny the need for arms control to stabilize the deterrent balance. But it is the destructive character of the arms that has prevented the war that in their absence would in all likelihood have broken out. Arms control is not a substitute for military strength, nor does it mean an end to the cold war. Rather, it supplements a national defense policy. The cold war is the product of forces more fundamental than the arms race; the arms race is the symbol of these forces. Eliminating or reducing weapons does not abolish the Soviet-American conflict of interests and values, the root cause of the arms race.

But the term *cold war* remains apt. The very use of the word *war* suggests the seriousness of the conflict, and *cold* that this war would have been waged by "hot" means at some point but for the revolution in military technology. The cold war is characterized, as it has been from the beginning, by a state of enmity in which force is not used to settle who is the victor. In that respect, it differs from the conflicts of previous major powers. Military power among the strongest nations since World War II has been used to deter, to pressure, and to intimidate; the U.S.-Soviet rivalry is "fought" at a level below that where actual violence is involved.

The East-West conflict is not the only conflict. There is also the North-South conflict. The Third World has its own set of attitudes and interests, primarily concerned with economics, that it asserts against the North. But the Third World is divided in many ways and is increasingly unstable. The growing frustration at the lack of development; the breakdown of religion and related tradition with whatever modernization occurs (often condemned, as in revolutionary Iran, as alien westernization); the rise of ethnic, racial, and religious ferment; the continuing unequal distribution of wealth, which tends to be accentuated in the early stages of economic development; the lack of legitimate and stable political institutions permitting peaceful change and transfers of power; and the ever-present possibility of national disintegration and territorial claims by neighboring states—all these problems lead to discontent, opposition, and the appearance of revolutionary ideas and regional conflicts. And most startling of all, the Third World will have more than 80 percent of the world's approximately 6 billion people by the end of the twentieth century. The majority of the globe's people will be nonwhite and poor.

The potential for an "international class war," the Marxist class struggle within nations projected worldwide as a struggle between poor nations and rich nations, means that the prospects for international stability are not high. The opportunities and enticements for superpower intervention and confrontation are, therefore, plentiful. Not all instability demands a U.S. reaction; some may not affect American interests or could be tolerated if it did. Much of it, however, may profoundly affect U.S. interests in a negative way and require a response, which may risk friction between the superpowers. But even if friction is avoided, the diffusion of military power in the world means that weaker states as well as nonstate actors can resort to terrorism and other means of limited violence against American interests. The Soviet Union is not the only country that perceives the United States as its enemy or that has the means to inflict damage on it.

Still, the Soviet Union remains the principal adversary of the United States, and events during the 1970s demonstrated vividly that the East-West and North-South conflicts cannot be divorced from each other; they interact. Even the regionalists in the Carter administration were concerned with solving problems in places like Zimbabwe, where failure to transfer power from the ruling tiny white minority to the black majority would have benefited the Soviet bloc. Any proposal for U.S. military intervention in 1972-1974 to seize the Persian Gulf oil fields was usually met with concern about Soviet intervention. Indeed, the fear that the Soviet Union, a "northern" state, might seek to dominate the nearby "southern" oil states was strengthened by the Soviet invasion of Afghanistan and led to the Carter Doctrine. Although the Soviet Union's motivation may have been completely different, Soviet power stands closer to the Gulf as a consequence of this invasion. And, of course, many Third World states voice strong anti-American sentiments. The nonaligned movement has embraced Communist states such as Vietnam, North Korea, and Cuba. Nonalignment, the declared foreign policy orientation of most Third World members, appears increasingly to be sheer hypocrisy, but it is also on the decline.

The Absence of a Foreign Policy Consensus

Among the most serious problems for the United States as it faces the future are the lack of a foreign policy consensus and the question of whether the American people still want to play an active and energetic role in the world. The key symptom of the public's increasing skepticism about foreign commitments is the fact that the two parties no longer share the same perception of the world and the U.S. role in it. Indeed, the two have essentially changed positions. During cold war I, the Democratic party was the most interventionist and most strongly anti-Soviet (and anti-Chinese during the days of the Sino-Soviet alliance) in its behavior. This reflected not only the views of its southern conservative anti-Communist wing and the party's efforts to ward off Republican accusations that it was the party of appeasement, but also the party's essentially dominant liberal orientation. The liberal wing, essentially northern and committed to democratic values and social justice at home, was equally concerned with the protection of democratic values from Soviet totalitarianism abroad. Because the Democratic party was essentially liberal, it was also a cold war party. The term *cold war liberalism* was the phrase usually used to describe this pattern of thought. By contrast, with the exception of its eastern moderate wing, which supported postwar Democratic foreign policy, the Republican party, primarily conservative, remained to a large extent isolationist, especially toward Europe. Its rhetoric was fiercely anti-Communist, but it was directed toward the Democrats, accusing them of "coddling communism." In 1952 Eisenhower ran for the Republican presidential nomination because he feared that if the conservative senator, Robert Taft of Ohio, were nominated and won the election, the party would abandon the nation's foreign policy commitments. Eisenhower's main task for eight years was in fact to gain his party's support for the nation's international role.

Since the Vietnam War, the two parties have flip-flopped. The Republicans are now interventionist in foreign policy, and the Democrats are much less willing to intervene abroad, to use force or the threat of force to support foreign policy objectives. Indeed, they are much more likely to define these objectives very selectively. The old cold war liberals, who belonged to the Hubert Humphrey-Henry Jackson wing of the party, have essentially disappeared. Liberalism—that is, the commitment to democratic fulfillment, social justice, and egalitarianism domestically—is now to a large extent divorced from a hard-line foreign policy stance. Ironically, this stance is now alive and well in the Republican party.

The Republicans, whether during Nixon's *détente* or Reagan's cold war II, still see the world as the Democrats used to. For them, the world is basically bipolar politically and militarily; international politics revolves mainly around issues of security; the prime focus for American foreign policy is the East-West conflict, including its manifestations in the Third World; and the principal threat is the Soviet Union, a totalitarian expansionist power whose military capability exceeds any conceivable defensive needs and endangers the military balance. In short, for the Republicans (except the small and dwindling number of moderates who are close to the Democratic liberal viewpoint), the key issue remains freedom versus tyranny, democracy versus totalitarianism. Containment of Soviet power cannot be abandoned.

The post-Vietnam or post-cold war liberal Democratic party defines the world as multipolar. It perceives the Soviet Union as a fundamentally conservative country, primarily concerned with preserving its gains; as militarily powerful but an essentially defensive power that is paranoid about its security because of past invasions; as willing to exploit opportunities for expansion in the Third World where opportunities arise. These opportunities could be reduced, according to the Democrats, if the United States pursued the correct policy. The reason the Soviet Union has such opportunities is that the United States is so frequently on the "wrong side of history" supporting the *status quo,* as in China, Indochina, and Nicaragua. The use of force is futile; to get on the "right side of history," the United States had to promote human rights and identify itself with social and economic change by supporting "progressive forces."

The Democrats' focus through the mid-1980s has not been on East-West issues, but on North-South issues. The problems the party wants addressed are poverty, overpopulation, hunger, ill-health, and lack of education. Once the party of cold war crusaders, it now regards the use of force with a distaste reminiscent of the Founding Fathers' attitude toward "entangling alliances." In turn, as noted earlier, this Democratic stance reflects the party's concern with interdependence and other global issues such as the inequitable distribution of wealth in the world, the Third World debt problem, the scarcity of natural resources, and environmental pollution, which cut across national boundaries. These problems confronting all humanity are said to be the critical issues for the future, more important than national and ideological differences among the superpowers and their allies. Building a new world order should, therefore, be the focus of attention and effort rather than the continuation of old-fashioned balance-of-power politics with its undue concentration on national interest, national security, and military power, all of which endanger the survival of the world. In an increasingly interdependent world, therefore, the Democrats, because of their commitment to social change in the Third World, are more sympathetic to left-wing forces who propose such changes and hostile to right-wing forces, even if they are pro-American.

Given their priorities and view of Soviet intentions, Democrats see U.S.-Soviet problems as negotiable. *Détente* and especially arms control can reduce superpower tensions, stabilize the deterrent balance, and allow resources that otherwise would have been invested in the arms race to be used to erase Third World poverty. In 1984 the Democratic platform stated that the "gravest political and security changes" stem from "poverty, repression, and despair." Economic aid, political and economic reform, and support for democratic values must be the "primary instruments" of U.S. influence in the Third World. Force would be of limited usefulness against such problems. Bayonets cannot create democracy. (Actually, a Democratic administration used precisely such instruments to create democracy in Germany and Japan.)

The Reagan administration, therefore, saw a Soviet-Cuban-Nicaraguan security threat to the United States in Central America, while the Democrats saw the problem in that area as essentially domestic. They viewed El Salvador and Nicaragua as the products of years of American-supported repressive rule. Their proposed solution was to bring democracy and the elimination of poverty to El Salvador and to attract Nicaragua away from Moscow and Havana by offering it help rather than opposing it and driving the Sandinistas into the arms of the Communists. In both cases, the Democrats were resolutely opposed to military intervention and very critical of the Reagan administration's deployment of carrier battle groups on both coastlines of Nicaragua, the covert intervention in that country, and the military assistance provided to the Salvadoran forces. Initially, the party was also very critical of the Grenada invasion, changing its mind only as it became clear that public opinion overwhelmingly supported the president. The evidence clearly indicates that since Vietnam the two parties have seriously disagreed on foreign and defense issues.

Indeed, the Democrats' anti-interventionist mood became very visible on one issue above all: multilateralism. During the Truman-Kennedy-Johnson presidencies, the Democrats' activist and interventionist policies had been conducted through various multilateral organizations: the United Nations, the Organization of American States (OAS), and SEATO. The United States had used these organizations to legitimate its actions: the intervention in Korea was carried out under the UN, the one in Vietnam under SEATO, and the one in the Dominican Republic under the OAS. In no case did these organizations act as a major restraint on the United States.

Since Vietnam, the Democrats have remained committed to multilateralism, but their purpose has changed. Advice to act through the UN or OAS are today advanced as substitutes for action because the majorities in these bodies usually disagree with U.S. policies. The Soviet bloc and Third World countries today constitute the majority in the UN General Assembly; even the OAS, which in 1964 formally supported the American intervention in the Dominican Republic, in 1983 would not have approved the U.S. invasion of Grenada. That is why the United States had to find the rather obscure Association of Eastern Caribbean States, an organization almost no one had heard of, to legitimate its action. The Republicans, now the party of interventionism, preferred to act unilaterally and viewed alliances and multilateral organizations mainly as constraints on America's freedom to do whatever was necesssary in its own interests.

The Economy: Is the United States Following Britain Again?

More damaging in the long run than even the absence of a genuine consensus on foreign policy is the deteriorating condition of the U.S. economy, as economic power, like military power, has diffused in the state system. Money has always been a basic underlying historic ingredient of international politics. The state with the most money could buy the largest army and navy. America's postwar role was based upon the same vigorous economy that had won World War II and created the highest standard of living in the world: a mass-production economy that built high-quality goods. Any product labeled "made in America" was sought after all over the world. But the United States did not depend upon overseas markets for its economic health; it did not need to export much or import many raw materials. Rich in resources, the nation's industry could provide the American consumer with abundant goods and create what in the 1950s was called the "affluent society." At the same time, it could sustain large-scale economic aid and rearmament plus two limited wars.

But even before the shock of the quadrupling of oil prices in 1973, the U.S. economy was showing signs of weakness. By the late 1970s the rise in energy prices had not only demonstrated brutally and swiftly that the economy was not immune to external events; it had also underlined the inability of America's industries to compete in the global economy. The flood of imports during the 1970s which so satisfied consumer demand had to be paid for; by the 1980s the trade deficit was still growing despite the sharp drop in oil prices.

The United States had become the world's largest debtor nation. Unfair trading practices by other countries, while certainly one factor, could not hide the weaknesses of industries ranging from the old smoke-stack factories to the latest high-tech products, including computer chips. America's farmers, who had been a mainstay in paying the nation's trade bills, suddenly found that they were too productive in a world in which even less-developed countries had learned the techniques of producing food. In addition, the lack of discipline in U.S. budget policy also damaged the economy. America's most conservative president, by cutting taxes while vastly increasing military spending, created the biggest deficits in U.S. history. High interest rates attracted foreign capital to cover the deficit, but made it more expensive for Americans to invest in industry. The accompanying high dollar and the subsequent flood of cheaper imported goods produced a further decline of U.S. economic growth and investment. But the president refused to raise taxes, and Congress, especially the Democrats, refused to make deeper cuts in the social programs the administration had already cut. The country apparently was unconcerned, wanting both social spending and low taxes, while continuing to indulge in mass consumption and saving little for future investment. With tax increases unlikely, Social Security untouchable, and domestic spending cut about as much as was politically tolerable, the United States was strategically and financially overcommitted.

The story of the industrial economy was frighteningly reminiscent of Britain's economic history. In 1887 Britain assembled the world's most powerful fleet to celebrate Queen Victoria's Diamond Jubilee. It was an impressive demonstration of power: 21 battleships and 54 cruisers among the total of 154 warships. But underneath this show of raw military power, the economy, which had made all this possible, was already showing signs of rot. Britain, the first nation to industrialize, often could not hold its own against German and American goods, even in its home market. With a large imperial market to sustain it and unused to competition, British industry had grown complacent.

Germany and the United States, admittedly, were larger countries with bigger industries, and, in the course of time, Britain would have declined relatively in world markets. But the decline of British industry was not inevitable and unavoidable. Having done so well for so long, British manufacturers saw no need to change traditional attitudes toward business management, production, labor relations, and salesmanship. These attitudes resulted in a lack of research and development and technological innovation; a low level of investment in new machinery, which was considered too expensive; an educational system that deemphasized science, technology and business management; and cultural values that frowned upon "commerce" and "business," the very activities that had energized Britain earlier in the nineteenth century. British power declined as a consequence, and that was a major reason why the United States was drawn out of its long isolationist stance.

In the late 1980s some of the symptoms of Britain's economic decay are evident in the U.S. economy: underinvestment and overconsumption; outdated machinery; a neglected infrastructure, especially education, which is better in all of America's major Western competitors; insufficient research and development, with too much of it going into military rather than economic needs; poor workmanship and a labor force not skilled enough; and poor management by bloated corporate bureaucracies that have not been receptive either to risk taking or to innovation. Is American power therefore fated to decline as did Britain's? When Britain became aware of Germany's growing might and challenge, it formed alliances to supplement its military power and defend its global commitments. Specifically, it organized alliances with Japan and with two former rivals, czarist Russia and France. This devolution of military responsibility failed. Russia suffered a revolution in 1917, France was defeated in 1940, and Japan turned into an enemy.

German power was simply too great, but, fortunately, Britain could fall back on the United States. Since the 1970s, with the vast improvement in the West European and Japanese economies, the United States has urged its allies to take over more of its defense burden as Soviet military power continued to grow and Soviet political influence expanded in the Third World. At the same time, the United States sought regional allies, such as Iran, and arrived at an accommodation with Communist China. But the U.S. effort to place some of its defense burden on NATO and Japan and smaller allies like Iran have failed. Upon whom could the United States rely to share its imperial burdens, if that should ever become necessary? This is no idle question, for the answer is intimately tied to the survival of democratic values.

The Purpose of American Foreign Policy

It is well to remind ourselves of the chief purpose of American foreign policy: the security of a *democratic* America. The balance of power, however defined and whatever its military ingredients, is not an end in itself, but the means to preserve security. In turn, successive administrations felt that this end required the maintenance of an international environment congenial to the survival of democratic societies. The fundamental orientation of American foreign policy, therefore, has been to support the democracies, old and new, in Western Europe and Japan through alliances—and to support one state, Israel, which has no formal alliance with the United States (although, for all practical purposes, it might as well have). Indeed, as the cases of West Germany, Italy, Austria, and Japan suggest, the expansion of American power and influence in the world is by and large associated with the promotion of democracy. Our former enemies, once dictatorial in nature, are today stable, free societies. This did not happen by accident. Our political leaders reflect the values of American society, and, when at times they seem to disregard these values in their conduct of foreign policy, they are usually criticized by other members of the executive branch, Congress, the opposition party, and the press. America's open society is its best insurance that, by and large, the nation "stays on course"; otherwise, its leaders had better have a convincing rationale for straying.

If we look at the societies liberated by the Soviet Union during World

War II, the contrast is striking. No East European country could be described as a "free society"; attempts to move toward greater freedom have been squashed by the Soviet army in East Germany, Hungary, and Czechoslovakia, and by the Polish army in Poland. East Germany had to build a wall across Berlin and a barbed wire fence along its entire border with West Germany to prevent its citizens from escaping. As South Vietnam was collapsing in 1975 before the advancing North Vietnamese armies, much of the population "voted with its feet," moving southward. After the unification of Vietnam, thousands more risked their lives fleeing from their country in small boats, and many were drowned. In neighboring Cambodia, the new Communist rulers killed more than one-quarter of the population. And when Cuba allows its people to leave, they do so by the hundreds of thousands.

Admittedly, over four decades the United States has acquired many dictatorial allies and friends, usually of right-wing coloration, which weakens Washington's democratic rationale and lays open its foreign policy to the charge of hypocrisy. The reason for this kind of alliance in the case of South Korea, for example, is that the security of another ally (Japan) required it. The United States therefore tolerated and supported its regime. Similarly in Europe, the desire for air and naval bases to strengthen NATO, composed of the principal remaining democracies in the world, led to the inclusion of Portugal as an ally and Spain as an associated power, when both were governed by right-wing authoritarian regimes. It is, of course, preferable to have democratic allies, but this is not always possible in a world in which most states are not democratic. Security and democracy occasionally are bound to appear as conflicting values. Which value is to be given priority is a difficult and often agonizing choice. If in the name of security a democracy somewhat indiscriminately picks up a large number of dictatorial allies to enhance its power, to acquire strategic position, or to play off one country against another, it may indeed corrupt its purposes. If in the name of democracy it refuses to align itself with any undemocratic regimes to keep its hands clean, it may remain pure but weaken itself against its principal adversary. In the real world, a democracy must at times sup with a dictatorship, be it of the right or left, although when it does so it should remember to eat with a long spoon.

The question is not whether a democracy should ever ally itself with an undemocratic government or come to its rescue if it sees that its *own* security is involved—as, for instance, Britain did when it went to the rescue of an undemocratic Poland attacked by Nazi Germany in 1939, or Britain and the United States when they were allied with the Soviet Union against Hitler, or the United States when it sought to bolster undemocratic Turkey and Greece against perceived Communist expansionist pressures from the Soviet Union in 1947—but how often, for what purposes, for how long, and at what level of commitment such an association should be forged. On these issues, honest men and women can and do differ vigorously. In the absence of war, it cannot be proven that America's relations with Portugal and Spain, for example, contributed to the prevention of hostilities and therefore to the protection of Western Europe. Perhaps the peace would have been kept without them and we need not have stained our cause. Perhaps the United States could have achieved its diplomatic objective of restraining the Soviet Union even without aligning itself with Tito's Yugoslav dictatorship after 1948 or, after 1972, with the regime in Communist China.

In any event, given the democratic nature of American society, the pros and cons of aligning with right- or left-wing despotisms tends to be debated so that the trade-offs between the values of democracy and security become clear, even if disagreements remain about the exact mix that policy should reflect. The pressure not to sacrifice democratic values on the altar of security, at least not in a permanent alliance, stems from the fact that America is a democratic society. This means first of all that the nation's leaders are products of American values and are committed to them. In addition, the watchfulness of Congress, the press, and private human rights groups constrains the ability of administration officials to align themselves with authoritarian regimes and then to look the other way when gross violations of basic human rights occur. This is not to say that such things do not happen; only that the pluralistic nature of U.S. society and the institutional system of checks and balances constrain political leaders from abusing their power or disregarding their nation's fundamental beliefs and values more than in any other society. Pressure from Congress and the press on El Salvador and the Philippines compelled the executive branch to concern itself with democratic reforms in these two countries.

Certainly, wherever possible, the United States should exert pressure for democratic reforms. South Korea is again an apt example. Strategically located, a country of 42 million, strongly anti-Communist as a result of the earlier war, it is now a highly urbanized society with a well-educated population. It is not currently, as in the past, threatened with an invasion from the North; neither Moscow nor Beijing have shown any support for a North Korean adventure, which would result in war with the United States. South Korea, therefore, has no reason to preserve its military dictatorship. The continued suppression of the widespread desire of the South Korean people for democracy resulted in widespread street demonstrations in 1987 with an overtone of anti-Americanism because of U.S. government support for the regime. As in the Philippines in 1986, it made sense from both the point of view of principle and power for the United States to be true to itself; the United States therefore privately encouraged a shift to more democratic rule, which the ruling party promised in response to the popular resistance.

In this connection, it is worth remembering that although not a single Communist state has ever evolved into a Western-style democracy or been overthrown by force from within in favor of a parliamentary form of government, a fair number of America's authoritarian allies and friends, such as in Portugal and Spain (and many of their "children" in Latin America, and the Philippines) as well as in Greece, have collapsed, been overthrown, or begun to evolve in a more democratic direction. This, in turn, suggests that it is not altogether hypocritical to say that there is an essential difference between left-wing Communist totalitarian and right-wing authoritarian regimes in terms of the permanence of government control and degree of oppression of the population. It is also worth a final reminder that the reformers who opposed U.S.-supported right-wing regimes often turned out to be left-wing revolutionaries who, once they did gain power, were at least as insensitive to democratic values and individual freedom as their American-supported predecessors had been. Indeed, usually they were more so. Fidel Castro, Ho Chi Minh, and the Sandinistas may have portrayed themselves as more humanitarian and democratic than the leaders they overthrew. But once in power, their suppression of the values they claimed to represent was efficient and total and, unlike those whom they deposed, they were not deposable. Their grip on the power and control of their societies was much more thorough and effective.

In any event, the principal thrust of American policy since World War II, as before the war, is still the preservation of a balance of power that would safeguard democratic values in the United States and other basically Western countries. Indeed, this has been a consistent policy since World War I, whether the threat came from the expansionism of the right or the expansionism of the left. American policy makers in the twentieth century have opposed both types of regimes, for they threatened not just U.S. security but, more broadly, the international environment in which democratic values could prosper. And this remains the crux of American opposition to the Soviet Union: that its great power is a threat to Western values and Western-style open societies. For communism, as reflected in the organization of all Communist societies, remains the antithesis of societies that believe in individual freedoms, whether of speech or religion, in free party competition and genuine political choice, and in a distinction between state and society. The basic purpose of American foreign policy, after all, is the preservation of a democratic social order in a hostile world, and it is America's counterbalancing power that has protected democratic values. Without that power, Soviet power and the Soviet Union's social values and order would have prevailed. Freedom in the world, in short, is intimately tied to American power and the economy that sustains that power. As Secretary of State Henry Kissinger succinctly expressed it, "If we do not lead, no other nation that stands for what we believe in can take our place."

Appendix A

U.S. Alliances in Europe and Asia

Alliance	Dates	Membership
NATO (15 members)	1949-	Belgium, Britain, Canada, Denmark, France, Greece, Iceland, Italy, Luxembourg, Netherlands, Norway, Portugal, Turkey, United States, West Germany
ANZUS [1] (3 members)	1951-	Australia, New Zealand, United States
Philippine Treaty (2 members)	1951-	Philippines, United States
Japanese Treaty (2 members)	1951-	Japan, United States
Republic of Korea (2 members)	1953-	South Korea, United States
Republic of China (2 members)	1954-1978	Nationalist China, United States
SEATO (8 members)	1954-1975	Australia, Britain, France, New Zealand, Pakistan, Philippines, Thailand, United States
METO (later CENTO minus Iraq), 1955-1979. (Initially 6, later 5, members if the United States is counted, although not a full-fledged member)		Britain (chief sponsor of this alliance), Iran, Iraq (until it pulled out after 1958 overthrow of monarchy), Pakistan, Turkey, United States

Note: The United States also has alliances in all but name with Israel, Egypt, and Saudi Arabia. Although no treaties of defense exist, long commitments and/or continued strategic or economic interests have made these countries virtual allies.

[1] The United States suspended the alliance in 1986 because of New Zealand's banning of visits by nuclear-powered and nuclear-armed ships. The United States stated that it therefore no longer felt obligated to come to New Zealand's defense.

Soviet Alliances in Europe and Asia

Alliance	Dates	Membership
Sino-Soviet (2 members)	1949-1979	Communist China, Soviet Union
Warsaw Pact[2] (7 members)	1955-	Bulgaria, Czechoslovakia, East Germany, Hungary, Poland, Romania, Soviet Union

Note: The Soviet Union has signed a number of treaties of friendship: Angola (1976), Mozambique (1977), Ethiopia (1978), Afghanistan (1978), Vietnam (1978), South Yemen (1979), and Syria (1981). Although Moscow has emphasized that the purpose of the treaties is consultation, the implication is that they involve defense commitments; the aim is certainly to deter the United States from any actions against these nations.

[2] The Soviet Union had signed bilateral alliances with Czechoslovakia, Poland, Romania, Hungary, and Bulgaria in the 1940s.

Appendix B

Selected Principal Events

Year

1945   The Yalta Conference seeks to organize postwar world.

World War II with Germany ends.

World War II with Japan ends after two atomic bombs are dropped.

President Franklin Roosevelt dies.

Vice President Harry Truman succeeds.

United Nations is established.

Soviet military forces occupy Poland, Romania, Bulgaria, Hungary, and Czechoslovakia.

1946   United States confronts the Soviet Union over Iran, and Moscow withdraws its troops.

Winston Churchill, Britain's wartime prime minister, delivers "iron curtain" speech at Fulton, Missouri, warning of Soviet threat.

1947   Truman Doctrine commits the United States to assist Greece and Turkey.

Plan for the economic recovery of Western Europe is devised by Secretary of State George Marshall, formerly U.S. chief of staff and architect of victory during World War II.

George Kennan, a Foreign Service officer, provides the government with the analysis that became the basis of the containment policy of Soviet Russia.

India becomes independent.

1948   Soviet *coup d'état* takes place in Czechoslovakia.

Soviets blockade all ground traffic from West Germany to West Berlin and the Western airlift starts.

Vandenberg resolution of U.S. Senate commits American support for the Brussels Pact of self-defense.

Marshall Plan is passed by Congress.

North and South Korea are established.

The state of Israel is established and receives immediate U.S. recognition.

Truman wins upset election.

Stalin expels Yugoslavia's Tito from Communist bloc.

1949   North Atlantic Treaty Organization (NATO) is formed.

Soviet Union ends Berlin blockade.

East and West Germany are established.

Soviet Union explodes atomic bomb.

Nationalist China collapses and Communist China is established.

U.S. troops are withdrawn from South Korea.

Truman announces Point Four foreign aid program for less-developed countries.

1950   Soviet Union and Communist China sign thirty-year treaty of mutual
            assistance.
            North Korea attacks South Korea by crossing the thirty-eighth parallel.
            United States intervenes on behalf of South Korea.
            Communist China intervenes after U.S. forces advance into North Korea
            toward China's frontier.
            European Coal and Steel Community is formed.
            Senator Joseph McCarthy begins his attacks on government for treason
            and "coddling communism."

1951   General Dwight Eisenhower is appointed Supreme Allied Commander in
            Europe and Truman sends U.S. forces to Europe.
            U.S.-Japanese mutual security pact is signed.
            Truman fires General Douglas MacArthur in Korea for proposing that
            the United States attack Communist China.

1952   Eisenhower is elected president.
            Greece and Turkey join NATO.
            Britain tests its first atomic weapon.

1953   Joseph Stalin dies.
            Armistice negotiated along thirty-eighth parallel in Korea.
            Soviet Union intervenes in East Germany to quell revolt.

1954   United States explodes first hydrogen bomb.
            France is defeated at Dienbienphu in Indochina.
            United States threatens to intervene in Indochina.
            Vietnam is partitioned at the seventeenth parallel at the Geneva Confer-
            ence.
            Southeast Asia Treaty Organization (SEATO) is formed.
            U.S.-Korean pact is signed to prevent a renewal of the war.
            U.S.-Nationalist China defense treaty is signed.
            Central Intelligence Agency overthrows Guatemala's left-wing govern-
            ment.

1955   Communist China shells the Nationalist Chinese islands of Quemoy and
            Matsu.
            The Formosa resolution authorizes Eisenhower to use force, if necessary,
            to protect Taiwan against a possible Communist Chinese invasion.
            Middle East Treaty Organization (Baghdad Pact) is formed.
            West Germany joins NATO, and Soviets establish "their NATO," called
            the Warsaw Pact.

1956   United States withdraws offer to help finance Egypt's Aswan High Dam.
            Egypt nationalizes the Suez Canal.
            Suez War breaks out after Israel attacks Egypt, and France and Britain
            intervene.
            UN forces are sent to Egypt to keep the peace between Israel and Egypt.
            Soviets suppress Hungarian revolt and almost intervene in Poland.
            Soviet leader Nikita Khrushchev attacks Stalin at twentieth Communist
            Party Congress.

1957   Soviet Union tests intercontinental ballistic missile (ICBM).
Soviets launch two Sputniks, or satellites, into space.
British test hydrogen bomb.
Eisenhower Doctrine commits the United States to assist Middle East countries that resist Communist aggression or states closely tied to the Soviet Union, such as Egypt.

1958   United States lands marines in Lebanon, and Britain lands paratroopers in Jordan after Iraqi revolution.
Soviet Union declares it would end the four-power occupation of Berlin and turn West Berlin into a "free city."
The European Economic Community (the Common Market) is established.
First of several Berlin crises erupts.
Communist China shells Quemoy and Matsu again.
Britain tests its first thermonuclear bomb.

1959   Khrushchev visits Eisenhower for Camp David meeting over Berlin issue.
Fidel Castro captures power in Cuba.
Central Treaty Organization (CENTO) replaces the Baghdad Pact.

1960   Soviets shoot down U.S. U-2 spy plane over the Soviet Union.
Paris summit conference collapses over U-2 incident.
The Congo becomes independent from Belgium, causing the first superpower crisis in sub-Sahara Africa.
UN forces sent to the Congo to help resolve the crisis.
France becomes an atomic power.
John Kennedy wins presidential election.

1961   Kennedy launches abortive Bay of Pigs invasion of Cuba.
Kennedy proposes Alliance for Progress for Latin America.
Kennedy holds summit conference with Khrushchev in Vienna.
Kennedy sends first military advisers to South Vietnam.
Soviets build Berlin Wall.

1962   In Cuban missile crisis, the United States blockades Cuba to compel the Soviets to withdraw their missiles.
Chinese-Indian frontier conflict erupts.

1963   French president Charles de Gaulle vetoes Britain's entry into the Common Market.
"Hot line" established between the White House and the Kremlin for direct emergency communications.
Atomic test-ban treaty is signed.
Kennedy is assassinated and Lyndon Johnson succeeds him.
Soviets place man in space.

1964   Congress passes Gulf of Tonkin resolution, raising the U.S. commitment to the defense of South Vietnam.
Khrushchev falls from power and is replaced by Prime Minister Aleksei Kosygin and Communist Party Secretary Leonid Brezhnev.

1965   United States starts bombing North Vietnam and sends American land forces into South Vietnam.

Protests against the war start.

United States intervenes in the Dominican Republic.

War erupts between Pakistan and India.

1966   Communist China becomes a nuclear power.

France withdraws its forces from NATO's integrated command structure but remains a member of the alliance.

1967   Six-Day War between Israel and its Arab neighbors takes place.

Greek colonels seize power in Greece.

1968   Tet offensive in South Vietnam escalates demand for U.S. withdrawal from Vietnam.

Johnson withdraws from presidential race.

Richard Nixon elected president.

Vietnamese peace talks begin in Paris.

Nuclear Non-Proliferation Treaty is made.

Soviet Union intervenes in Czechoslovakia to squash revolt.

1969   Brezhnev Doctrine is proclaimed asserting the right of Soviet Union to intervene in Soviet sphere to suppress "counterrevolution."

ABM deployment is narrowly voted by Senate.

United States tests MIRV.

SALT talks start.

"Vietnamization" program starts. South Vietnamese are to do more of the fighting while the United States begins troop withdrawal.

Ho Chi Minh dies.

United States lands men on moon.

Lt. William Calley, Jr., stands trial for My Lai massacre of civilians in South Vietnam by U.S. troops.

First of several Sino-Soviet border clashes occurs.

1970   West Germany concludes treaties with Soviet Union and Poland recognizing Poland's western border and acknowledging Germany's division into East and West Germany.

Senate repeals Gulf of Tonkin resolution.

U.S. invasion of Cambodia causes widespread student protests, which escalate after National Guard kills four students at Kent State University.

Chile elects a Marxist, Salvador Allende, president.

1971   India and Pakistan go to war over the Bangladesh (East Pakistan) secession effort.

Communist China joins the United Nations.

Four-power Berlin settlement is reached ensuring Western access to Berlin.

1972   Nixon visits Communist China, beginning a process of normalizing relations after two decades of hostility.

North Vietnam invades South Vietnam.

Nixon retaliates by expanding air war against North Vietnam and blockading the harbor of Haiphong.

Nixon visits Moscow for summit conference with Soviet leaders, signs

Strategic Arms Limitation Treaty (SALT I) and ABM treaty.

Watergate affair starts with police arrest of five men who had broken into Democratic party headquarters.

Soviets buy enormous quantities of U.S. grains, raising U.S. domestic prices.

Britain, Denmark, and Ireland join Common Market, increasing membership to nine countries.

Paris peace talks, close to success, break down, and the United States bombs North Vietnam heavily during Christmas season.

Nixon reelected president in a landslide that carried every state but Massachusetts.

1973　Henry Kissinger is appointed secretary of state while remaining the president's national security assistant.

Vietnamese peace agreement is signed.

United States and China establish liaison offices, or informal embassies, in Washington and Beijing.

Yom Kippur War breaks out in Middle East.

Arab members of the Organization of Petroleum Exporting Countries embargo oil to the United States because of U.S. support for Israel.

OPEC quadruples oil prices.

U.S.-Soviet Mutual and Balanced Force Reductions talks in Europe start.

West and East Germany exchange recognition and ambassadors, acknowledging Germany's division into two countries.

Congress passes the War Powers Resolution over Nixon's veto.

Vice President Spiro Agnew resigns and Gerald Ford succeeds him.

Allende is overthrown by military in Chile.

1974　India explodes "peaceful" nuclear device.

Congress asserts right to veto large arms sales to other nations.

Annual Nixon-Brezhnev summit conference further reduces small numbers of ABMs the United States and Soviet Union are allowed by SALT I.

Kissinger negotiates first agreements between Israel and Egypt and Syria as part of his "step-by-step" diplomacy intended to achieve a comprehensive regional peace.

Nixon visits Egypt, Syria, and Israel.

Nixon resigns and Ford becomes unelected president; New York governor Nelson Rockefeller becomes vice president.

Ford and Brezhnev set Vladivostok guidelines for SALT II negotiations.

1975　Soviet Union rejects American-Soviet trade agreement because of the Jackson-Vanik amendment.

South Vietnam collapses and a unified Communist Vietnam is established.

Cambodia falls to Cambodian Communists.

Cambodians seize U.S. merchant ship *Mayaguez,* and the United States reacts forcefully to free crew and ship.

SEATO dissolves itself.

Helsinki agreements, including Western recognition of Europe's division (and Soviet domination in Eastern Europe), arrived at by Western and Eastern states.

Congress passes arms embargo against Turkey.

Lebanese civil war erupts.

Francisco Franco dies and King Juan Carlos starts to lead Spain to democracy.

In Angola three major factions struggle for control as Portugal gives Angola independence.

1976   Soviet-Cuban forces in Angola win victory for Marxist-led faction over pro-Western factions.

Syrian forces intervene in Lebanon.

Mao Zedong dies.

Jimmy Carter elected president.

1977   Carter announces U.S. withdrawal from South Korea (to be reversed later).

Carter sends letter to leading Soviet dissident, and another dissident visits the White House.

Soviets denounce Carter's human rights campaign as violation of Soviet sovereignty.

Carter submits new SALT II plan to Soviet Union, which quickly rejects it because it is not based on Vladivostok guidelines.

Carter halts plans to produce B-1 bomber and instead chooses to deploy air-launched cruise missiles on B-52 bombers.

United States and Panama sign Panama Canal treaties.

Somalia expels Soviet advisers and denounces friendship treaty with Soviet Union.

Soviet-Cuban military help for Ethiopia grows.

Menachem Begin is elected prime minister in Israel.

Egyptian president Anwar Sadat pays historic visit to Israel, offering peace and friendship. Other Arab states denounce him.

1978   Soviet-Cuban military intervention in Ethiopia's war against Somalia forces latter out of Ogaden.

Soviet-inspired *coup* occurs in Afghanistan.

Camp David meeting of the United States, Israel, and Egypt arrives at "framework for peace" between two former enemies. Other Arab states denounce framework because it did not provide for a Palestine solution.

Senate approves sale of jet fighters to Israel, Egypt, and Saudi Arabia.

Panama Canal treaties approved by Senate.

Carter postpones neutron "bomb" (tactical warhead) production.

United States ends arms embargo on Turkey.

Shah leaves Iran.

Rhodesian prime minister Ian Smith announces "internal solution" to the race problem—the formation of a black-led government.

1979   United States officially recognizes the People's Republic of China. It also breaks ties with government on Taiwan as official government of China and ends mutual defense treaty.

China briefly invades Vietnam to punish it for the invasion of Cambodia in 1978, which overthrew a regime friendly to China and replaced it with a pro-Soviet and pro-Vietnamese one.

Shah's regime in Iran replaced by Islamic republic led by Ayatollah Ruhollah Khomeini.

U.S. Embassy in Tehran seized and employees held hostage by militant Islamic students after shah is hospitalized in United States for cancer treatment.

United States freezes Iran's financial assets in United States and boycotts Iranian oil.

Oil prices shoot upward as Iranian oil production drops and world supplies tighten.

SALT II Treaty signed by Brezhnev and Carter at Vienna summit conference.

Soviets send 80,000 troops into Afghanistan to ensure survival of pro-Soviet regime.

NATO decides to deploy 572 theater nuclear weapons to counter Soviet "Eurostrategic" missile buildup.

1980   U.S. mission to rescue hostages in Tehran ends in disaster before it reaches embassy.

SALT II "temporarily" withdrawn from Senate by Carter after Soviet invasion of Afghanistan.

Carter embargoes shipments of feed grain and high technology and declares United States will boycott summer Olympic games in Moscow.

Carter Doctrine commits United States to security of Persian Gulf oil-producing states if they are externally threatened.

United States organizes Rapid Deployment Force to back up the Carter Doctrine.

Iraq attacks Iran.

Ronald Reagan elected president.

1981   U.S. hostages released moments after Reagan assumes presidency.

AWACS deal with Saudi Arabia is approved by Senate.

Reagan declares United States will not allow Saudi Arabia to become "another Iran."

Begin reelected in Israel.

Sadat assassinated in Egypt.

Reagan decides on large program to rebuild U.S. military power, including 100 MX missiles and 100 B-1 bombers.

Polish government imposes martial law.

United States imposes economic sanctions on Poland and on Soviet Union, believed to be behind the Polish crackdown.

1982   Reagan announces an economic assistance plan for the Caribbean Basin (the Caribbean and Central America) as he supports El Salvador's government against rebel forces and attempts to isolate the Sandinistas in Nicaragua despite congressional criticism.

Israel invades Lebanon, attempting to destroy the PLO.

U.S. marines are sent into Beirut as part of a multinational peace-keeping force to supervise the PLO's leaving.

China and the United States sign agreement on the reduction of U.S. arms sales to Taiwan.

Brezhnev dies and is succeeded by Yuri Andropov, former head of the Soviet secret police.

Argentina invades the British Falkland Islands, long claimed by Argentina. Britain reconquers the islands.

United States imposes—and later, lifts—sanctions on U.S. and European companies selling equipment to the Soviets for building a natural gas pipeline to Western Europe.

Secretary of State Alexander Haig resigns.

1983   Reagan denounces the Soviet Union as an "evil empire."

Bipartisan Scowcroft Commission recommends deployment of 100 MX missiles and eventual replacement of missiles equipped with MIRVs with mobile, smaller missiles with single warheads. Congress accepts these recommendations.

Catholic bishops in pastoral letter deplore nuclear deterrence for its immorality. French bishops endorse deterrence as "service to peace."

Two hundred forty-one marines killed in suicide truck-bomb attack on their barracks in Beirut.

Soviet Union shoots down Korean 747 airliner with 269 passengers after it strayed into Soviet airspace.

U.S. forces, together with troops from six Caribbean states, invade the island of Grenada. They depose the Marxist government, return Cuban worker-soldiers to Cuba, and withdraw.

United States begins deployment of Pershing II and ground-launched cruise missiles in Europe. Soviet Union responds by breaking off all arms control talks.

1984   Bipartisan Kissinger Commission recommends extensive economic and military assistance to Central America to combat domestic poverty and Soviet-Cuban intervention. Congress critical of administration policy.

Andropov dies and Brezhnev's confidant, Konstantin Chernenko, succeeds him.

Reagan is reelected.

United States pulls marines out of Lebanon.

Napoleón Duarte wins Salvadoran presidency, defeating right-wing candidate.

Congress cuts off all military assistance to the contras in Nicaragua.

Latin American debtor countries meet at Cartagena to discuss the debt problem and repayment.

United States declares Iran a supporter of international terrorism.

1985   Chernenko dies and is succeeded by Mikhail Gorbachev.

Africa, especially Ethiopia, which is engaged in a civil war, suffers from widespread starvation.

Christian Democratic party, led by Duarte, wins majority in Salvadoran National Assembly.

Various terrorist groups hijack a TWA plane flying from Athens to Rome, seize an Italian cruise ship, and attack Israel's El Al passengers at the Vienna and Rome airports.

Reagan orders limited economic sanctions against South Africa; Congress imposes harsher sanctions in 1986.

Reagan and Gorbachev hold their first summit conference in Geneva, Switzerland.

1986   Ferdinand Marcos and Jean-Claude Duvalier are forced to flee their respective countries, and the Reagan administration proclaims its new human rights policy, opposing dictatorships of the left and right.

Congress approves $100 million for the Nicaraguan contras.

The United States attacks Libya for terrorist acts. Syria is shown to be involved in terrorism, and Britain breaks diplomatic relations with Syria after abortive attempt to blow up Israeli airliner.

World's worst nuclear accident takes place at Chernobyl in the Ukraine.

Sweden broke news of radioactivity coming from the Soviet Union.

Reagan and Gorbachev meet in Iceland, and Reagan refuses to trade limitations in SDI research for deep cuts of Soviet strategic missiles and a mutual elimination of all intermediate-range missiles in Europe.

United States exceeds SALT II limits and declares that the unratified 1979 treaty is no longer "operational."

Iran-contra scandal breaks.

OPEC's oil price falls to $9 to $10 a barrel, but then stabilizes at $18 a barrel.

Spain and Portugal join the European Economic Community.

U.S. dollar is allowed to drop substantially against Japanese yen and West German mark to improve U.S. exports and reduce huge trade deficit, but action proves ineffective.

1987   Congressional hearings into Iran-contra scandal raise doubts about Reagan's effectiveness for the remainder of his term.

The United States and the Soviet Union agree to a worldwide ban on shorter- and intermediate-range missiles, the so-called double zero option, ending years of tension over Soviet SS-20 missile deployment.

The United States reflags Kuwaiti oil tankers in the Persian Gulf and escorts them with U.S. warships. This move is widely seen as an administration effort to appear more neutral in the Iran-Iraq war.

Five Central American presidents devise a plan for peace in their area.

Selected Bibliography

Most of the entries in this bibliography are books. Readers who wish to keep up with contemporary foreign and defense policies will find the articles in *Foreign Affairs, Foreign Policy,* and *International Security* useful and relevant. This is especially so for *Foreign Affairs'* annual *America and the World 198-.*

American Society and Style in Foreign Policy

Almond, Gabriel A. *The American People and Foreign Policy.** New York: Praeger Publishers, 1960.

Boorstin, Daniel J. *The Genius of American Politics.** Chicago: Phoenix Books, 1953.

Crabb, Cecil V. *Policy Makers and Critics.** New York: Praeger Publishers, 1976.

Dallek, Robert. *The American Style of Foreign Policy.* New York: Alfred A. Knopf, 1983.

Hartz, Louis. *The Liberal Tradition in America.** New York: Harvest Books, 1955.

Herberg, Will. *Protestant, Catholic, and Jew,* rev. ed.* New York: Anchor Books, 1960.

Hofstadter, Richard. *The Paranoid Style in American Politics.** New York: Vintage Books, 1967.

Kennan, George F. *American Diplomacy 1900-1950.** Chicago: University of Chicago Press, 1951.

Krasner, Stephen D. *Defending the National Interest.** Princeton, N.J.: Princeton University Press, 1978.

Morgenthau, Hans J. *In Defense of the National Interest.* New York: Alfred A. Knopf, 1951.

Osgood, Robert. *Ideals and Self-Interest in America's Foreign Relations.* Chicago: University of Chicago Press, 1953.

---

* Asterisked titles are available in paperback editions.

Packenham, Robert A. *Liberal America and the Third World.** Princeton, N.J.: Princeton University Press, 1973.

Potter, David M. *The People of Plenty.** Chicago: Phoenix Books, 1954.

American Foreign Policy

Allison, Graham T. *Essences of Decision.* Boston: Little, Brown & Co., 1971.

Aron, Raymond. *The Imperial Republic.** Cambridge, Mass.: Winthrop Publishers, 1974.

Bell, Coral. *The Diplomacy of* Détente. New York: St. Martin's Press, 1977.

Brzezinski, Zbigniew. *Game Plan.* Boston: Atlantic Monthly Press, 1986.

Clemens, Diane S. *Yalta.* New York: Oxford University Press, 1970.

Draper, Theodore, and others. *Defending America.* New York: Basic Books, 1978.

Fleming, D. F. *The Cold War and Its Origins, 1917-1960,* 2 vols. Garden City, N.Y.: Doubleday, 1961.

Fulbright, J. William. *Old Myths and New Realities.** New York: Vintage Books, 1964.

——. *The Arrogance of Power.** New York: Vintage Books, 1967.

——. *The Crippled Giant.** New York: Vintage Books, 1972.

Gaddis, John L. *The United States and the Origins of the Cold War, 1941-1947.** New York: Columbia University Press, 1972.

——. *Russia, the Soviet Union and the United States.** New York: John Wiley & Sons, 1978.

——. *Strategies of Containment.** New York: Oxford University Press, 1982.

Gati, Charles, ed. *Caging the Bear.* New York: Bobbs-Merrill, 1974.

George, Alexander, ed. *Managing U.S.-Soviet Rivalry.** Boulder, Colo.: Westview Press, 1983.

Gilbert, Felix. *To the Farewell Address.* Princeton, N.J.: Princeton University Press, 1961.

Halle, Louis J. *The Cold War as History.** New York: Harper & Row, 1967.

Harbutt, Fraser J. *The Iron Curtain.* New York: Oxford University Press, 1986.

Hilsman, Roger. *To Move a Nation.* Garden City, N.Y.: Doubleday, 1967.

Hoffmann, Stanley. *Primacy or World Order.* New York: McGraw-Hill, 1978.

Hyland, William G. *Mortal Rivals.* New York: Random House, 1987.

Kennan, George F. *American Diplomacy, 1900-1950.** New York: Mentor Books, 1952.

——. *Memoirs.* Boston: Little, Brown & Co., 1967.

——. *The Clouds of Danger.** Boston: Atlantic/Little, Brown & Co., 1977.

Kuniholm, Bruce R. *The Origins of the Cold War in the Near East.* Princeton, N.J.: Princeton University Press, 1980.

Larson, Deborah Welch. *Origins of Containment.* Princeton, N.J.: Princeton University Press, 1985.

Mandelbaum, Richard, and Strobe Talbott. *Reagan and Gorbachev.** New York: Vintage Books, 1987.

May, Ernest R. *Lessons of the Past.** New York: Oxford University Press, 1973.

Morgenthau, Hans. *A New Foreign Policy for the United States.** New York: Praeger Publishers, 1969.

Muravchik, Joshua. *The Uncertain Crusade.* New York: Hamilton Press, 1985.

Osgood, Robert, and others. *America & the World.** Baltimore: Johns Hopkins University Press, 1970.

——. *Retreat from Empire?** Baltimore: Johns Hopkins University Press, 1973.

Rosenau, James N., and Ole R. Holsti. *American Leadership in World Affairs.** Boston: Allen & Unwin, 1984 (see also *International Studies Quarterly,* December 1986).

Sainsberry, Keith. *The Turning Point.* New York: Oxford University Press, 1985.
Schlesinger, Arthur, Jr. *The Imperial Presidency.** Boston: Houghton Mifflin, 1973.
Smith, Gaddis. *Morality, Reason, and Power.* New York: Hill & Wang, 1986.
Steel, Ronald. *Pax Americana.** New York: Viking Press, 1967.
Talbott, Strobe. *The Russians and Reagan.** New York: Vintage Books, 1984.
Tucker, Robert W. *The Purposes of American Power.** New York: Praeger Publishers, 1981.
Wildavsky, Aaron, ed. *Beyond Containment.* San Francisco: Institute for Contemporary Studies, 1983.
Wilmot, Chester. *The Struggle for Europe.* New York: Hayes & Brothers, 1952.
Yergin, Daniel. *Shattered Peace.** Boston: Houghton Mifflin, 1977.

Revisionist or New Left Histories

Alperovitz, Gar. *Atomic Diplomacy.** New York: Vintage Books, 1967.
Barnet, Richard. *Roots of War.** New York: Atheneum, 1972.
Kolko, Gabriel. *The Roots of American Foreign Policy.** Boston: Beacon Press, 1969.
Kolko, Gabriel, and Joyce Kolko. *The Limits of Power.** New York: Harper & Row, 1972.
La Feber, Walter. *America, Russia, and the Cold War 1945-1980.** New York: John Wiley & Sons, 1981.
Oglesby, Carl, and Richard Schaull. *Containment and Change.** New York: Macmillan, 1967.
Paterson, Thomas G. *Soviet-American Confrontation.* Baltimore: Johns Hopkins University Press, 1973.
___. *On Every Front.** New York: W. W. Norton, 1979.
Sherry, Michael. *Preparing for the Next War.* New Haven, Conn.: Yale University Press, 1977.
Williams, William Appleman. *The Tragedy of American Diplomacy.* rev. 2d ed. New York: Delta, 1972.

Critical Evaluations of New Left Histories

Maddox, Robert J. *The New Left and the Origins of the Cold War.* Princeton, N.J.: Princeton University Press, 1973.
Richardson, J. L. "Cold War Revisionism: A Critique," *World Politics,* July 1972, 579-612.
Schlesinger, Arthur, Jr. "The Origins of the Cold War," *Foreign Affairs,* October 1962, 22-52.
Tucker, Robert W. *The Radical Left and American Foreign Policy.** Baltimore: Johns Hopkins University Press, 1971.

American Military Policy

Abel, Elie. *The Missile Crisis.** New York: Bantam Books, 1966.
Blechman, Barry M., and Stephen S. Kaplan. *Force Without War.** Washington, D.C.: The Brookings Institution, 1978.
Dinerstein, Herbert. *The Making of a Missile Crisis.** Baltimore, Md.: Johns Hopkins University Press, 1976.
Epstein, William. *The Last Chance.* New York: Free Press, 1976.
Freedman, Lawrence. *The Evolution of Nuclear Strategy.** New York: St. Martin's Press, 1983.
George, Alexander L. *The Limits of Coercive Diplomacy.** Boston: Little, Brown & Co., 1971.
George, Alexander L., and Richard Smoke. *Deterrence in American Foreign Policy.** New York: Columbia University Press, 1974.

Gompert, David, Michael Mandelbaum, Richard Garwin, and John Barton. *Nuclear Weapons and World Politics.** New York: McGraw-Hill (for the Council on Foreign Relations,1980s Project), 1977.

Gray, Colin. *The Soviet-American Arms Race.* Lexington, Mass.: Lexington Books, 1976.

Harvard Nuclear Study Group. *Living with Nuclear Weapons.* Cambridge, Mass.: Harvard University Press, 1983.

Horelick, Arnold L., and Myron Rush. *Strategic Power and Soviet Foreign Policy.* Chicago: University of Chicago Press, 1966.

Kahan, Jerome H. *Security in the Nuclear Age.** Washington, D.C.: The Brookings Institution, 1975.

Kissinger, Henry A. *Nuclear Weapons and Foreign Policy.** New York: Harper & Brothers, 1957.

___. *The Necessity for Choice.** New York: Anchor Books, 1961.

___. *The Troubled Partnership.** New York: Anchor Books, 1966.

Krepon, Richard. *Strategic Stalemate.* New York: St. Martin's Press, 1984.

Newhouse, John. *Cold Dawn.* New York: Holt, Rinehart and Winston, 1973.

Payne, Keith P. *Strategic Defense.* Lanham, Md.: Hamilton Press, 1986.

Scoville, Herbert, Jr. *MX.** Cambridge, Mass.: M.I.T. Press, 1981.

Smoke, Richard. *National Security and the Nuclear Dilemma.* 2d ed. New York: Random House, 1987.

Stares, Paul B. *The Militarization of Space.* Ithaca, N.Y.: Cornell University Press, 1985.

Talbott, Strobe. *End Game.* New York: Harper & Row, 1980.

Thayer, Charles W. *Guerrilla.** New York: New American Library, 1963.

Tirman, John, ed. *The Fallacy of Star Wars.* New York: Vintage Books, 1984.

Tucker, Robert W. *The Nuclear Debate.* New York: Holmes & Meier, 1985.

Wolfe, Thomas W. *The SALT Experience.* Cambridge, Mass.: Ballinger Publishing, 1979.

American Policy in Postwar Europe

Barnet, Richard J. *The Alliance—America, Europe, Japan.* New York: Simon & Schuster, 1983.

Calleo, David P. *The Atlantic Fantasy.* Baltimore: Johns Hopkins University Press, 1970.

___. *Europe's Future.** New York: W. W. Norton, 1967.

De Porte, A. W. *Europe Between the Superpowers.* New Haven: Yale University Press, 1979.

Flanagan, Stephen J., and Fen O. Hampton, eds. *Securing Europe's Future.* Dover, Mass.: Auburn House, 1986.

Gelb, Norman. *The Berlin Wall.* New York: Times Books, 1987.

Goldsmith, Walter, ed. *Reagan's Leadership and the Atlantic Alliance.* New York: Pergamon-Brassey's, 1987.

Grosser, Alfred. *The Western Alliance.* New York: Vintage Books, 1982.

Hoffmann, Stanley. *Gulliver's Troubles or the Setting of American Foreign Policy.** New York: McGraw-Hill, 1968.

Holborn, Hajo. *The Political Collapse of Europe.* New York: Alfred A. Knopf, 1951.

Jones, Joseph. *The Fifteen Weeks.* New York: Viking Press, 1955.

Kleiman, Robert. *Atlantic Crisis.** New York: W. W. Norton, 1964.

Krauss, Melvyn. *How NATO Weakens the West.* New York: Simon & Schuster, 1986.

Mally, Gerhard. *Interdependence.* Lexington, Mass.: Lexington Books, 1976.

Mander, John. *Berlin, Hostage for the West.** Baltimore: Penguin Books, 1962.

Newhouse, John, ed. *U.S. Troops in Europe.** Washington, D.C.: The Brookings Institution, 1971.

Osgood, Robert E. *NATO.* Chicago: University of Chicago Press, 1962.

Pierre, Andrew J., ed. *Nuclear Weapons in Europe.** New York: Council on Foreign Relations, 1984.

Pipes, Richard, ed. *Soviet Strategy in Europe.* New York: Crane, Russak, 1976.

Speier, Hans. *Divided Berlin.* New York: Praeger Publishers, 1961.

Steel, Ronald. *The End of Alliance.** New York: Delta Books, 1966.

Talbott, Strobe. *Deadly Gambits.** New York: Alfred A. Knopf, 1984.

Treverton, Gregory F. *Making the Alliance Work.* Ithaca, N.Y.: Cornell University Press, 1986.

Tucker, Robert W., and Linda Wrigley. *The Atlantic Alliance and Its Critics.** New York: Praeger Publishers, 1983.

Williams, Phil. *The Senate and U.S. Troops in Europe.* New York: St. Martin's Press, 1985.

American Policy in Asia

Barnett, A. Doak. *China Policy.** Washington, D.C.: The Brookings Institution, 1977.

———. *China and the Major Powers in East Asia.** Washington, D.C.: The Brookings Institution, 1977.

Clough, Ralph N. *East Asia and U.S. Security.** Washington, D.C.: The Brookings Institution, 1975.

Clubb, O. Edmund. *China and Russia.** New York: Columbia University Press, 1971.

Cohen, Warren I. *America's Response to China.* 2d ed.* New York: John Wiley & Sons, 1980.

Dulles, Foster R. *American Foreign Policy Toward Communist China.** New York: Crowell, 1972.

Fall, Bernard B. *The Two Viet-Nams,* 2d rev. ed. New York: Praeger Publishers, 1967.

Feis, Herbert. *China Tangle.** Princeton, N.J.: Princeton University Press, 1953.

Gelb, Leslie, and others. *The Pentagon Papers.** New York: Bantam Books, 1971.

Gurtov, Melvin. *The First Vietnam Crisis.** New York: Columbia University Press, 1967.

Halberstam, David. *The Best and the Brightest.** New York: Random House, 1969.

Hammer, Ellen J. *The Struggle for Indochina, 1940-1955.** Stanford, Calif.: Stanford University Press, 1966.

Hellman, Donald C. *Japan and East Asia.** New York: Praeger Publishers, 1972.

Hinton, Harold C. *Three and a Half Powers.** Bloomington: Indiana University Press, 1975.

Hoopes, Townsend. *The Limits of Intervention.** New York: McKay, 1969.

Karnow, Stanley C. *Vietnam.* New York: Viking Press, 1983.

Kim, Samuel S., ed. *China and the World.* Boulder, Colo.: Westview Press, 1984.

Lake, Anthony, ed. *The Vietnam Legacy.* New York: New York University Press, 1976.

Lewy, Guenter. *America in Vietnam.** New York: Oxford University Press, 1978.

Lomperis, Timothy J. *The War Everybody Lost—and Won.** Washington, D.C.: CQ Press, 1987.

Meisner, Maurice. *Mao's China.* New York: Free Press, 1977.

Oksenberg, Michel, and Robert Oxnam, eds. *Dragon and Eagle.* New York: Basic Books, 1978.

Schell, Orville. *To Get Rich Is Glorious.* New York: Pantheon, 1984.

Spanier, John W. *The Truman-MacArthur Controversy and the Korean War,* rev. ed.* New York: W. W. Norton, 1965.

Sutter, Robert. *Chinese Foreign Policy After the Cultural Revolution.* Boulder, Colo.: Westview Press, 1978.

Thompson, Sir Robert. *No Exit from Vietnam.* New York: McKay, 1969.

Thompson, W. Scott, ed. *The Third World,* rev. ed. San Francisco: Institute for Contemporary Studies, 1983.

Tsou, Tang. *America's Failure in China, 1941-1950,* 2 vols.* Chicago: Phoenix Books, 1963.

American Policy in the Middle East-Persian Gulf

"America in Captivity: Points of Decision in the Hostage Crisis," *New York Times Magazine,* May 17, 1981.

Christopher, Warren, and others. *American Hostages in Iran.* New Haven, Conn.: Yale University Press, 1985.

Doran, Charles, *Myth, Oil and Politics.* New York: Free Press, 1977.

Golan, Galia. *Yom Kippur and After.* New York: Cambridge University Press, 1977.

Golan, Matti. *The Secret Conversations of Henry Kissinger.** New York: Quadrangle/Times Books, 1976.

Herring, George C. *America's Longest War.* New York: John Wiley & Sons, 1979.

Quandt, William. *Decade of Decisions.* Berkeley: University of California Press, 1977.

___. *Saudi Arabia in the 1980s.** Washington, D.C.: The Brookings Institution, 1981.

___. *Camp David.* Washington, D.C.: The Brookings Institution, 1986.

Sadat, Anwar. *In Search of Identity.* New York: Harper & Row, 1978.

Safran, Nadav. *Israel: The Embattled Ally.** Cambridge, Mass.: Harvard University Press, 1978.

___. *Saudi Arabia: The Ceaseless Quest for Security.* Cambridge, Mass.: Harvard University Press, 1985.

Schiff, Ze'ev, and Ehud Ya'ari (edited and translated by Ina Friedman). *Israel's Lebanon War.* New York: Simon & Schuster, 1984.

Shipler, David K. *Arab and Jew.* New York: Times Books, 1986.

Sick, Gary. *All Fall Down.* New York: Penguin Books, 1986.

Spiegel, Steven L. *The Other Arab-Israeli Conflict.* Chicago: University of Chicago Press, 1985.

Wright, Robin. *Sacred Rage: The Crusade of Modern Islam.* New York: Touchstone, 1986.

American Policy in Africa and Latin America

Blasier, Cole. *The Giant's Rival: The U.S.S.R. and Latin America.* Pittsburgh: University of Pittsburgh Press, 1983.

Christian, Shirley. *Nicaragua: Revolution in the Family.* New York: Random House, 1985.

Duncan, W. Raymond. *The Soviet Union and Cuba.* New York: Praeger Publishers, 1985.

El-Khawas, Mohamed, and Barry Cohen, eds. *The Kissinger Strategy for Southern Africa.* Westport, Conn.: Lawrence Hill, 1976.

Erisman, H. Michael. *Cuba's International Relations.* Boulder, Colo.: Westview Press, 1985.

La Feber, Walter. *The Panama Canal: The Crisis in Historical Perspective.** New York: Oxford University Press, 1978.

____. *Inevitable Revolutions: The United States in Central America.* New York: W. W. Norton, 1983.

Lake, Anthony. *The "Tar Baby" Option.* New York: Columbia University Press, 1976.

Leiken, Robert S., ed. *Central America.* New York: Pergamon Press, 1984.

Lemarchand, René, ed. *American Policy in Southern Africa.* Washington, D.C.: University Press of America, 1978.

Rangel, Carlos. *The Latin Americans.* New York: Harcourt, 1977.

The Report of the President's National Bipartisan Commission on Central America. New York: Macmillan, 1984.

Sigmund, Paul. *The Overthrow of Allende and the Politics of Chile.* Pittsburgh: University of Pittsburgh, 1977.

International Economics and The New International Politics

Atlantic Council Working Group on the U.S. and the Developing Countries. *The United States and the Developing Countries,* Boulder, Colo.: Westview Press, 1977.

Baldwin, David A. *Economic Statecraft.* Princeton, N.J.: Princeton University Press, 1985.

Bhagwati, Jagdish, ed. *The New International Economic Order.* Cambridge, Mass.: M.I.T. Press, 1977.

Blake, David, and Robert Walters. *The Politics of Economic Relations.* 3d ed.* Englewood Cliffs, N.J.: Prentice-Hall, 1987.

Brown, Harrison. *The Human Future Revisited.* New York: W. W. Norton, 1978.

Cohen, Benjamin J. *In Whose Interest?: International Banking and American Foreign Policy.* New Haven, Conn.: Yale University Press, 1986.

Fishlow, Albert, Carlos Diaz-Alejandro, Richard Fagen, and Roger Hansen. *Rich and Poor Nations in the World Economy.* New York: McGraw-Hill (for the Council on Foreign Relations, 1980s Project), 1978.

Keohane, Robert O. *After Hegemony.** Princeton, N.J.: Princeton University Press, 1984.

Keohane, Robert O., and Joseph Nye. *Power and Interdependence.** Boston: Little, Brown & Co., 1977.

Krasner, Stephen D. *Structural Conflict.* Berkeley, Calif.: University of California Press, 1985.

Lewis, Arthur. *The Evolution of the International Economic Order.** Princeton, N.J.: Princeton University Press, 1978.

Lewis, John P., and Valeriana Kallab, eds. *Development Strategies Reconsidered.* New Brunswick, N.J.: Transaction Books, 1986.

Morse, Edward. *Modernization and the Transformation of International Relations.* New York: Free Press, 1976.

Report of the Independent Commission on International Development Issues under the Chairmanship of Willy Brandt, *North-South: A Programme for Survival.* Cambridge, Mass.: M.I.T. Press, 1980.

Rothstein, Robert. *The Weak in the World of the Strong.* New York: Columbia University Press, 1977.

Spero, Joan. *The Politics of International Economic Relations.* 2d ed.* New York: St. Martin's Press, 1981.

Thurow, Lester C. *The Zero-Sum Solution.* New York: Simon & Schuster, 1985.

Tucker, Robert. *Inequality of Nations.* New York: Basic Books, 1977.

Vernon, Raymond, ed. *The Oil Crisis.** New York: W. W. Norton, 1976.

Wriggins, Howard, and Gunnar Adler-Karlsson. *Reducing Global Inequities.* New York: McGraw-Hill (for the Council on Foreign Relations, 1980s Project), 1978.

Memoirs, Biographies, and Histories of American Statesmen and Administrations

Acheson, Dean. *Present at the Creation*. New York: W. W. Norton, 1969.

Ambrose, Stephen E. *Eisenhower*. 2 vols. New York: Simon & Schuster, 1983 and 1984.

Brown, Harold. *Thinking About National Security*. Boulder, Colo.: Westview Press, 1983.

Brzezinski, Zbigniew. *Power and Principle.** New York: Farrar, Strauss & Giroux, 1983.

Bundy, McGeorge, ed. *The Pattern of Responsibility*. Boston: Houghton Mifflin, 1952.

Burns, James MacGregor. *Roosevelt*. New York: Harcourt Brace Jovanovich, 1970.

Byrnes, James F. *Speaking Frankly*. New York: Harper & Brothers, 1947.

Cannon, Lou. *Reagan*. New York: Random House, 1981.

Carter, Jimmy. *Keeping Faith*. New York: Bantam Books, 1982.

Churchill, Winston S. *The Second World War*. 6 vols. Boston: Houghton Mifflin, 1948-1953.

Dallek, Robert. *Franklin D. Roosevelt and American Foreign Policy, 1932-1945*. New York: Oxford University Press, 1979.

Eisenhower, David. *Eisenhower at War*. New York: Random House, 1986.

Eisenhower, Dwight D. *Mandate for Change.** New York: New American Library, 1965.

——. *Waging Peace*. New York: Doubleday, 1965.

Feis, Herbert. *Churchill, Roosevelt, Stalin*. Princeton, N.J.: Princeton University Press, 1957.

Ferrell, Robert H. *George C. Marshall*. New York: Cooper Square Publishers, 1966.

Gerson, Louis. *John Foster Dulles*. New York: Cooper Square Publishers, 1967.

Guhin, Michael. *John Foster Dulles*. New York: Columbia University Press, 1972.

Haig, Alexander. *Caveat*. New York: Macmillan, 1984.

Harriman, W. Averell. *Special Envoy to Churchill and Stalin, 1941-1946*. New York: Random House, 1975.

Hoopes, Townsend. *The Devil and John Foster Dulles.** Boston: Atlantic/Little, Brown & Co., 1975.

Isaacson, Walter, and Evan Thomas. *The Wise Men*. New York: Simon & Schuster, 1986.

Johnson, Lyndon B. *The Vantage Point.** New York: Popular Library, 1971.

Kalb, Marvin, and Bernard Kalb. *Kissinger.** Boston: Little, Brown & Co., 1974.

Kearns, Doris. *Lyndon Johnson and the American Dream.** New York: Harper & Row, 1976.

Kennedy, Robert S. *Thirteen Days.** New York: W. W. Norton, 1971.

Kissinger, Henry A. *The White House Years*. Boston: Little, Brown & Co., 1979.

——. *Years of Upheaval*. Boston: Little, Brown & Co., 1982.

Manchester, William. *American Caesar*. Boston: Little, Brown & Co., 1978.

McLellan, David S. *Cyrus Vance*. Totowa, N.J.: Rowman & Allanheld, 1985.

Nixon, Richard. *RN*. New York: Grosset & Dunlap, 1978.

Parmet, Herbert S. *Eisenhower and the American Crusades*. New York: Macmillan, 1972.

Pogue, Forrest C. *George C. Marshall*. New York: Viking Press, 1987.

Schlesinger, Arthur M., Jr. *A Thousand Days.** New York: Crest Books, 1967.

Sherwood, Robert E. *Roosevelt and Hopkins*. New York: Harper, 1948.

Smith, Gaddis. *Dean Acheson*. New York: Cooper Square Publishers, 1972.

Sorensen, Theodore C. *Kennedy.** New York: Bantam Books, 1966.
Stoessinger, John. *Henry Kissinger.** New York: W. W. Norton, 1976.
Truman, Harry S. *Memoirs.* 2 vols.* New York: New American Library, 1965.
Vance, Cyrus. *Hard Choices.* New York: Simon & Schuster, 1982.

Soviet Foreign Policy

Adomeit, Hannes. *Soviet Risk-Taking and Crisis Behavior.** Boston: Allen & Unwin, 1982.
Bialer, Seweryn. *The Soviet Paradox.* New York: Alfred A. Knopf, 1986.
Byrnes, Robert F., ed. *After Brezhnev.** Bloomington: Indiana University Press, 1983.
Caldwell, Dan, ed. *Soviet International Behavior and U.S. Policy Options.* Lexington, Mass.: Lexington Books, 1985.
Dallin, Alexander. *Black Box.* Berkeley.: University of California Press, 1985.
Daniels, Robert V. *Russia, The Roots of Confrontation.* Cambridge, Mass.: Harvard University Press, 1985.
Dibb, Paul. *The Soviet Union.* Champaign: University of Illinois Press, 1986.
Dinerstein, Herbert S. *The Making of a Missile Crisis.* Baltimore: Johns Hopkins University Press, 1976.
Donaldson, Robert H., ed. *The Soviet Union in the Third World.* 2d ed. Boulder, Colo.: Westview Press, 1984.
Duncan, W. Raymond, ed. *Soviet Policy in the Third World.* New York: Pergamon Press, 1980.
Garthoff, Raymond L. *Détente and Confrontation.* Washington, D.C.: The Brookings Institution, 1985.
Gati, Charles. *Hungary and the Soviet Bloc.* Durham, N.C.: Duke University Press, 1986.
Goldman, Marshall I. *U.S.S.R. in Crisis.* New York: W. W. Norton, 1983.
___. *Economic Reform in the Age of High Technology.* New York: W. W. Norton, 1987.
___. *Gorbachev's Challenge.* New York: W. W. Norton, 1987.
Hammond, Thomas T. *Red Flag Over Afghanistan.** Boulder, Colo.: Westview Press, 1984.
Hough, Jerry. *The Struggle for the Third World.* Washington, D.C.: The Brookings Institution, 1986.
Luttwak, Edward. *The Grand Strategy of the Soviet Union.** New York: St. Martin's Press, 1984.
Krickus, Richard J. *The Superpowers in Crisis.* New York: Pergamon-Brassey's, 1987.
MacFarlane, S. Neil. *Superpower Rivalry and Third World Radicalism.* Baltimore: Johns Hopkins University Press, 1985.
Mastny, Vojtech. *Russia's Road to the Cold War.* New York: Columbia University Press, 1979.
Nogee, Joseph L., and Robert H. Donaldson. *Soviet Foreign Policy since World War II,* 2d ed. New York: Pergamon Press, 1984.
Nye, Joseph S., Jr., ed. *The Making of America's Soviet Policy.* New Haven, Conn.: Yale University Press, 1984.
Papp, Daniel S. *Soviet Policies Toward the Developing World During the 1980s.* Maxwell Air Force Base, Ala.: Air University Press, 1986.
Pipes, Richard. *Survival Is Not Enough.* New York: Simon & Schuster, 1984.
Rubinstein, Alvin Z. *Soviet Foreign Policy Since World War II.** Cambridge, Mass.: Winthrop Publishers, 1981.

Rush, Myron. *Strategic Power and Soviet Foreign Policy.* Chicago: University of Chicago, 1966.

Saivetz, Carol R., and Sylvia Woodby. *Soviet-Third World Relations.* Boulder, Colo.: Westview Press, 1985.

Taubman, William. *Stalin's American Policy.* New York: W. W. Norton, 1982.

Valkenier, Elizabeth K. *The Soviet Union and the Third World.* New York: Praeger Publishers, 1984.

Index